READING GANDHI

Anil Dutta Mishra

Pearson

Assistant Editor–Acquisitions: Kaushal Kumar Jajware
Assistant Editor–Production: Saima Ghaffar

ISBN 978-81-317-6956-0

First Impression, 2012
Eighth Impression, 2022
Ninth Impression

Published by Pearson India Education Services Pvt.Ltd., CIN: U72200TN2005PTC057128.

Head Office: World Trade Tower, 15th Floor, Plot No: C – 01, Sector – 16, Noida 201301 U.P., India.

Registered Office: 7th Floor, SDB2, ODC 7, 8 & 9, Survey No.01 ELCOT IT/ ITES SEZ, Sholinganallur,
Chennai – 600119, Tamil Nadu, India. Website: in.pearson.com, Email: companysecretary.india@pearson.com

Compositor: Country Caramels

Printing In india : India Binding House, Noida

Contents

Preface

Mohandas Karamchand Gandhi, popularly known as Mahatma Gandhi or Bapu or Father of the Nation, is tallest among the leaders of the world of the 20th century.

He was a creative man, creating history for himself and for the rest of the world to follow. He was the most complex thinker and a unique personality. He was greatly admired but has also been greatly misunderstood. His concerns were contemporary but timeless. Gandhi who is considered as an iconic personality, has inspired millions of people during his lifetime, is still inspiring people round the globe. His thoughts are everlasting, time-tested, and have been written for a common man. He brought awareness of political, social, and human freedom to millions of people and also gave them a practical method for achieving redressal against the wrongs, by practising non-violent assertion of rights. In short, Gandhi was travelling from truth to truth and was the first person in the history of world who gave the culture of non-violence for a change.

He is remembered all over the world for his love of peace, non-violence, truth, honesty, pristine purity, compassion, and success in using these instruments to bring together the people and helping the country attain independence from the colonial yoke. He gave the world new techniques of non-violent protest.

Gandhi changed the course of history and created history. He was a man of principles and great convictions and always practiced what he preached. There was no dichotomy between theory and practice and between his public and private life. He left an everlasting impact on the world at large because he always spoke and understood the language of the masses, socially deprived, and the downtrodden. Even after his death, Gandhi continues to attract the attention of scholars, social activists, media, policy makers and dreamers not only in India, but abroad too.

He was a great man in every sense and many ways. It is said that it is difficult to understand a great person. Bhavbhuti, a great scholar of Sanskrit, has rightly said 'Who indeed can claim to know and understand the mind of the great?'. This is true is case of Gandhi.

This book is an outcome of two decade of research, teaching, and administrative experience in the field of Gandhian Studies/institutions. *Reading Gandhi* analyses in depth the fundamental postulates of Mahatma Gandhi which are being echoed world wide. In this book, a humble attempt has been made to reassess and reinvent Gandhi. A reader-friendly book, written in a simple and lucid style provides new insight into the subject. The volume is addressed to a wide range of readers in the field of social science, humanities, and Gandhian Studies. It will be a must book for students of Delhi University opting for the Reading Gandhi Paper as well as pan-India demands on Gandhi.

This work would not have been possible in the present form without the support and help from friends and well-wishers. I acknowledge all of them from the core of my heart. I am thankful to Mr. Kaushal Jajware and the entire team of Pearson for bringing out the book in present form and that too within record time.

Mohandas Karamchand Gandhi was a creative man, creating history for himself and the rest of the world. He was a most complex thinker and a unique personality. He was greatly admired but misunderstood. His concerns were contemporary but timeless.

Step by step, Gandhi reached at the pinnacle of existence, where no one has reached before. Gandhi, who motivated millions of people during his lifetime, continues to inspiring people around the globe. His thoughts are everlasting, time tested and written for the common man in a simple language. He emerged as a giant among men and brought about awareness of political, social and human freedom to millions of people and gave them a practical method for achieving redressal against the wrongs, through the practice of non-violent assertion of rights. In short, Gandhi was traveling from truth to truth and was the first person in the history of the world who gave the culture of non-violence for change.

A reader-friendly book, written in a simple and lucid style, *Reading Gandhi* provides a new insight on the subject. This volume is addressed to a wide range of readers in the field of social science, humanities and Gandhian Studies. It will be a must read for the students of Delhi University, who have opted Reading Gandhi as well as pan India demands on Gandhi.

Anil Dutta Mishra

About the Author

Anil Dutta Mishra, a rare combination of activist and Gandhian scholar, started his career as an Assistant Professor in the Department of Non-violence and Peace Studies, Jain Vishva Bharati University, Ladnun, Rajasthan.

He held various offices in his professional life time, chief among them being the General Secretary of Indian Society of Gandhian Studies, Alliance for Sarvodaya, Member of the Board of Studies, Nagpur and Punjab Universities and is Member of Gandhian Studies Centre of different colleges and universities across India sponsored by the University Grants Commission and Executive Member IIPA Regional Branch. He has authored and edited 30 books and published a number of research papers. Presently, he is the Deputy Director, National Gandhi Museum, Rajghat, New Delhi.

1

Introducing Gandhi

Introduction

Mohandas Karamchand Gandhi was the most prominent leader of pre-independence and post-independence India, who changed the course of history during the Indian freedom struggle. A pioneer of satyagraha, or resistance to tyranny through mass civil disobedience—a philosophy firmly founded upon ahimsa in thought, action and deed—Gandhi not only led India to independence, but also inspired movements for civil rights and freedom across the globe. Mahatma Gandhi was a most complex thinker as well as a unique personality. He was greatly admired but sometimes misunderstood. Nobel Laureate Rabindranath Tagore bestowed upon him the title 'Mahatma' and Netaji Subhash Bose addressed him as the 'Father of the Nation'. On the other hand, Winston Churchill called Gandhi 'a half-naked, seditious fakir'. Lord Wavell and Lord Willingdon called him the most dangerous enemy of the British rule. M. A. Jinnah called him a great Hindu, whereas Rightists like Vinayak Damodar Savarkar, Dr. K. B. Hedgewar and M. S. Golwalkar believed him to be a noble soul but pro-Muslim. Lord Mountbatten called him a one-man army. The *Time* magazine referred to personalities like Dalai Lama, Lech Wałęsa, Martin Luther King, Caesar Chavez, Aung San Suu Kyi, Benigno Aquino, Jr., Desmond Tutu and Nelson Mandela as the Children of Gandhi as well as his spiritual heirs to non-violence. Gandhi was a man whose concerns were contemporary but timeless.

Gandhi was a prolific writer and wrote several books, notable among them being *An Autobiography or The Story of My Experiments with Truth; Satyagraha in South Africa; Hind Swaraj or Indian Home Rule*; and *Sarvodaya* a paraphrase in Gujarati of John Ruskin's Unto This Last. Gandhi wrote a commentary on the *Bhagvad Gita* in Gujarati which was translated into English by Mahadev Desai and published in 1946. He wrote extensively on vegetarianism, diet and health, religion, social reforms, etc. Gandhi's writing was essentially in Gujarati.

For decades, he edited several newspapers, including *Harijan* in Gujarati, in Hindi and in the English language; *Indian Opinion in English, Telegu, Hindi and Gujarati* while in South Africa; *Young India*, in English; and *Navajivan*, a Gujarati monthly, on his return to India. Later, *Navajivan* was also published in Hindi. Gandhi wrote letters almost every day to individuals and newspapers. His complete works were published by the Indian government under the name *The Collected Works of Mahatma Gandhi* published in a set of hundred volumes.

Family and Childhood

Mohandas Karamchand Gandhi was born on October 2, 1869 at Sudamapuri in Porbandar, a coastal town in Gujarat. His father, Karamchand Gandhi (1822–1885), who belonged to the Hindu Modh Bania community, served as the *diwan* of Porbander State, a small princely State in the Kathiawar region of British India. He was truthful, brave, honest and a man of principles. Karamchand Gandhi never had any ambition to accumulate wealth and had bequeathed his family very little by way of property. Mohandas' grandfather was Uttamchand Gandhi. His mother, Putlibai, who came from the Hindu Pranami Vaishnava community, was Karamchand's fourth wife, the first three wives having apparently died in childbirth. Growing up with a devout mother and the Jain traditions of the region, the young Mohandas quickly absorbed the influences that would play an important role in his life. Gandhiji's mother Putlibai was an epitome of religious faith and devotion. She had strict rules about alcohol and tobacco. She was deeply religious and never took her food without offering her daily prayers. Mahatma inherited these qualities from her. The devotion of his mother in adhering to the religious rites and vows made an indelible mark on Gandhi.

Gandhi's primary and high school education was done at Rajkot. At the age of 12 he was shifted to the Alfred High School. He was a mediocre student, shy and slow to mix with others. During his school days, he was known to have never lied to his teachers or anybody else. He was influenced by an ancient play *Shravana Pitribhakti*, portraying the boundless love of Shravan for his parents. Thereafter, obedience to parents became Gandhi's motto. Further, a play about King Harischandra influenced him to lead a truthful and sincere life.

In May 1883, the 13-year-old Mohandas was married to 14-year-old Kasturbai Makhanji, the daughter of Shri Gokuldas Makan, a merchant. Later on, she came to be known as 'Kasturba', and affectionately as 'Ba'. It was an arranged child marriage, as per the custom of the region. Recalling the day of their marriage, Gandhi once said, 'As we didn't know much about marriage, for us it meant only wearing new clothes, eating sweets and playing with relatives'. However, as was also the custom of the region, the adolescent bride was to spend a lot of time at her parents' house, and away from her husband. In 1885, when Gandhi was 15, the couple's first child was born, but survived only for a few days. Also, Gandhi's father Karamchand had died earlier that same year. Mohandas and Kasturba had four more children, all sons: Harilal, born in 1888; Manilal, born in 1892; Ramdas, born in 1897; and Devdas, born in 1900. Kasturba stood by Gandhi through all his struggles and proved to be his firm and stoic supporter till her death.

In Pursuit of Knowledge

Gandhi passed the matriculation exam from Samaldas College at Bhavnagar, Gujarat .On September 4, 1888, he travelled to London, England, to study law at University College, London and to train as a barrister. Gandhi took a vow to his mother in the presence of the Jain monk Becharji, upon leaving India, to observe the Hindu precepts of abstinence from meat, alcohol and promiscuity. While in London, Gandhi experimented with adopting certain 'English' customs, like taking dancing lessons. In England, he read a book titled *Plea for Vegetarianism* by Salt. This influenced him to become a vegetarian not only because of his vow taken before his mother but also by principle. From then, the spread of the message of vegetarianism became a mission for him, making him more sociable and popular. He was introduced to poet Narayan Hunachandra, who requested Gandhi to teach English. Gandhiji undertook the task of becoming an English gentleman, but maintained the disciplined life of a student.

Gandhiji came across theosophists who told him about the Bhagdvad *Gita.* Later in his life, *Gita* became a book of his daily reading. The *Gita*, to Gandhiji, was the 'key to the scriptures of world'. He described the *Gita* as his 'mother', and referred to it as 'My Kamdhenu, my guide, my open sesame'. He also started reading the bible and took great interest in the New Testament, particularly the Sermon on the Mount. He was attracted by the teachings of Buddha through Edwin Arnold's *The Light of Asia.* A friend recommended Carlyle's *Heroes and Hero Worship*, which gave him the impetus to learn more about Prophet Mohammed.

Gandhi's three years in London were a time of social, moral and intellectual ferment. He was confronted not only with the academic opportunities that he was seeking, but also with a bewildering array of intellectual, religious and cultural influences, as well as moral 'temptations' from the view point of his tradition. For him, it was the first time he had the opportunity and the necessity of taking charge of his own life, of sorting out his priorities and values. Freed from the constraining if comforting continues of his family and its cultural setting, apart from the triple vow which he rigorously observed, he had to work out who and what he was and wanted to become, and what it meant to be an Indian adrift in the cultural and economic capital of the empire whose influences had only just reached the home he had left.[1]

Gandhi was called to the bar on June 10, 1891. Two days later, he left London for India, where he learned that his mother had died while he was in London and that his family had kept the news from him.

In Search of Livelihood

Mohandas' attempts at establishing a law practice in Bombay failed and later, after applying and being turned down for a part-time job as a high school teacher, he returned to Rajkot to make a modest living by drafting petitions for litigants, a business he was forced to close when he ran foul of a British officer. In his autobiography, Gandhi refered to this incident as an unsuccessful attempt to lobby on behalf of his older brother. It was in this climate that in April 1893, Gandhi accepted a year-long contract from Dada Abdulla & Co., an Indian firm, to a post in the Colony of Natal, South Africa, then part of the British Empire.

In South Africa

In April 1893, Mohandas sailed for South Africa without his family. It was in South Africa that he came face to face with racial prejudices and a racially oppressive atmosphere. Here, Indians were treated as slaves and servants. One incident in his life changed his thinking and showed the way to fight for injustice. While he was on his way to Pretoria, from Durban, at Maritzberg Railway station, he was detrained from the first class compartment even though he was holding an appropriate ticket. The train left the station without him, and he was left alone on the platform. It was a severely cold winter. That sleepless night, Gandhi determined to fight the indiscrimination and root out the social evils and suffer any amount of hardship for this cause. He decided to work on removing racial discrimination and subordinated his legal practice to public work.

Incidents in South Africa aroused Gandhi's sense of social justice and motivated him to mobilize the Indian community in South Africa to take action against such outrage. At a public meeting, he asked them to fight for their rights; to rise above the barriers of caste, creed and religion; and to form an association to look after the interests of the Indian community. Mohandas offered them his professional time and services for free. Though he completed his assignment for Dada Abdulla and Co., he stayed on for 20 years in South Africa, becoming increasingly involved in fighting for the rights of the Indian community.

It was during his stay in South Africa that Gandhi's mode of living underwent a sea change. His lifestyle became increasingly simpler. He began doing his chores himself and spent less money on his clothes. He did voluntary work in hospitals. He felt very strongly about issues that directly impacted people's lives such as apartheid, poverty and inequality.

In South Africa, Gandhi fought a case for social justice and ultimately won the defense. After reading John Ruskin's *Unto This Last*, he decided to change his lifestyle and create a commune called Phoenix Settlement. He founded the Phoenix Settlement near Durban and Tolstoy Farm. In January 1915, Gandhi finally returned to India not as a lawyer but as a well-experienced organizer in the cause of social justice and equality. He spoke at the conventions of the Indian National Congress but was introduced to Indian issues, politics and the Indian people primarily by Gopal Krishna Gokhale, a respected leader of the Congress Party at the time.

Gandhi earnestly believed that a person involved in public service should lead a simple life. He first displayed this principle when he gave up wearing Western clothes, which he associated with wealth and success. When he returned to India, he renounced the Western lifestyle he had been leading in South Africa, where he enjoyed a successful legal practice.

Satyagraha in India

After returning from South Africa, Gandhi spent the first year in India touring all over the country and studying the regions with 'his ears open but his mouth shut'. In 1917, he launched the first Satyagraha in Champaran, Bihar, where he received impressive success. This was followed by Ahmedabad Textile mill workers' strike on the bonus issue. The strike went on for 21 days. During the strike, Gandhi initiated his maiden fast for three days and his intervention had the desired effects. The problem was soon settled through arbitration between the labourers and owner. His next Satyagraha was in Kheda district of Gujarat. Owing to failure of the crops, the farmers wanted certain concessions in regard to tax. Many leaders of national eminence took part in this Satyagraha and finally the Government suspended the revenue assessment for the poor farmers. This example demonstrates Gandhi's popularity, the importance of peoples' participation in the freedom movement. 'Non-cooperation' enjoyed widespread appeal and success, increasing the feeling of excitement and participation from all strata of Indian society.

On March 11, 1930 Gandhi along with other satyagrahis started from Sabarmati Ashram to Dandi, a distance of 240 miles on foot. Gandhi and his followers broke the Salt Law on April 6, 1930. No part of India remained untouched by the Dandi March, and virtually every aspect of the campaign elicited some public response and soon the entire nation was with Gandhi. This satyagraha laid the foundation of the road to *swaraj* and the beginning of the end of British Empire not only from India but from the whole world.

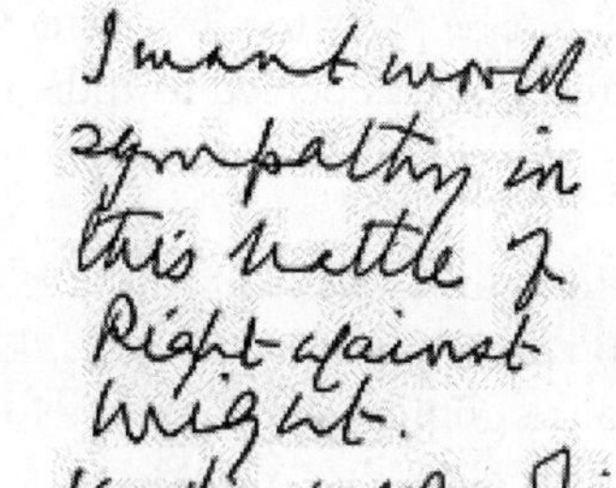
I want world sympathy in this battle of Right against Might.
Dandi M.K.Gandhi
5.4.'30

'I want world sympathy in this battle of right against might'.

– Dandi, April 5, 1930

The government, represented by Lord Edward Irwin, decided to negotiate with Gandhi. The Gandhi-Irwin Pact was signed on March 1931. The British Government agreed to free all political prisoners, in return for the suspension of the Civil Disobedience Movement. Also, as a result of the pact, Gandhi was invited to attend the Round Table Conference in London as the sole representative of the Indian National Congress. The conference was a disappointment to Gandhi and the other nationalists, because it focused on the Indian princes and Indian minorities rather than on transfer of power.

In 1932, the government granted the caste of untouchables separate electorates under the new constitution. In protest, Gandhi embarked on a six-day fast in September 1932. The resulting public outcry successfully forced the government to adopt an equitable arrangement through negotiations mediated by Palwankar Baloo. This was the start of a new campaign by Gandhi to improve the lives of the untouchables, whom he named Harijans, the children of god. On May 8, 1933, Gandhi began a 21-day fast of self-purification to help the Harijan movement, and continued from then on for the upliftment of the dalits.

Gandhi returned to active politics again in 1936, with the Nehru presidency and the Lucknow session of the Congress. Although Gandhi wanted to totally focus on the task of winning independence and not speculate on India's future, he did not restrain the Congress from adopting socialism as its goal. Subhash Bose was elected the president in 1938. Bose won his second term despite Gandhi's criticism, but resigned from the Congress when the All-India leaders resigned en masse in protest of his abandonment of the principles introduced by Gandhi.

Towards Freedom

World War II broke out in 1939. Gandhi favoured offering 'non-violent moral support' to the British efforts in the war, but other Congressional leaders were offended by the unilateral inclusion of India in the war, which had been done without consultation of the peoples' representatives. All Congressmen resigned from office. After long deliberations, Gandhi declared that India could not be party to a war ostensibly being fought for democratic freedom, while that very freedom was denied to India itself. As the war progressed, Gandhi intensified his demand for independence, drafting a resolution calling for the British to Quit India.

Quit India became the most forceful movement in the history of the Indian struggle, with mass arrests and violence on an unprecedented scale. Thousands of freedom fighters were killed or injured by police gunfire, and hundreds of thousands were arrested. Gandhi and his supporters made it clear they would not support the war effort unless India was granted immediate independence. He even clarified that this time the movement would not be stopped if individual acts of violence were committed, saying that the 'ordered anarchy' around him was 'worse than real anarchy'. He called on all Congressmen and Indians to maintain discipline via ahimsa, and believe in the tenet *Karo Ya Maro* ('Do or Die') in the cause of ultimate freedom.

The British arrested Gandhi and the entire Congress Working Committee in Bombay on August 9, 1942. Gandhi was held for two years in the Aga Khan Palace in Pune. It was here that he suffered two terrible blows in his personal life. His 50-year-old secretary Mahadev Desai died of a heart attack and 6 days later, Kasturba died after 18 months' imprisonment on February 22, 1944. He was released before the end of the war on May 6, 1944 because of his failing health.

One after another Gandhiji achieved success and finally, under his leadership, India got Independence on August 15, 1947.

While the Indian National Congress and Gandhi called for the British to quit India, the Muslim League passed a resolution in 1943, for the British to divide India and then quit. Gandhi is believed to have been opposed to the partition during independence and suggested an agreement which required the Congress and Muslim League to cooperate and attain independence under a provisional government. Thereafter, the question of partition could be resolved by a plebiscite in the districts with a Muslim majority. When Jinnah called for Direct Action, on August 16, 1946, Gandhi was infuriated and personally visited the most riot-prone areas to stop the massacres. He made strong efforts to unite the Indian Hindus, Muslims and Christians and struggled for the emancipation of the 'untouchables' in Hindu society.

On August 14 and 15, 1947, the Indian Independence Act was invoked and the following carnage witnessed a displacement of up to 12.5 million people in the former British Indian Empire, with an estimated loss of life varying from several hundred thousand to a million.

Martyrdom

Gandhi regularly followed the practice of conducting the prayer meeting where persons of all faiths and religions were free to assemble. On January 30, 1948, at the prayer meeting, Gandhi was assassinated by Nathu Ram Godse. He fell on the ground uttering the word 'Hey Ram'. Thus, the apostle of non-violence had himself fallen victim to violence. On the evening of January 31, 1948, his body was reduced to ashes on the bank of Yamuna. On January 30, Jawaharlal Nehru addressed the nation through the radio:

> '… the light has gone out of our lives, and there is darkness everywhere…The light has gone out, I said, and yet I was wrong. For the light that shone in this country was no ordinary light… that light represented something more than the immediate present, it represented the living, the eternal truths, reminding us of the right path, drawing us from error, taking this ancient country to freedom… A great disaster is a symbol to us to remember all the big things of life and forget the small things of which we have thought too much. In his death he has reminded us of the big things of life, the living truth, and if we remember that, then it will be well with India.'[2]

Summing Up

Gandhi influenced many important leaders like Martin Luther King, James Lawson, Nelson Mandela, Khan Abdul Ghaffar Khan, Steve Biko, Aung San Suu Kyi and Benigno Aquino, Jr. In 1955, Martin Luther King Jr. said 'Christ gave us the goals and Mahatma Gandhi the tactics'. Barack Obama, the President of the United States at the Wakefield High School speech in September 2009, said that his biggest inspiration came from Mahatma Gandhi. Barack Obama in an address to a Joint Session of the Parliament of

India, 2010 said that: 'I am mindful that I might not be standing before you today, as President of the United States, had it not been for Gandhi and the message he shared with America and the world.'

Gandhi's life and teachings inspired many who specifically referred to him as their mentor or those who dedicated their lives to spreading Gandhi's ideas. Joseph J. Doke wrote the first biography entitled *Gandhi: A Patriot In South Africa*, published in the London Indian Chronicle in 1909 when Gandhi was not a particularly well-known figure. In Europe, Romain Rolland was the first to discuss Gandhi in his 1924 book *Mahatma Gandhi*, and Brazilian anarchist and feminist Maria Lacerda de Moura wrote about Gandhi in her work on pacifism. Several biographers have undertaken the task of describing Gandhi's life. Among them are: D. G. Tendulkar with his *Mahatma: Life of Mohandas Karamchand Gandhi* in eight volumes, and Pyarelal and Sushila Nayar with their *Mahatma Gandhi* in 10 volumes.

Mahatma Gandhi has been portrayed in film, literature and also in theatre. Ben Kingsley portrayed Gandhi in the 1982 film *Gandhi*. Gandhi is also the central theme in the 2006 Bollywood film *Lage Raho Munna Bhai*. The 2007 film, *Gandhi, My Father* explores the relationship between Gandhi and his son Harilal. The 1996 film, *The Making of the Mahatma*, documents Gandhi's stay in South Africa. There is also another documentary, titled Mahatma: *Life of Gandhi*, 1869–1948, which has 14 chapters and is 6 hours long.

Time magazine named Gandhi the Man of the Year in 1930. Gandhi was also the runner up to Albert Einstein as the 'Person of the Century' at the end of 1999. In 2011, *Time* magazine again named Gandhi as one of the top 25 political icons of all time. On June 15, 2007, the United Nations General Assembly unanimously adopted a resolution declaring 2nd October as 'the International Day of Non-Violence'. Every year, 30 January is observed as the School Day of Non-violence and Peace in schools of many countries. Gandhi's birthday, October 2, is a national holiday in India, and referred to as Gandhi Jayanti. India observes January 30, the day of his assassination, as Martyr's Day, to commemorate those who gave up their lives in service of the nation. There are two temples in India dedicated to Gandhi. One is located at Sambalpur in Orissa and the other at Nidaghatta village near Kadur in Chikmagalur district of Karnataka. Gandhi also appears on every Indian Rupee note.

Gandhi climbed the stages to self enlightenment step by step right to the top where no one has reached before. Gandhi, who inspired millions of people during his lifetime, continues to inspire people around the globe. His thoughts are everlasting, time tested and written for the common man in a simple language. He emerged as a giant among men and brought about an awareness of political, social and human freedom to millions of people, and also gave them a practical method for achieving redress against wrongs, through the practice of nonviolent assertion of rights.

In short, Gandhi was traveled from truth to the higher truth and was the first person in the history of the world who focussed on the culture of nonviolence for change. We have buried Gandhi, along with our self respect and self esteem. Now the time has come to follow the basic tenets of Gandhism, which is the core of all religious thoughts and is essential for human centric approach.

References

1. Brown Judith M., Gandhi: *Prisoner of Hope*, Delhi: Oxford University Press, 1990, p. 23.
2. Ibid., p. 384.

Summary

- M. K. Gandhi was born on October 2, 1869 at Porbandar. His father was Karamchand Gandhi and his mother was Putlibai.
- He did his primary education in India and higher education in England.
- Gandhi got a job in Dada Abdulla & Co., an Indian firm in South Africa, where he got firsthand experience of racial discrimination. That was the birth of Satyagraha. Gandhi founded the Phoenix Settlement near Durban and Tolstoy Farm. In January 1915, Gandhi finally returned to India not as a lawyer but as a well-experienced organizer in the cause of social justice and equality.
- Certain books and extracts from books that greatly influenced Gandhi's thinking and behaviour and helped him understand people better were The Holy Bible; The Bhagvad Gita; Sir Edwin Arnold's *The Song Celestial* (the English translation of The Bhagvad Gita); The Light of Asia (a book on the Buddha's life); A S Ali's *Spirit of Islam*; NK Bhatt's *Biography of The Prophet;* Henry S Salt's *A Plea for Vegetarianism*; John Ruskin's *Unto This Last*; and Henry Thoreau's *Civil Disobedience.*
- A prolific writer, Gandhi wrote several books; namely, *An Autobiography or The Story of My Experiments with Truth; Satyagraha in South Africa; Hind Swaraj or Indian Home Rule;* A paraphrase in Gujarati of John Ruskin's *Unto This Last*; and commentary on the Bhagvad Gita in Gujarati. He also edited *Harijan*, *Opinion, Young India*, and *Navajivan.*
- In 1917, the first Satyagraha in India was launched at Champaran in Bihar, followed by Ahmedabad Textile mill workers' strike, Kheda Satyagraha, Dandi March, Quit India Movement and, finally, under his leadership, India got Independence on August 15, 1947.
- On January 30, 1948, at the prayer meeting, Gandhi was assassinated by Nathu Ram Godse. The apostle of non-violence had fallen victim to violence.

Further Readings

Gandhi, M. K., *An Autobiography* or *The Story of My Experiment With Truth*, Ahmedabad: Navajivan Publishing House, 1927.

Gandhi, M. K., *Satyagraha in South Africa*, Ahmedabad: Navajivan Publishing House, 1928.

Brown, M. Judith, *Gandhi Prisoner of Hope*, Delhi: Oxford University Press, Delhi, 1992.

Fischer, Louis, *The Essential Gandhi*, London: George Allen and Union Limited, 1962.

Kripalani, J. B., *Gandhi: His Life and Thought*, New Delhi: Publications Division, Ministry of Information and Broadcasting, Government of India, 1968.

Nanda, B.R., *Mahatma Gandhi: A Biography*, London: George Allen and Unwin Ltd., 1959.

Rolland, Romain, *Mahatma Gandhi, The Man Who Became One With The Universal Being* (Translated by Catherine D. Groth), Agra: Shiva Lal Aggarwala & Co. Ltd.

2

Text and Context

Introduction

There is a stark contradiction between theory and practice. Reality is not the same as appearance and appearance is not reality. This statement is true in the case of books as well. When one reads any book, one must read between the lines and go beyond words and figures. From time to time, scholars and social scientists have raised the question of how to interpret a text. The moot question is whether it is possible to lay down any general or specific rules about how to decipher a text. For this, one must understand what is text and what is its interpretation.

According to the *Oxford Advanced Learner's Dictionary*, text means 'the main printed part of a book or magazine, not the notes or pictures,' or 'any form of written material, or the written form of a speech, a play and an article'. In other words, any written word, sentence, paragraph, story, novel or any book may be considered as a text. Text is different from the spoken words and covers a wide range of written expressions. However, some postmodernists of the deconstruction strain define text as to encompass not just written words, but also the entire spectrum of symbols and phenomena. The *Longman Dictionary of Contemporary English* defines interpretation as 'the way in which someone explains or understands an event, information or someone's actions,' or 'the way in which someone performs a play or even a piece of music, and shows what they think and feel about it'. Interpretation varies from person to person, from one scholar to another and from one philosopher to another. Interpretation differs in terms of time and space. Interpretation is also relative. There are many ways of reading a text. The two most popular methods are the textual and the contextual.

In the textual method, the reader needs only to read the text in order to understand its meaning. The writer in his/her wisdom makes an all out effort to convey to the reader whatever he/she wishes to convey and there is, therefore, no need to even identify the writer of the text, or even when and under what social and political circumstances was it written. According to Daniel Chandler, there are three ways in which the textual method is interpreted. According to objectivists, the meaning of the text 'is contained' in the text and must be 'extracted' by the reader. Such a model of communication is 'transmissive', i.e., the meaning of a text can be transmitted from the sender to the passive receiver. The second type of textual reading is 'constructivist', where in method, a text is an interplay between writers and readers. This means that a text cannot speak for itself. It needs a reader and writer. The other method of reading text is 'subjectivist', which believes that meaning is entirely in its interpretation by readers, that it is 'recreated'. Andrew Hacker supports the textual approach. According to him, the 'Great Books' are timeless for both causal and ethical theories. First, they can go a long way towards explaining the political situation of today. They do this because of its universal application. For example, Aristotle's writings on the role of middle class, or on the causes of revolution, can tell us much about those phenomena in the Indian society. Second, various classics prescribe norms which are as worthy of attention now as they were never before. For example, J. S. Mill's views on liberty and Plato's ideas of justice have enchanted the people in every age. The textualists highlight the eternal, universal issues and the timeless problems and solutions found in the classic texts. The texts can be and should be studied autonomously without referring to the socio-historical context of their origin. For example, Plamenatz focuses on the text, because in the classic texts the general problems of life of man are discussed in a style which is particular to its author. Leo Strauss emphatically writes that political philosophy is a non-historical endeavour. The classic texts should be interpreted while keeping in mind the eternal and universal principles.

In the contextual method, while reading a text, one must keep in mind the social and historical environment in which the text was written. It attempts to understand a philosophical position in terms of its relation to the intellectual movements of its time and those earlier philosophies that may have influenced its development. The contextual approach leads to the development of transferable skills and stimulus to critical thinking. M. J. Osler in the article *The History of Philosophy and the History of Philosophy: A Plea for Textual History in Context*, said that contextual studies could be of two types: focusing upon the context of other philosophical ideas surrounding a philosophical argument; and focusing upon the social and historical context within which a philosopher has developed his arguments. The context is important and useful because it helps us in two ways. First it throws light on some hidden meaning in the book which would not otherwise be revealed. Secondly, it is important in so far as it emphasizes the totality of social process in which the world is integrally related to consciousness as a part of this process. In other words, a context has two aspects. First comes the objective and subjective, and second, the intellectual history of the society.

In the succeeding pages, Terence Ball on *Reappraising Political Theory* and Quentin Skinner on *Meaning and Understanding in the History of Ideas* have discussed the matter in great detail.

Terence Ball on Reappraising Political Theory[1]

Terence Ball is a leading political theorist who has contributed immensely to the theory of interpretation. Ball, in his work, *Handbook of Political Theory* wrote that 'Interpretation is, so to speak, a kind of triangulation between the text and two (or more) interpretations of it. Hence, we cannot but take others' interpretations into account, reappraising their adequacy and value.' Terence Ball gave his own strategy for interpretation in his prominent work, *Reappraising Political Theory,* published in 1995. An important hypothesis of this book is that if the horizon of knowledge and wisdom is to be expanded ceaselessly, we have to engage ourselves in the task of reappraising, reinterpreting and even reinventing political theory on a continuous basis. His article *Reappraising Political Theory* has been paraphrased below for the readers.

Need and the Way to Study a Classic

The question arises as to why scholars specializing in political theory continue to write about the classics or the great thinkers, of the past. Why no one had a last word on Plato, Aristotle, Kautilya, Rousseau, Mill, Marx or Gandhi? Why could we not have a definitive work about these classics of politics? Why has there been so much fuss about understanding and/or interpreting these great texts in the right context? Why should we read or bother to revise them or their interpretations instead of going straight to the text and see the articles and books about the great political thinkers in order to survive as academicians in the age of publish or perish?

These were often repeated yet unsettling questions to which one could hardly provide satisfactory answers except for the eternal value of the classics for understanding the most fundamental questions regarding the origin and nature of man, society and state. One would also argue about the perennial fascination of classic works for succeeding generations of scholars, each of which reads them anew and from their own point as well as the world view. Further, these classics comprise political and literary traditions, which one renews and enriches by reading, analyzing and criticizing textually as well as contextually.

However, these answers could never fully satisfy any one. Firstly, scientifically minded political scientists complained that the worship of long-dead thinkers was impeding the development of genuinely scientific theories of political behaviour. Nowadays, however, such criticisms come more often from quarters that one would normally expect to be sympathetic to the historical study of political thought. Among them are advocates and practitioners of analytical political philosophy, some of whom see a sustained and systematic interest in the history of political thought as an antiquarian distraction and an obstacle to our thinking for ourselves in more modern and, presumably, more fruitful ways about the pressing political concerns of our own time. They tend to favour not the historical study and interpretation of old texts, but the application of economic, rational choice and game-theoretic models and theories to questions of freedom, justice, political participation, and other concerns. Or, if they do study classic works, it is to either look for insights or for forerunners and ancestors who share their views. Thus (to mention merely two of the many examples),

Hobbes became a proto-rational choice theorist and the Hobbesian state of nature a model of decision-making under conditions of perfect rationality and imperfect information; and Kautilya became a guide to a perfect art of statesmanship and administration.

A second set of objections comes from proponents of multiculturalism in the modern curriculum. We should not, they say, be in the thrall of old books by dead white men, since these canonical texts tend to preserve and legitimize the power of living white males, and to marginalize the views of women, blacks, gays and other minorities. The imperative need, they feel and argue, first is to deconstruct this canon in order to show how it functions to empower some while disempowering or oppressing others; and then to discard, or at least delegitimize and move to the margins, the very idea that there are classic works in political theory that have made a careful study by both sexes, regardless of race or nationality or sexual preference.

Such sweeping criticism has, usually, provoked protest from defenders of the great books and the timeless truths that they teach to the fortunate few. The disciples of late Leo Strauss have been particularly vocal on this score and have also succeeded in conforming closely to the stereotype or caricature created by postmodern critics of the texts comprising the canon.

The Inescapability of Interpretation

Consider first the matter of method. There is in modern academic discourse much ado about one's method or approach to the interpretation of texts. Being aware of, and attentive to, matters of method is no doubt necessary, and to proceed methodically is surely an admirable trait for a scholar (as indeed it could be for a motor mechanic or a carpenter or anyone who practices a skilled craft). The danger is that these means have a way of becoming ends in themselves: method becomes methodology, and a driving force in its own right. Hence, Terence Ball feels that ours is for better or worse an age in which method precedes matter and sometimes pre-empts substance. If one's enquiries are to be both intelligible and legitimate, one must conform to the norms of one's own age and culture, and ours requires that one to begin by describing and defending one's method or approach.

Any reappraisal or interpretation of a text, theory, philosophy—textual or contextual—has to begin with a belief that interpretation is both inescapable and necessary. Next, several strategies of interpretation compete for attention and even, one might say, allegiance as to be considered and even debated. One may find several of these strategies to be mutually compatible, in as much as each answer to quite different but entirely legitimate interests. Therefore, one may have to look for a problem-centred and multi-method approach to interpretation, leading to reappraisals and, at times, revisionist critiques or interpretations.

Disputes over interpretation are almost certainly as old as the human species itself. Although unwritten, the first 'texts'—omens and portents, animal bones and entrails—had to be 'read' and their meaning made clear. Later still, the singers of tales told and retold stories whose meaning was interpreted and reinterpreted from one generation to another. With the advent of the written word came new and even more intractable problems of interpretation, and along with it, there also emerged a written record of the sorts of difficulties faced by interpreters, commentators and critics. Aristotle's *Poetics* is perhaps the most famous, if not the earliest, example of the genre. It could not be said any more that questions of interpretation were merely pleasant pastimes enjoyed by the idle and affluent because lives were often at stake in the interpretation of legal and religious texts. What counts as a capital crime, or as heresy or blasphemy, is a matter of interpretation not only of legal or religious texts, but of the intent of the accused. Thus, questions of interpretation constitute what Terence Ball has called 'deadly hermeneutics'—deadly in as much as people's lives, liberties and happiness hang in the balance.

Another feature of this long history of ideas is the periodic and recurring call to 'get back to basics'—to the text, the author, the author's intention, or whatever—and eschew interpretation altogether. This is the call made with almost predictable regularity by fundamentalists in law and literature as well as in religion. The law or the scripture, they say, has become encrusted with interpretation, each successive layer of which skews or distorts the original or true meaning of the text and/or its author and in the case of holy scriptures, the author. The first task must accordingly be to undo the damage done by earlier commentators. It is in this context that Luther claims interpretation to be the scum of holy scripture and calls for a return to the straight road of scripture, unadorned and undistorted by commentary or interpretation. He explains in the preface to his translation of the New Testament that his own preface is necessary only because earlier interpreters 'have perverted the understanding of Christian people till they have no inkling of the meaning of the gospel... This distressing state of affairs calls for some sort of guidance by way of preface, to free the ordinary man from his false though familiar notions [and] to lead him into the straight road. The irony Ball feels is, that Luther's fulmination against interpretation is itself inescapably interpretive, in as much as it amounts to a defense of one kind of interpretive strategy against other alternatives.

Even now, in one version or another, variations on Luther's complaint can be heard not only from religious fundamentalists, but from judges, lawyers and literary critics. In the United States, some conservative jurists have called even for a return to the original intent of the Founders. And among literary critics some, such as Susan Sontag, take their stand against interpretation.

But surely it is as absurd to be against as it is to be for interpretation, much less to love it, as Professor Fish professes to do. Whether one likes or dislikes interpretations is quite beside the point, for one really has no choice in the matter. The decision to interpret or not to interpret is not an option open to human beings, but a requirement that comes, so to speak, with the territory of being human. For our language-using and meaning-seeking species, interpretation is inescapable. Heidegger put the point with absolute clarity when he said that for human beings, interpretation is an ontological category. Also, Gadamer has underscored the point by saying that hermeneutics—the art and practice of interpretation—is a matter not of method but of ontological necessity.

The world we inhabit and the texts we read, says Gadamer, are never raw sense-data or some ideal *objet trouve* but are always already interpreted and invested with meaning.

We are born and grow into a world made meaningful by the language we speak and the traditions we inherit. And these, in turn, supply us with our own culturally and historically specific standpoint or set of 'prejudices' acting as the vantage-point from which we make sense of our world and the creatures, texts, signs and artifacts that comprise the world for us. But Gadamer also insists that this standpoint, far from being static and unchanging, is historically situated and subjected to criticism and alteration. Indeed, the central thrust of Gadamer's hermeneutics is that, while we necessarily begin with our own present-day prejudices, we need not end them unchanged and forever intact. We extend or expand our present horizon of understanding by encountering and attempting to understand prejudices and practices that at first sight seem strange or alien.

By encountering and trying to come to some understanding of the alien and unfamiliar, we gain a better sense of the historically specific limitations of our own parochial horizon. We attempt to make a distant horizon compatible with our own. In thus effecting, or at least attempting, a 'fusion of horizons' (Horizont verschmelzung), we at once appreciate our distance from and kinship with those whose perspectives differ markedly from our own. And in so doing, we also come to appreciate our common, if differently expressed, humanity. Thus, the art of interpretation, according to Gadamer, is an essential part of the art of living the life of a human being.

This art, however, is not a luxury but a necessity. We cannot dispense with interpretation or get by without it. As communicating and interacting social agents, each of us must in our daily lives interpret the meaning of the actions, practices, and utterances of other people. Suppose, for instance, I see coming towards me a large man, knife in hand and wearing a blood-smeared smock. How I respond depends on how I interpret the meaning of what I see. Placing that sight in a larger interpretive context constituted by certain customs, conventions, and social roles—this is a meat market, that man is the butcher, and I am a customer—permits me to arrive at a correct interpretation and to act accordingly. Instead of fleeing in terror, if engaged in a series of socially appropriate and recognizable acts like placing an order, making a purchase, paying for it, things remain clearer. Of course, such aspects of the everyday taken-for-granted life are ordinarily unproblematic so far as they are pre-interpreted; that is, we do not see a situation and then interpret it, but see and interpret it as a single seamless activity.

However, matters are much more difficult, if we find ourselves in an alien age or culture with whose concepts, categories, customs and practices we are completely unfamiliar. In such situations we are often at a loss to know what is being done, why it is so or what its meaning may be. We therefore need a translation, which is neither more nor less than an interpretation and, moreover affected by fusing that culture's horizon of meaning, with ours. A good translation or interpretation is one that decreases the strangeness of the sight, making it more familiar and accessible to an otherwise puzzled or perplexed observer. To provide such cross-cultural translations is usually the aim of the anthropologist, among others.

The historian of political thought also finds himself or herself in a situation analogous to that of the anthropologist studying an alien culture. The artifacts or texts produced in political cultures preceding and differing from our own do not readily reveal their meanings even to the most careful reader. To read a text over and over again, as some advise, is no doubt necessary. But it is hardly sufficient to enable us to arrive at anything like an adequate understanding of what, say for example, Machiavelli meant by virtue or what Rousseau was trying to do in devising his scheme for a 'religion civile' or what Vico and Marx meant in saying that human beings make their own history or what Gandhi wanted to convey in *Hind Swaraj*. To try to make sense of such terms and actions requires that we interpret their meaning. There is no understanding without interpretation, and no interpretation without the possibility of multiple understandings or/and misunderstandings.

There is hardly a neutral standpoint or Archimedean point from which to interpret and appraise any text, classic or otherwise. All interpretation implies, and originates in, some vantage-point or standpoint or, to use Gadamer's term, prejudice. Every interpretation, in short, implies an interest not simply in the sense that one is interested in an author of text, but rather in the deeper or the transcendental sense that an interest provides the ground for and possibility of an interpretation—a standpoint from which enquiry can begin and interpretation proceed. These interests are usually multiple and varied. One's interests can be contemporary: What (for example) can Gandhi teach us about liberty? Or they may be more historical: Why did Kautilya's arguments in *Arthashastra* take the form they did? Who were Gandhi's main targets, and his intended audience? Or one's interests may be more narrowly linguistic or literary: What tropes and rhetorical stratagems did Gandhi employ, and with what effect? What oppositions and antinomies did Gandhi set up ('liberty' versus 'authority'; self versus other-regarding acts) and which ones did he deny or explicitly eschew ('liberty' versus 'necessity', modernity versus traditions,)? Or one's interests may be logical or philosophical: Were Gandhi's arguments in *Hindi Swaraj* or the curse of untouchability internally coherent and logically consistent? Were there gaps or lacunae in the argument? Did Gandhi construct a compelling case?

None of these interests necessarily excludes the others. But they do construct what will count as a problem, what constitutes an interesting or important question, and what method might be most appropriate and fruitful for dealing with these matters. One would not, for example, assess the logical adequacy of Gandhi's argument by examining his use of tropes. Nor would one be able to answer questions posed from a historical interest or vantage-point by looking only at the logical structure of his argument.

One's method, in short, is dictated by the problem at hand and the interest that one seeks to serve. Thus, all interpretations are, in a word, interest laden. And because they necessarily answer to some interest or other, they cannot be normatively neutral or value-free. Or, to put the point more plainly, all interpretation implies appraisal; and all reinterpretation implies reappraisal. What is in these instances reappraised is not merely the text and author in question, but the adequacy or inadequacy of other interpretations that seek to satisfy a similar interest. Indeed, one's own attempts at interpretation and reappraisal typically begin with some sort of confusion arising in one's reading the text or in going through various interpretations of it.

That much, at least, seems to be fairly obvious and unproblematic. But by what means are we, as students of political theory, to interpret, criticize and perhaps even appropriate for our own use the texts that comprise our contested cannon or 'currency' or 'tradition of discourse'? These are contentious questions, and one has to accept that the terrain on which they are addressed is hotly contested. There are many contestants, in the words of Ball. One part of the battlefield is occupied by neo-Marxists, an adjoining part by realists, another by 'assorted post-structuralists' and deconstructionists, yet another by Straussians, and still another by the 'new historians' of political thought. Each takes a distinctive approach to the history of political thought, and each is highly critical of the others.

Marxists interpret all political theories, past and present—save their own, perhaps—as ideological masks concealing and/or justifying the domination of one class by another. Realists, some of whom are Marxists of one or another sort, view political ideas and theories as playing a causal role in reproducing and legitimating the structures comprising the social world. Post-structuralists would like to deconstruct works by this or that author in order to show how his search for 'foundations' was actually an arbitrary construct. It is such a construct that multiculturalists and critics contend, which contributed to oppression of one or another sort (women by men and blacks by whites).

Straussians, however, claim that a canon of works by Plato and a handful of other authors contain the whole truth about politics, a truth which is eternal, unchanging, and accessible only to the fortunate few. The 'new historians' of the Cambridge School, on the contrary, tend to view texts on political theory as forms of political action, grasping the point or meaning of which requires that one recover the intentions of the actor/author as well as the linguistic resources and conventions available to him or her.

These are just brief outlines of the different broad perspectives available to interpret and reappraise political ideas. Such sketches do not do justice to the insights offered by proponents of these perspectives. But they do suggest something of the diversity of views and vantage-points from which we reinterpret the meaning and reappraise the value of a rich and varied heritage.

Strategies of Interpretation

There are a number of fault-lines that separate the several modern theories of interpretation. One of the most obvious of these is the question of authorial intent. Some of the most perplexing and recurring questions in legal, literary and other kinds of interpretation are these: Can we identify an author's intention in writing this or that work? If we can, should we? What weight, if any, is to be assigned to an author's intentions? Have we discovered the 'meaning' of a text or, more typically, a particular passage, once we discover what the author intended or meant to do in writing it? Or is the meaning to be found in (the reading of) the text itself? Or do we forget the author's intent altogether and look instead at the consequence—often unintended—of an utterance or argument or text?

These are not abstractly academic questions. For example, some American jurists and constitutional scholars contend that the discovery of the original intent of the framers of the Constitution settles the matter of meaning, once and for all. And a similar argument is advanced, albeit in different ways and for different reasons, by Quentin Skinner and Cambridge's new historians. It can be argued that the proponents of original intent are wrong about legal or constitutional interpretation, which differs in important respects from the interpretation in the history of political thought. Here, however, one can try to defend the new historians against often heard criticisms—criticisms to which they have not been able to offer a wholly satisfactory reply.

For instance, one criticism leveled repeatedly against Skinner and the new historians of political thought is that the recovery of an author's intention is unimportant or irrelevant, even if possible in principle. The argument of these critics is that even if we accept Skinner's claim that political writing is a species of action, the fact remains that these sorts of actions—like all human actions—produce consequences unintended, unforeseen and perhaps even unforeseeable by the actor/author. Hence, to recover an author's aims or intentions, even if possible, is besides the point. The history of political thought is, or at any rate should be, the story of the consequences of authorial actions. It should, also, be about the uses to which a writer's ideas were later put by actors whose interpretation of the meaning of a term—be it some utterance, phrase, passage, or entire text—may not and need not accord with the authors own intentions. Or, to put it in other words, the historian's task is to trace the unintended consequences of purposive political action which, in this instance, is the action of writing a political tract or treatise.

While it is true that actions, including the act of writing, often produce unintended consequences, the contention that intentions are irrelevant or do not matter simply does not follow. It is so because logically one cannot validly contention that a certain consequence X was unintended unless one can do two things. One must first be able to show what the author did intend or could conceivably have intended; and then one must be able to demonstrate that X differs from the end(s) that the author intended or could conceivably have intended to bring about. In other words, the very identification of a consequence as unintended requires that one be able to identify what the author's intentions actually are, or were. Hence, it cannot be presumed or concluded that reference to an author's intention(s) is irrelevant or beside the point—particularly for anyone wishing to write the history of political thought or problems or episodes therein as the story of unintended consequences!

This does not, in any case, mean that the historian of political thought should cease enquiries once he/she has succeeded in identifying an author's ideological-linguistic context and the intentions(s) that emerge as possible or likely. That may only be taken to show what a term or utterance, or even an entire text meant for its author, and perhaps for his or her audience; and so it may help to recover the 'historical identity' of the text; but it can hardly be taken as sufficient to show how it was received and interpreted by subsequent reader-authors and their audiences. Here, the reception or reader-response theories of interpretation can become significant.

One has to keep in mind that text is not merely an artifact produced by an author; it is also a communication received by a reader. Its meaning, at least in some part, has to be the product of this process—the 'fusion of horizons' which can, at once be illumination and confusing for readers, interpreters and commentators. It is illuminating in as much as it suggests that there is a vast distance to be bridged. But the metaphor is also confusing, in the sense that a 'horizon' in the visual-perspective sense is one thing, not two and, therefore, not the sort of thing that could be joined or 'fused'.

However, Alan Ryan seems to offer a more prosaic, and perhaps better, way of putting the matter. He says that in reading an earlier work of political theory we are usually tugged in two different directions at once. On the one hand, we want to know what the author was up to and what he or she meant in saying something. But, on the other hand, we also have to recognize that:

> 'Once the essay or book in which we are interested has been put before the public, it takes on a life of its own. Whatever the copyright laws, an author has only a limited control over his own writings. What he writes will have implications which he did not see—implications in the narrow sense of more or less logical inferences from what he says to the consequences of what he says... Works outlive their authors, and take on lives their writers might be perturbed to see.'

As the most obvious instance of this process, Ryan cites the history of how Machiavelli's major works were read, from 1520 to the 1980s with a sidelong glance at Marx's (mis)reading of Hegel.

In fact, what Ryan seems to refer to above are some of the manifold ways in which purposive political actions can, and typically do, produce unintended consequences. And certainly, these do present problems for the historian who takes an internationalist tack towards textual interpretation. These problems are not, however, insoluble or insurmountable, and need not pose any grave difficulty for an approach to interpretation via authorial intention. To appreciate just how and why this might be so, one has to look outside the immediate purview of political theory.

'Suppose I arrive home late one evening. Entering my house, I flip the light switch and several things happen. The light comes on, as I intended that it should. But the light's coming on also wakes the cat, alerts a burglar in the adjoining room, annoys a neighbour, causes the dial in the electric meter to rotate, and raises my electric bill. Flipping the switch is my basic action. The light's coming on is my action under an internationalist description; that is what I was doing, or trying to do, when I flipped the switch. I did not intend, and could not have intended, to wake the cat or to frighten the burglar, since I was in no position to know that the cat was asleep or that the burglar was hiding in the adjoining room. And yet I did, that is, brought about, all these things, not all of which were intended but all of which were made possible by my acting intentionally.

The above example beautifully and quite unambiguously depicts the difference between intended and unintended consequences of action.

The performance of a political action—including the act of writing—is not much unlike flipping the light switch. The basic action of putting pen to paper can be given an internationalist description: the author was doing, or attempting to do, a certain thing—to defend or to criticize royal absolutism, to justify or decry democracy/modernity to promote or oppose religious toleration, or any number of other things. But an author's action may well produce unintended consequences. His argument might, for example, later be used for purposes that the author did not address, and did not or perhaps could not have intended or even foreseen. The concepts used in constructing that argument, and the linguistic conventions according to which it was constructed, may well be misunderstood or deliberately ignored by later writers who wish to extend or perhaps amend what they understood or took this earlier writer to have been doing. Some of these misunderstandings and/or rank misrepresentations may prove fruitful for other writers with their other, doubtless very different, aims and agendas. Two examples might serve to make this point clearer.

Some modern feminists have interpreted Locks as a proto-feminist, in as much as he was, as they are, critical of patriarchalism. Thus, Melissa Butler for one, contends that Locke's critique of Filmer's *Patriarchia* in the *Two Treatises* lays the groundwork, as it were, for modern feminist critiques of male dominion or patriarchy. Locke may himself be surprised to find himself enlisted as an early forerunner of feminism, and he might well be appalled at the prospect. But, while it would be a mistake to claim that, in criticizing Filmer, Locke meant or even could conceivably have intended to add arguments to the arsenal of modern feminists, there is nothing necessarily wrong or illegitimate in taking the view that arguments constructed for one purpose may subsequently be put to some altogether different use. And this, most probably, has happened in the case of Locke's critique of patriarchalism. Locke has, as it were, no copyright or exclusive title to his ideas and arguments. They are part of the public domain, and may be interpreted, appropriated and applied in almost any way by any political actor theorist or critic who finds them to be congenial or useful.

The second example comes from Margaret Leslie's critique of Gandhi and her defiance of the 'anachronistic' readings of earlier thinkers. Strained analogies, and even anachronisms may, in the hands of an ingenious writer such as Antonio Gramsci, prove to be politically persuasive when addressed to a certain sort of audience. In redescribing the Communist Party as the 'modern prince', Gramsci adapted and made creative use of what he took to be Machiavelli's notion of a ruthless and all-powerful Principe. On Gramsci's reading, the Communist Party, like Machiavelli's prince, must be prepared to use guile, cunning, deceit and violence to achieve worthy ends. By substituting 'Party' for 'prince', Gramsci was able to adapt Machiavelli's arguments to a more modern and distinctly different context. That Gramsci's use of Machiavelli's text was admittedly anachronistic is beside the point. As a political actor, Gramsci had, and used, the political equivalent of poetic license.

Skinner's contention, broadly, is that no such license is granted to historians of political thought. If we, as historians, are to understand the meaning that particular terms, utterances, claims and arguments had for certain authors and their audiences, then surely we must, at a minimum, know something about the linguistic conventions of the day and the political concepts, languages, or idioms available to them. Thus, it would be important to note, for example, that the modern concept of the political party, as understood by Gramsci and his audience, was not available to Machiavelli and his contemporaries. One might also note that certain key concepts in Machiavelli's vocabulary, such as fortuna, have no place in—and are arguably at odds with—Gramsci's own rather more deterministic Marxian framework.

To make these observations is, of course, to take nothing away from Gandhi, who wrote not as a scholar but as a practicing social reformer and activist who was, in Skinner's sense, an 'innovating ideologist'. Gandhi, in other words, used an existing and already well-known stock of concepts and images to redescribe and lend legitimacy to an institution widely regarded as suspect. An interpretation like Gandhi's may be adjudged good, indigenous, innovative, ingenious, path-breaking, persuasive and popular on political grounds even as it is adjudged deficient on scholarly grounds, and vice versa.

We must remember that political actors, past and present, are most likely to fight conceptual ideological battles by at times even misrepresenting the opponent's views, constructing arguments, and using almost any rhetorical weapon that comes to hand. And success in such endeavours depends, as often as not, upon one side's skill or sheer good luck in hitting upon an illuminating image or telling metaphor to make its case persuasive or at least palatable. But it is also important to note that such arguments and appeals must be tailored to the tastes, standards and outlook of the audience at which they are aimed. If one fails to take one's audience's standards into account, one runs the grave risk of having one's actions viewed as unintelligible and/or illegitimate. Both intelligibility and legitimacy are for political agents considerations of utmost importance. As Skinner notes, 'the problem facing an agent who wishes to legitimize what he is doing at the same time as gaining what he wants cannot simply be the instrumental problem of tailoring his normative language in order to fit his projects. It must in part be the problem of tailoring his projects in order to fit the available normative language.'

However revolutionary the ideologist, he will nevertheless be committed, once he has accepted the need to legitimate his behaviour, to attempting to show that some of the existing range of favourable evaluative-descriptive terms can somehow be applied as apt descriptions of his own apparently untoward actions. Every revolutionary is to this extent obliged to march backward into battle.

At the same time, however, a political actor and/or author—particularly one on whom we retrospectively bestow the honorific title of political theorist—does things not only with language, but to language in that his or her actions produce changes sometimes intended, sometimes not, in the vocabulary available to his or her audience and to subsequent speakers of the language. Through the use of argument, analogy, metaphor and many other means, he or she may be able to alter the language of description and appraisal in certain ways, perhaps by extending the meaning of a term, or even by coining a new one. But any author daring to do so is likely to proceed cautiously and perhaps even apologetically, as Locke does, for example, in the *Second Treatise*. 'It may perhaps be censured as an impertinent criticism in a discourse of this nature' he writes, ' to find fault with words and names that have obtained in the world: And yet possibly it may not be amiss to offer new ones when the old are apt to lead men into mistakes'... The concept in question is 'paternal power', which in the political-linguistic context of late-17th-century England was being put to a particular political use, namely, justifying royal absolutism. Locke's refutation of arguments in favour of royal absolutism relies rather less upon the coining of new terms than upon showing that 'paternal power', as used by Filmer and other apologists, was by the logical and linguistic standards of the day contradictory and incoherent, rested on misreading or misunderstandings of scripture.

Many other examples could be offered, but it seems quite clear that the history of political thought is in no small part the story of one theorist's commentary on, or criticisms of, a predecessor or a contemporary and among the most powerful weapons in any theorist's arsenal are argument, like Locke's against Filmer, whose objective is to show that an opponent has otherwise contradicted himself. Such Socratic questioning and criticism has been and remains, the political theorist's stock in trade. In so far as its practitioners attend closely and critically to matters of logic and language, political theory is at once a form of political action and a species of philosophical enquiry. But the latter, far from being separate from the former, is an integral part of the enterprise. And both, in turn, play an integral role in the process of political innovation and conceptual change. As Alasdair MacIntyre aptly observes:

> 'Philosophical inquiry itself plays a part in changing moral [and political] concepts. It is not that we have a straightforward history of moral concepts and then a separate and secondary history of philosophical comment. To analyze a concept philosophically may often be to assist in its transformation by suggesting that it needs revision, or is discredited in some way. Philosophy leaves everything as it is—except concepts. And since to possess a concept involves behaving or being able to behave in certain ways in certain circumstances, to alter concepts, whether by modifying existing concepts or by making new concepts available or by destroying old ones, is to alter behaviour. A history, which takes this point seriously, which is concerned with the role of philosophy in relation to actual conduct, cannot be philosophically neutral.'

It is in part the hybrid character of political theory that makes its history, or any particular episode therein, so difficult to interpret and so instructive to study and reflect upon.

There are many different ways of interpreting and understanding what earlier thinkers were doing, and why, and what consequences (intended and unintended) followed from their actions. Let us try to sketch the outlines of the pluralistic and problem-centred approach taken in the present volume.

Meanings and Contexts

In trying to understand any aspect of or episode in the history of political thought, one does not and cannot return to the scene directly. The way back has been illuminated—or littered—by an intervening history of commentary and interpretation of both the political and scholarly varieties. In reading Filmer, for example, one cannot but be aware of the uses to which *Patriarcha* (1680) was put some three decades after his death by defenders of royal absolutism, nor can one be blind to or uninterested in the criticisms that Locke leveled against these latter-day Filmerians. These subsequent uses, interpretations and criticism have, for us, come to be part of what *Patriarcha* means and the place it occupies in the history of political thought. These are facts about an author named Filmer and a text bearing the title *Patriarcha.* The fact that they emerged or developed only after the text's publication and well after its author's death does not detract from impugning their status as facts: that, on the contrary, is the nature of historical fact.

But no reading is innocent or naïve; it is not a direct return to the text and/or context but is filtered through, and coloured by, other readers' reading. The methodological moral to be drawn form this is that we need to be aware of the ways in which our own readings are apt to be beholden to someone else's—and not so that we can be grateful to them, but so that we can critically assess and perhaps disagree and differ with them, in the hope of overcoming the limitations that they impose upon our understanding of (say) Locke or Rousseau or Gandhi. We need, in short, periodically to reappraise the value and validity of the interpretations we have inherited from earlier writers.

Perhaps surprisingly, this task is in one crucial respect like that of the natural scientist. As Imre Lakatos noted, a scientific theory offers a framework for interpreting the data. But these data do not exist wholly independently of the theory: which data are to count as (relevant) data are determined, in part, by the theory (or interpretive framework) itself. Even our most direct observations are impregnated with expectations generated by the theory we hold. Thus there is no neutral or natural dividing line between observational and theoretical statements. All observation is theory laden and involves interpretation of some kind. But if that is true, how can a scientist favour one theory or interpretation over another? Is no theory better or worse than any other? The answer, according to Lakatos, is that science is a search for truth, and this search takes the form of a three-cornered fight between the data and two (or more) competing interpretations of it. Competing theories are not redundancies or luxuries, but are necessary to the enterprise of science itself. So, too, are competing interpretations of texts essential to the enterprise of political theory.

We approach a text, in part, by way of other readings or interpretations of it, against which we counterpoise our own or someone else's alternative reading. Out of these competing readings comes a new, and mostly better, interpretation. This process is sometimes aided by the appearance of better and more accurate versions of a particular text, and even by the discovery of new, non-textual 'data'-such as, for example, the fact that Marx did not try to dedicate *Das Kapital* to Darwin. But, these exceptions aside, we more typically begin by puzzling over a text, aided—or, we may come to believe, hindered—by someone else's attempt to make sense of the same work. And we come to reinterpret the former by taking issue with the latter.

Lakatos' three-cornered fight is characteristic of all interpretive enquiries and has indeed served as an implicit standard among political theorists for quite some time. We have alluded already to Locke's critique of Filmer, a critique necessitated by the use to which Filmer's text was then being put by proponents of royal absolutism. One could also add many other examples, including Gandhi's critique to modern civilization, Marx's critique of capitalism, which proceeded by way of a critique of political economy, in as much as Adam Smith, David Ricardo, and others had supplied some of the concepts and categories in which capitalist production and distribution was re-described, defended—and, not least, legitimated—in supposedly scientific terms.

But such multi-cornered fights are fought not only by political theorists turned activists, but by academic political theorists as well: the form of the fight remains the same, whether the subject be science, political action or political theory. For scholars, the fight must be fair and be conducted according to the academic equivalent of the Marquis of

Queensbury rules. One may not, for example, deliberately misquote or misleadingly paraphrase an author; one must not conceal or suppress counter-evidence that might weigh against one's interpretation, and so on.

These rules for fighting fair do not always or necessarily apply to political actors and activists themselves. The hermeneutical battles waged by innovating ideologists are often far from fair, are rarely scholarly, and are typically conducted by almost any means available. All these were primarily political rather than scholarly works; none can be trusted as reliable guides to the thinkers about whose views they were writing. And that is simply because politics is not scholarship, neither is scholarship politics. It seems to me a mistake—and an inexcusable conceit—to say, as some now do, that all scholarship is somehow political or is 'itself' politics practiced by other means. That view tends to demeans both politics and scholarship.

However, this is not to say that a scholar's motives must not be political; it is only to emphasize that the methods and results of his/her researches must be judged according to scholarly standards, not political ones. The aim of scholarship is to seek and to tell the truth, as best one can discern it, and not to promote any particular partisan cause. Of course, if telling the truth about (say) the sources of Mill's feminism should in some way promote (say) the cause of feminism, well and good; but, as a scholar, one should not suppress or fail to tell the truth simply because one's cause might somehow be sullied or undermined.

One may take up a topic or a thinker out of political interest or ideological preference without thereby forfeiting one's scholarly credentials; indeed, it is probably fair to say that most students of political theory, myself included, have been motivated by political concerns. But the worth of one's work is to be judged, not according to its political correctness (or lack thereof), but according to its scholarly (in) adequacy. One historian of political thought may agree with another about politics but disagree strongly about the other's use of evidence and argument.

It is here, and on these grounds, that the three-cornered fight is waged. It may be, and most often is, a friendly fight between cordial combatants. But, friendly or not, the form is always the same: one interpretation of the data is challenged by another, and both are put to test according to the available evidence (textual, linguistic and historical). But, since such evidence is rarely, if ever, self-evident, it requires interpretation to decipher, uncover, tease out its meaning and significance for and bearing on the problem at hand. And for this purpose, a rival interpretation is indispensable. The second or rival account proceeds not only as reference to these data, but also by way of critique of the first's interpretation of it. This critique is not a distraction or an unfortunate necessity, but is instead an essential feature of the history of political thought.

This is exactly the form in which Macpherson, for example, makes his case against the interpretations supplied by commentators who sketch a picture of the tolerant, democratic and liberal Locke. And the critics who have tried to recover the historical identity of the *Two Treatises* have worked their way back to Locke's texts and context by way of a critique of Macpherson and other interpreters. Although this is not a move supported in the abstract methodological manifestos of the new historians, it is nevertheless one made with thorough regularity in their actual practice. Their programme, in practice, is not a fundamentalist one, deliberately avoiding any reference to an intervening history of interpretation but is, on the contrary, one which takes off from—by taking issue with—prevailing interpretations that they consider to be defective or deficient. We see this kind of three-cornered fight even in the earlier and more militant phase of the 'new history' of political thought.

Consider, for example, John Dunn's preface to the *Political Thought of John Locke* (1969). His is, he says, a 'historical ... account of what Locke was talking about, not a doctrine written (perhaps unconsciously) by him in a sort of invisible ink which becomes apparent only in the writings of a succession of determined philosophers'.

Yet the interpretive principles prescribed in Dunn's highly puritanical preface actually make possible the richness, subtlety, and suggestiveness of the reading of the *Two Treatises* that follows—a reading motivated by, and mounted against, what he takes to be the misreading offered by Macpherson and Strauss, amongst others.

Not that Dunn is alone in following this route. Quentin Skinner's manifesto of 1969, prescribing what historians of political thought ought (not) to do, proceeds by way of a critique of the ways in which historians have heretofore carried their trade. And elsewhere—for example in his enquiry into the ideological context of Hobbes's theory of obligation—Skinner makes his case, not by discarding intervening interpretations altogether and somehow returning directly to the original text and its context, but by way of a critique of contemporary interpretations of Hobbes's account of obligation, such as those proposed by Taylor and Warrender, amongst others. Exactly the same sort of move is made in his other historical works, including his studies of Machiavelli, More and other seminal figures in early modern political thought.

What are we to make of this? Are we to understand the pronouncements and the practices of the new historians? We must, I think, view them in much the same way that they view the writings and actions of historical actors. Their methodological prescriptions must be understood, in part, as polemics directed against a certain sort of historian or commentator. On the one side those 'textualists' who read a piece of political theory as a timeless text of the sort imagined and idealized by New Critics who held that historical context and authorial intention are utterly irrelevant (indeed they claimed that to look for meaning in authorial intention is to commit something they called 'the intentional fallacy'). On the other side one finds contextualists, including conservative Namierites and radical Marxists who, despite their differences, are alike in agreeing that ideas are epiphenomenal, mere flotsam floating on an eternal sea of self, or class or party or national interest.

The purpose here, however, is neither to expound nor to defend the views of the historians but to suggest several affinities between their approach and the tack taken in the present volume. Foremost among these are the following: we are alike in agreeing about the importance; indeed the indispensability of the intellectual, political and linguistic contexts in which political texts appear and do their work. These contexts, in which a text was composed, but also the successive contexts in which it was received, are read, interpreted, criticized, reread and reinterpreted. These we might call the context of a text's composition and the subsequent contexts of its reception, respectively.

From this more complex conception of context, several implications follow. For one, authorial intentions, although important, are not in all cases all-important. For certain purposes, one may wish to discover, recover and restate an author's intentions so as to show what he or she was trying to convey in using a certain word or phrase, or constructing a particular argument in a particular way, or even composing an entire treatise. This is especially important in those instances in which one seeks to understand an author as a political actor. But sometimes we are less interested in Locke, say, than in what subsequent author-actors made of Locke's text, and quite possibly in ways that Locke would not or even could not have intended, did not foresee, and almost certainly would not have approved of. Political actions—including the act of writing—often produce unintended consequences. And this again for the simple reason that the very identification of an outcome as unintended logically requires that we be able, first, to describe the original intention and, secondly, show that the outcome differs from the one initially intended.

More than that, we are less likely to be interested in authors, tests, and/or contexts per se than we are in particular problems that arise as we attempt to understand them. As a rule we do not come to Plato, Locke, Rousseau or even Gandhi wanting to know all about them or their texts or their times, but because we are puzzled or troubled about something on which a certain sort of enquiry might shed some light. Did Locke really mean to defend the property rights of a rising bourgeoisie? How are we to understand the role of a religion civile in Rousseau's Contract Social? What are the probable sources of John Stuart Mill's feminist sympathies? What was the nature of Marx's debt to Darwin and what are its implications for his view of science and social theory? Did Gandhi really think the Indian economy could be made real through rural and cottage industries?

Such problems can come from any source and be of almost any sort. One might be interested in Mill because one is sympathetic to or highly critical of the liberal tradition, or because one believes that liberty is under threat and that Mill might shed some light on our modern predicament. Or one might wish to assess the (in)adequacy of the Western and liberal conception of tolerance in the light of some contemporary question or issue, such as the Salman Rushdie affair, and find it both necessary and desirable to reread and reappraise Locke on toleration and Mill on liberty. In short, the problem-driven 'context of discovery' is wide open, and the 'context of justification' is comparatively restricted. The problems can come from anywhere and be addressed via a variety of strategies; but the (in) adequacy of the solutions must be assessed according to more stringent scholarly criteria.

The historical study of political theory is, in sum, a problem-solving activity. It takes other interpretations as alternative solutions to some puzzle or problem, and then goes on to assess their adequacy vis-à-vis each other and in relation to one's own proposed solution. Interpretation is indeed a three-cornered fight. Hence, we cannot but take others' interpretations into account, reappraising their adequacy and value.

This process of reappraisal is not incidental to the practice of political theory but is, instead, an indispensable, if not indeed defining, feature of theorizing. This craft is in an important sense backward looking. Political theory, more than any other vocation, takes its own past to bc an essential part of its present. Its past includes a history not only of theorizing, of great (and not-so-great) books, but of commentary on and interpretation of those thinkers and tests. It is through the latter that the former are reconsidered, criticized and reevaluated—in short, reappraised. One might even put the point more strongly by saying that the seminal works of political theory are kept alive and vivid by not being worshipped at academic shrines but rather through carefull and criticall reappraisal.

It might, therefore, appear that political theory, at least as regards its reappraisive function, is a benign and harmless enterprise and the modern student of the subject a mildly curious creature in the academic zoo. Yet political theory is not without critics from various quarters, some of whom are occasionally quite vociferous. Some political scientists think of the political theorists in their midst as historians or perhaps philosophers. Historians, however, may not wish to claim them as colleagues, and philosophers might not understand political theorists' interest in history and, stranger still, in politics. All, moreover, are suspicious of the claim that thinkers long dead might somehow be connected with, and might in some respects illuminate, the darker recesses of our present condition.

Such suspicion sometimes erupts into open hostility. During the 'behavioural revolution' of the 1950s and 1960s, many political scientists went on the offensive against the aliens in their midst. Political theory was charged with being antiquarian, non-empirical, and, worst of all normative—that is, concerned with the values or subjective preferences of this or that long dead thinker and/or his or her present-day interpreter. This bill of indictment, as I attempt to show in this chapter, was predicated on the philosophy of sciences and a conception of cognitive meaningfulness that has long since been repudiated by philosophers of science. But academic political theorists were also attacked from the other side by critics who claimed that the classics of political theory were the antiquated, sexist, racist, homophobic texts of dead white men, all sharing the aim of perpetuating and legitimating the dominance of themselves and their descendants. There was, accordingly, a call to disavow, if not eliminate from the curriculum, the classics, the canon of 'Great books' that, when read and taken seriously by students, can only serve to justify the unjustifiable.

Since the present work is intended, in part, to be an answer to contextualize, the classics and political theory therein, I would say that I do not think of it as ridiculous or entirely ill founded. There are, if not texts, then certainly ways of reading or interpreting them, that give aid and comfort to those who wish the worst for some of their fellow human beings. One need to only think, for example, of the ways in which Hitler and the Nazis used (and arguably abused) the works of Nietzsche—or Stalin the works of Marx—to justify genocidal policies. But it is no less important to note that the disclosure and criticism of such misunderstandings is itself an integral part of political theory. Far from being the sort of hagiographic exercise portrayed by some of its present-day detractors, the study of political theory is, above all, a relentlessly critical enterprise. As such, one of its essential features is its attention to the ways in which authors and texts are appropriated and used—or, as often as not, misappropriated and abused—by would-be defenders or disciples.

Five points merit particular mention in appreciating any perspective which can be adopted in reappraising political theory. The first and most important, as I have noted already, is that of choosing a method. A method of interpretation varies with and is usually dictated by the particular interpretive problem being addressed, and not the other way round. A method is not like a stretch sock: one size does not fit all feet. Nor, by the same token, can any single method or approach—textual, contextual, Marxist, realist, Strauss Ian, or whatever—possibly illuminate, much less resolve, every conceivable problem of interpretation.

Second, these interpretive problems can come from any source, historical, contemporary, literary or political. These problems provide the interest or vantage point from which interpretation proceeds. Ball's enquiries proceeded not only from problems within the text, but, no less importantly, from questions raised and interpretations advanced and defended by subsequent commentators, often in idioms that were unavailable to the author. Charges that the theories of Plato or Rousseau were totalitarian or that Bentham was a feminist fall under this heading. Although anachronistic, these characterizations are not necessarily illegitimate. They may be useful and illuminating in some contexts but not in others, and at times act as a stimulus to the reinterpretation and reappraisal of a theorist and his or her work.

Third, it may be worth trying, in so far as possible and where appropriate, to place the text within two contexts, the first being the context of its composition, which necessarily includes some reference to its author's intentions and the second being the various contexts of its reception which may or may not take account of authorial intent.

A fourth feature is that an attempt be made, wherever possible, to show how an earlier theorist, and/or a subsequent interpretation casts light on contemporary problems. The light must, of necessity, be indirect or reflected—Machiavelli and Marx, for example, are not our contemporaries—but no less valuable for that. A particular way of reading Thucydides or Machiavelli, for instance, could conceivably illuminate the darker corners of our present condition as no reading of a modern self-styled realist such as Henry Kissinger can.

Fifth, and finally our aim should invariably be to try to show what a pluralist and problem-driven approach to the history of political thought can (and cannot) hope to achieve. If the proof of the pudding be in the eating, then nothing is to be gained by talking about pudding in the abstract, or various recipes for pudding, or what various culinary experts—imported from France or elsewhere—have to say about the matter. Nor will a General Theory of Pudding be of much use. One must sample for oneself and, in so far as possible, trust one's own taste-buds, whether the result be retching or, as I [Ball] hope, the kind of curiosity that leads one to one's own, and doubtless better readings and reflections.

Quentin Skinner on Meaning and Understanding in the History of Ideas[2]

Quentin Skinner is a well-known political theorist. He published a seminal essay *Meaning and Understanding in the History of Ideas* which turned out to be a milestone in the art of interpreting the history of ideas. Skinner pointed out the inadequacies of earlier methods of textual interpretations. Ideas reflect historical stages in the growth of society. Taking a contextual approach, Skinner provided his own perspective—a historically more sensitive approach to reading and interpreting a classical text. In the succeeding pages, Quentin Skinner's *Meaning and Understanding in the History of Ideas* has been paraphrased for reader.

This essay tries to discuss some of the problems created due to a certain way of reading the classical texts. The approach that is being discussed here is that of having a history of ideas. The author has attempted to bring out the flaws of this approach through various arguments and examples.

What do the Historians of Ideas do?

The task of the historian of ideas is to study and interpret the classical texts. The attempt is towards bringing out the 'dateless wisdom' or 'universal ideas' present in moral, political and religious writings. The idea is to gain from these 'timeless elements,' as they are believed to be of significance in all times, irrespective of the period in which they were written. The focus is kept on what was 'said' about certain 'fundamental concepts' related to morality, politics, religion and social life. These texts are re-read as though they were written by some contemporary thinker for the present times. It is believed that while undertaking such studies, one must not go into the details of when and in which social context were these written, as this would divert attention unnecessarily from the main concept and thus lessen their importance and value.

The Problem with this Approach

This point of view is being questioned in this essay. It has, for long, been believed that the classical theorists have a command over certain 'fundamental concepts'. This has caused much confusion over the years in the history of ideas. There are various ways in which this thought is misleading. First of all, the problem is that a certain continuity of ideas in a given field of thought is unavoidable. The new concepts do have some links with the earlier concepts. Without these resemblances, it would be difficult to relate activities to each other. History would become meaningless if we do not recognize these connections. Actually, this leads to greater confusion.

Now, the problem can be clearly pinpointed. If we just concentrate on what the classical texts 'say' about certain concepts then actually we will not be able to understand what those theorists meant by that concept. Our own preconceptions are bound to colour that concept (and in that case, it would certainly loose its original meaning). Psychologists face this dilemma very often as an observer, sometimes his own mental set up, sees the reality in that specific way.

Put in other words, the problem is that in order to understand, classification has to be done but in order to classify, we must take the help of familiar categories. This poses the danger of seeing the new material through the old categories, which might not be the right categorization. May be we could have come up with some new forms of categorization otherwise. And we could be imposing our meaning on someone else's thought, someone else's concepts.

The Problem with the Paradigm

A preset pattern or understanding is called a paradigm and this essay attempts to show that although such paradigms are important and have often brought out significant results, sometimes such paradigms create an illusion where the concepts from the past are wrongly, forcibly conjoined with the study of morality, politics and religion in the present times. So much so that sometimes such accounts seem less of history and more of *mythology*.

This also involves assuming that a certain classical writer said such and such thing about an issue.

History or Mythology?

One such way through which the historians come up with mythologies is that of assuming that each classical writer must have had a doctrine of his own on all the concepts related to his area of study. Such attempts sometimes even create these doctrines. This happens in various ways.

Concepts Reinterpreted or Wrongly Interpreted

Any chance remarks by a theorist would be taken up and used as a point 'from his doctrine'. Such an erroneous connection could be established by some biographer or historian of ideas who is working on building up some 'unique idea' or concept.

In the first situation, a biographer can interpret a remark or comment made by a classical thinker in a way entirely unintended by the thinker himself. There have been such instances of gross misinterpretation or superimposition of one's own notions on somebody else's words. For example, Marsilius of Padua in his *Defensor Pacis*, remarked that the executive role of rulers is in contract with the legislative role of the people. Now some modern commentator, who is familiar with the doctrine (popular since the American Revolution) that one condition of political freedom is the separation of executive from legislative power, would propose that Marsilius should be taken to be the founder of this doctrine. Marsilius was not referring to the question of political freedom while making that comment and yet, thanks to this form of imagined connection-making exercises, it is a point of debate whether he was or was not referring to that doctrine, although he was clearly not familiar with that line of events.

Similarly a statement, given by Sir Edward Coke on the Bonham case was that the common law of England may sometimes override statute. The modern commentator (specifically American) would associate it with the doctrine of judicial review which came much later. Coke knew nothing of such a doctrine. He was making that statement in an entirely different context where a party politician of law is custom and not, as James believed, the will of the sovereign. What follows after such erroneous interpretations is that a debate follows whether he meant to say so or not. People who disagree with this deep-connection between the past and the present also ironically base their conclusion on Coke's text and do not question the attempt which in the first place assumed that Coke must have meant to say this.

Another danger such suppositions pose is that of finding doctrine in the classical texts where none existed.

For example, Richard Hooker commented in Book I of his *Of the Laws of Ecclesiastical Polity* upon natural sociability. Now he was merely distinguishing between the godly origins of church from the mundane origins of civil associations. But that comment was seen as the first step towards the 'theory of social contract'. Or when John Locke makes a remark somewhere in his *Two Treatises of Government* about trusteeship, he is believed to be coming up with the doctrine of the political trust.

The point is that if the writer meant to propose such a theory, why did he himself not do so and why is it that the historian has to reconstruct their ideas through guesses and hints.

The Danger of Half Truth-Half Imagination

How half truth-half imagination brings out absurd notions can be seen from an illustration of what the pioneer of this approach, Arthur Lovejoy, has to say about the method of this approach. First of all, one must create an ideal type of the doctrine to be traced back in history—it could be that of equality, progress, reason of state, the social contract and the separation of power. Then one must trace its roots back in history and for that, each and every part of history where this was mentioned in any form must be noted.

The danger with this approach is that the doctrine to be searched becomes an entity in itself, and then the historian starts treating it as though it has always been present in the past too. It is argued that it has always been there but could not come up strongly, because maybe it was not understood properly then, or maybe it faced obstacles or maybe it dropped from sight several times.

Emergence of a doctrine is presented as though the story of development of an organism is being told. For example, we are told that the birth of the idea of progress was quite an easy one; it overcame the difficulties presented by the 16th century and gained ground through the next hundred years. But the idea of the separation of powers came into the world with greater difficulty. Although it almost emerged during the English civil war, it took another century for the three-fold division to emerge fully.

The Absurdities Created Due to this Mythicization

Whenever this kind of approach is followed, two kinds of absurdities arise. The writers of the past are credited with having extraordinary, almost magical, capacity of foreseeing the doctrine of the future much before they actually emerged. For example, Marsilius of Padua is considered notable for his contributions because he foresaw the emergence of Machiavelli's theory. Machiavelli is notable because he 'laid the foundation' for Marx. John Locke's theory of signs is notable as an anticipation of Berkeley's metaphysics. They are even praised or criticized for 'being like us' or 'not being like us'. Machiavelli's political ideas are very much like our own so he is praiseworthy. But other thinkers of his time were not like us, so their views are completely unreal.

Another absurd thing that happens as a result of such an approach is that extensive debates begin regarding whether that unit idea/concept was really present in the past in that form or not. An imagined course of movement is debated upon causing further absurdity. When the history of ideas takes up the theory of separation of powers and 'traces' its past—the debate begins whether the doctrine was present in the works of George Buchanan? No, he did not clearly express it, but he was the only one to come closest to it. So, it must have come up clearly by the royalists during the English Civil War, when they presented their constitutional proposals. No, it is not in its pure from even there on. Or consider the theory of social contract; was it there in the pamphlets produced during the French religious wars? No, because there it was incompletely developed. So, was it there in the works of the Catholics at that time? No, not even there but definitely better expressed than the others.

So, the mythology of doctrines tends to convert stray, scattered remarks into hints of doctrine by the classical writers—and, interestingly, these discovered doctrines are the ones that the historian had set to *discover* at the outset. They claim to have found what they started with.

The Other Aspect of the Problem

The *opposite* of this also happens when this kind of approach is followed. A classical theorist who 'fails' to provide any such clues of doctrine in his work, is criticized either for not having a vision for the future or for having serious drawbacks. Thomas Hobbes or sometimes Niccolo Machiavelli is made responsible for man's first disobedience. His works are termed 'immoral and irreligious' by Leo Strauss, a chief proponent of this approach.

Basically, however, what these historians of ideas do is to supply the classical theorists with beliefs which were not there in the first place. Thomas Aquinas may not have called 'civil disobedience' foolish but that he would not have approved of it. Marsilius of Padua would have approved of democracy since the sovereignty he espoused pertained to the people. Such attempts are dangerous because through these, the historian presents his own prejudices as the ideas of more popular thinkers in the name of understanding their works. Through this, history is made into a dirty game where the ideas of the writers *who are no more* are hugely misrepresented.

The most usual practice is to take up a doctrine, criticize some classical writer for having failed to mention it and show how incompetent that theorist was. This approach is so dominant in the field of history of political ideas that even the most anti-essentialist of theorists, T. D. Weldon has not questioned it. In the first part of his book *'State and Morals,'* he has presented various definitions of state as 'formulated' by several political theorists. He maintains that all the theories of the state fall into two main groups: 'some define it as an organism, others as a machine' and further adds that even the theorists considered to be the leading thinkers fail to present a clear, consistent theory of state. Their works are full of inconsistencies. Only Hegel comes closer to using one of the two main models of describing a state. Without these models, what sort of theory can one hope to come up with? So, in his opinion, he has clearly cracked the code of what the theory of state should be like and he has discovered that none of the earlier political theories have had the clarity of thought to think on those terms. Everyone except Weldon himself has been confused.

The literature on history of ideas is full of such imagined, constructed misguidances. Let us take up, for example, the question of importance of voting, role of public opinion in the political theory. Now, these questions have gained importance in modern times with the introduction of representative democracies. This does not matter to commentators and they go on criticizing Plato's *Republic,* for leaving out any discussion on the influence of public opinion. Or for criticizing John Locke's *Two Treatises* for not being clear on his understanding of the question of universal suffrage. In a historical context, where popular rule was not an issue of discussion, how can the historian find flaws with the writers of that time about not having paid any attention to points related to modern day issues like universal suffrage, voting, public opinion and people's rule?

Another aspect of such mythological constructions is that it is assumed that these classical writers wanted to put forth some great theories of modern concern. And then, when obviously their writings do not show that level of contribution, they are criticized for presenting a flawed work, a weak theory or an unclear concept. For example, it is first assumed that one of Machiavelli's basic concerns in *IL Principe* was to explain the characteristics of men in politics then obviously his work would seem one sided and unsystematic. Again, if it is first assumed that Locke's *Two Treatises* talks of natural law and political society, then clearly his work would seem to be of poor quality since he fails to talk of a world state. The question is whether, in the first place, these writers intended or even could have intended to do what then are criticized for not doing.

A Second Type of Mythology

Another aspect of the mythical constructions by the historians of ideas is that they usually set out searching for theories in the works of the classical writers where there were none. In other words, it may not at all be necessary that those writers did not express themselves very coherently or did not elaborate much upon a certain point. Now, these historians of ideas often take on the responsibility of providing coherence to these theories of the classical writers, that is, they fill up the 'gaps' in the theory, thereby not only dangerously changing the meaning of what the original writer wanted to say, but also coming up with an abstract message which can be passed on because it is clear.

In writing about the history of moral and political philosophy, this coherence is most essential. This they create by all means, at all costs, by every effort. So, if Hobbes' political philosophy is not clear, his work *Leviathan* must be read, re-read till some coherence is visible. Or, if Hume's work does not seem consistent, an effort should be made to go through all the works of his until consistency is displayed at all costs. If Herder's political ideas are scattered throughout his work, then it is the duty of the historian 'to present these ideas in some coherent form.' The attitude of the historian of ideas is that of effort and quest to find coherence where there may not be, need not be, could not be.

Who Needs the Details? Just Find Some Coherence

This attitude tends to restrict and close the ideas provided by these thinkers. A forced coherence misrepresents their contributions which could have been very expansive and wide ranging originally. If it is assumed that a study of Rousseau's philosophy must search for most fundamental thought, then it would belittle his contribution over several decades to several fields of enquiry. If Hobbes is assumed to have presented his views mainly on a general 'Christian' system, then it hides his major contributions to the relations between ethics and political life. If Edmund Burke is supposed to have worked on a coherent moral philosophy then the variety of thoughts put forth by him would go absolutely unnoticed.

It could be so that a certain writer was interested in various issues and has reflected on a variety of topics but to force a coherent structure out of these would be incorrect. In their attempt to come out with some clear theory and not finding one the works of the classical writers, these historians of ideas criticize them for being incoherent, unsystematic. Great effort is made towards systematizing Marx's various remarks and ideas, but such an activity is difficult because Marx was concerned with a wide range of different issues at different times. After failing to systematize his work he is accused of having presented his ideas in a fragmentary manner.

First these writers are categorized as having a certain model of thought and then criticized for not really coming up to that model thought. First it is assumed that all conservative thinkers must hold some organic conception of the state and then Lord Bolingbroke is criticized for not having that sort of an idea of the state. First it is assumed that any philosopher who writes about the theory of justice, would write about one of the three basic points on that subject and then, Plato or Hegel are shown to be rather incoherent about these points. It becomes completely unimportant that they were not writing in today's context or that they were expressing their views in an entirely different socio-political context. It does not remain a historical study anymore; it becomes something far from it, a mythological construction by the historian.

Even stating this problem clearly with illustrations has not had an impact. It still goes on and misguides in two ways. One, there is an attempt to dismiss what the writer himself wanted to say. His points are overlooked if they seem to disrupt the line of thought discovered by the historian. Due to this, sometimes complete works are ignored. Locke is treated as a liberal political theorist but the information ignored here is that in his thirties he favoured conservative and authoritarian stances. It was only in his fifties that his views changed. He is not considered 'Locke' till his fifties.

Then there is Hobbes who has quite clearly presented his political theory on the issue of Civil Rights in '*The Sovereigns and the Duty and Liberty of Subjects*' and has undoubtedly related it to the mutual relation between Protection and Obedience. This work has been seen as indirectly referring to the 'religious character' of the whole system and the historian wonders why Hobbes was not forthright about it.

Another related tendency, in this manner of thinking, is that a contradictory less, clear theory must be extracted out of the varied works of the classical writers. It is believed that there has to be a single line of thought specific to that theorist. No consideration is paid towards the path of development that his ideas took. He might have changed his views under different intellectual influences over the time, but those complexities are forcibly ironed out. A simple, generalized theory is created using the works of the thinker. Machiavelli's two works, *IL Principe* (1513) and *Discorsi* (1519) are quite different in their notions and yet the usual attempt is to come up with a general theory of Machiavelli that integrates both the works in a manner where the two do *not* show any contradiction between them. Similarly, Karl Marx is not allowed to have changed his pattern of thinking from his days of Economic-Philosophical Manuscripts to *Das Kapital.* Instead of presenting the changes his ideas underwent over the time, the historian of ideas informs us that Marx was actually 'obsessed with a moral vision of reality' and is not a scientist of society but a moral-religious thinker.

Complexity of Work Reduced to Contradictions in Work

Leo Strauss, a promoter of this approach, maintains that often whenever such contradictions in the works of a writer are observed, they are explained as an attempt by the writer to avoid persecution, social and intellectual criticism. He is only pretending to stand by those ideas in order to be away from any controversy. It is for the readers, the historians to see his true opinions and overlook the seeming contradictions.

Such a defense of the historian's approach is problematic because it assumes two things at the outset. One is that the original works must have been against the popular ideas of that period. Two, uncovering the real theory behind the presented work of the writer is a very intelligent thing to do. Those who feel that two aspects of a writer's work are plainly contradictory, are simply being careless and unintelligent.

Does the Author Know Better or the Interpreter?

Till now, we saw how having certain preconceived notions about the works of a certain writer can lead to misjudgements about his work. It is believed that such incorrect, misguiding references would only be possible at an abstract level. However, it has been observed that even while describing the finer details of some writer's work, preconceived notions exercise their influence.

When a historian describes the work of a certain author, he leaves no space for what the author himself had to say. In discussing the importance of relevance of that work in present context, he completely overlooks the context in which that work was put forth by the author at that time. For example, it is often suggested that with Petrarch's ascent of Mount Ventoux, the age of Renaissance dawned. But whether Petrarch himself intended to show this through his act does not concern the historian of ideas. Another crude version of such attempts is where Plato's political views in *The Republic* are said to be one of a 'totalitarian party politician'. Similarly, Rousseau is held responsible for the emergence of totalitarianism.

There is another less-noticeable fashion in which such misrepresentation of historical works takes place. For example, Machiavelli is called the founder of 'modern political orientation' (this bit is historically significant) but where this phrase is used as a starting point of a discussion of the modern elements in Machiavelli's thought, then it becomes problematic. Not only are certain ideas discovered through this but also the original meanings of that author's thoughts are lost. Similarly, Locke is seen as one of the founders of modern liberal school of political thought. But to then go on to say that he was himself a liberal political theorist would be going beyond the fact/truth.

While explaining the meaning of these writings, the interpreter might describe the meaning of it in an incorrect manner if he fails to connect the writings with the socio-political circumstances in which those were written. The usual mistake made is that of mixing up the classical works with the concepts the interpreter is familiar with. It is like trying to understanding some other culture *purely* on the basis of knowledge about one's own culture. It is unavoidable to use one's own knowledge but the problem begins when only that is used and the context in which the original work was created is totally ignored.

This sort of attitude leads to two kinds of problems. One, unnecessary links are assumed between two works where there is no link. The interpreter would find some similarity in a modern and a classical work and would then assume that the modern work must have been inspired by the classical one. It is true that works are inspired by other works but the connection must not just be assumed; it must be proved. The connections should not be mythological or imagined but real. For example, Edmund Burke's political views were supposed to be an answer to Bolingbroke's work, who himself is said to have written under the influence by Hobbes who, in turn, is said to have been influenced by Machiavelli.

Such connections are purely imagined. If real connections are to be seen, then three conditions must exist, first, the inspired author must have read the works of the earlier author. Secondly, that inspiration could not have come from any other writer and finally the inspired writer could not have come up with those ideas for sure, on his own.

None of the writers discussed above who are said to be linked by a chain of inspiration fulfill these conditions. They have not read the work they are supposed to be inspired by; the influence in none of the cases is specifically from the said authors (it could have come from many other writers of that time) and about the third test, one can never tell as to how far an idea can be called original (because somewhere or the other, the direct/indirect influence does exist).

Putting Meaning Where there is None

The other misguiding impact that a flimsy connection between theories of the past and concept of the present can have is that such give a certain meaning to the past activities or events which was never there.

For example, if a historian decides that a fundamental feature of the radical political thinking of the English Revolution during the mid-17th century was to ensure the right to vote to all, then he will show that Leveler's demands were also along the same lines when the demand of democracy was raised. The danger arises when the concept of a 'philosophy of liberal democracy' is used as a blanket term for understanding the Leveler movement. In such a case, some of the very important characteristic elements of Levelers ideology cannot be explained; they will seem out of line. For instance, then we cannot understand why did he raise his voice for monarchy, or why did he appeal to people's religious sentiments, because if he was for democracy then both these elements of his ideology go against democratic values, and they are the characteristic features of his ideology. Leveler is, by some imagined connection, associated with the fight for right to vote while he was not into any such efforts.

Similarly there is the example of Locke's *'Two Treatises'*. In his work, he has talked about the right to resist tyrannical governments. A historian who thinks that this argument is about the importance of consent in any lawful political community would lead the readers towards a wrong argument. He has used a modern concept of 'government by consent' to explain the work of Locke's but what the concept really stands for and what Locke was talking about are actually two entirely different things. The words may seem similar somewhere but the context and meaning of the two thoughts are absolutely unconnected.

While the concept of 'government by consent' talks of the legal arrangement that must be there if a civil association is to be called legitimate; Locke's concept of consent arises in connection with a description of the *origins* of legitimate political societies.

Can We Avoid Paradigms or Reference to the Past?

The problem discussed till now is that a historian of ideas cannot avoid being influenced by the present-day paradigms in discussing the earlier works and that it is also dangerous. However, what can be done to surpass this danger is to understand that there are certain considerations that must be kept in mind before making statements or before understanding the statements made by other people. What follows is a methodological solution to this unavoidable problem.

If the author himself was so clear about the future significance of his ideas or if he was presenting a certain concept, he is the best person to tell what exactly he means by his concept. If he himself has not connected it with some larger theory or idea, then no one else has the authority to assume what he wanted to say. If at all a need to interpret his concept arises then such an attempt must be very careful in doing so. It must be described within the range of descriptions that the author himself would have used. The interpretation should remain clearly within the context given by the author himself. Otherwise, the interpretation cannot represent author's idea.

And if this consideration is kept in mind while interpreting some classical theorist's work, then the criticism that he did not present his theory properly or clearly would also disappear because it is wrong to criticize a theorist for not being theoretically clear when he did not intend to discuss that aspect. There is no sense in asking questions which the theorists did not seek to ponder upon, in the first place. They were not writing in response to modern day queries; their works must be seen in their specific context if their real, actual meaning is to be understood.

The problem that arises due to imagined connections between the works of different theorists is that they mislead. They are more like stories, created, or made up. They are far from the truth.

One last consideration that must be kept in mind while interpreting some thinker's work is that it must be realized that thinking is not an effortless activity. In the course of thinking of problems, various sorts of activities and ideas come up. There are contradictory ideas that fight with each other; there emerge ideas that are beyond our pattern of thinking and they sometimes tend to create confusion in the mind of the thinker. He ponders over them, changes his earlier ideas and presents something totally new. So, while he may come up with a coherent theory, he may also given certain unclear concepts. This effort and this pattern are ignored when an attempt is made towards systematically presenting the scattered thoughts of a classical writer. It must be kept in mind that this confusion or un-clarity are equally important while discussing someone's work. These confusions actually explain how the ideas developed and what influenced them to come up. They form the context in which these works emerged originally.

Is Having a History of Thoughts a Good Idea?

Till now, the dangers of understanding the classical texts at a very surface level have been shown. (The danger lies in just picking up words from those texts and assuming their meanings). Now, it has also been argued that with some care, such dangers can be overcome. But actually the point remains that such an approach of interpreting the classical texts in the context of modern concepts is basically wrong.

From now on, the attempt would be on putting forth an argument even stronger than the one given till now. The approach being discussed here, in principle, cannot help us to arrive at an adequate understanding of the texts we study in the history long of ideas.

The basic reason behind this is that if we wish to understand any such classical text, we must be able to not only give the meaning of what was said but also of what the writer himself may have meant by saying what he said. A study that focuses just on what a writer *said* about some doctrine would be inadequate and misleading because the meanings of terms we use to express our concepts sometimes change over time. So, what a writer meant to say then may mean something else in today's context, if we just concentrate on what he said. For example, when Bishop Berkeley's doctrine of immaterialism was called by the critics as having 'egoism' in it, they did not mean to say that it had 'Hobbism' in it (which a historian of ideas would interpret). When they used the term egoism, they meant to say what we today mean by solipsism (a theory that the self is the only existing thing).

Another way in which what a writer said and the interpretation of his work fail to connect is when a certain irony is observed in their statements.

Using this argument that ironically what they said seems totally different from what they meant or would have meant is also misguiding.

Taking the statements and remarks made by a classical theorist at their face value is misleading. For example, Thomas Hobbes, while discussing the laws of nature, somewhere claims that the laws of nature are the laws of god, and that we are obliged to obey the laws of nature. Now this is a statement that uses the term god to bring forth the importance of the laws of nature (just as people who believe in god follow his rules so everyone should follow the rules of nature). He was a known skeptic (critical of established traditions) and usually this statement is not taken too seriously by those who know his work. But the promoters of this approach (of having a history of ideas) insist that Hobbes must have meant what he said and that he was actually a believer. Similarly, Pierre Bayle whose *Dienonnam* contains theories appropriate to a Calvinist theology (a sect in Christianity opposed to the Catholic Sect) is not known as an anti-Catholic but some commentators argue that he was not a non-believer, but a man of faith.

Now, the inadequacy of the approach used by the revisionist interpreters is being pointed out through these examples. The revisionists (the historians of ideas) claim that a study of the texts by these theorists in itself can show what they meant to say. Such an analysis wrongly assumes certain notions, not just about the writers, but also about the times they were living in. Their contemporaries, both the critics as well as the sympathizers, believed that Hobbes and Bayle were against the prevailing religious orthodoxies. Both these writers were well aware of the dangers of being against the religious orthodoxy in those times. Two assumptions follow: one, either they were in favour of religious orthodoxies (as the revisionists claim); or two, they were against the religious orthodoxy. The revisionists' argument does not stand because the two writers lived in fear of being attacked for their writings at various points in their life and also, if they were so in favour of religious orthodoxy, then why did they not change the major sections of their works which talk against religious orthodoxy.

How to Read a Classical Text?

So, just by reading the texts written by those writers again and again, we cannot hope to get to the meaning of their works. We would have to connect it with the information beyond the text; the information about the socio-political conditions in which they were writing.

Basically, the argument is that while trying to understand the meaning of any serious remark, just a study of what he said is not sufficient. To understand the meaning, we need to know: What is said? What is the intended force with which it is said? We need to know not just what these writers were *saying* but also what they were *doing in* saying it.

It is very important to know *what they meant by saying it,* and not just what is the meaning of their words.

The Problems with the 'Unit Idea' Quest

The approach that says that individual works from the past can be understood keeping in mind the development of a certain 'unique idea' can be questioned by an argument of

Wittgenstein. According to him, it is very important to ask the question: What were the writers doing when they made those statements? What was the problem that they were addressing while presenting those remarks? It is only then that the meaning of their work can be understood properly.

For example, Descartes in his *Meditations* has argued in favour of the idea of unquestioned knowledge. The historians of philosophies have never asked the question why and under what circumstances did Descartes present this idea. Everyone takes for granted that he was a philosopher who dealt with the question of certainty, so in that context he must have talked of this as well. It was later found out by some of the scholars working on Descartes' theory (when he asked the question: 'Under what circumstances did this remark/idea come up'?). It was, in fact, in response to a very strong belief in skepticism (a belief that one should question each and every idea). This information throws a new light on the meaning of Descartes' works; it explains the special character of his work.

When Lovejoy (a promoter of the approach of history of ideas) attempts to 'track the development of a unique idea through several individual texts', he is taking us in a wrong direction, because he is assuming that conditions in which an idea develops are not important and also that an idea has existed on its own and different works have just 'approached' it differently. It also assumes that an idea exists beyond the individual works where it has been found.

For example, an attempt was made to write the history of the idea of nobility in early modern Europe. In one context, it has been used to refer to a marked noble quality; in another, it stands for a class; in yet another context it means that one can have noble qualities even if not being noble by birth; in another it means nobility is a quality attained by deeds but is often seen in people noble by birth; and in yet another context it is used in a disreputable sense.

It is not sufficient to understand a term in one context, if a history of that idea is to be written. It must be studied in all the contexts wherever it appeared, all the points that it was then trying to make in different contexts.

The mistake that historians of ideas like Lovejoy make is that of looking for the 'essential meaning of the idea', as something that 'remains the same'.

The second problem that such approach causes is that it ignores the theorist's contributions. They are merely shown to be contributors towards the development of that idea. This sort of approach ignores many important questions like: What role did this idea play in the thought of those thinkers? What place did that idea hold in the intellectual climate of a given period? If these questions are asked, then we get to know a lot.

We come to know how this idea was an answer to some problem of its time and what is its significance and what are the reasons that still make it relevant.

This exercise would actually show that there cannot be a history of a unique idea. There is no unique idea, the ideas that have emerged at different points in time have had their specific contexts and have not necessary emerged out of each other.

But Connections with the Past are Important

To say so does not mean that we are saying that continuities in philosophies have not existed or there have never been certain key concepts in philosophies. What we are saying is that we need to move beyond the study of those continuities.

One reason is that they were not really answering similar questions when they gave their individual ideas.

The second reason for moving beyond such histories is that these tend to block out the individual contributions, the actual meaning of the ideas presented by a given thinker.

Two Conclusions

The appropriate method of studying the history of ideas involves an understanding of what these works wanted to say when they were put forward. The context in which that work appears is the best judge of what the writer intended/wanted to say.

The importance of studying the history of ideas lies in a possibility of mutual enrichment between historical evidence and philosophical analysis. How, with time, the meaning and concepts change form. The issues raised in the past and the solutions offered can guide the philosophers of today.

The main conclusion is that instead of looking for the answers, the classical texts gave for the problems of that time and directly using those for our present-day problems we should do our own thinking for ourselves.

But this does not mean that the study of the history of idea is useless. What we can learn from them is how there exist various ways of thinking about issues. Different periods had different types of problems and the answers were also different for each of those problems. This tells us that each case is unique, each social period has its own specificities and this must be kept in mind while looking for an answer to their problems. It is most important to learn that there are no timeless issues or evergreen answers; and that issues and concepts are the specific truth of specific societies at a certain point of time. This is the best lesson we can learn, that we should learn from the history.

Summing up

The theory of interpretation has made significant movement. Leo Strauss and others have favoured the textual approach as against the contextual approach of Sabine. Skinner, through broadly the contextual approach, extended its meaning and scope by bringing in linguistic and ideological aspects in its fold. Further, Skinner underscores the crucial importance of authorial intent. Terence Ball has moved a step further by bringing the context of the reception of given text within the broad fold of the context, though not totally ignoring the original intent of the writer. Quentin Skinner's approach to interpretation has several positive aspects. Firstly, it has led to the study of various minor historical texts which might have been otherwise ignored by scholars. Secondly, Skinner's main argument that classical texts are not that monolithic and context-free is useful in analyzing the contemporary issues. James Tolly rightly said that Skinner is not solely concerned with history and the method; he uses both to throw light on the present. The approaches made by Quentin Skinner and Terence Ball are very useful in analyzing, locating and understanding Gandhi's writings.

Notes and References

1. Paraphrased version of the Terence Ball article, *'Reappraising Political Theory'* in *Reappraising Political Theory*, Oxford:, Clarendon Press, 1995.
2. Paraphrased version of the article by Quentin Skinner titled *'Meaning and Understanding in the History of Ideas'* in *Visions of Politics* Vol. I, Cambridge, 2002.

Summary

- From time to time, scholars and social scientists have raised the question of how to interpret a text. The two most popular methods are the textual and the contextual.
- In the textual method, the reader needs only to read the text in order to understand its meaning.
- In the contextual method, while reading a text one must keep in mind the social and historical environment in which the text was written.
- Terence Ball was a leading political theorist who has contributed a lot to the theory of interpretation.
- Ball's important hypothesis is that if the horizon of knowledge and wisdom is to be expanded ceaselessly, we have to engage ourselves in the task of reappraising, reinterpreting and even reinventing political theory on a continuous basis.
- Terrence Ball mentioned five points which can be adopted in reappraising political theory.The first and most important is that of choosing a method.Second, the interpretive problems can come from any source, whether historical, contemporary, literary, political or whatever. These problems provide the interest or vantage point from which interpretation proceeds.Third, it may be worth trying, to place the text within two contexts, the first being the context of its composition which necessarily includes some reference to its author's intentions and the second being the various contexts of its reception which may or may not take account of authorial intent.A fourth, to show how an earlier theorist, and/or a subsequent interpretation casts light on contemporary problems.Fifth, to show what a pluralist and problem-driven approach to the history of political thought can (and cannot) hope to achieve.
- Quentin Skinner is a well-known political theorist. Ideas reflect historical stages in the growth of society. Taking a contextual approach Skinner provided his own perspective—a historically more sensitive approach to reading and interpreting a classical text.

- The task of the historian of ideas is to study and interpret the classical texts. The attempt is towards bringing out the 'dateless wisdom' or 'universal ideas' present in moral, political and religious writings. The idea is to gain from these 'timeless, elements', as they are believed to be of significance in all times, irrespective of the period in which they were written.
- The appropriate method of studying the history of ideas involves an understanding of what these works wanted to say when they were put forward. The context in which that work appears is the best judge of what the writer intended/wanted to say.
- The importance of studying the history of ideas lies in a possibility of mutual enrichment between historical evidence and philosophical analysis. How, with time, the meaning and concepts change form. The issues raised in the past, the solutions offered can guide the philosophers of today.
- Instead of looking for the answers that the classical texts gave for the problems of that time and directly using those for our present-day problems, we should do our own thinking for ourselves.
- The theory of interpretation has made significant movement. The approaches made by Quentin Skinner and Terence Ball are very useful in analyzing, locating and understanding Gandhi's writings.

Further Readings

Rothy, R., J. B. Schneewind, and Q. Skinner (eds.), *Philosophy in History*, Cambridge, 1984.

Suleiman, S. R. and I. Crosman (eds.), *The Reader in the Text,* Princeton, NJ, 1980.

Schochet, G. J., *Patriarchalism in Political Thought,* New York, 1975.

3

Hind Swaraj

Introduction

Hind Swaraj is Mahatma Gandhi's unique, fundamental and unparalleled work. It is India's contribution to political theory after Kautilya's *Arthashastra.* Gandhi was a political activist who responded creatively to the socio-political and economic circumstances in which he was situated. *Hind Swaraj* is an alternative to modern socio-economic-political thought. It is a book, which cannot be ignored in any discussion or any debate on issues such as human progress, socio-economic development and contemporary problems. It is a key to understanding not only Gandhi's life and thoughts but also the present dilemmas arising out of technology, industrialization and globalization. Even now, *Hind Swaraj* continues to evoke critical interest across the world. It is not only a book on how to win political freedom for India, it is a Magna Carta for the freedom of the mind and the evolution of human species from conscious and material beings to super-conscious and moral beings.[1] In fact, *Hind Swaraj* is a manifesto for a new world order based on supremacy of ethics and morality over matter. It continues to represent the voice of the voiceless, that of the common man of India, and even of the common people of the whole world. *Hind Swaraj* gives power to the powerless and provides nonviolent techniques of change and social transformation.

Hind Swaraj is one of the earliest of the few books that Gandhi wrote during his hectic public life. All his other writings are in the form of articles, statements, letters and speeches. *Hind Swaraj* has a pivotal position in his writings, because in this small but 'severe' booklet is contained Gandhi's ideas, and which Mahadev Desai has aptly termed 'seminal'. The book, in Gandhi's own words, has had a 'chequered career'.[2]

Raghavan Iyer says, *Hind Swaraj* is 'the point d'appui [fulcrum] of Gandhi's moral and political thought'. Margaret Chatterjee called *Hind Swaraj* 'a very basic document for the study of Gandhi's thoughts'. B. R. Nanda called it Gandhi's 'confession of faith'. Erik Erikson called it 'a rather incendiary manifesto'. Dennis Dalton called it 'a proclamation of ideological independence.' Judith Brown called it 'the nearest he came to producing a sustained work of political theory'. Similarly, Gerald Heard compared *Hind Swaraj* with Rousseau's *Social Contract.* George Catlin (1950) compared it with *The Spiritual Exercises* of St. Ignatius Loyala.[3] K. Swaminathan has remarked in the Preface to the tenth volume that 'Hind Swaraj… occupies in the Gandhi story much the same place as Chapter 4 of St. Matthew or St. Luke in the New Testament'. John Middleton Murry hailed it as 'one of the spiritual classics of the world'.

Hind Swaraj is a work which Gandhi himself translated from Gujarati into English. It is the seed from which the tree of Gandhian thought has grown to its full stature. For those readers who are interested in Gandhian thought in a general way, it is the right place to start; for it is here that he presents his basic ideas in their proper relationship to one another. And for those who wish to study his thoughts more methodically, it remains the norm by which to assess the theoretical significance of his other writings, including his autobiography.[4]

The unique beauty of *Hind Swaraj* lies in its capacity to present a very scientific and philosophical discourse in the most ordinary language. In other words, the book is written in perfect Gandhian style—terse, simple and logical. The principal theme of *Hind Swaraj* is the moral inadequacy of Western civilization, especially its industrialism, as a model for free India. The basic feature here is that every time you go through the book, you will gain a new interpretation and a new insight. It is in *Hind Swaraj* that we find Gandhi first announcing his own life's mission. This is nothing other than showing the way for the moral regeneration of Indians and the political emancipation of Mother India. *Hind Swaraj* teaches 'the gospel of love in place of that of hate. It replaces violence with self-sacrifice. It puts soul force against brute force'.[5]

Context of *Hind Swaraj*

The immediate context of writing the booklet was Gandhi's encounter with the Indian anarchists in England and their cult of violence. It is not only the cult of violence that provoked Gandhi to write this tract. On the contrary, it goes much deeper and is more comprehensive in its sweep. The entire Western or material civilization forms the very backbone of his critique.[6]

One can discover three issues clearly emerging in *Hind Swaraj.* First is the then current politics in India, its leaders and political events and Gandhi's own position in relation to them. Second, and rather the most crucial issue is the entire question of material or 'modern' civilization. And, lastly, there is the question of passive resistance that is positioned as an alternative to what Gandhi calls the brute force.[7]

In *Hind Swaraj*, three streams of thought merge and what finally emerges is a manifesto warning against what Gandhi called the mad race after civilization or (according to more recent usage) modernization. *Hind Swaraj* is a critique of modernization, which in Gandhi's words, is identified with the Western, material, modern civilization. The critique does not stop there. One can discover the contours of what he called, 'the whole theory of life', emerging from the discussion recorded therein. It is a theory of life, which is not static. No theory, which seeks to build up an alternative to the one in vogue, can be static. It is, indeed, a dynamic model theory, which acquires greater precision as Gandhi's experiences through his public life accumulate. Mahatma Gandhi considers 'Parliament' and 'machinery' to be the mainstay of modern civilization and, therefore, warns against their importation.[8]

On October 9, 1909, Gandhi[9] wrote a letter to Lord Ampthill, which contains the very ideas which formed the basis of *Hind Swaraj:*

- Impatience with the British rule was widespread in India and so was the hatred of the British.
- The above being the case, repression would be counter productive.
- British people were obsessed with commercial selfishness and, hence, the British Government would not concede to the rights of the Indians.
- The fault lies not with the British people but with modern civilization which is a negation of the sprit of Christianity.
- All that shines as modern—the railways, machines, the style of life and other things, are a true badge of slavery of the Indian people, as they are of Europeans.
- Rise of large cities like Calcutta and Bombay was a matter of sorrow, not of congratulation.
- India has lost because her villages are destroyed.
- Violent methods are built in the modern civilization and so is immorality.
- I share the national sprit but I do not agree with those who want to use violence directly or indirectly to win freedom for the country because it is immoral and against the sprit of Indian civilization.
- Rulers must rule according to the wishes of the people; the moment they fail in their primary duty, people must refuse to recognize them and cooperate with them.

Hind Swaraj raises some fundamental questions. India's encounter with Britain was not political and economic but civilizational. Even today, the situation is no different from the one when Gandhi wrote *Hind Swaraj*. For proper understanding of *Hind Swaraj*, it is necessary to refer to its historical context which, in the main, consisted of six situations or developments:

- The general developments in India since 1857.
- The emergence of new professional classes.
- The circumstances prevailing in India with special reference to the partition of Bengal.
- The Russia-Japanese War, and the revolutionary fervour in Czarist Russia.
- The situation in South Africa and Gandhi's experiences and experiments there
- The immediate provocation for Gandhi to write *Hind Swaraj*.[10]

The book was addressed to a mixed audience: the expatriate Indians who were greatly attracted to terrorism and political violence, the Extremists and Moderates of the Indian National Congress, the Indian nation (means ordinary Indians), and the English (means both the British ruling class living in India and Britons living in Great Britain).

As to why Gandhi wrote the book there was, first of all, the question of an inner illumination and the consequent urge to communicate. Gandhi's intentions in writing *Hind Swaraj* have been grouped by Anthony J. Parel[11] under six rubrics. These are:

- Gandhi harboured the ideas contained in *Hind Swaraj* for quite some time. Gandhi was impatient to communicate them to the people around him and world over, especially the Indians who were his immediate concern.
- He wanted to clarify the meaning of Swaraj, which was far wider and deeper than political independence.
- Gandhi wanted to reopen a peaceful path of conflict resolution perfected by Indian civilization and convince the people of India, especially the youth, to abjure terrorism and return to the Indian way.
- Gandhi wanted to tell his countrymen that it was not the British colonialism which was their real enemy. The real enemy was Western civilization. So long as they remained mesmerized by Western civilization, they would remain slaves even if they get political independence.
- Gandhi was keen to see that Indians and British part political company as friends, not as enemies. He did not consider the British to be the enemies of Indians; the enemy was the modern (industrial) civilization, which afflicted them both
- He wanted to use *Hind Swaraj* as a vehicle to give to India an updated version of *dharma*, which even a common man could understand and which would fit its people for life in the modern world. 'I have used the language of politics, but I have really tried to offer a glimpse of dharma'. Thus, Gandhi wanted to make British occupation of India as an opportunity to fully realize the potential of Indian civilization.

Parel[12] then looks into the historical contexts in which Gandhi wrote *Hind Swaraj*. These contexts include:

- The hold of modern industrial civilization on the minds of the people all over the world, especially in the West. *Hind Swaraj* challenged this civilization and branded it as satanic. According to Parel, 'Its critique of that civilization is one of its main contributions to modern political thought'. While criticizing modern civilization, Gandhi was not negative and vindictive. He commended some of its contributions which Indian civilization lacked or did not pay the attention they deserved—civil liberty, equality, human rights, prospects of improving the economic conditions of the poor, emancipation of women from tradition and religious toleration. He was critical because its tendencies were lopsided, because its concept and practice of freedom did not amount to Swaraj. In fact, it negated it. It promoted rights at the cost of duties, economic progress at the cost of moral and spiritual progress, and divided the world into us and them using religion, political dispensation, economic status, military might and education as dividers. It negated human brotherhood and the concept of *Vasudhaiva Kutumbakam*.

- The political situation in South Africa where Gandhi evolved as a Mahatma was another historical context in which *Hind Swaraj* was written. It was in South Africa that he first acquired the vision of Indian nationalism. In fact, South Africa was the foundation on which he realized himself as a leader. Parel rightly says that South Africa enabled him to transcend colonialism as the cause of the plight of Indians there. The culprit was the modern civilization, which had grabbed the entire humanity by its neck.

  South Africa freed Gandhi from many of the constraints he would have got, had he been in India. He could not work without any social and religious pressures but also experiment with his ideas in places like the Phoenix Settlement. But for his being in South Africa, he would not have got the opportunity to go to London on lobbying missions in 1906 and 1909 and thus acquire his diplomatic skills.
- The third historical context that Parel identifies is the politics of the expatriate Indians, especially of those based in London, which was centred on preparation for violent struggle against the British. This brought Gandhi closer to many of the revolutionaries and prompted him to write *Hind Swaraj*.
- The Indian nationalist movement was yet another context in which Gandhi wrote his book.
- Gandhi's acquaintance with Western people, philosophers and thoughts was a major factor that shaped and sharpened the views contained in the *Hind Swaraj*.

The above-mentioned ideas were developed in *Hind Swaraj* or *Indian Home Rule*, a small book of about 30,000 words (96 pages), written in Gujarati on board the ship RMS Kildonian Castle during Gandhi's return trip from England to South Africa after an abortive mission to London. It was written in ten days from November 13 to 22, 1909. The whole manuscript was written on the ship's stationery, and the writing went on at such a furious pace that when the right hand got tired Gandhi continued with the left. He worked day and night on the manuscript. An astounding 40 of the 275 manuscript pages were written with the left hand. And Gandhi wrote as if under inspiration. In the entire autograph, only sixteen lines have been scratched out and only a few words changed here and there.[13] As stated by Gandhi himself: 'I wrote the entire *Hind Swaraj* for my dear friend Dr. Pranjivan Mehta. All the arguments in the book are reproduced almost as it took place with him.'[14]

The book first appeared serially in the *Indian Opinion* and later it was published in book form, to be proscribed in March 1910, by the Bombay Government, because it contained 'matter declared to be seditious'.[15] On that, Gandhi published the English translation from Natal to show the innocuous nature of its contents. The ban was finally lifted on December 21, 1938. When Gokhale saw the translation, he thought it to be so crude and hastily conceived that he prophesied that Gandhi himself would destroy the book after spending a year in India. In 1921, Gandhi said: 'with deference to the memory of the great teacher, I may say that his prediction has failed to come true.' Gandhi, speaking about writing of the book said: 'I withdraw nothing except one word of it, and that in deference to a lady friend'.[16]

The *Hind Swaraj or Indian Home Rule* is a severe condemnation of modern civilization. It is divided into twenty chapters and two appendices. It deals in detail with Swaraj, civilization, lawyers, doctors, machinery, education, passive resistance and other matters. It answers practical questions in the most scientific and original way. It is written in dialogue form, reaching great heights in some places. It is a faithful record of conversations that Gandhi had with workers, one of whom was an avowed terrorist.

Divided into four themes elaborated or enunciated in various parts of the book, namely core concepts: nonviolence, education, and technology; criticism of Parliament, of machinery and of the Congress view of Swaraj; *Hind Swaraj* as an assessment and a critique of the Western civilization with reference to non-Western civilization with non-Western criteria; and prescription.[17] *Hind Swaraj* is the quintessence of all that Mahatma Gandhi had read, thought and experienced by the age of forty. While a student in England, he came in contact with radical and liberal groups and individuals. It was there that he read extensively, thought deeply and gained firsthand experience of the working of Western civilization. The most distinctive influence on the formation of his ideas was through the works of Tolstoy, Ruskin, Thoreau and Edward Carpenter, all vehement critics of industrial life and advocates of simplicity.

The substance of Gandhi's attacks in *Hind Swaraj* is 'machinery', that is, technology. It 'is the chief symbol of modern civilization; it represents a great sin'.[18] In *Hind Swaraj* Gandhi declared 'Parliament' as a 'prostitute and a sterile woman'. He indicates that *Hind Swaraj* posits an ideal state of things in which there will be no machine, no railways, no doctors, no lawyers and other such things as are the symbols of modern civilization. It is not Rousseau's state of nature, but the ideal society of Marx in which the state will wither away, minus the modern type of technology (machinery) to which the former (Marx) was wedded unconditionally.[19]

Gandhi's thinking about the whole question of industrialization seemed to be running along two parallel levels. At one level, he seemed to be concerned with the problem of poverty and unemployment. Gandhi was very clear about this issue. He knew that the Western pattern of industrialization involved per capita investment of a magnitude, which India could hardly afford to generate unless it took to either authoritarian or totalitarian methods. Gandhi's aim was to revive cottage and village industries. In other words, what he was seeking was the resuscitation of the village through the revival of its handicrafts. It must not be supposed that Gandhi believed in the static, archaic mode of production in the village prevalent in the past. He welcomed every improvement in the village craft (small unit) if it led to increase in productivity. The only condition attached was that the improvement must not render people unemployed. He was even willing to accept the use of energy in the form of electricity, if it could be useful for village industries, in case the village owned the power plant. At another level, Gandhi had a more fundamental objection to Western patterns of industrialization. It is in this respect that his approach differed both from the liberal and the Marxian approach that put their faith in an ever-growing material standard of life. And for this very purpose, they depend upon an intensive exploitation of natural resources, minerals and fossil fuels. This leads them to multiply machinery which Gandhi called the 'craze for machinery'. Agriculture, therefore, becomes the backbone for pushing ahead with such a pattern of industrial development. Exploitation of agriculture leads to the growing desolation and ruination of the villages and the pauperization of the village population, which eventually finds its sanctuary in the cities, in the slums and in overcrowded, cramped spaces. This further leads to an unrestrained urbanization with all its attendant evils of crime, prostitution and has been aptly termed as 'street corner societies'.[20]

A very critical element in Gandhi's critique of modern machine technology is that it leads to conflict among nations and ultimately to war. 'Blueprint for Survival,' a collection of statements by thirty-three of Britain's most distinguished scientists have reaffirmed the faith in Gandhi. Recent critics who question the very basis of its dependence on the present-day technology reinforce Gandhi's objection to modern civilization. Since technology is predicated upon increasing consumption of natural resources, which, the critics point out, are limited, the entire superstructure of the so-called civilization is threatened with destruction. Gandhi cried a halt to this mad pursuit after indiscriminate multiplication of machinery.[21]

Gandhi questioned all these assumptions. He was not against science as such. Modern science is grounded on two fundamentals. The first is the kind of science which penetrates the nature of reality, tries to go deep into problems of the universe, raises issues of a philosophical nature and tries to establish or reject them through its experiments, and makes an effort through its findings at unification of man with the deeper reality in which he has his being and becoming. But there is yet another dimension of science, that is, the dimension of its application to solving the physical needs of the humankind.[22]

Gandhi warned against all these appoints and suggested moderation and restraint. It is in this context that he prescribed the application of science only when its usefulness had been assessed in all its multi-dimensional relationship with man, society and nature. Today, we are witnessing a civilizational crisis because the entire system of machine technology is threatened with a crash as sensitive minds, scientists and others are warning us today. Gandhi was perhaps the first in the previous century who realized the deeper and long-range implications of this technological progress. His entire response to it is one of caution, restraint and limitation. It originated in *Hind Swaraj* as a response of a particular civilization, namely, of the Indian civilization to the Western. Gandhi's thinking evolved within the orbit of the world developments (including the two World Wars); his response acquired a universal character, embracing the whole mankind and verging on a precipice where the large-scale high technology has brought it.[23]

Gandhi could easily reconcile it with his basic philosophical position. What emerged from this was a way out of the present civilizational crisis. We may now chart out the basic ingredients of the Gandhian scheme. In Gandhi, man emerges at the centre of all social, economic and political development. This man is the spiritual man, aligned and wholly integrated with his community and his surroundings.[24]

Hind Swaraj is a warning against indiscriminate large-scale mechanization of life and a pointer to the future. The rudimentary model presented therein is, as we have indicated, not static. It is, on the contrary, dynamic in so far as it assumes a more sharply defined shape as Gandhi's thinking becomes global in character through time. *Hind Swaraj*, therefore, must be placed within the framework of Gandhi's thought as it developed through his active life.[25]

In *Hind Swaraj*, Gandhi reopens the debate, which had raged in India in the second half of the 19th century, and raised his voice against modern, Western civilization. He also offered a concept of normal society having its roots in India's past along with its values. Gandhi revalidated the essence of Indian civilization; he made the plea that it be accepted as the starting point of the next phase of India's growth in order to transform it in the long run. Two other factors determined the format and the content of *Hind Swaraj*. The patriotic Indians in London had come to the conclusion that India should 'adopt modern methods of violence and modern civilization to drive out the British'.[26]

Gandhi had evolved a different approach to life on the basis of his experiments in South Africa; he disagreed with the patriotic Indians about their diagnosis and prescription.[27] As a point of clarification, we should like to point out that Gandhi's denunciation of railways, lawyers, doctors, parliaments, machinery and brute force should not be taken literally. These have only an emblematic or metaphorical significance. Gandhi means more than what he says.[28] Gandhi enunciates a 19-point programme of action entitled *Chhutkara*, which means 'the emancipation'.[29]

Hind Swaraj provides a scathing critique of Western civilization. The three recurrent themes are colonial imperialism, industrial capitalism, and rationalist materialism.[30] According to Gandhi, colonialism triumphed in India not because of its strength but because of Indians' inherent weaknesses, which allowed 'this intimate enemy' to take root. Gandhi was the first person to have attributed the British rule in India to a 'moral decline' affecting the entire nation.[31] Attributing colonialism in India to 'our weakness', Gandhi thus argued that 'The English have not taken India; we have given it to them. They are not in India because of their strength, but because we keep them…'[32]. According to Gandhi, the British conquest of India was solely due to the Indians' moral failure.[33] In *Hind Swaraj*, Gandhi produced the most effective trans-cultural protest against the hyper-masculine worldview of colonialism. In other words, *Hind Swaraj* is the most creative response to the perversion of industrial capitalism.[34] For Gandhi, industrialization remained the driving force behind Western civilization. 'Machinery is the chief symbol of modern civilization; it represents a great sin… If the machine craze grows in our country, it will become an unhappy land.'[35] 'It is necessary to realize that machinery is bad. We shall then be able gradually to do away with it… If, instead of welcoming machinery as a boon, we look at it as an evil, it would ultimately go.'[36] According to Gandhi, 'a snake-bite is a lesser poison than the mill industry because, while the former merely harmed the body, the latter destroys body, mind and soul.'[37] According to Gandhi, there remained a tension between true civilization and a civilization based on machines. While the former is based on brute rationalist materialism, the latter draws its sustenance from dharma. In modern civilization, artha (money) and *kama* (desire) are totally divorced from dharma on the basis of the alleged superiority of rational materialism.[38]

On the one hand, *Hind Swaraj* was Gandhi's creative response to the theoretical basis of Western civilization. Drawing on the civilizational resources of Hindu religion and its tradition, he put forward a new theoretical framework to conceptualize both colonialism and industrial capitalism. On the other hand, he developed the fundamental precepts of what later became Gandhism. The three important themes that recur not only in his writings but also in his deeds are Swaraj, *swadeshi* and *satya*. Swaraj was rule of self by the self. It was, therefore, more than a political idea. For the Mahatma it meant India's spiritual liberation through a fundamental change in each individual's perception. Swadeshi, which meant self-respect, self-realization and self-reliance, was not merely glorification of traditional and indigenous methods of production but a creative application of the available means meaningful to the people in consideration. His debate is not on 'whether India needs technology'; his debate is on 'the kind of technology that India needs'. *Satya* is truth-force and only *ahimsa*. Together with *ahimsa*, *satya* constituted *Satyagraha*. It was a method of securing rights by personal suffering. *Satyagraha* was an indigenous combination of reason, morality and politics; it appealed to the opponent's head, heart and interests.[39]

Contents of *Hind Swaraj*

The opening chapters 1-3 deal with the Indian National Csongress and the Indian awakening. Chapter 4 explains the true meaning of Swaraj. A critique of modern industrial civilization is presented in chapters 5 and 6. The pitiable condition of India is elaborated in chapters 7-12. The reason why Gandhi considered Indian civilization to be a truly modern civilization is given in chapter 13. The potency of *Satyagraha* or passive resistance is explained in chapters 14-17. The following chapters 18 and 19 discuss the problems associated with modern education and technology. The last chapter concludes with a summary of the entire book. Appendix I lists twenty references for further reading, including six by Tolstoy, two by Thoreau, two by Ruskin, one by Plato (*Defense* and *Death of Socrates*), and one by Mazzini (*Duties of Man*), and one each by Dadabhai Naoroji, and R. C. Dutt on the economic condition of colonial India.

In a letter to a friend in India, Gandhi[40] summarized the contents of *Hind Swaraj* in the following words:

- There is no impassable barrier between the East and the West.
- There is no such thing as Western or European civilization, but there is a modern civilization which is purely material.
- The people of Europe—before they were touched by modern civilization—had much in common with the people of the East; anyhow even today Europeans who are not touched by modern civilization, are far better able to mix with Indians than the offspring of that civilization.
- It is not the British people who are ruling India, but it is modern civilization, through its railways, telegraph, telephone, and almost every invention, which has been claimed to be a triumph of civilization.
- Bombay, Calcutta, and other chief cities of India are the real plague spots.

- If British rule was replaced tomorrow by Indian rule based on modern methods, India would be no better, except that she would be able to retain some of the money that is drained away to England; but then India would only become a second or fifth nation to Europe or America.
- East and West can really meet when the West has thrown overboard-modern civilization, almost in its entirety. They can also seemingly meet when East has also adopted modern civilization, but that meeting would be an armed truce, even as it is between, say, Germany and England, both of which nations are living in the Hall of Death in order to avoid being devoured, the one by the other.
- It is simply impertinent for any man or any body to being or to contemplate reform of the whole world. To attempt to do so by means of highly artificial and speedy locomotion is to attempt the impossible.
- Increase of material comforts—it may be generally laid down—does not in any way whatsoever conduce to moral growth.
- Medical science is the concentrated essence of black magic. Quackery is infinitely preferable to what passes for high medical skills as such.
- Hospitals are the instruments that the devil has been using for his own purpose, in order to keep his hold on his kingdom. They perpetuate vice, misery and degradation and real slavery. I was entirely off the track when I considered that I should receive a medical training. It would be sinful for me in any way whatsoever to take part in the abominations that go in the hospitals. If there were no hospitals for venereal diseases, or even for consumptives, we should have less consumption, and less sexual vice against us.
- India's salvation consists in unlearning what she has learnt during the past fifty years or so. The railways, telegraphs, hospitals, lawyers, doctors, and such like have all to go, and the so-called upper classes have to learn to live consciously and religiously and deliberately the simple life of a peasant, knowing it to be a life giving true happiness.
- India should wear no machine-made clothing, whether it comes out of European mills or Indian mills.
- England can help India do this and then she will have justified her hold on India. There seems to be many in England today who think likewise.
- There was true wisdom in the ages of old having so regulated a society as to limit the material conditions of the people: the rude plough of perhaps five thousand years ago is the plough of the husbandman today. Therein lies salvation. People live long under such conditions, in comparative peace much greater than Europe has enjoyed after having taken up modern activity, and I feel that every enlightened man, certainly every Englishman, may, if he chooses, learn this truth and act according to it.

Similarly, R. P. Misra[41] summarizes the contents of Hind Swaraj beautifully in a nutshell:

- The so-called modern civilization is not Western civilization because there was no difference between East and West before the modern industrial civilization engulfed the West

- The exploitation of the East by the West is not because of the civilization they have been bitten by
- India has not been invaded by the British; the Indians were so lured by the industrial civilization that they invited the British to rule over them.
- Exploitative urbanization symbolizes modern civilization.
- The problem is not the removal of the British and their replacement by Indians but how to change the system to bring in a truly modern civilization.
- Improvement in the material welfare does not, in any way, uplift man morally. Improvement in the moral standards of life ennobles even materials progress.
- Medicine, as it is practiced, is the major cause of diseases.
- Legal system generates discord among the people; it rarely brings people together
- Craze for machinery is a dangerous proposition; labour-saving machinery is good if everyone has work for livelihood and creativity.
- Violence breeds violence; *Satyagraha* is the weapon of the strong, not of the weak
- Ends and means are inseparable; we cannot achieve noble ends by wrong means. Right means will always lead to correct ends.
- 'Simple living and high thinking' alone can bring peace and harmony.
- Primary education means moral education.
- There was true wisdom in the saying of the sages having so regulated a society as to limit the material conditions of the people.
- India will be free the moment Indians cast away the lure of modern civilization.

Gandhi on *Hind Swaraj*

Writing the introduction to the Gujarati edition, translated and published in the *Indian Opinion* on November 22, 1909, Gandhi said, 'The views I venture to place before the reader are, needless to say, held by many Indians not touched by what is known as civilization but I ask the reader to believe me when I tell him that they are also held by thousands of Europeans.'[42] However, when the English translation was published, Gandhi wrote a comparatively longer introduction on March 20, 1910: 'The British Government in India constitutes a struggle between the modern civilization, which is the kingdom of Satan, and ancient civilization, which is the kingdom of God.' In the same year he wrote to Gokhale that the ideas contained in the book 'have been matured in the course of the struggle…' Again, writing to Maganlal Gandhi, he said, 'My present state of mind is such that even if the whole world is against what I have written, I would not be depressed.'[43]

Gandhi published Mr. Wybergh's criticism written in the form of a letter dated May 3, 1910 in the *Indian Opinion* issue of May 21, 1910.[44] In reply, Gandhi, in his letter dated May 10, 1910 concentrated mainly on an exposition of passive resistance, because most of the remarks in Mr. Wybergh's letter centred round it. However, in answer to Wybergh's criticism of his views on modern civilization, Gandhi categorically stated: 'I have ventured utterly to condemn modern civilization because I hold that the spirit of it is evil. It is possible to show that some of its incidents are good but I have examined its tendency in the scale of ethics.'[45] In 1914, when the second Gujarati edition was brought out, Gandhi wrote: 'I find that the convictions I started in the book have grown stronger.'[46] Further, 'The key to an understanding of *Hind Swaraj* lies in the belief that worldly pursuits should give way to ethical living.'[47] Writing to Maganlal Gandhi in 1919, Gandhi said: 'Besides, the more experience I gain, the more I realize that machinery will keep us in personal slavery and I find that what I said in *Hind Swaraj* is literally true'.[48] In 1920, answering the critics, he said: 'I do not ask India to follow today the methods prescribed in my booklet. If they could do that, they would have Swaraj not in a year but in a day. What I am doing today is that I am giving the country a pardonable programme for the attainment of parliamentary Swaraj'.[49]

In 1921, he carried the explanation still further. In his foreword to the book, he sounded a note of caution to the reader.

> 'But I must warn the reader against thinking that I am today aiming at the Swaraj described therein. I know that India is not ripe for it. It may seem an impertinence to say so. But such is the conviction. I am individually working for the self- rule pictured therein. But today, my corporate activity is undoubtedly devoted to the attainment of parliamentary Swaraj in accordance with the wishes of the people of India. I am not aiming at destroying railways or hospitals, though I would certainly welcome their natural destruction. Neither railways nor hospitals are a test of a high and pure civilization. At best, they are a necessary evil. Neither adds one inch to the moral stature of a nation. Nor am I aiming at a permanent destruction of law courts, much as I regard it as a "consummation devoutly to be mills. It requires a higher simplicity and renunciation than the people are today prepared for".'[50]

In 1924, answering some objections, Gandhi wrote:

> 'I have nothing to withdraw from what I have written in the Indian Home Rule… It must be remembered that it is not the Indian Home Rule depicted in that book that I am placing before India. I am placing before the nation parliamentary, that is, democratic Swaraj. I do not suggest today a destruction of all machines, but I am making the spinning-wheel the master machine. The *Indian Home Rule* depicts an ideal state… The fact that I cannot come up to the ideal condition of things laid down therein is to be attributed to my weakness.. What I have said about hospitals is also true. And yet I suppose I shall resort to the few medicines I hold lawful so long as I retain the least attachment for my body.'[51]

In 1929, Gandhi wrote to Satish Chandra Dasgupta that 'there is not one word in *Hind Swaraj* that cannot be substantiated if I have to rewrite it today, I may change the language but never the thought.'[52] In 1938, the *Aryan Path* bought out its special number devoted to *Hind Swaraj*. Giving a message to the *Aryan Path* on the eve of the publication of its special number, Gandhi categorically stated:

> 'I may change the language here and there, if I had to rewrite the booklet. But after the stormy thirty years through which I have passed, I have seen nothing to alter the views expounded therein.'[53]

In 1939, a friend, according to Gandhi, pointed out the contradiction between what he wrote in the *Hind Swaraj* and what he practiced. Gandhi commented with his usual forthrightness.

> 'The key to understand that incredibly simple (so simple as to be regarded foolish) booklet is to realize that it is not an attempt to go back to the so-called ignorant dark ages. But it is an attempt to see beauty in voluntary simplicity, poverty and slowness. I have pictured that as my ideal. I shall never reach it myself and hence cannot expect the nation to do so. But the modern age is for variety, for flying through the air, for multiplicity of wants, which have no fascination for me. They deaden the inner being in us. The giddy heights which man's ingenuity is attempting, take us away from our maker who is nearer to us than the nails are to the flesh which they cover.'[54]

In October 1939, Gandhi had a discussion with the members of the Executive of Gandhi Seva Sangh. He told the members present on that occasion: 'I would ask you to read *Hind Swaraj* with my eyes and see therein the chapter on how to make India nonviolent. You cannot build nonviolence on factory civilization, but it can be built on self-contained villages.'[55]

Two of Gandhi's last pronouncements on *Hind Swaraj* need to be extensively quoted. Both of them are in the form of letters. In a letter to one Mr. Krishnachandra on June 14, 1945, he wrote:

> 'I still abide by whatever I wrote about railways in *Hind Swaraj*. But that applies to be an ideal state. It is possible that we may never reach that state. Let us not worry about it. It is for this reason I said if we do not feel unhappy. At the same time, we should also not make a duty of giving up these things. We should have a free and easy attitude in such matters. We must use these facilities as little as possible. There will be all types of people in the society. There certainly are today. We have to live with them. Non-attachment is the only proper dharma under these circumstances. The only thing we must be careful about is that we do not deceive ourselves. Your statement that trains should be shunned, even as theft, adultery and falsehood, is not correct. The important reason for this is that even society considers theft and other sins to be immoral. Trains have not been, nor need they be so considered. All that we may say is that we should not consider trains as means of enjoyment.'[56]

The last letter he wrote was to Jawaharlal Nehru in which he explicitly referred to *Hind Swaraj*. 'I have said', he wrote, that 'I fully stand by the kind of governance I have described in Hind Swaraj…My experience has confirmed the truth of what I wrote in 1909.'[57] Then he went on:

> 'It is better that I redraw the picture today in my own language… What is worth knowing is only what I have to say today. I believe that if India, and through India the world, is to achieve freedom, then sooner or later we shall have to go and live in village—in huts, not in places. Millions of people can never live in cities and places in comfort and peace… We

can have the vision of that truth and nonviolence only in the simplicity of the villages. That simplicity resides in the spinning wheel and what is implied by the spinning wheel… The sum and substance of what I want to say is that the individual person should have control over the things that are necessary for the sustenance of life.'[58]

One can analyze from the above statements that Gandhi's own evaluation of *Hind Swaraj* has undergone a change.

Methodology

In studying *Hind Swaraj*, the first problem that confronts a student is that of methodology. Is *Hind Swaraj* to be taken as a final blueprint, which the Mahatma was trying to realize in reconstructing the Indian society? Or is it the outburst of an Indian disgusted with the ills of modern civilization and its institutions, for example, the parliament? Or is it a message that calls for rethinking of the entire approach of linear progress, which was the hallmark of the nineteenth and early twentieth centuries?[59]

All these questions immediately arise as soon as one goes through the *Hind Swaraj*. In order to understand *Hind Swaraj* both with reference to India and the world at large, we will have to put the tract in a historical perspective. But before we do so, a word about the methodology of studying it is called for.[60]

From the point of view of methodology, *Hind Swaraj* cannot be taken to be the final blueprint along which Gandhi wanted to refashion Indian society as well as the world order. *Hind Swaraj* 'has reference to an ideal state.' Gandhiraj was an ideal condition, and he warned the reader 'against thinking that I am today aiming at the Swaraj described therein'.[61]

One can see that Gandhi had a flexible mind. Yet from the series of citations, which we have mentioned above, it is clearly visible that the Mahatma was not willing to yield ground on the ideas propounded in the booklet. In the letter written to Nehru, which perhaps suggests his latest thoughts, he said he fully stood by the kind of governance he described in *Hind Swaraj* and went on to say, 'what is worth knowing is only what I have to say today.' And then he proceeded to redraw the picture that he had in mind.[62]

It will appear, therefore that the Mahatma expresses apparently contradictory opinions, which, it is assumed in some quarters, persisted till the end. Yet in Gandhi's own words:

'I am not at all concerned with appearing to be consistent. In my search after truth, I have discarded many ideas and learnt many new things. Old as I am in age, I have no feeling that I have ceased to grow inwardly or that my growth will stop at the dissolution of my flesh. What I am concerned with is my readiness to obey the call of Truth, my God, from moment to moment, and, therefore when anybody finds any inconsistency between any two writings of mine… he would do well to choose the later of the two on the same subject.'[63]

And Mahadev Desai very aptly expressed this when he said that while 'the views expressed in the first edition of *Hind Swaraj* have remained in substance unchanged, they have gone through a necessary evolution.'[64]

This only means that there are some very basic and fundamental propositions on which Gandhi tried to build up what he called the entire theory of life. These basics remained unchanged and unmodified. In response to challenges posed to him by the limitations with which both the individual 'man and the 'social situation' were constrained, he was willing to compromise on details.[65] We have made an attempt to explore the fundamental propositions of Gandhi right from *Hind Swaraj* until his death in 1948. What we are aiming at is to show that while the basic model he conceived remained the same in working it out it was open to adaptation.

Studies on *Hind Swaraj*

It was only in 1919, that *Hind Swaraj* became widely known in intellectual circles in India. All of them, however, did not like it. S. A. Dange, a noted communist leader, in his book *Gandhi versus Lenin* (1921) and M. N. Roy in his book *India in Transition* (1922) dismissed it as mere humanitarianism based on ignorance of the laws of class struggle. It is quite another thing that at least Dange changed his views so enormously in the later stages of his life that he almost became a Gandhian. Sir Shankar Nair, a leading lawyer of India (he was also the president of Indian National Congress) in his book *Gandhi and Anarchy* (1922), castigated Gandhi for advocating anarchism through Satyagraha.

Gandhi's *Hind Swaraj*, which contains his seminal ideas and basic approach to the problems of contemporary civilization, has not received the attention it merits. It is notable that during the period 1920–47, when Gandhi dominated the national movement, the book *Hind Swaraj* was widely ignored. Even the intellectual community in the universities and in other centres of learning, research and public education did not evince much interest in Hind Swaraj. We know of only five major studies. First, in 1938, Sophia Wadia devoted an entire issue of *Aryan Path* (London) to *Hind Swaraj*. Secondly, T. K. Mahadevan in 1973 brought out a special number of *Gandhi Marg* (New Delhi) on *Hind Swaraj*. Third, in 1981 Ashis Nandi, wrote a lengthy article called *From Outside the Imperialism: Gandhi's Cultural Critique* of the '*West*'. Fourth, Nageshwar Prasad brought a book entitled *Hind Swaraj*: *A Fresh Look* in 1985. Fifth, in 1993 Partha Chatterjee devoted a chapter 'The Movement of Manoeuvre: Gandhi and the Critique of Civil Society' to *Hind Swaraj* in his work *Nationalist Thought and the Colonial World: A Derivative Discourse*. Sixth, in 1997, Anthony J. Parel brought a book entitled *Gandhi*: *Hind Swaraj And Other Writings*. Seventhly, in 2007, R. P. Misra made a deep study of *Hind Swaraj*. More recently, Anil Dutta Mishra published a book *Revisiting Hind Swaraj* in 2010.

Summing Up

Hind Swaraj is one of the most significant treatises that Gandhi wrote to clarify his views. It is perhaps the most systematic exposition of Gandhi's ideas of state, society and nation. Although *Hind Swaraj* is an original tract, while writing it Gandhi was heavily influenced by some of the leading Western thinkers[66] as well as Indian philosophy. It contains a statement of some of the most fundamental tenets in Gandhi's politics. In other words, Gandhi stated his position quite clearly in *Hind Swaraj* and held onto it all his life. In fact, *Hind Swaraj* laid the most crucial theoretical foundation of his entire strategy for winning Swaraj for India.[67] It is also the most authentic text of Gandhian social and political ideas dealing with Swaraj and Satyagraha. In Hind Swaraj, Gandhi depicted the dichotomies between the spiritual, moral fabric of Indian society, and the violent, politically corrupt nature of European states more dramatically than any of his predecessors.

The aim of *Hind Swaraj* was 'to confront the anarchist and violence-prone Indian nationalists with an alternative to violence, derived from Gandhi's earliest experiments with *Satyagraha*'. *Hind Swaraj* served two purposes: on the one hand, it was a detailed commentary on Western civilization that thrived on naked force; it also laid down, on the other, the fundamental pillars that were to later become the basic precepts of Gandhi's social and political ideas.[68]

Hind Swaraj is a foundational text for understanding Gandhi and his ideology. An outcome of a cross-fertilization of ideas, Indian and Western, *Hind Swaraj* was perhaps the most powerful exposition of Gandhian social and political ideas.[69] It is a significant text with refreshing ideas on critiquing the Western civilization, and also seeking to build 'a vernacular model of action' that the people of India understood.[70]

Gandhi's *Hind Swaraj* is not a rejection of the liberative contribution of modernity: civil liberties, religious tolerance, equality, poverty alleviation. Rather, his effort can be interpreted as an attempt to integrate these positive elements with a liberating reinterpretation of tradition. With his critique from within the tradition, Gandhi becomes the great synthesizer of contraries within and across traditions.[71]

In *Hind Swaraj* or *Indian Home Rule*, Gandhi set a goal for himself and for Indians. Through *Hind Swaraj*, Gandhi wanted to establish self esteem of individual and moral regeneration of India. In other words, through *Hind Swaraj*, Gandhi wanted to transform India as a nation and polity and Indians. It is a source book for evaluation of India and Indians, a manual of action for people and a critique of excessiveness of materialistic western society. It is a pointer to down side of modern civilization, that is, colonialism, neo-colonialism, violence and alienation. It is also a pointer to political democracy because political democracy without social democracy is not a democracy at all.

Hind Swaraj is Gandhi's response to the immediate, contemporary problems arising out of inner and outer conflicts at individual, state and society level. This volume also provides a vision, strategies, blueprint to future and an alternative to solve the contemporary problems. Gandhi outlined in the *Hind Swaraj* a remarkable, constructive, and inward-looking programme based on ethical and moral values. Future hope lies in *Hind Swaraj*.

Hind Swaraj is echoed in recent well-known studies like *The Ages of Gaia* by James Lovelock; *The Turning Point* by Fritjof Capra; *Entropy: A New Worldview* by Jeremy Refkin; *Human Destiny* by Le comte Du Nouy; *Clash of Civilization* by Samuel P. Huntington; *The Third Wave* by Elwin Toffler; *Deschooling Society* by Evan Ellich and *Mega Trends* by John Naisbitt. It is high time for both our policy makers and the people to turn the torch within so that they may be inspired to adopt the way shown in *Hind Swaraj*, if not for any other consideration, but for its pragmatic strength to solve our present-day maladies of India as well as of the whole world. T. K. Mahadevan, a Gandhian scholar, in his book *Dvija: A Prophet Unheard* pleads:

> Read *Hind Swaraj* if you love the human family and this earth which is our home. Read it if you wish to do your little bit to halt man's mad race towards self-extinction.

Notes and References

1. Misra, R. P., *Hind Swaraj, Gandhi's challenge to modern civilization*, New Delhi: Concept Publishing Company, 2007.
2. Prasad, Nageshwar (Ed.), *Hind Swaraj: A Fresh Look*, New Delhi: Gandhi Peace Foundation, 1985, p. 1.
3. Parel, Anthony J., *Hind Swaraj and Other Writings*, Cambridge: Cambridge University Press, 1997, p. XII.
4. Ibid., p. XIII.
5. Gandhi, Mohandas Karamchand, *Hind Swaraj or Indian Home Rule*, Ahmedabad: Navajivan Publishing House, 1938, p. 13.
6. Prased, Nageshwar op. cit., p. 16.
7. Ibid.
8. Ibid. pp. 16–17.
9. Tendulkar, D. G., *Mahatma*, Vol.1, Bombay: Vithalbhai K. Jhaveri, 1951, pp. 127–28.
10. Devdutt, 'Hind Swaraj: Context and Text', in Nageshwar Prasad (Ed.), *Hind Swaraj: A Fresh Look*, New Delhi: Gandhi Peace Foundation, 1985, p. 30.
11. Misra, R. P., op. cit.
12. Ibid.
13. Parel, Anthony J., op. cit., p. XIV.
14. CWMG, Vol. 71, p. 238.
15. CWMG, Vol. 10, p. 245.
16. CWMG-CD, Vol. 22, p. 260.
17. Devdutt, op. cit., p. 33.
18. Gandhi, M. K., op. cit., p. 94.
19. Prasad, Nageshwar, op. cit. p. 17.
20. Ibid., pp. 18–19.
21. Ibid., pp. 20–23.
22. Ibid., p. 23.
23. Ibid, pp. 3–24.
24. Ibid., p. 24.
25. Ibid., p. 28.
26. Devdutt, op. cit., p. 32.
27. Ibid.
28. Ibid., p. 35.

29. Ibid., p. 38.
30. Chakrabarty, Bidyut, *Social and Political Thought of Mahatma Gandhi*, London: Routledge, 2006, p. 24.
31. Ibid.
32. Gandhi, M. K. op. cit., p. 24.
33. Chakrabarty, Bidyut, op. cit. p. 25.
34. Ibid.
35. Gandhi., M. K. op. cit., p. 81.
36. Ibid., pp. 83–84.
37. Ibid. p. 82.
38. Chakrabarty, Bidyut, op. cit., p. 26.
39. Ibid., pp. 26–27.
40. Tendulkar, D. G. op. cit., pp. 129–31.
41. Misra, R. P. op. cit.
42. CWMG, Vol. 10, p. 7.
43. CWMG, Vol. 10., p. 139.
44. CWMG, Vol 10., pp. 507–11.
45. CWMG, Vol. 10, p. 247.
46. CWMG, Vol. 12, p. 411.
47. CWMG, Vol. 12, p. 412.
48. CWMG, Vol. 15, p. 340.
49. Tendulkar, D. G. op. cit., p. 17.
50. CWMG, Vol. 19, pp. 277–78.
51. CWMG, Vol. 24, p. 548.
52. CWMG, Vol. 42, p. 125.
53. CWMG, Vol. 67, pp. 169–70.
54. CWMG, Vol. 70, p. 242.
55. Ibid., p. 296.
56. CWMG, Vol. 80, p. 325.
57. CWMG, Vol. 81, p. 319.
58. CWMG, Vol. 81, pp. 319–20.
59. Prasad, Nageshwar, op. cit., p. 12.
60. Ibid.
61. Ibid.
62. Ibid., pp. 12–13.
63. CWMG, Vol. 55, p. 61.
64. Gandhi, M. K. op. Cit., p. 5.
65. Prasad Nageshwar, p. 13.
66. Chakarabarty, Bidyut p. 23.
67. Ibid.
68. Ibid., p. 24.
69. Ibid.
70. Ibid.
71. Heredia, Rudolf C., 'Interpreting Gandhi's Hind Swaraj', in *Economic and Political Weekly*, Vol. XXXIV, No. 24, June 12–18, 1999, p. 1501.

Summary

- *Hind Swaraj* or *Indian Home Rule* is a small book of about 30,000 words, written in Gujarati on board the ship RMS Kildonian Castle during Gandhi's return trip from England to South Africa. It was written in ten days in the period November 13–22, 1909.
- This polemical book first appeared serially in the *Indian Opinion* and later on, it was published in book form, to be proscribed in March 1910 by the Bombay Government, because it contained 'matter declared to be seditious'. On that, Gandhi published the English translation from Natal to show the innocuous nature of its contents. The ban was finally lifted on December 21, 1938.
- *Hind Swaraj* is Mahatma Gandhi's unique, fundamental, unparallel work and an Indian contribution to Political Theory after Kautilya's *Arthashastra.*
- Gandhi was a political activist responding creatively to the socio-political and economic circumstances in which he was living.
- *Hind Swaraj* is an alternative to modern socio-economic political thought.
- The principal theme of *Hind Swaraj* is the moral inadequacy of Western civilization, especially its industrialism, as a model for free India.
- It is in *Hind Swaraj* that one finds Gandhi first announcing his own life's mission.
- The immediate context of writing the booklet was Gandhi's encounter with the Indian anarchists in England and their cult of violence.
- The issues clearly emerging in *Hind Swaraj* are: First is the then current political situation in India, its leaders and political events and Gandhi's own position in relation to them. Second, the most crucial issue is the entire question of material or 'modern' civilization. And, third, there is the question of passive resistance
- The *Hind Swaraj* is a severe condemnation of modern civilization. It is divided into twenty chapters and two appendices. It deals in detail with Swaraj, civilization, lawyers, doctors, machinery, education, passive resistance and other matters.
- Divided into four themes elaborated or enunciated in various parts of the book, viz., core concepts: nonviolence, education, and technology; criticism of the parliament, of machinery and of the Congress' view of Swaraj, *Hind Swaraj* as an assessment and a critique of the Western civilization with reference to non-Western civilization with non-Western criteria; and prescription.
- *Hind Swaraj* is the quintessence of all that Mahatma Gandhi had read, thought and experienced by the age of forty.
- In *Hind Swaraj*, Gandhi reopens the debate, which had raged in India in the second half of 19th century, and he raised his voice against modern Western civilization.
- *Hind Swaraj* provides a scathing critique of Western civilization. The three recurrent themes are: colonial imperialism; industrial capitalism; and rationalist materialism. Gandhi thus argued that 'The English have not taken India; we have given it to them. They are not in India because of their strength, but because we keep them…'.

According to Gandhi, the British conquest of India was solely due to the Indians' moral failure.

- *Hind Swaraj* is one of the most significant treatises that Gandhi wrote to clarify his views. It is the most systematic exposition of Gandhi's ideas of state, society and nation.
- *Hind Swaraj* is a foundational text for understanding Gandhi and his ideology, an outcome of a cross-fertilization of ideas, Indian and Western.
- Through *Hind Swaraj*, Gandhi wanted to establish self esteem of individual and moral regeneration of India. Gandhi through *Hind Swaraj* wanted to transform India as a nation and polity and Indians.
- It is a source book for evaluation of India and Indians. It is a manual of action for people and a critique of excessiveness of materialistic Western society. It is a pointer to down side of modern civilization, that is, colonialism, neo-colonialism, violence and alienation. It is also a pointer to political democracy because political democracy without social democracy is not a democracy at all.

Further Readings

Brown, M. Judith, *Gandhi Prisoner of Hope*, Delhi: Oxford University Press, 1992..

Chakrabarty, Bidyut, *Social and Political Thought of Mahatma Gandhi*, London: Rutledge, 2006.

Chatterjee, Partha, *Nationalist Thought and the Colonial World*, Delhi: Oxford University Press, 1986

Mishra Anil Dutta, *Revisiting Hind Swaraj*, New Delhi: Concept, 2010.

Parekh, Bhikhu, *Colonialism, Tradition and Reform: An Analysis of Gandhi's Political Discourse*, New Delhi: Sage Publications, 1989.

Parel, Anthony J., *Hind Swaraj and other Writings*, Cambridge: Cambridge University Press, 1997.

Parel, Anthony J., *Gandhi, Freedom, and Self-Rule*, New Delhi: Vistaar Publications, 2000.

Prasad, Nageshwar, *Hind Swaraj A Fresh Look*, New Delhi: Gandhi Peace Foundation, 1985.

Vinobha, Bhave, *Swaraj Sastra*, Varanasi: Sarva Seva Sangh Prakashan, 1963.

Weber, Thomas, *Gandhi As Disciple And Mentor*, New Delhi: Cambridge University Press, 2004.

4

Satyagraha with Special Reference to Bhiku Parekh

Introduction

Satyagraha was not originally coined by Gandhiji. Even before him, the idea of *Satyagraha* was found in religious books like the *Upanishads*, the *Ramayana*, the *Mahabharata*, the *Gita*, the *Quran* and many others. This belief was also practiced by Indians as well as Westerners including Prahlad, Raja Harishchandra, Socrates, Plato, Jesus, Ashoka, etc and many other great men., Prahlad, the first individual *satyagrahi*, offered *Satyagraha* against the tyranny of his cruel father. It was not known then that it was what *Satyagraha* meant.[1] According to Gandhiji, 'the principle called *Satyagraha* came into being before that name was invented. Indeed, when it was born, I myself could not say what it was'.[2] Some of the Westerners believe that Gandhiji derived the idea of *Satyagraha* from Christ's *New Testament*, specially the Sermon on the Mount. Some others believe that he got this idea from the writings of Tolstoy, though Tolstoy himself deduced it from the *New Testament*. In fact, Gandhi derived his idea of *Satyagraha* neither from Christ nor from Tolstoy, but from his own Vaishnavite faith.[3]

Satyagraha: Meaning and Genesis

The word *Satyagraha* is Sanskrit in origin. It is a compound word formed of *Satya*, meaning truth and *Agraha*, meaning clinging, holding fast, adherence, and insistence. In other words, *Satyagraha* means clinging to truth, holding fast to truth, insistence on truth or firm adherence to truth, come what may. Defining the term *Satyagraha*, Gandhi once wrote:[4]

> 'Truth (*Satya*) implies love and firmness (*agraha*) engenders and, therefore, serves as a synonym for force. I thus began to call the Indian movement *Satyagraha*, that is, the

> force which is born of truth and love or non-violence and gave up the phrase passive-resistance in connection with it.'

Gandhiji described *Satyagraha* as 'firmness in a good cause'[5] in the *Indian Opinion*. In *Young India*, he pointed out that *Satyagraha* was just a new name for 'the law of self-suffering'.[6] And in *Hind Swaraj*, he proclaimed that 'sacrifice of self is infinitely superior to sacrifice of others', and that a self sufferer does not make others suffer for his mistakes.[7]

Satyagraha, which was Gandhi's supreme invention, discovery or creation, stands for a ceaseless and relentless pursuit of truth without resorting to hatred, rancour, ill-will or animosity. His concept does not imply passivity, weakness, helplessness or expediency. It is essentially an attitude of mind and a way of life based on the firm desire for vindicating just causes, correcting wrongs and converting among the doers by voluntary self-suffering as well as by patient and active use of the means that are non-violent and intrinsically just. In J. B. Kripalani's words, '*Satyagraha* is strike plus something more. This something makes for better morals amongst those who carry on the fight. It also means greater loss of morals for the opponent. A *satyagrahi* is a better non-cooperator than a striker'.[8] In fact, *Satyagraha* is an action-oriented search for and adherence to truth and a non-violent fight against untruth.

Satyagraha also implies an assertion of the power of the human soul against political and economic domination, because domination amounts to a denial of truth since it takes recourse to falsehood and manipulation for maintaining itself. Thus, *Satyagraha* is the vindication of the glory of the human conscience. The latter (conscience) reinforces the non-violent battle for the victory of truth.[9]

Satyagraha is utter self-effacement, greatest humiliation, greatest patience and brightest faith. It is its own reward.[10] *Satyagraha* is a relentless search for truth and a determination to arrive at the truth.[11] It is a force that works silently and apparently slowly. In reality, there is no force in the world that is so direct or so swift in working.[12] It implies the exercise of the purest soul-force against all injustice, oppression and exploitation. Literally, it means 'truth pressure' and denotes the operation of the soul or spirit suffering, confidence, self-purification and trust are attributes of soul-force.

The theory of *Satyagraha* is not a new innovation. It is as old as Patanjali. Gandhiji emphatically asserted that its origin had deep linkages with the idea of purity. Calling *Satyagraha* as Kamadhenu, he believed that it was useful both for a *satyagrahi* as also his adversary.[13] *Satyagraha* has also been linked with *Yajna* of Indo-Aryan days. Between the original form of human and animal sacrifice and its contemporary manifestation in *Satyagraha*, it has 'undergone the intellectual refinement of the Upanishads and humanistic transfusions from Jainism and Buddhism'.[14]

Gandhi discovered this term during his endless non-violent resistance movement against racial discrimination in South Africa. In 1906, Gandhi organized the Indians in South Africa and led a new kind of resistance movement against the unjust laws under which the people were then suffering. In the beginning, Gandhi used the term 'Passive Resistance', but as the time passed and his struggle for justice advanced, this phrase gave rise to confusion and was considered as the weapon of the weak. As a result, it appeared shameful to use an English word which could not be easily understood. Gandhi felt that the movement he had started was essentially different from what was ordinarily known as passive resistance. Gandhi, thus, felt the need for an appropriate word for the new kind of resistance and announced a small prize in his weekly, *Indian opinion* for the best suggestion in this regard. One of the competitors, Shri Maganlal Gandhi, suggested the word *Sadagrha* meaning firmness in a good cause. Gandhi liked the word but he felt it did not represent the whole idea he wished to connote, namely truth-force or the power of truth, force born of truth and love or non-violence. He, therefore, corrected it to '*Satyagraha*', which literally means insistence or truth or the pursuit of truth.

Discussing the origins of *Satyagraha* with Joseph J. Doke, Gandhi is represented to have stated:

> 'I remember', he said, 'how one verse of a Gujarati poem, which, as a child, I learned at school, clung to me'. In substance it was this:
> 'If a man gives you a drink of water and you give him a drink in return, that is nothing. Real beauty consists in doing good against evil.' As a child, this verse had a powerful influence over me, and I tried to carry it into practice'. Then came the sermon on the mount.
> 'But, said I, 'surely the *Bhagavad Gita* came first? 'No', he replied. Of course I knew the *Bhagavad Gita* in Sanskrit tolerably well, but I had not made its teaching in particular a study. It was the New Testament which really awakened me to the rightness and value of passive resistance. When I read in the sermon on the mount such passages as "Resist not him that is evil but whosoever smiteth thee on thy right cheek turn to him the other also", and "love your enemies and pray for them that persecute you, that they may be sons of your Father which is in heaven", I was simply overjoyed, and found my own opinion confirmed where I least expected it. The *Bhagavad Gila* deepened the impression, and Tolstoy's *The Kingdom of God is Within You* gave it permanent form.'[15]

Satyagraha and Passive Resistance

Until the invention of this term *Satyagraha*, the South African movement was called 'Passive Resistance'. But so long as the phrase passive resistance was used, *Satyagraha* was mistaken to be a danger to person and property, which the suffragists in England were, and the movement was regarded as a weapon of the weak. Gandhi apprehended the possible psychological effect of characterizing the South African movement as a weapon of the weak and the helpless and sharply contrasted *Satyagraha* to passive resistance:

> 'The power of suggestion is such that a man at last becomes what he believes himself to be. If we continue to believe in ourselves and let others believe, that we are weak and helpless and therefore offer passive resistance, our resistance would never make us strong, and at the earliest opportunity we would give up passive resistance as a

> weapon of the weak... Again, while there is no scope for love in passive resistance, on the other hand, not only has hatred no place in *Satyagraha* but is a positive breach of its ruling principle. While in passive resistance there is a scope for the use of arms when a suitable occasion arrives, in *Satyagraha,* physical force is forbidden even in the most favourable circumstances'.[16]

Thus, if a passive resister does not use violence, it is due to his incapacity or under the force of circumstances, whereas a *Satyagrahi* refrains from using violence even if he were in a position to use violence effectively. A *Satyagrahi* never seeks to take advantage of the opponent's weakness. Passive resistance may, therefore, sometimes be looked upon as a preparation for the use of force while *Satyagraha* can never be utilized as such. It may also be offered side by side with the use of arms. *Satyagraha* and brute force, being each a negation of the other, can never go together.

Passive resistance is a new technique of fighting wrongs or a policy resorted to by the unarmed against superior force, while *Satyagraha*, as seen by Gandhi, is a matter of faith or creed. Hence, the latter is grounded in an integrated philosophy of the universe life and fundamental ethical principles.

In passive resistant, the aim is to embarrass and harass the adversary and eventually to defeat him; but in *Satyagraha* the effort is towards not causing the slightest harassment or injury to the other party. In passive resistance, the resister's aim is to gain a victory over the adversary, while terms like 'victory' or 'defeat' have no place in the *satyagrahi's* vocabulary. The latter's aim is the moral and mental conversion of the other party.

Passive resistance may be undertaken against persons while *Satyagraha* is never directed against any one person as such. It is directed only against institutions, systems, political and other vested interests, and wrongdoings (and not strictly against the wrong doer).

Passive resistance may arise from hatred, anger or frustration and may thus be motivated by a feeling of retribution or retaliation, but not so with *Satyagraha* which is accompanied with love for the other party and possibly with a prayer that he may see reason without coming to personal harm.[17]

Satyagraha may be offered to one's nearest and dearest; passive resistance can never be offered to them unless, of course, they have ceased to be dear and become an object of hatred to us.

Satyagraha goes beyond passive resistance in the stress on a spiritual and moral teleology because the final source of hope and consolation for the *Satyagrahi* is God. Hence, Gandhi wrote:

> '*Satyagraha* differs from passive resistance as the North Pole from South. The latter has been conceived as a weapon of the weak and does not exclude the use of physical force or violence for the purpose of gaining one's end whereas the former has been conceived as a weapon of the strongest and excludes the use of violence in any shape or form'.[18]

Thus, passive resistance is, according to Gandhi, a 'negative concept and has little in common with the active principle of love on which *Satyagraha* is based'.[19]

Basic Postulates of *Satyagraha*

There are some essentials or basic postulates of *Satyagraha* like truth, non-violence, faith in God, brotherhood of man, supremacy of moral law, and purity of means.[20] These are discussed below:

Truth

Truth is the core of Gandhian philosophy of *Satyagraha*. *Satyagrahi* minus the truth or *satya* is zero. In fact, *Satyagraha* is based on truth or soul force. Inner voice is the voice of truth and justice. Howsoever man might be selfish or crooked, the voice of truth resides in his innermost depth and the *satyagrahi* tries to appeal to that voice of reason and truth.

Truth is derived from the Sanskrit word *Sat* which means being, existing, or living. Thus, truth means 'that which exists'. Since the existence of nothing is more obvious than that of the various laws governing the universe, truth, according to Gandhi, is nothing but a law operating in the universe. 'The world', he says, 'rests upon the bedrock of *satya* or Truth'.[21]

For Gandhi, it was not mere perception of the truth which mattered; what was more important for him was speaking the truth, acting the truth and realizing the truth in every breadth of life and action. Self-realization was another name for realization and establishment of the truth of life and being.

Gandhi identified God with truth. Hence, his famous proposition 'God is truth'. The reason for his identification, according to Gandhi, was that God alone is that law which governs all life. But in 1929, he reversed the earlier proposition and asserted that 'truth is God'. This inversion of the proposition does not change its basic meaning, yet there was a reason behind this change of formulation. Gandhi said 'I found that the nearest approach to truth was through love. Love has many meanings in the English language. But I never found a double meaning in connection with truth and even the atheists had not demurred to the necessity or power of truth. And it was because of this reason that I saw that rather than say that 'God is Truth' I should say that 'Truth is God'. Accordingly, in our fight for social change, we must hold fast to truth and truth alone'.[22]

Non-Violence

To Gandhi, the path of truth is narrow as it is straight.[23] As a result, truth and non-violence are inseparable and it is impossible to realize perfect truth. So long as we are imprisoned in the moral frame without non-violence, it is not possible to seek and find truth. Hence, non-violence and truth are so intertwined that it is practically impossible to disentangle and separate them. So, *Satyagraha* is impossible without non-violence.[24]

Non-violence literally means non-killing or non-injury. According to Gandhi, every act of injury to a living creature and endorsement of such an act should be restrained with non-violent effort, whenever possible.

Historically, or chronologically speaking, to prevent it, is a breach of *Ahimsa*.[25] Gandhi's active non-violence emerged as a result of his experiences in South Africa, especially his painful experience at Maritzburg. But, it also followed logically from his conception and quest for truth. Gandhi said, 'without non-violence it is not possible to seek and find truth... They are like the two sides of a coin. Truth is the end.'[26] The principle of non-violence is hurt by every evil thought, undue haste, lying, hatred and wishing ill-will to anybody. It is such a state of physical and mental discipline that can move the chord of human heart and bring a change of heart in the so-called enemies.

Supremacy of Moral Law

Satyagraha does not depend upon physical or brutal force. It is based on moral force—the force of truth and justice, the force of self-purification and self-suffering, love and service, courage and discipline. Gandhi says, 'Purity of means is based upon the recognition of the supremacy of moral law'. Therefore, the entire gamut of the philosophy of *Satyagraha* is based on the fact that truth and morality alone can be victorious, and we cannot adopt immoral principles to create a moral society. Hence, Gandhi made *Satyagraha* 'the moral equivalent of war'. It is a way of life based on the laws of love and holiness.[27] However, insistence on moral means does not imply that evil, injustice, tyranny and exploitation are to be tolerated. On the other hand, Gandhi believed that evil must be resisted and eliminated but it should be done through means that are in consonance with morality, not with hate, war, violence and ill-will.

Faith in God

Gandhi emphasizes that a *satyagrahi* must be a believer in God. A *satyagrahi* has no other stay but God, arid one who has any other stay or depends on any other help, cannot offer *Satyagraha.* Such a person may be a passive resister, a non-cooperator and so on, but he cannot be a true *satyagrahi.*

Brotherhood of Man and Faith in the Goodness of Man

Gandhi believed in the principle of one universal soul. To Gandhi, brotherhood of man means, 'that we are one of another'. It means that you cannot injure your neighbour without injuring yourself or vice-verse. Hence, the entire edifice of *Satyagraha* rests on the faith in the goodness of man. *Satyagraha* aims at a change of heart through non-violent, noble and friendly action.

Gandhi mentions the following as the basic assumptions for successful *Satyagraha.*[28]

- There must be common honesty among the *satyagrahis.*
- They must render heart discipline to their commander. There should be no mental reservation.
- They must be prepared to lose all, not merely their personal liberty, not merely their possessions, land, cash, and other valuables but also the liberty and possessions of their families, and they must be ready cheerfully to face bullets, bayonets, or even slow death by torture.
- They must not be violent in thought, word or deed towards the 'enemy' or even among themselves.

Vows of *Satyagraha*

For the success of *Satyagraha* and in order to make the *satyagrahi* intellectually, morally and spiritually strong enough to withstand enough temptations, provocations and inflictions, Gandhi prescribed certain cardinal disciplines (eleven vows), or codes of conduct, to be observed by them—more by the Satyagrahi leaders than by the Satyagrahi masses—in their daily life. The vows fall into two categories—principal and subsidiary.[29]

Principal Vows

Truth

Of all disciplines, the observance of the vow of truth comes first. The observance of the vow of truth is generally understood as merely confined to speaking the truth. But, according to Gandhi, it really means that we must be truthful in thought, word and deed. Thus, the observance of truth rules out the practice of secrecy, cunningness and deception. Truth is to be realized by devoted constant practice and indifference to all other interests in life. It means ceaseless striving and complete detachment. The realization or *darshan* of truth, Gandhi said, 'can only be attained by the man of pure detachment. Anger, greed, pride, fear, all these things draw a veil across the seeker's eyes'.

Ahimsa (Non-injury)

Ahimsa or non-violence literally means non-killing or non-injury. It is not enough that one does not take the life of any living being. The follower of this vow cannot hurt physically or mentally even those whom he believes to be unjust. He cannot be angry with them; he must love them. Thus, he would oppose the tyranny and injustice, whether of parents, governments or others, but will never hurt the tyrant. The follower of truth and *ahimsa* will conquer the tyrant by love; he will not carry the tyrant's will but he will suffer punishment even unto death for disobeying his will until the tyrant himself is conquered.

Celibacy or Brahmacharya

It is highly impossible to observe the foregoing two vows unless celibacy is also observed; for this vow, it is not enough that one does not look upon any woman with a lustful eye; he has to control his animal passions so that they will not move him even in thought. If he is married, he should not have a carnal mind regarding his wife but consider her as his life-long friend and establish with her the relationship of perfect purity.

Control of the Palate

Until one has overcome the temptations of the palate, it is difficult to observe the foregoing vows, more especially that of celibacy. Control of the palate is the first essential in the observance of the vow of *brahmacharya*. Sex is, indeed, so tightly bound up with the palate that one who has not mastered taste cannot control animal passion either. An aspirant and striver for *brahmacharya* should, therefore, cultivate a feeling that he is eating not to satisfy the palate but just to keep body, mind and soul in perfect health.

Non-Stealing

To take another person's property without his knowledge or permission or in the belief that it is an unclaimed property is, no doubt, an act of stealing. But stealing according to Gandhi, also includes taking of something from another without really needing and working for it, or taking it in a larger quantity than is required for the immediate use, or to use it for a purpose different from one intended by the leader or to use it for a period longer than fixed with him, needless multiplication of wants and needless accumulation and hoarding for future use while others are in need of it at the moment. In his opinion, all amassing of wealth, above and beyond one's legitimate requirements, is theft.

Non-possession or Aparigraha

It is not enough not to possess and keep much, but it is also necessary not to keep anything which may not be absolutely necessary for our bodily wants. Thus, if one can do without chairs, one should do so. The follower of this vow will, therefore, as a result of constant reflection, simplify his life.

Subsidiary Vows

Social and Religious Equimindedness

A *satyagrahi*, according to Gandhi, should be a firm believer in social and religious equality as well as in the equality of sexes. He should cultivate perfect equimindedness towards all people, irrespective of their caste, colour, occupation, sex, religion, birthplace and habitation and should cultivate equal reverence for all the principal religions of the world. He should try to eradicate all kinds of unreasonable distinctions and discriminations—including untouchability—from the society; should try to establish communal harmony and to elevate the position of the fallen sections of the society, including those of the untouchables, the aboriginals and the women.

Bread Labour

The vow of bread-labour means that everybody, especially a *satyagrahi*, must earn his bread and other primary needs of life by labouring with his hands, since production of every essential article involves bodily labour. Bread labour is a veritable blessing to one who would observe non-violence, worship truth, and make the observance of *brahmacharya* a natural act. It develops habits of obedience, self-respect and reliance, tenacity of will, sense of unity with others, endurance of hardships, sense of order and cooperation, energy, courage, equanimity, and practice in handling moral equivalents of weapons. Gandhi recommended hand spinning as the only universal form of bread labour. But he never ceased to regard agriculture to be the ideal. In addition to spinning, everybody must, according to Gandhi, be his own scavenger. He felt that 'there must be something radically wrong where scavenging has been made the concern of a separate class in society'. Everyone should, therefore, commence bread labour as a scavenger. Scavenging, if intelligently taken up, will help one to a true appreciation of the equality of man.

Swadeshi

It is inconsistent with truth to use articles about which or about whose makers there is a possibility of deception. Therefore, for instance, a votary of truth will not use articles manufactured in the mills of Manchester, Germany or even in his own country, for he does not know that there is no deception about them. The vow of Swadeshi requires the use of simple clothing to the exclusion of even fancy buttons and foreign styles and so the belief of Swadeshi will be applied to every department of life.

Fearlessness

Truth and non-violence or love are the principal keystones of *Satyagraha* and these require sufficient fearlessness. One who fears cannot seek and follow the truth. A *satyagrahi* will, therefore, endeavour to be free from the fear of kings, people, caste, families, thieves, robbers, ferocious animals such as tigers and even death. Cultivation of courage and preparedness for sacrifice and sufferings which are necessary for a non-violent fighter also demand fearlessness. 'He who has not overcome all fear cannot practice *ahimsa* to perfection'.[30] A truly fearless man will defend himself against others by truth force or soul force.

Humility

Arrogance, egotism, self-importance, anger, and the pride of achievement—all these draw a veil across a truth seeker's eyes. Detachment, openness and tranquility of mind, absence of prejudice and of the idea of doership in action, mildness, sublimity, forgiveness, fortitude—these are the real attributes of the dispassionate seeker after truth and a follower of non-violence. All these qualities, taken together, are called humility. Hence, Gandhi writes in his *Autobiography*: 'The instruments for the quest of truth are as simple as they are difficult. They may appear quite impossible to an arrogant person, and quite possible to an innocent child, the seeker after truth should be humbler than the dust'.[31]

Code of Satyagraha

After discussing vows of *Satyagraha* in detail in the preceding pages, we now take up the code of *Satyagraha*. It is as follows:

A *satyagrahi* bids good-bye to fear. He is, therefore, never afraid of trusting the opponent. Even if the opponent plays him false twenty times, the *satyagrahi* is ready to trust him the twenty-first time, for an implicit trust in human nature is the very essence of his creed.[32]

A *satyagrahi* is nothing if not instinctively law-abiding, and it is his law-abiding nature which exacts from his implicit obedience to the highest law, that is the voice of conscience which overrides all other laws.[33]

Since *Satyagraha* is one of the most powerful methods of direct action, a *satyagrahi* exhausts all other means before he resorts to *Satyagraha*. He will, therefore, constantly and continually, approach the constituted authority. He will appeal to public opinion, educate public opinion, state his case calmly and coolly before everybody who wants to listen to him, and only after he has exhausted all these avenues will he resort to *Satyagraha*. But when he has found the impelling call of the inner voice within him and launches out upon *Satyagraha*, he has burnt his boats and there is no receding.[34]

The *satyagrahi,* whilst he is ever ready for fight, must be equally eager for peace. He must welcome any honourable opportunity for peace.[35]

My advice is *Satyagraha* first and *Satyagraha* last. There is no other or better road to freedom.[36]

In the code of the *satyagrahi*, there is no such thing as surrender to brute force. Or the surrender then is the surrender of suffering and not to the wielder of the bayonet.[37]

As a *satyagrahi*, I must always allow my cards to be examined and re-examined at all times and make reparation if an error is discovered.[38]

Qualifications of a Satyagrahi

The following are the qualifications that Gandhi held as essential for every *satyagrahi* in India:

- He must have a living faith in god, for he is his only rock.
- He must believe in truth and non-violence as his creed and, therefore, have faith in the inherent goodness of human nature which he expects to evoke by his truth and love expressed through his suffering.
- He must be leading a chaste life and be ready and willing for the sake of his cause to give up his life and his possessions.
- He must be a habitual *khadi*-weaver and spinner. This is essential for India.
- He must be a teetotaler and be free from the use of other intoxicants in order that his reason may be always unclouded and his mind steady.
- He must carry out with a willing heart all the rules of discipline as may be laid down from time to time.
- He should carry out the jail rules unless they are specially devised to hurt his self-respect.

These qualifications are not to be regarded as exhaustive. They are illustrative only.[39]

Forms and Techniques of *Satyagraha*

The technique of *Satyagraha* admits of various methods to be used in successive stages—and many of them simultaneously—the most important being basic education and other items of the constructive programme, persuasion through reason, persuasion through change of heart by self-suffering and persuasion through non-violent direct action or non-violent non-cooperation which may take the forms of strike, picketing, boycott and *hijrat*, ultimately culminating in civil disobedience.

Basic Education

Gandhi wanted every individual to be a full-blooded, fully developed member of society and aimed at the all-round development of man's personality, that is, his physical, mental, moral and spiritual faculties. He knew that 'man is neither mere intellect, nor the gross animal body, nor the heart or soul alone. A proper and harmonious combination of all the three is required for the making of the whole man'.[40] Thus, he devised a scheme of basic education which aimed at 'an all-round drawing out of the best in child and man—body, mind and spirit. He aimed at a perfect, well-balanced, all-round education in which the body, the intellect and the heart have all simultaneous and full development into a natural harmonious whole. He described the system of basic education as 'the spearhead of a silent social revolution fought with the most far-reaching consequences'[41] which will lay the foundation of a more just social order in which there is no unnatural division between the haves and the have-nots.

Constructive Programme

Constructive programme was an integral and positive aspect of Gandhi's post-1920 *Satyagraha* movements. It was adopted for the achievement of economic self-sufficiency and inculcation of the Swadeshi spirit amongst the masses. It was employed for the promotion of communal harmony and removal of social evils like untouchability, unemployment and illiteracy.

Any constructive programme, according to Gandhi, is designed to build up the nation from the very bottom… it must mean complete independence in every sense of the expression. Indeed, his claim was that Civil Disobedience is not absolutely necessary to win freedom through pure non-violent effort if the cooperation of the whole nation is secured in the constructive programme. For Gandhi, constructive work was the heart of the matter. He described it as the permanent part of the non-violent effort. Handling of *Satyagraha* without the constructive programme will be, in his words, 'like a paralyzed hand attempting to lift a spoon.'[42]

Gandhi adopted constructive programme as a method of *Satyagraha* for the first time during his Non-violent Non-cooperation Movement of 1920. In the course of this movement, national schools and institutions were started, arbitration courts and panchayats were established, and spinning was done on *charkha,* all with the sole object of replacing government schools and colleges, law courts, and foreign goods which were to be completely boycotted.

Spinning and social welfare activities were continued throughout the Bardoli *Satyagraha* of 1928 with an emphasis upon the entire *khadi* programme. Even during Gandhi's Salt *Satyagraha* of 1930, the wearing of hand-spun cloth was imperative for all *satyagrahis*, and welfare and self-sufficiency work was undertaken as a way of achieving Swaraj. However, the constructive programme as a definite method of achieving complete independence found its clear and full exposition only in the post-individual *Satyagraha* period of December 1941.

Constructive programme was not conceived by Gandhi for a single day. It took several years to give shape and form to the programme. It was during the post-individual *Satyagraha* period that Gandhi expounded his entire philosophy of constructive programme and published a 25-page booklet entitled *Constructive Programme.* In 1941, Gandhi listed the following thirteen items:

- Communal Unity
- Removal of Untouchability
- Prohibition
- *Khadi*
- Other village industries
- Village sanitation
- New or basic education
- Adult education
- Upliftment of women
- Education in health and hygiene
- Provincial languages
- Propagation of *Rashtra Bhasha*
- Promotion of economic equality

On February 15, 1945, Gandhi addressed the Kasturba Nidhi workers. The booklet on Constructive Programme was revised with some more items added to the already existing thirteen. The items added were:

- *Kisans*
- Labourers
- *Adivasis*
- Lepers
- Students[43]

After Gandhi's death, the following items were added by his followers to strengthen the movement:

- Cow protection
- Nature cure
- *Bhoodan*
- *Gramdan*
- Shanti Sena[44]

Conversion through Persuasive Argumentation

Simultaneous with mass education and other constructive activities, in order to bring about any lasting revolution or radical change, it is necessary first to change the attachment of individuals and groups to certain ideas, sentiments and assumptions. This is possibly only by conversion through rational and gentle persuasion, not by coercion and compulsion.

In *Satyagraha*, persuasion takes two forms, to be applied in successive stages. The first stage is largely characterized by rational argumentation. The opponent is sought to be convinced by reason. Gandhi said: 'I have no desire to carry a single soul with me if I cannot appeal to his or her reason. My conventionality I carry to the point of rejecting the divinity of the oldest *Shastras* if they cannot convince my reason.'[45] In his opinion, one of the greatest qualities of a *satyagrahi,* particularly a *satyagrahi* leader, is to possess the capacity for independent thinking and convincing others by reason. Thus, a *satyagrahi* has first of all to try to convince his opponent by reason and mobilize public opinion against the evil which he is out to eradicate. When public opinion is sufficiently roused against an evil, the strongest will not dare to practice or openly to lend support to it. An awakened and intelligent public opinion is the most potent weapon of a *satyagrahi.*[46]

Conversion through Self-Suffering

According to Gandhi, the next step that the *satyagrahi* has to take in the direction of weaning the evil-doer from the evil is to appeal to his heart by patient self-suffering, sympathy, sincerity, chivalry and humility. 'You cannot inject new ideas into a man's head by chopping it off; neither will you infuse a new spirit into his heart by piercing it with a dagger'.[47] Voluntary self-suffering opens the eyes of the evil-doer which are otherwise shut to the voice of reason. Thus, a *satyagrahi* has to appeal continuously to the evil doer's head and heart combined.[48] Having failed to convince the evil doer merely by reason or in case he refuses even to listen to his arguments, the *satyagrahi* seeks—by means of self-suffering—to get through to his unprejudiced judgement so that he may willingly come again onto a level where he may be persuaded through reason. '...the hardest metal yields to sufficient heat. Even so must the hardest heart melt before sufficiency of the heat of non-violence. And there is no limit to the capacity of non-violence to generate heat.'[49]

Fasting

The most delicate form of *Satyagraha* is fasting. Unlike some other forms of *Satyagraha*, Gandhi was himself the author of fasting. Fasting is chiefly a way of personal cleansing and penance.[50] It is a potent and 'infallible weapon in the armoury of *Satyagraha*'. It is a fiery weapon.

Gandhi enunciated certain general principles and conditions under which a *satyagrahi* could resort to fasting: 'A *satyagrahi* should fast only as a last resort when all other avenues of redress have been explored and failed. Suffering even unto death and, therefore, even through a perpetual fast is the last weapon of a *Satyagrahi.* That is the last duty which is open to him to perform.'[51] Gandhi was of the considered view that fasting should be undertaken only by an 'expert' and by him, too, only according to his capacity to fast. Fasting should be undertaken either for self-purification or self restraint, or for appealing to the better nature of the opposite party, in order to make him reconsider his stand and realize his wrong. It may be undertaken to check acts of violence, to remove bitterness or even purify the political atmosphere. It should, however, be employed only as 'a species of *tyaga*, and never as a method of exercising under pressure on the opposite party'.

As an expert in *Satyagraha,* Gandhi himself undertook fasts on as many as seventeen different occasions during his life, but he warned his friends and followers against imitating him blindly or out of false or hysterical sympathy. Of these fasts, three of them were against official injustice, four against the institution and practice of untouchability, three against Hindu-Muslim riots, and four against other acts of violence. Further, three of his fasts were for self-purification and penance,[52] and one to encourage the Ahmedabad Mill workers in the strike which they were continuing on his advice in order to secure an increase in their wages.[53]

Non-Violent Non-Cooperation

Gandhi admittedly learnt the technique of non-violent non-cooperation from Leo Tolstoy. Non-violent non-cooperation is a sacred duty and an alternative to anarchy. It is the most expeditious method known to the world for winning over opponents. Non-cooperation with the evil-doer is a mild form but can become an immensely potent technique when undertaken on a mass scale. It is the activization of love for the redress of wrongs. There can be non-cooperation between a father and his sons as well between an imperial oppressor and the citizens. Non-cooperation, indeed, means renunciation of the benefits of a system with which we non-cooperate. A non-cooperator has, therefore, to renounce the benefits of schools, corporations, courts, titles, legislatures and other institutions set up under an evil system.

Gandhi's scheme of non-cooperation presupposed the ability on the part of *satyagrahi* masses to control all the forces of evil. His scheme also presupposed suffering and losses to the non-cooperator. According to Gandhi, non-cooperation was a 'measure of discipline and self-sacrifice, without which no nation can make real progress.'[54]

Gandhi started his first Non-cooperation Movement in India in 1920. It aimed to redress the wrongs of the Khilafat and the Punjab massacres and for the attainment of Swaraj. The items of the programme were as follows:[55]

- Surrender of titles and honorary offices and resignation of nominated posts in local bodies.
- Refusal to attend government levies, *durbars* and other official and semi-official functions held by government officials, or in their honour.
- Gradual withdrawal of children from school and colleges in the various provinces.
- Gradual boycott of British courts by lawyers and litigants and establishment of private arbitration courts by them for settlement of private disputes.

- Refusal on the part of the military, clerical and labouring classes to offer themselves as recruits for service in Mesopotamia.
- Withdrawal by the candidates from election to the reformed councils and refusal on the part of the voters to vote for any candidate who may, despite the Congress' advice, offer himself for election.
- Boycott of foreign goods, laying down of arms and the suspension of taxes were the two last stages of non-cooperation.

Non-violent non-cooperation may take the form of strike, picketing, boycott, *hartal* and *hijrat*, ultimately culminating, in Civil Disobediences.

Strikes

According to K. L. Shridharani, the strikes as such 'are a labourer's instrument for the acquisition of a desired standard of treatment and living from the employer'.[56] Strikes may be employed directly and openly to achieve political ends. For example, during his South African *Satyagraha* Movement, Gandhi first advised and then himself conducted a strike of Indian Coalmine workers and railway men in the months of October-November, 1913, for the singular object of persuading the Government to repeal the £ 3 tax.[57]

However, whether the strike method is employed to achieve economic ends, or to secure political betterment, it must fulfill certain preliminary requisites in order to find a definite place in the *Satyagraha* scheme. Firstly, a peaceful strike must be limited to the actual sufferers and must, at the same time, be justifiable on its own merits. Secondly, it should be spontaneous and not manipulated. During his Ahmedabad *Satyagraha*, Gandhi laid down the conditions of a successful strike. These were:[58]

- Never to resort to violence.
- Never to molest black legs[59].
- Never to depend upon alms.
- To remain firm, no matter how long the strike continued, and to earn bread, during the strike by any other honest labour.

Gandhi, however, warned against the use of strikes in the public utility services. He thought that strike or abstention from work in essential services was against the spirit of *Satyagraha* for it puts the community, or at least a substantial section of it, to loss, harassment or inconvenience. He thought that dislocation of these would dislocate public life.[60]

Hartal

Hartal or peaceful stoppage of work is another form of *Satyagraha. Hartal* means voluntary suspension of business in protest against some evil authority. It is a way of signifying protest, and its purpose is to strike the imagination of all—the people as well as the government. According to Gandhi, it is an 'act of self purification'.[61] 'It is the best method of making our strong disapproval of the action of the government. It is a means, more powerful than monster meetings expressing national opinion.'[62] *Hartals*, however, should be absolutely voluntary; otherwise, they would cease to be non-violent. *Hartal*, if forcibly brought about, cannot be considered to be *satyagrahi hartal.* It should be brought about by persuasion, gentle argument and propaganda.

In any case, there should be no element of compulsion or force in it. Besides, *hartals* should not be organized too frequently, for then they would be hardly effective.

Boycott

Another *Satyagraha* method advocated by Gandhi was the boycott of economic, social, political, educational, legal and other institutions with the object of lodging protest against—and putting pressure on—the opposite party in order to ultimately seek redress of grievances. It is a sort of punishment and is conceived in a vindictive spirit.

Economic boycott is implied in the vow of a *Swadeshi.* It implies the boycott of commodities of universal use, for they must always be locally produced. According to Gandhi, foreign cloth is such a commodity. Hence, in 1920–1922, he went so far as to urge the destruction of foreign cloth in India. Gandhi himself inaugurated the bonfires of foreign cloths in Bombay in July 1921.

In the social sphere, boycott takes the form of non-violent social ostracism. But Gandhi tells us that in the complex conditions of the modern world, social ostracism is of a very limited application. It may be employed only in extreme cases 'when a defiant minority refused to bend to the majority, not out of any regard for principle, but from sheer defiance or worse'.[63] Social boycott should be applied only in such a way that it is not felt as a punishment by the object of boycott. 'It must cause pain to the party using it, if it causes inconvenience to its object.'[64]

In the political sphere, boycott takes the form of civil disobedience. It includes resignation of offices and titles and refraining from making use of the services of those who do not represent popular will and flout public opinion. Voters 'must ratify their verdict by complete abstention from any encouragement of the so-called representatives. The public will be bound—if they are non-cooperationists—to refrain from giving these representatives any prestige by attending their political functions or parties'.[65]

The boycott of educational, legal and other institutions means setting up of such parallel institutions on the non-violent model in the light of the ideal.

Picketing

Peaceful picketing is also a valid and useful form of *Satyagraha.* Picketing, like *hartal*, should also be persuasive and coercive. Both during the Non-cooperation Movement and the Civil Disobedience Movement of 1930–1934, Gandhi urged picketing, preferably by women, of foreign as well as country liquor shops and foreign cloth shops. However, Gandhi did not favour *dharna* as a method of picketing. He considered *dharna* as a form of barbarity, a crude and cowardly way of using coercion. Picketing as a species of *Satyagraha* has to be entirely non-violent.

Hijrat

Hijrat or deshatyaga is an age-old technique—individual as well as corporate—of meeting wrongs. It means voluntary emigration by people from the land they have hitherto believed to be theirs,[66] when they are grievously oppressed and terrorized and when they have no other recourse. But in Gandhi's opinion, in the purest form of *Satyagraha*, there is no need of doing *hijrat*. But in case of incapacity of offering non-violent or even violent resistance to the oppressor, Gandhiji's alternative to cowardly submission to oppression and demoralization was *hijrat*. 'It is wisdom to vacate houses or places that are plague infected. Tyranny is a kind of plague and when it is likely to make us angry or weak, it is wisdom to leave the scene of such temptation.'[67]

Gandhi advised *hijrat* to the Hindus of the Sindh province during communal riots in 1939–1940.[68] He also advised *hijrat* to the city women of India during the Second World War to escape criminal assaults and violation by foreign soldiers stationed in India.[69] Earlier he had commended *hijrat* to the *satyagrahis* of Bardoli in 1928, and those of Junagadh and Vitthalgad in 1939.[70]

Hijrat, however, should be resorted to in extreme cases. It should be a planned, and not a cowardly fight. But 'planned *hijrat* requires courage and forethought'.[71]

All these various species of non-cooperation culminate in civil disobedience, which is the next logical weapon.

Civil Disobedience

Civil Disobedience is an active, strong and extreme form of *Satyagraha*. According to Gandhiji, civil disobedience is a necessary part of non-cooperation.[72] Gandhi conceived it as 'a substitute for violence or armed rebellion. It is a non-coercive method which any law-abiding citizen can adopt, provided he is saturated with the spirit of non-violence and is ready for the utmost sacrifices'.[73]

According to Gandhi, complete civil disobedience, implying a refusal to render obedience to every single state-made law, can be a very powerful movement.[74] In Gandhiji's opinion, civil disobedience should be 'so complete that if an order was issued on us by the government saying go to the right, we must not hesitate to move leftward'. It is a complete, effective and bloodless substitute of armed revolt.

Civil disobedience can be undertaken for the deliberate breach of certain unmoral statutory enactments, or as the symbolic non-violent revolt against the state. In either case, it does not reflect want of respect for the constituted authority. Its ultimate aim is to substitute voluntary cooperation for involuntary cooperation and willing obedience for forced obedience. This underlying objective alone can make the *satyagrahis* adhere to their inner voice.[75] Civil disobedience can be practiced only as the last resort and by a selected few in the first instance at any rate.[76]

Civil disobedience is primarily of two types—offensive or assertive and defensive. Either of the two types may be offered by single individuals as completely independent units or by masses collectively. But whereas individual civil disobedience is self-led, mass civil disobedience needs a leadership. Gandhi considered civil disobedience as essentially an individual affair and he regarded individual civil disobedience as more effective, almost irresistible. According to him, 'offensive compromise is based on give and take, but in *Satyagraha* "there can be no give and take in fundamentals. Any compromise on fundamentals is a surrender because it is all give and no take".'[77]

However, this list like any other list, cannot be said to be complete and exhaustive. There can be as many forms and techniques of *Satyagraha* as there are forms of injustices, different grades of intensity, different nature of the agents and their relations with others. It is through the advocacy and use of these techniques that Gandhi delivered his supreme message of substituting willing obedience to forced obedience and voluntary cooperation for involuntary cooperation. In the words of Diwakar, 'It is not Gandhiji who made *Satyagraha* but *Satyagraha* which has made Gandhiji...' If it is a matter of obligation between two, it is *Satyagraha* which has obliged Gandhiji rather than it reverse.[78]

Bhikhu Parekh on *Satyagraha*[79]

For Gandhi, rational discussion and persuasion were the best ways to resolve conflict. This was peaceful, non-coercive and respected the moral integrity and autonomy of each party. Gandhi acknowledged that, when taken to its logical extreme, his theory of 'relative truth' undermined the very basis of action, for no man could ever act if he constantly entertained the nagging doubt that he might be wholly mistaken. However, he thought that one should at least acknowledge one's fallibility and leave room for reflection and reconsideration, and that, being irreversible and emotionally charged, violence did not allow this.

Gandhi also rejected violence on moral grounds. Morality consisted in doing what was right because one believed it to be right, and required unity of belief and conduct. Since the use of violence did not change the opponent's perception of truth, it compelled him to behave in a manner contrary to his *swabhava* and sincerely held beliefs, and violated his moral integrity.

Gandhi further argued that violence rarely achieved lasting results. An act of violence was deemed to be successful when it achieved its immediate objectives. However, if it were to be judged by its long-term consequences, our conclusion would have to be very different.

Finally, for Gandhi the means-end dichotomy lying at the heart of most theories of violence was false. In human life, the so-called means consisted not of implements and inanimate tools but of human actions, and by definition these could not fall outside the jurisdiction of morality. Besides, the method of fighting for an objective was not external to but an integral part of it. The so-called means were really the ends in an embryonic form, like seeds, of which the so-called ends were a natural flowering. As such, the fight for a just society could not be conducted by unjust means.

Gandhi argued that we needed a new method to fight against injustice, as the two methods—rational discussion and persuasion—were inadequate or deeply flawed. The new method, according to Gandhi, should activate the soul, mobilize its enormous latent energy, and generate a new kind of spiritual power that had hitherto not been given its due place in political life. The new method should aim to open up the opponent's mind and heart so that rational discussion could take place in a climate of goodwill and critical self-reflection. He thought that his method of *Satyagraha* met this requirement.

Gandhi first discovered *Satyagraha* and tried it out during his campaigns against social discrimination in South Africa. In the course of his struggles against British rule in India and the unjust practices of his own society, he kept on perfecting it. According to Gandhi, *Satyagraha* meant civil insistence on or tenacity in the pursuit of truth. It aimed to penetrate the barriers of prejudice, ill-will, dogmatism, self-righteousness and selfishness, and to reach out to and activate the soul of the opponent. Every human being had a soul, however, degenerate or dogmatic he might be. Thus, he had the capacity to feel for other human beings and to acknowledge their common humanity.

Satyagraha was a 'surgery of the soul, a way of activating the soul-force'. For Gandhi, 'suffering love' was the best way to do this, and formed the inspiring principle of his new method. The *satyagrahi*, whenever confronted with an injustice, sought a dialogue with his opponent. He did not confront the latter with a dogmatic insistence on the justice of his demands; rather, he invited his opponent to join him in cooperatively searching for the truth of the matter in dispute, as he knew he could be partial and biased. Since his sole concern was to evoke a moral response in his opponent, he did everything possible to put him at ease and nothing to harass, embarrass, anger, or frighten him, hoping thereby to trigger in him a slow, intensely personal, and highly complex process of self-examination. He suspended the struggle the moment his opponent showed willingness to talk in a spirit of genuine goodwill, and gave reason a chance to work in a more hospitable climate.

Gandhi, like Kant and John Rawls, argued that every community required a widespread sense of justice to hold it together. But unlike them, he argued that the sense of justice was highly cerebral and needed a deeper and emotionally charged sense of shared humanity to give it depth and energy. The sense of humanity consisted in recognition of the fundamental ontological fact that human well-being was indivisible, that in degrading and brutalizing others, people degraded and brutalized themselves, and that they could not sustain a communal life without a spirit of mutual concern and love.

Gandhi observed certain basic principles in all his *Satyagrahas*. They were preceded by a careful study of the situation, patient gathering of facts, a reasoned defense of the objectives, a popular agitation to convince the opponent of the intensity of the satyagrahi's feeling, and an ultimatum to give him a last chance for negotiation. Throughout the *Satyagraha*, the channels of communication with the opponent were kept open, the attitudes on either side were not allowed to harden, and intermediaries were encouraged. A pledge—not to use violence or to resist arrest or confiscation of his property—was to be taken by the *satyagrahi*. The *satyagrahi* prisoner, too, was to follow these rules. He was expected to be courteous, to ask for no special privileges, to do as he was ordered, and never to agitate for conveniences 'whose deprivation does not involve any injury to his self-respect'.

The effectiveness of *Satyagraha* was explained by Gandhi in terms of the spiritual impact of suffering love. The *satyagrahi's* love and moral nobility disarmed his opponent, weakened the feelings of anger and hatred, and mobilized his higher nature. His uncomplaining suffering denied his opponent the pleasure of victory, mobilized neutral public opinion, and created in him a mood conducive to calm introspection. The two together triggered the complex process of critical self-examination on which a *satyagrahi* relied for its ultimate success. Neither love by itself nor suffering by itself was enough. Love spiritualized suffering, which in itself had only a psychological value; suffering gave love its psychological energy and moral power. According to Gandhi, it was not easy to explain rationally how non-violence worked, as we knew so little about the operations of the human soul. 'There is nothing invisible in violence. On the other hand, non-violence is three-fourth invisible', and it acted in a 'silent and undemonstrative' manner.

Although Gandhi continued to maintain that suffering love was omnipotent and, when pure, capable of 'melting even the stoniest hearts', he knew that reality was quite different. Not surprisingly, Gandhi introduced such other forms of pressure as economic boycott, non-payment of taxes, non-cooperation, and hartal (cessation of work), none of which relied on the spiritual power of suffering love alone. Even his vocabulary increasingly underwent a radical change, at times becoming merely an obverse of the language of violence. He started talking about 'non-violent warfare', 'peaceful rebellion', a 'civilized form of warfare', a 'war bereft of every trace of violence', and 'weapons' in the 'armory' of the *satyagrahi*, all intended to 'compel' and 'force' the opponent to negotiate. Gandhi's political realism triumphed over his moral idealism and, despite his claims to the contrary, the *Satyagraha* was not always a purely spiritual method of action.

Apart from these methods, Gandhi introduced the method of fasting, which was highly controversial. He argued that his fast was a form of suffering love which had a four-fold purpose. First, it was his way of expressing his deep sense of sorrow and hurt at the way in which those he loved had degraded themselves and disappointed him. Second, as their leader he felt responsible for them, and his fast was his way of atoning for their misdeeds. Third, it was his last desperate attempt, an 'intense spiritual effort', to 'stir their sluggish conscience', to 'sting them into action', and to mobilize their moral energies. Finally, the fast was intended to bring the quarrelling parties together and to get them to resolve their differences themselves, thereby both deepening their sense of community and developing their powers of self-determination and conflict resolution.

Gandhi agreed that his fasting exerted considerable pressure on his intended target, but thought it fully justified on balance. The fast did exert moral pressure, but there was nothing improper in it. And it was not coercion or blackmail because it did not threaten others with personal harm.

Gandhi imposed strict limits on fasting as it could be misused for selfish purposes and even degenerate into blackmail. These limits were: it could not be undertaken against those with whom one was bound by the ties of love; it must have a concrete and clearly specified purpose and not vague and abstract goal; the purpose must be morally defensible in the eyes of its intended target; it should not in any way be designed to serve one's own interests; it should not ask people to do what they are incapable of doing, or involve great sacrifices; and it should only be undertaken by one who is an acknowledged moral leader of his people, has a long record of working for their welfare, and an unblemished moral character.

The Limits of Satyagraha

Gandhi's *Satyagraha* had moral and political significance, but it also suffered from several limitations. Although he was right to stress the unity of reason and morality—or the head and the heart as he called it—he was wrong to think that all or even most social conflicts could be resolved by touching the opponent's heart. They sometimes occur because men of goodwill take very different views of what human well-being consists of. It is difficult to see how Gandhi's method can resolve these differences and the consequent conflicts.

Gandhi rightly argued that human beings are generally affected by the suffering of others and regret that suffering even if they are unable or unwilling to do anything about it. However, he overlooked the fact that, if they thought the suffering deserved, their reaction would be different. Not the suffering per se but one's judgement of it determines one's response to it, and hence it has different effects on different individuals, depending on their beliefs and values.

Gandhi was wrong to argue that *Satyagraha* never failed and that it was effective under all conditions. If he had said that it was as a self-chosen way of being in the would and that one would die rather than kill, is view would have made moral but not political sense. To his credit, he insisted that it was meant to succeed and achieve results. And that subjected his claim to a different kind of scrutiny. It was an article of faith for him that all human beings had souls which could be 'touched' and 'activated'. As a result, he did not and could not acknowledge that some souls might be profoundly distorted and pathological. Contrary to what he said, *Satyagraha* presupposes a sense of decency on the part of the opponent, an open society in which his brutality can be exposed, and a neutral body of opinion that can be mobilized against him.

Gandhi's *Satyagraha* has much to be said for it, but it cannot be a catholicon. Although Gandhi insisted otherwise, violence need not be accompanied by hatred and ill-will or be uncontrolled. Like non-violence, it too can be restrained, measured, born out of love for both the victims and the perpetrators of injustice, and used to arrest human degradation.

Although Gandhi's *Satyagraha* had its limitations and he was wrong to claim 'sovereign efficacy' for it, it is a powerful, novel, and a predominantly moral method of social change. Not surprisingly, it has been borrowed and tried out in different countries with suitable adjustments to local circumstances. The United States is an excellent example of this.

Summing Up

Satyagraha is, in fact, a growing science. Gandhi has demonstrated the efficiency and efficacy of *Satyagraha* not only in getting political freedom but against exploitation, oppression, social injustice and social evils in his life time. *Satyagraha,* moreover, is not the weapon of the weak or coward; rather, it is a weapon of the strong or brave which demands for a new real civilization and culture for the humanity as a whole.

In fact, *Satyagraha* is the most powerful and permanent weapon to solve political, social and economic as well as religious problems. It holds good even today in our democratic setup against any perpetrated evil. Gandhi claimed that the Sarvodaya social order would be free from moral degradation, economic exploitation and political subjugation. Recently, Anna Hazare has used *Satyagraha* to fight against corruption in India. He successfully mobilized the masses and forced the Government to accept his demand for passing the bill for Lokpal.

Notes and References

1. Thakur, Gouri Kant, *Mahatma Gandhi's Philosophy of Satyagraha,* Varanasi: Kishore Vidya Niketan, 1988, p. 3.
2. Gandhi, M. K., *An Autobiography or the Story of* My *Experiments with Truth,* Ahmedabad: Navjivan, 1956, p. 239.
3. Thakur, Gouri Kant, o*p. cit.,* p. 3.
4. Gandhi, M. K., *Satyagraha in South Africa,* Ist Edition, S. Ganesan, Madras, 1928, p. 173.
5. *The Collected Works of Mahatma Gandhi,* Vol. VIII, The Publications Division, Ministry of Information and Broadcasting, Government of India, Delhi, 1962, pp. 22–23.
6. *Ibid.,* Vol XVIII, 1965, p. 133.
7. Gandhi, M. K., *Hind Swaraj* or *Indian Home Rule,* II Edition, III Reprint, Ahmedabad: Navjivan, 1958, p. 79.
8. Kripalani, J. B., *Gandhian Terminology* (Unpublished MSS) AICC Papers, File No. 15, 1936, p. 27.
9. Varma, V. P., *The Political Philosophy of Mahatma Gandhi and Sarvodaya,* Agra: Lakshmi Narain Agarwal, IV Edition, 1980–81, p. 162.
10. *Young India,* 26-2-1925, p. 73.
11. *Young India,* 19-3-1925, p. 95.
12. *Young India,* 4-6-1925, p. 189.
13. *Tire Collected Works of Mahatma Gandhi,* Vol. XIII, p. 522.
14. K. L. Shridharani, *War Without Violence,* Bombay, 1962, p. 162.
15. V. P. Varma, *op. cit.,* pp. 163–164.
16. Gandhi, M. K., *Satyagraha in South Africa,* op. cit., p. 114.
17. Gangal, S. C., *Gandhian Thought and Techniques* in *tire Modern World,* New Delhi: Criterion Publications, 1988, pp. 154–155.
18. Varma, V. P., op. cit, p. 168.
19. *Harijan,* 14.5.1938, p. 111.
20. Singh, Ramjee, *Gandhi and tire Modern World,* New Delhi: Classical Publishing Company, 1988, p. 79.
21. Gandhi, M. K., *Satyagraha in South Africa, op. cit.,* p. 433.
22. Mishra, Anil Dutta,, *Fundamentals of Gandhism,* New Delhi: Mittal Publication, 1955, p. 22.
23. Gandhi, M. K., *Satyagraha, Ahmedabad:* Navajivan, 1954, p. 40.
24. Sharma, M. L., 'Mahatma Gandhi's View of *Satyagraha*', *Gandhi Bhavan News Letter,* University of Delhi, Vol. II, No.1, January 1989, p. 52.
25. *Young India,* 11-8-1920.
26. Gangal, S. C., *op. cit,* p. 152.
27. Singh, Ramjee, *op. cit,* pp. 82–83.
28. *Harijan, 22-10-1938.*
29. Diwakar, R. R., *Saga of Satyagraha,* New Delhi: Gandhi Peace Foundation, 1969, p. 225.

30. *Harijan, 1-9-1940.*
31. Gandhi, M. K., *Autobiography, op. cit,* p. 15.
32. Gandhi, M. K., *Satyagraha in South Africa,* 1950 Edition, *op. cit,* p. 159.
33. *Speeches and Writings of Mahatma Gandhi,* G. A. Natesan and Company, Madras, 1933, 4th Edition, p. 465.
34. *Young India,* 20-10-1927, p. 353.
35. *Young India,* 19-3-1931.
36. *Harijan,* 15-9-1946, p. 312.
37. *Young India, 30-4-1931,* p. 93.
38. *Harijan,* 11-3-1939, p. 44.
39. *Harijan,* 25-3-1939, p. 64.
40. *Harijan,* 8-5-1937.
41. *Harijan,* 9-10-1937.
42. Gandhi, M. K., *Constructive Programme,* 1941, p. 29.
43. *Ibid.,* p. 3.
44. Mishra, Anil Dutta,, *op. cit,* p. 77.
45. *Young India,* 14-7-1920.
46. *Young India,* 8-8-1929.
47. Fischer, Louis, *The Life of Mahatma Gandhi* (Bhavan's Library), Vo1. I, p. 93.
48. Quoted in D. G. Tendulkar, *Mahatma,* Vo1. II, p. 265.
49. *Harijan,* 7-1-1939.
50. Gandhi, M. K., *Autobiography, op. cit,* p. 419.
51. *Harijan,* 18-2-1933.
52. For details see Ram Rattan, *Gandhi's Thought and Action,* Delhi: Kalinga Publications, 1991, pp. 289–292.
53. *The Collected Works of Mahatma Gandhi,* Vol. XIV, *op. cit,* 1965, pp. 254 and 268.
54. Tendulkar, D. G., *op. cit,* p. 13.
55. *Ibid.,* p. 12.
56. Shridharani, M. L., *War Without Violence:* A *Study of Gandhi's Method and its Accomplishments,* I Edition, London: Victor Gollancz Ltd., 1939, p. 36.
57. The *Collected works of Mahatma Gandhi, op. cit,* Vo1. XII, 1964, pp. 658–68.
58. Gandhi, M. K., *Autobiography, op. cit,* p. 27.
59. Black-leg is a person who offers to work when the regular workers are on strike.
60. *Harijan,* 10-8-1947, p. 274.
61. Gandhi, M. K., *Autobiography, op. cit.,* p. 562.
62. Tendulkar, D. G., *op. cit.,* Vol.1, p. 312.
63. Tendulkar, D. G., *op. cit.,* Vol.1, p. 312.
64. *Young India,* 16-2-1921.
65. *Young India,* 8-12-1920, p. 298.
66. *Young India,* 31-5-1928.
67. Gandhi, M. K., 'Bardoli on Trial', *Young India,* 31-5-1928.
68. *Non-Violence Peace and War,* Vol. I, Ahmedabad: Navjivan Publishing House, 1948, pp. 253–54.
69. *Ibid.,* Vol. II, p. 377.
70. *Harijan,* 20-5-1939.
71. *Non-Violence in Peace and War, op. cit.,* p. 253.
72. *Young India,* 27-3-1920.

73. *Harijan,* 24-6-1939, pp. 159-60.
74. *Young India,* 4-8-1921.
75. *Harijan,* 15-10-1938, p. 290.
76. *Young India ,* 23-3-1921.
77. *Harijan, 30-4-1940.*
78. Diwaker, R. R., *Satyagraha: Its Technique And History, History,* Bombay: Hind Kitabs, 1946, p. 91.
79. Excerpts from Bhikhu Parekh, *Gandhi*, London: Oxford University Press, 1997.

Summary

- *Satyagraha* was not originally coined by Gandhiji. Even before him, the idea of *Satyagraha* was found in religious books, like the *Upanishads*, the *Ramayana*, the *Mahabharata*, the *Gita*, the *Quran* and many others.
- It was also practiced by Indians as well as Westerners like Prahlad, Raja Harishchandra, Socrates, Plato, Jesus, Ashoka and numerous others.
- *Satyagraha* is a compound word formed of *Satya*, meaning truth and *Agraha*, meaning clinging, holding fast, adherence and insistence. Gandhiji described *Satyagraha* as 'firmness in a good cause'. *Satyagraha* also implies an assertion of the power of the human soul against political and economic domination, because domination amounts to a denial of truth since it takes recourse to falsehood and manipulation for maintaining itself.
- Basic postulates of *Satyagraha* are: truth, non-Violence, faith in god, brotherhood of man, supremacy of moral law and purity of means.
- Gandhi prescribed certain cardinal disciplines (eleven vows) a code of conduct, to be observed by them-more by the *satyagrahi* leaders than by the *satyagrahi* masses, in their daily life. The vows fall into two categories—principal and subsidiary. Principal vows are: truth, a*himsa* (non-injury), celibacy or *Brahmacharya*, control of the palate, non-stealing, non-possession or *Aparigraha*. Subsidiary vows are: social and religious equimindedness, bread labour, swadeshi, fearlessness and humility.
- Code of *Satyagraha*: A *satyagrahi* bids good-bye to fear. He is never afraid of trusting the opponent. A *satyagrahi* is instinctively law abiding. *Satyagraha* is one of the most powerful methods of direct action, so a *satyagrahi* exhausts all other means before he resorts to *Satyagraha*. The *satyagrahi,* whilst he is ever ready for fight, must be equally eager for peace. He must welcome any honourable opportunity for peace. In *Satyagraha* there is no such thing as surrender to brute force.
- Qualifications of a *satyagrahi* are : He must have a living faith in God, must believe in truth and non-violence, must be leading a chaste life and be ready and willing for the sake of his cause to give up his life and his possessions, must be a teetotaler and be free from the use of other intoxicants , must carry out with a willing heart all the rules of discipline as may be laid down from time to time. He should carry out the jail rules unless they are specially devised to hurt his self-respect.
- Forms and techniques of *Satyagraha*: The most important being basic education and other items of the constructive programme, persuasion through reason, persuasion

through change of heart by self-suffering and persuasion through non-violent direct action or non-violent non-cooperation which may take the forms of strike, picketing, boycott, and hijrat, ultimately culminating in civil disobedience.

- *Satyagraha* is, in fact, a growing science. Gandhi has demonstrated the efficiency and efficacy of *Satyagraha* not only in getting political freedom but against exploitation, oppression, social injustice and social evils in his life time.
- *Satyagraha* is the most powerful and permanent weapon to solve political, social and economic as well as religious problems. It holds good even today in our democratic setup against any perpetrated evil.

Further Readings

Appadorai, A., *Documents on Political Thought in Modern India*, Vol. 1, New Delhi: Oxford University Press, 1981.

Ashe, Geoffrey, *Gandhi: A Study in Revolution*, Bombay: Asia Publishing House, 1968.

Bondurant, Joan, *Conquest of Violence The Gandhian Philosophy of Conflict*, Bombay: Oxford University Press, 1959.

Brown, Judith M., *Gandhi and Civil Disobedience*, London: Cambridge University Press, 1977.

Diwakar, R. R., Saga of *Satyagraha*, New Delhi: Gandhi Peace Foundation, 1969.

Gandhi, M. K., *Satyagraha in South Africa*, Ahmedabad: Navajivan Publishing House, 1975.

Gregg, Richard B., *The Power of Non-Violence*, Ahmedabad: Navajivan Publishing House, 1960.

Ostergaord Geoffrey, *Non-violent Revolution in India*, New Delhi: Gandhi Peace Foundation, 1985.

Weber, Thomas, *Conflict Resolution and Gandhian Ethics*, New Delhi: The Gandhi Peace Foundation, 1991.

5

The Critique of Modernity with Special Reference to Bhiku Parekh

Introduction

Gandhi rejected modern civilization. The civilization which India has evolved is not to be beaten in the world. Nothing can equal the seeds sown by our ancestors. Rome went, Greece shared the same fate; the might of the Pharaohs was broken; Japan has become Westernized; of China, nothing can be said; but India is still, somehow or other, sound at the foundation. The people of Europe learned their lessons from the writings of the men of Greece or Rome, which do not exist in their former glory any longer. In trying to learn from them, the Europeans imagined that they would succeed in avoiding the mistakes of Greece and Rome. Such is their pitiable condition. In the midst of all this, India remains immovable and that is her glory. For Gandhi, civilization is the mode of conduct which points out to man the path of duty.

Gandhi was one of the most fundamental critics of modernity. In his opinion modernity, unless unchecked, will sweep away everything that stands in its way as it tries to take 'charge of the world'. Taking charge of the world implies that we can organize the world (through science and rational, neutral theorizing) and implement our plans (through research, technology and instrumental reasoning). At the heart of modernity is a questioning of dissatisfaction with the present. It is a faith that reason and the changes it fosters will lead to a progressively better future. In mounting his challenge, Gandhi confronts the foundational principles of the modern world and, in their place, he offers an idealized conception of traditional life in rural India, which he sees providing an alternative to the complexity, materialism and poverty he detects in modern society.

Critique of Modernity

The usual reading of Gandhi presents him as relentlessly anti modernist. The fact is that Gandhi was not anti modernist in its totality. Rather, he was against the down side of modernism and excessiveness of materialism resulting in exploitation, domination and conquest. Ramashray Roy has rightly said, 'Gandhi's critique of modern civilization is total'.[1]

Gandhi built on important modern conceptions such as secular equality and universal rights; his encounters with modernity did not prompt him to merge it with tradition. His reconceptualization of autonomy and equality—allied as they are with community, duty and cohesion—are oppositional to modern ones, and he seeks to buttress these goods by mounting a critique of modernity and modernization that is simultaneously conservative and radical. He wants a reformed tradition to stand, erectly and resolutely, to confront modernity. Only in this way, he reasons, can the dangerous elements of modernity be exposed and the modern project be made to explain itself. In advancing his position, Gandhi seeks to complicate modernity and rob it of its certainty.[2]

Modernity is a complex phenomenon, with a layered history of meanings. Modernization as a conscious and deliberate pursuit has acquired currency in the post-war world. Modernization indicates swift widespread change and transformation of societies and the broad lines of the process are industrialization, urbanization and mass communication.

The major trends indicative of modernity are that: peoples' commitments and associations change from the local to the universal; the individual, as a unit of society, begins to play a more important role as against groups; association, depending upon the accident of birth, is replaced by association of choice; in place of fatalistic beliefs, there comes a sense of mastery over environment; individual and group identities are not ascribed but chosen and achieved; an individual's work is less influenced by his family, residence and community; rational and scientific attitudes replace emotions and non-rational approaches; there is a change in social life in the sense that authority is not necessarily associated with seniority or sex; youth and women acquire a new place and identity; and the government, far from being a manifestation of power, come to be regarded as an instrument of society with more popular participation, element of consent and accountability. A modern society is differentiated, pluralistic, and is broadly participatory and democratic.[3]

But the dichotomy between tradition and modernity has limited validity applicability. Tradition and modernity are to be viewed as a continuum rather than two extreme and exclusive poles. A traditional society may have aspects of modernity and even the most modern society may have traits of traditionalism. The process of modernization may take various paths. Some traditions persist, some undergo change and some of them, indeed, may help in the very process of modernization. Modernization as a social process is an entire gamut that carries forward the past traditions and brings about a new pattern, a fresh combination. Since there never is a complete divorce between tradition and modernity, transition to modernity has often been effected through the use of traditional idiom, symbol and behaviour.

Under Gandhi's leadership, India's traditions were refurnished, mobilized and galvanized to serve new goals and objectives. Gandhi was a great builder. He built numerous institutions: women's institutions; labour unions; institutions like the Satyagraha Ashram and Sevagram Ashram; political institutions like the Indian National Congress, Harijan Sevak Sangh, Hindi Bhasha Pracharini Sabha and Khadi Gramodyog Sangh; and political movements like the Non-cooperation Movement and Dandi March and all this along with his ubiquitous contacts with India's millions. Gandhi was keen to apply the most appropriate techniques in his agricultural and artisan-related activities. Ashramities were, for example, sent from Phoenix to learn from Trappists to learn how to make sandals, the resulting product providing a valuable source of income for the institution. Gandhi advocated a careful study of horticulture and the establishment of model farms that would provide an example for the surrounding farmers. He encouraged his followers to undertake socio-economic surveys of villages, so as to be able to obtain the facts on which appropriate campaigns for rural improvement could be based. 'Gandhi did not therefore reject rational and scientific approaches to problems', admitted David Hardiman, 'so long as they accorded with his moral principles'.[4]

It was the singular genius of Gandhi that he perceived India's traditions with an instinct of a leader who knew what to do with them and how to do it. He was a strange mixture of the old and the new. Some of the richest and highest traditions of Indian civilization were embodied in him. His prayer meetings, his revival of songs of worship, were all indicative of his deep roots in India's traditions of *bhakti,* asceticism and self sacrifice.

In his personal life, Gandhi was a saint who abjured worldly pleasures and lived a life of self-denial and devotion. The symbols he popularized, the technique he adopted, all contained rich elements of past traditions. He wanted to provide work for the half starved and half-naked millions unemployed and underemployed, living in lakhs of villages in India. This, he thought, could be done through the revival of the spinning wheel and other cottages and village industries. Viewed uncritically in an age of highly, sophisticated technology, this looks like 'reaction', or even a 'revivalism'. The putting back of the clock of progress or whatever else the so-called modernist may choose to call it.

The reintroduction of Khadi and other crafts was a necessity but not in the same sense as it was in the past. It was not a physical necessity but a moral social economic and political necessity, if unmitigated poverty resulting from unemployment and semi-employment was to be relieved. Here also, Gandhi took the help of science. He offered a prize of one lakh of rupees to a scientist or technologist who invented a *charkha*, which could yield more yarn and which could be produced and repaired in the villages. What Gandhi objected to was a mad craze for industrialization which would replace our human beings.

Gandhi is also dubbed as conservative on account of his approach to religion. No doubt, he believed in God whose existence he admitted, he could not logically prove. For him, truth was God. The moral law was God. He held that whoever believed in truth and non-violence was spiritual and godly. This, he held, could not be practiced in a cave or on a mountain top. It must manifest itself in every activity of man within a society. It was not a personal God that the Mahatma believed in. He had the very, very deep and profound

Hindu concept of Brahma, the all-pervading reality, which is god in its various manifestations. To quote his own words, 'To me God is Truth and love: God is ethics and morality: God is fearlessness: God is the source of life; Light and Life, and yet he is above and beyond all this. He is even the atheism of the atheist: he transcends speech and reason.'[5]

Gandhi named his autobiography as '*An Autobiography or my Experiments with Truth*'. The idea of experimentation was in itself modern. All through his life, Gandhi experimented with himself. His experiment was truth to truth. He experimented with food, apparel, medicine, personal hygiene, social customs, language, public sanitation and sex. His ceaseless endeavour to strike new paths and make fresh efforts evoked in the minds of people a symbolism of successful change and transformation.

The way Gandhi struggled within himself for the attainment of perfection was a story that helped in the revival of national self-respect. The most subtle and pervasive influence of the British Raj lay in spreading the psychology of self-defeatism among the Indian people. The root of Indian slavery, according to Gandhi, was in the psychology of fear; and his personal life served to eradicate it and revive the ego and self-esteem of the Indian people.

Before Gandhi's entry into Indian politics, the freedom struggle had proceeded along two broad channels: the terrorist methods; and the constitutional approach through appeal to the good sense of the British. Both the approaches had failed dismally and the country was in need of new leadership and a fresh approach. Here was a call for innovation, for channeling the hopes, aspirations and energies of the people into new but acceptable ways. India had reached a blind alley and was groping in the dark. Gandhi's new technique of non-violent non-cooperation suddenly illumined the minds of the people. Here was a technique that grew out of India's traditions. It was perfectly applicable to a disarmed nation and it was based upon Gandhi's understanding of, and insight into, the British political culture.

Like J. S. Mill, Gandhi clearly understood that a liberal government—in his case free India—cannot be sustained without a liberal society. Gandhi never used the term modernization. But his programmes, movements and approach gave eloquent proof of his perception of the need for modernity in India. Modernization was necessary from three points of view. Firstly, it was the emergent need in as much as India had considerably lagged behind during the years of dependence and the lag had to be bridged. Secondly, the idea of nationalism, in itself new and modern, needed modernism as its pre-condition. India had to be a modern society before it could successfully fight against the foreign rule. This needed mobilization and activization of a vast number of people. India had to reform itself socially and religiously before it could think of demanding freedom. Lastly, as Gandhi realized, a modernized society alone could stand the stress and strain of independent nationhood, the goal of the Indian national movement. Modernization was necessary for the self-sustaining, integrative growth of India's nationalism.[6]

Gandhi appears to be a strange mixture of tradition and change. Perhaps it is one of the reasons of his wide appeal, national stature and general acceptability, Gandhi symbolized India in transition, the India that found herself to be then and the India that welcomed modernism. Some of the deepest and most significant founts of tradition were tapped to support and legitimize the newest needs of national awakening and exertion. Gandhi was a perfect specimen of *Bhagavad Gita*'s *karmayogi,* a Kautilya in action. Traditional in his exterior, Gandhi breathed modernism in every sector of national life. There was, for instance, the time factor. India was to be modernized within a time span that Gandhi laid down as it were. Every minute counted, every gesture mattered, and every move was significant in the overall plan that had to be fulfilled. Gandhi perceived his role in the context of the total situation that prevailed in India. Otherwise traditional in appearance, Gandhi dangled on his waist a watch, the symbol and emblem of modernity. Time was the essence and the given tasks were to be performed in a given period of time. Punctual to the minute, Gandhi had a fetish for cleanliness and order. People close to him have remarked that he was never seen unshaven; his nails were always cut; he did not use soap but his standards of cleanliness were very high.

Through personal example of self-discipline and self-development, embodying in his self the predispositions and cultural configurations of India's traditions, Gandhi successfully carried out a thrust of modernity into the otherwise dull and stagnant society. With his arrival, India's politics gained primacy, involving a larger number of people. With Gandhi, politics became participative, national and largely secular.

Gandhi acquired wide and convincing legitimacy for himself, reinforced national identity, achieved a rare degree of political penetration among the vast masses of India and brought forth an unusual degree of popular participation through empathy and mobility. All this was richly indicative of a fast pace of modernization.

The extent to which Gandhi went beyond his predecessors, especially the so-called conservatives, was evident in the way he defined the nature of the cultural encounter between Britain and India. While they had argued that the conflict was between the Indian and European or between the Eastern and Western civilizations, Gandhi insisted that it was really between the ancient and modern. As he put it, there is 'no such thing as Western or European civilization, but there is a modern civilization'.

Gandhi's apparently trivial redefinition according to Bhikhu Parekh was, in fact, intended to alter the terms of the debate in his favour and achieve several ideological and political advantages. First, he was able to reject the currently fashionable view among many British and Indian writers that the East and the West were radically different and shared nothing in common. For Gandhi, such a doctrine had no basis in facts, denied the fundamental unity of mankind and bred cultural parochialism. Second, he was able to attack modern civilization without attacking the West. He greatly admired Socrates and Christianity, modern writers such as Tolstoy, Ruskin and Thoreau and several Western values and practices, and wished to exclude them from his criticism. Third, the distinction enabled Gandhi to argue that modern civilization was of relatively recent origin in the West and that its pre-modern counterpart was very different and more like Indian. He hoped, thereby, to remind the West of its earlier traditions and values, evoke its temporarily suppressed historical memories and elicit its support for his fight against modern civilization. He was able to argue that since Indian civilization stood for values to which the West had itself for centuries subscribed and was only trying to preserve their common heritage, by attacking and undermining it, the West had not only betrayed its own great past but also damaged its chances of future redemption. Fourth, by arguing that industrial civilization was modern and 'still very young', Gandhi intended to suggest that it lacked the wisdom and maturity conferred by age, an important argument in a country that revered age. Finally, Gandhi hoped to convince his countrymen that in fighting modern civilization they were not being reactionary. They were only combating the arrogance and impetuosity of an historical upstart and helping to preserve the permanent values of the whole of mankind, including the West. The idea of saving the soul of their misguided masters tickled Indian pride and made Gandhi's harsh message more acceptable.[7]

For Gandhi, at that time, India was a great battlefield, the modern Kurukshetra on which the modern and ancient civilizations, the past and the present, were locked in a momentous battle for the future. The British were the best representatives of modern civilization and the Indians of the ancient. The former had fancied themselves as the missionaries of modern civilizations; Gandhi turned the Indians into missionaries of universal civilization based on the great ancient values enriched by some of the valid insights of the modern. The hold of the colonial ideology was such that even its shrewdest critic did not transcend but largely reinterpreted its terms of debate.

Gandhi's critique of modern civilization was far more complex than is generally imagined and quite different from that of such other writers as Rousseau, Carlyle, Ruskin, Tolstoy and Thoreau, by the last three of whom he was deeply influenced. In his view, modern civilization was grounded in a fatally flawed theory of man. Unlike ancient civilization which was soul- or spirit-centred, the modern was body-centred and, in that sense, 'materialistic'. For Gandhi, the body had two basic characteristics. First, it was distinct, self-enclosed and separated from and only capable of preserving its integrity by maintaining its separateness from other bodies. As such, it was the ontological basis of the human sense of particularity, and the source of the illusion that each individual was an independent and self-centred ego only externally and contingently related to others and constantly concerned to preserve his identity by keeping the invasive others at a safe distance. Second, the body was the seat of the senses, and thus of wants and desires. By their very nature, desires recurred with rhythmic regularity and were never satiated. They were also interrelated and one desire always gave rise to others. [8]

A body-centred or materialist view of man, thus, attributed two basic properties to him and regarded them as natural and legitimate, namely 'selfishness' and an 'infinite multiplicity of wants'. A civilization based on such a flawed view necessarily suffered from several basic and interrelated limitations. First, it lacked moral and spiritual depth. Second, since it had no guiding principles to decide what desires deserved to be satisfied and within what limits, it led to a way of life devoid of meaning and purpose. Third, it de-humanized man and had a profound anti-human bias. Fourth, it perverted the human psyche and was suffused with the spirit of violence. Finally, it reduced wisdom to knowledge and the latter to a form of power only useful as an instrument of control over nature and other men. It thereby not only perverted the pursuit of truth but also lacked a system of knowledge capable of 'critically evaluating its basic assumptions and objectives'.[9]

For Gandhi, modern civilization was propelled by the two inter-related principles of greed and want. It was controlled by 'a few capitalist owners' who had only one aim: to make profit, and only one means to do so: to produce goods that satisfied people's wants. They had a vital vested interest in constantly whetting jaded appetites, creating new wants and creating a moral climate in which not to want the goods daily pumped into the market and to keep pace with the latest fashions was to be abnormal and archaic. Indeed, since self-discipline or restriction of desires, the very emblem of human dignity, threatened to cause mass unemployment, throw the economic system out of gear and cause human suffering, it was seen as anti-social and immoral. Not surprisingly, men saw themselves not as self-determining moral subjects but as consumers or vehicles for the satisfaction of externally induced wants.[10]

The capitalist search for profits led to mechanization and industrialism. For Gandhi, machines relieved drudgery, created leisure, increased efficiency and were indispensable when there was a shortage of labour. Their use must, therefore, be guided by a well-considered moral theory, indicating how men should live, spend their free time and relate to one another.[11]

Modern civilization rested on and was sustained by massive violence. It involved violence against oneself. Each felt threatened by others and desperately sought to keep them at a manageable distance. He had to rely on the use of threat of verbal, emotional, moral and even physical violence, ultimately backed by the concentrated violence of the modern state. Modern civilization also involved an egregious amount of violence against nature, which was largely seen as man's property to do so with it what he liked.

In Gandhi's view, the exploitation of one's fellow men was built into the very structure of modern civilization. For Gandhi, a civilization properly placed man at its centre and measured its greatness in terms of its ability to produce men and women possessing such distinctively human powers as self-determination, autonomy, self-knowledge, self-discipline and social co-operation. Modern civilization did the opposite.

Hind Swaraj is a trenchant critique of modern civilization but it also contains a statement of Gandhi's alternative to modern civilization and a programme for Indians to actualize such an alternative.[12]

The critique attacked all the major aspects of the 'modern philosophy of life'. Gandhi especially liked Carpenter's argument that the ever-increasing powers of production engendered by modern science and technology alienated man from nature, from his true self and from his fellows and it worked 'in every way to disintegrate and corrupt man… to break up the unity of his nature'.[13]

The question that arises now is: 'Was Gandhi Modern?' J. B. Kripalani has very rightly said that if adherence to truth and supremacy of the moral law is modern, Gandhi was modern. If keeping one word and fulfilling one's engagement; eating for the sake of not satisfying a sophisticated palate but keep one's body fit for work recognition of the dignity of physical labour; tolerance and good understanding; feeling at home with those who differ from one or who are opponents; identification with the lowly and lost; untiring work for the poor, needy and downtrodden, the unfortunate Daridranaryana, and last but not least, dying for a noble cause is modern, Gandhi was definitely modern. If, however, the adoption of Western forms in dress, food, drinking and smoking, dinning in fashionable and costly hotels and restaurants; using pleasure houses and night clubs; wasting time in scandal mongering and gossip is modern, surely Gandhi was not modern.[14]

Bhikhu Parekh on the Critique of Modernity[15]

Modern industrial civilization emerged in the early years of the 19th century. Its characteristic features were rationalism, secularization, industrialization, the scientific culture, individualism, technological mastery of nature, globalization and liberal democracy. Whether it happened for good or bad is a point of debate since then. The answers to it varied, depending on the viewpoint of the commentator. Writers like J. S. Mill, Tocqueville, Thoreau, Tolstoy, Marx, Max Weber and Emile Durkheim viewed it in their own ways but theirs was a European standpoint.

Gandhi was familiar with both the European as well as the non-European viewpoints but found the non-European perspective more significant. Gandhi clearly separated the term modern from Western, because although modernity evolved in the West, the West had seen another form of civilization also before the advent of modernity. Modernity is a period that came in the West at a certain point in time; West has not been modern all along.

No Self-Restraint

Gandhi found modern civilization to be basically, fundamentally flawed as it gave no respect to the basic nature, the qualities, and the *swabhawa* of the individuals. It gave more importance to the body and neglected the soul. It was imperialist, violent, exploitative, unhappy and had no sense of purpose.

Since the modern civilization gave more importance to the body, it also gave greater importance to the idea of individualism and to greed. It encouraged unending desires, an unsatisfied want for more and more material goods and gave no importance to morality. The centre of this material civilization was the capitalist economy which produced for the market, where people were tempted to keep buying with no sense of self-discipline or regulation of desires.

Capitalism encouraged the use of machines. Mechanization could have been a good source of betterment of human lives but due to a lack of moral principles, and with the only aim of gaining profit, it caused suffering for many. It threw many out of work when introduced in places where there was an abundance of human labour. Mechanization and modern economic life created a new kind of slavery towards material goods.

Modern civilization believes in always being on the move. The sense of identity that comes with social roots and established communities is being replaced by emptiness, mutual indifference and even hostility.

Moral life is been seen as a burden to be endured, just a means of keeping people from harming each other. Morality is much more deeper than just this. It shows the way to human dignity but, in modern times, it is seen just as a set of rules to be followed. Morality should be driven by sentiments of goodwill and mutual concern; instead, it is now being driven by a non-moral element, fear. Morality is seen, in modern times, as a means to self-interest. Modernity has robbed the morality of its most key quality—the quality of the soul. The only aim of the modern man is to somehow get on in the world, even at the cost of the purity of soul. Qualities like sensitivity, generosity and tender heartedness have been rendered unimportant. Instead, aggression, ambition, toughness, self-centredness are considered important.

Modern civilization exploited the poor and the weak European imperialism was a key expression of the aggressive and exploitative modernity. It rested on violence, both personal and collective. It even exploited nature and earth. Gandhi feared that after a certain time, the modern man may become so used to this violence that he will not even notice its damaging existence. Although modernity claims to be based on values like freedom and equality, it was actually violent and exploitative.

The Limits of Rationality

Although Gandhi understood and appreciated the importance of reason, he was critical of the way it was treated in modern times. Modernity was considered the reason to be the ultimate test of all knowledge, while its own flaws and limits were overlooked grossly. Reason has its own place since it questions but not all aspects of human life are governed by reason. There is faith which goes beyond reason. Morality, wisdom, tradition, intuition, conscience are some faculties which are as valuable as reason. In fact, they are sometimes a step ahead of reason.

This attitude of modernity tends to consider all those systems of knowledge which are different from reason, as inferior, backward and useless. It has no respect for diversity of thought patterns. It believes that rationalism is the best form of thinking, everything else is lesser, lower.

State Culture

Since modernity promotes aggressive perusal of self-interest at all costs, such a system has to be managed by an equally ruthless, violent state. Such a system is governed by impersonal rules through a powerful bureaucracy.

The centralized economy created problems of a higher magnitude, requiring a centralized political power. The state becomes all powerful; it does not let individuals or groups solve their own problems. It creates greater problems and shows that only a big power has the capacity to solve them. It also monopolizes all morality. Since people are no more bound by values, morality and ethics, they are controlled by the state. State became the highest body of moral order—whoever followed its rules was good and the rest were bad. Gandhi argued that although the state claimed to be the supreme power that worked in the interest of the larger good, it was just a battleground where powerful groups fought amongst themselves for power. It was in the hands of morally shallow people, who were hungry for power. The modern democracy was hardly democratic. In the name of people, some grabbed the power and misused it and no one was concerned about the interests of the common man.

The Three Achievements of Modernity in Gandhi's View

Despite being critical of modernity, Gandhi appreciated it for its three good qualities: its scientific spirit; greater human control over the material world; and a new culture of respect for rules.

What Gandhi found problematic about modernity was that it brought these three things but it failed to see the limitations of these aspects. It is very important to know where and how do these qualities can prove to be weak. For example, it is right to emphasize on the importance of rules but it is wrong to not see that they are useless if the basic morality, basic value system is weak.

Gandhi could see the problems with the modern civilization better because he belonged to that part of the world which had suffered due to it. He clearly saw that the Europeans were very biased in the implementation of their great humane values like freedom, dignity and equality. They believed that only their people were entitled to these values.

Gandhi's viewpoint was special for another reason also—the fact that he belonged to a different culture, a different civilization.

Summing Up

Gandhi's perspective was unique because of his position—his being a non-European—which, in a way, was also a disadvantage. He oversimplified it. Although modern civilization is materialistic, it also promotes the search for personal independence. It promotes social justice and discourages social inequality in its own ways. It does promote greed but it also encourages creativity, equality, liberty, and an all-round human development. Modernity has its own morality.

Gandhi failed to see that the good qualities of modernity were a result of the total structure of modernity and these were not just accidental by-products. In order to understand the true spirit of modernity, both its virtues and vices need to be seen in a complete context. They are not exclusive of each other. Modern civilization should not just be criticized; its positive potentials need to be appreciated.

Gandhi's critique of modern civilization has a strong resemblance to the criticisms of such writers as Rousseau, Ruskin, Carlyle, Tolstoy, Nietzsche and Marx. Gandhi's critique contained original and important insights derived from the two great advantages he enjoyed over them. First, as a colonial native belonging to a despised race and an oppressed country, Gandhi experienced the darker side of modern civilization not directly accessible to the Westerners. Second, as an heir to the rich and differently structured Indian civilization, he brought to his critique an intellectual perspective and moral sensitivity not available to its Western critics.

Indeed, it is like a paradox that a man who was once regarded as an avowed critic of modern civilization is being acclaimed today as the saviour of the modern world. Only a few years ago more than sixty Noble prize winners, in a joint statement—while expressing their concern and anxiety over the deepening of world crisis—have looked towards Gandhi as the hope of humanity. The modern world is facing an unprecedented crisis. Violence has replaced the law of love; machine has replaced man and individual has become a mere cog in the wheel of the state. The old world is worn out and dead but the new world is yet to be born. The values of materialism, industrialism and consumerism are being challenged but the manifesto of the alternative civilization remains hazy. In such a dismal scenario, Gandhi provides a ray of hope for a better future and humanized world.

Notes and References

1. Roy, Ramashray, *Self and Society*, New Delhi: Sage, 1985, p. 38.
2. Terchek, Ronald, J., *Gandhi's Struggle for Autonomy*, New Delhi: Vistar Publications, 2000, p. 78.
3. Rudolph, Lloyd, I. and Susanne, Hoeber, Rudolph, *The Modernity of Tradition*, Chicago, University of Chicago Press, 1967, p. 3.
4. Hardiman, David, *Gandhi in His Time and Ours*, New Delhi: Permanent Black, p. 77.
5. *Young India*, March 5, 1931.
6. Pathak, D. N., 'Gandhiji: Tradition and Change' in S. Biswas (ed.), *Gandhi : Theory and Practice, Social Impact and Contemporary Change*, Shimla: Indian Institute of Advanced Study, 1969, p. 154.
7. Parekh, Bikhu, *Gandhi's Political Philosophy: A Critical Examination*, New Delhi: Ajanta, 1995, p. 20.
8. Parekh, Bhikhu, *Gandhi's Political Philosophy: A Critical Examination*, London: MacMillan Press, 1989, p. 21.
9. Ibid., pp.21–22.
10. Ibid., p. 22.
11. Ibid., p. 22.
12. Mukherjee, Rudrangshu, *Gandhi Reader*, New Delhi: Penguin Books, 1993, p. XI.
13. Carpenter, Edward, *Civilization: Its Cause and Cure*, London: George Allen & Unwin, 1921, pp.46–49.
14. Kripalani, J. B., *Gandhi: His Life and Thought*, New Delhi: Publications Division, Government of India, 1991, p. 423.
15. Paraphrased version of the chapter, The critique of Modernity, written by Bhikhu Parekh in his book.

Summary

- Gandhi provides one of the most fundamental critics of modernity. The fact is that Gandhi was not anti modernist. Rather, he was against the down side of modernism and excessiveness of materialism resulting in exploitation, domination and conquest.
- Gandhi built on important modern conceptions such as secular equality and universal rights; his encounters with modernity do not prompt him to merge it with tradition. His reconceptualization of autonomy and equality, allied as they are with

community, duty, and cohesion, are in opposition to modern ones, and he seeks to buttress these goods by mounting a critique of modernity and modernization that is simultaneously conservative and radical.

- Modernity is a complex phenomenon, with a layered history of meanings. Modernization as a conscious and deliberate pursuit has acquired currency in the post-war world. Modernization indicates swift widespread change and transformation of societies and the broad lines of the process are industrialization, urbanization, and mass communication.
- Under Gandhi's leadership, India's traditions were refurnished, mobilized and galvanized to serve new goals and objectives.
- Gandhi was a great builder. He built institutions—women's institutions, labour unions and institutions.
- Gandhi acquired wide and convincing legitimacy for himself, reinforced national identity, achieved a rare degree of political penetration among the vast masses of India and brought forth an unusual degree of popular participation through empathy and mobility. All this was richly indicative of a fast pace of modernization.
- According to Bikhu Parekh, Gandhi was able to reject the currently fashionable view among many British and Indian writers that the East and the West were radically different and shared nothing in common. For Gandhi, such a doctrine had no basis in facts; it denied the fundamental unity of mankind and bred cultural parochialism.
- Second, he was able to attack modern civilization without attacking the West.
- Third, the distinction enabled Gandhi to argue that modern civilization was of relatively recent origin in the West and that its pre-modern counterpart was very different and more like Indian.
- Fourth, by arguing that industrial civilization was modern and 'still very young', Gandhi intended to suggest that it lacked the wisdom and maturity conferred by age, an important argument in a country that revered age.
- Finally, Gandhi hoped to convince his countrymen that in fighting modern civilization they were not being reactionary.
- Gandhi's critique of modern civilization was far more complex than is generally imagined and quite different from that of such other writers as Rousseau, Carlyle, Ruskin, Tolstoy and Thoreau, by the last three of whom he was deeply influenced. In his view modern civilization was grounded in a fatally flawed theory of man.
- For Gandhi, modern civilization was propelled by the two inter- related principles of greed and want.
- Modern civilization rested on and was sustained by massive violence. Modern civilization also involved an egregious amount of violence against nature, which was largely seen as man's property to do with it what he liked.
- In Gandhi's view, the exploitation of one's fellow men was built into the very structure of modern civilization.
- *Hind Swaraj* is a trenchant critique of modern civilization but it also contains a statement of Gandhi's alternative to modern civilization and a programme for Indians to actualize such an alternative.

- Gandhi was familiar with both the European as well as the non-European viewpoints but found the non-European perspective more significant.
- Modern civilization gave more importance to the body, it gave importance to the idea of individualism and to greed. Modernity has robbed the morality of its most key quality—the quality of the soul.
- Modern civilization exploited the poor and the weak European imperialism was a key expression of the aggressive and exploitative modernity.
- Modernity considered reason to be the ultimate test of all knowledge, while its own flaws and limits were overlooked grossly.
- Despite being critical of modernity, Gandhi appreciated it for its three good qualities. One, its scientific spirit; two, greater human control over the material world; three, a new culture of respect for rules.

Further Readings

Brown, Judith M., *Gandhi's Rise to Power, Indian Politics*, 1915-22, London: Cambridge University Press, 1972.

Chatterjee, Partha, *Nationalist Thought and the Colonial World*, New Delhi: Oxford University Press, 1986.

Hardiman, David, *Gandhi In His Time and Ours*, New Delhi: Permanent Black, 2003.

Kripalani, J. B., *Gandhi: His Life and Thought*, New Delhi: Publications Division, Ministry of Information and Broadcasting, Government of India, 1968.

Mishra, Anil Dutta, *Understanding Mahatma Gandhi: Speeches and Writings that Reveal his Mind, Methods and Mission*, New Delhi: Concept, 2012.

Parekh, Bhikhu, *Colonialism, Tradition and Reform: An Analysis of Gandhi's Political Discourse*, New Delhi: Sage Publications, 1989.

Parekh, Bhiku, *Gandhi's Political Philosophy: A Critical Examination*, London: MacMillan Press, 1989.

6

The Philosophy of *Sarvodaya*

Introduction

Sarvodaya, today, does not represent a mere vision or a Utopian notion but makes an attempt of reorienting the human mind to reconstruct human society. It has assumed the dimensions of a movement and a socio-economic force of great potentialities. It is a dynamic philosophy, which can make possible the advent of a radically transformed humanity. *Sarvodaya* seeks to build a new society on the foundations of old, spiritual and moral values of India and attempts to meet the challenge of the contemporary problems.[1] The world has witnessed the propagation, experimentation and implementation of various socio-economic ideologies—capitalist, socialist and communist—from time to time. But, in overall consideration, *Sarvodaya* is undoubtedly far more superior to other attributive models. It envisages a well-balanced and integrated development of the nation with no distinction among have and have-nots, privileged and under-privileged, ruler and ruled. The essence of *Sarvodaya* thought lies in socializing matter through the strength of the spirit. Dogmas have no place in *Sarvodaya*. 'The philosophy of *Sarvodaya* is not a set of dogmas; in its essence; it is compatible with an attempt of the spirit to prevail over matter and to socialize itself.'[2] *Sarvodaya* is a redeemer's philosophy of social and political orientation; where suffering is, *Sarvodaya* goes to mitigate it. It is the culmination of human emotional integration and the highest intellectual aspiration. It is a symbol of platonic detachment and the *Gita*'s *Anasakti*.[3] It is the highest manifestation of love and attempts at a mental transformation of the people. Gandhi denounced the utilitarian principle of the greatest good of the greatest number, and advocated the *Sarvodaya* philosophy.

Gandhi did not originally coin the word *Sarvodaya*. Even before him, the idea of *Sarvodaya* was found in religious books: the *Vedas*, *Upanishads*, the *Ramayana*, the *Gita*, the *Holy Quran* and many others. It was also preached by Indian and Western saints as well as philosophers. But Gandhi gave to these age-old principles and ideals an extended meaning and application. In fact, after the death of Gandhi, the word *Sarvodaya* came into greater prominence, when his fellow-workers assembled at Sevagram (Wardha) in March 1948, and decided to form an organization named Sarvodaya Samaj. This name was chosen in preference to Satyagraha Mandal (Satyagraha Circle) because the word *Satyagraha* had come to acquire a restricted meaning which did not include constructive work. Since then, the school of thought which accepts Gandhi's philosophy in all its aspects and of which the central figure is Vinoba Bhave, has come to be known as the *Sarvodaya* School and its philosophy as the *Sarvodaya* Philosophy.[4] The prominent thinkers of this school were Acharya Vinoba Bhave, Kishorlal Ghanshyam Mashruwala, J. C. Kumarappa, Kaka Kalelkar, Shankerrao Deo, Dhirendra Mazumdar, Loknayak Jayaprakash Narayan and Acharya J. B. Kripalani. Except for Jayaprakash Narayan, all of them had been associated with Gandhi in his constructive work.

Sarvodaya: Meaning and Genesis

Sarvodaya is Sanskrit in origin, which is comprised of *Sarva*, meaning all and *Udaya*, meaning rising. The etymological meaning of *Sarvodaya* is the rising of all. This includes all living beings.[5] In other words, *Sarvodaya* as a word means welfare of all. The word first appeared in the form of the title for the Gujarati translation of John Ruskin's book entitled 'Unto this Last'.[6] *Sarvodaya* was also the title of a series of nine articles, which Gandhi wrote and got published in Gujarati in the *Indian Opinion* weekly in South Africa in 1908.[7]

Sarvodaya is essentially a spiritual activity, which has two meanings, namely negative and positive. As a negative concept, *Sarvodaya* is not limited to one person or to one group of persons. Nobody is excluded from enjoying anything from other.[8] It is not something which one man or set of men can gain or enjoy to the exclusion of others.[9] As a positive concept, *Sarvodaya* implies the participation of all kinds of people irrespective of class, caste, creed and religion. It also stands for the total blossoming of all the faculties—physical, mental and spiritual of the human being. It is an activity in which all may partake if it is to amount to a full realization of the human faculties of the human soul.[10]

According to Acharya Vinoba Bhave, the term *Sarvodaya* commands a two-fold meaning. Firstly, *Sarvodaya* means making everyone happy by removing suffering and poverty with the help of scientific knowledge. Secondly, establishing a world state full with divinity, kindness and equality is called *Sarvodaya.*[11] *Sarvodaya* aims not at the rise of the few or the many or, for that matter, the rise of the greatest number. It is not utilitarianism, which stands for the greatest good of the greatest number. It contains the germ of minority and majority. Contrary to utilitarianism, *Sarvodaya* stands for the good of one and all, of the high and the low, of the strong and the weak, the intelligent as well as the dull. As against the Laissez -faire theory, that is, the survival of the fittest, *Sarvodaya* believes in the survival and development of all. To Vinoba, 'The idea of *Sarvodaya*, as preached by the *Gita* is to merge oneself in the good of all.'[12]

Apart from connoting the welfare of all, *Sarvodaya* commands two more meanings, firstly, the universal welfare and secondly, the integrated development of all. The laissez-faire philosophy stands for the exploitation of many by a few. The utilitarian school supports the majority, totally neglecting the minority. *Sarvodaya* rejects these theories—which stand for the joy of few—advocates the welfare of all, irrespective of class, costs, creed, colour, race, region or religion. The philosophy of *Sarvodaya* makes the attempt of reorienting the human mind, of reconstructing human society. It means welfare and prosperity of all. All must progress together without collision of interest.[13] Interpreting the purport of *Sarvodaya*, Dada Dharmadhikari said: '*Sarvodaya* is a term with a wider connotation since it conceives of assimilation of all and not only of many or most.[14] *Sarvodaya* is a philosophy, which provides checks against the imperfections of human mind and soul.

As regards the meaning of the word *Sarvodaya*, there are broadly two views: the first, in its micro-form, means simply the rise of one and all; secondly, the macro-form connotes the rise of all, the universal welfare and the all round development of all.[15] But it connotes several other meanings. In its negative sense, it never omits even a single person from enjoying anything from the rest of the mankind. As a positive concept, it promotes the development of all the faculties of man. According to Vinoba Bhave, it stands for not only making everyone happy by eliminating suffering from all but also for bringing a world state based on equality. For Gandhi, *Sarvodaya* as a broader concept stands for the merger of one in all with self-sacrifice and a selfless service. It aims at not only fulfilling the minimum material needs but also developing the ethico-spiritual aspects of all people.

Sources of *Sarvodaya*

The following sources helped Gandhi to develop his concept of *Sarvodaya.* These were: Ruskin's book *Unto This Last*, Tolstoy's *The Kingdom of God is Within You*, Thoreau's *Civil Disobedience*, *The Bhagvad Gita*, *Isavasyopanisad*, Buddhism, Jainism, and Islam.

Ruskin's Unto This Last

The Gandhian philosophy of *Sarvodaya* can be traced to the central teachings of India's spiritual and religious heritage, although Gandhi admits the fact that he had immediate inspiration from Ruskin's *Unto This Last* of which the term *Sarvodaya* is his rendering.[16] The welfare of all became the basic idea of Gandhi's philosophy right from the days when he wrote in Gujarati his most world famous thirty thousand words' book *Hind Swaraj* or *Indian Home Rule* in 1909.

Gandhi called one of the chapters of his Autobiography 'The Magic Spell of Book', wherein he describes the effects of Ruskin's *Unto This Last* (meaning uplift of the last). He translated it later into Gujarati, claiming it *Sarvodaya.* It is a book from which Gandhi drew great inspiration and he at once determined to change his view of life in line with the ideals embodied in Ruskin's book *Unto This Last.*[17]

The central teaching of *Unto This Last*, according to Gandhi are:

- That the good of the individual is contained in the good of all
- That a lawyer's work has the same values as the barber's in as much as all have the same right of earning their livelihood from their work

- That a life of a labourer, that is, the life of the tiller of the soil and the handicraftsman is the life worth living

There is a controversy with regard to the meanings of the terms 'Unto This Last' and *Sarvodaya.* Gandhi himself acknowledged that he translated it later into Gujarati, entitling it *Sarvodaya.* On the one hand, Benudhar Pradhan opines that the idea of welfare of all formed a part of Gandhi's mental make-up even before he read this book.[18] This view is further strengthened from what Gandhi has expressed in his own words, 'The first of these I knew'[19]. On the other hand, Geoffrey Ashe doubted whether the idea of *Sarvodaya* is contained at all in Ruskin's *Unto This Last.* Persons like Benudhar affirm that 'it will be a travesty of truth to say that the objective of 'welfare of all' does not remain couched in the pages of *Unto This Last* of Ruskin.'[20]

Ruskin and Gandhi both were earnestly concerned with social welfare. While Ruskin aimed at the social welfare of the greatest number, Gandhi aimed at the welfare of all. Therefore, Vinoba Bhave feels that Gandhi is the real author of the term *Sarvodaya*, since the term 'Unto This Last' would mean only the upliftment of the last (*Antyodaya*). In fact, one has to accept that Ruskin's *Unto This Last* had directly or indirectly had a profound influence on Gandhi in fulfilling the ideal of *Sarvodaya*, which he had already cherished as his life's mission.

Leo Tolstoy's The Kingdom Of God Is Within You

Gandhi was greatly influenced by Leo Tolstoy, through his book *The Kingdom Of God Is Within You* and his essay on 'Christianity and Patriotism'. Tolstoy's simplicity of life and purity of purpose influenced Gandhi deeply. His views on Christianity, its church, its teachings aroused Gandhi's feelings. Tolstoy accepted love to be the law of life. The principles of non-violence are based on love for the entire mankind. Tolstoy and Gandhi both adopted the instrument of love to solve all problems in their lives. In Tolstoy's celebrated book *The Kingdom of God is Within You*, we find a political force creating an indelible mark on Gandhi. Gandhi confessed that its reading cured him of the skepticism and made him a firm believer of *ahimsa.* Both Tolstoy and Gandhi firmly believed that non-violence could cure all social maladies, remove political ills, and establish peace on the earth and goodwill among mankind. In fact, both Tolstoy and Gandhi believed in the efficacy of love for the cure of evil and suffering in this world. Tolstoy perceived the truth, love and non-violence and Gandhi grasped the essence of these virtues and led his life directed towards these paths.[21]

Tolstoy also impressed upon Gandhi's mind the importance of bread-labour. For Tolstoy, the man who abstains from manual labour is a thief of the society. Gandhi acknowledged his debt to Tolstoy. He says, 'the law that to live man must work, first came to me after reading Tolstoy's writing, 'On Bread Labour'. Only those men deserve to eat bread who actually till the ground, spin cloth and produce things'. Tolstoy says, 'let us get off the shoulder of our neighbours' and Gandhi adds that if everyone performed that simple operation, he would have rendered all the service that God requires of him. Since every man has an obligation to himself as well as to the society, bread labour becomes an imperative duty which must be performed by each and every man.[22]

Gandhian philosophy of *Sarvodaya* comes very close to Tolstoyan philosophy of anarchism. The pure ideal of Gandhi's conception of *Sarvodaya* is an ideal of philosophical anarchism, a stateless society marked by voluntary co-operation. Profound faith in God, commiseration from the exploited, inherent aversion to violence, deep-rooted belief in the dignity of man led the two philosophers to the same goal and objective. But Gandhi is not a through-going Tolstoyan. The difference between the two philosophers arises out of the fact that Gandhi is far more practical than Tolstoy. Tolstoy recoils from all expressions of violence. Gandhi permits violence, provided of course, that motive for violence is not anger but true love. Thus, the moral content of Gandhi's doctrine of *ahimsa*—which forms the fulcrum around which the entire doctrine of *Sarvodaya* ideology is based—has a higher significance than that of Tolstoy's. This is due to the fact that Gandhi was greatly influenced by *Gita*'s ideal of *niskamakarma*, that is, action without attachment.[23]

Thoreau's Civil Disobedience

The American pacifist Thoreau was a champion of the free sprit and was repelled by the established political and economic routine of time. In him we discover an element of moral individualism culminating in his concept of 'civil disobedience'. Thoreau used this term in his speeches in 1849. It is obvious that Gandhi did not derive his idea of 'civil disobedience' from the writings of Thoreau. In fact, the resistance to authority in South Africa preceded before Gandhi read the essay of Thoreau on 'civil disobedience'. This movement was then known as 'passive resistance'. Gandhi was not satisfied with the term 'civil disobedience' because it failed to convey the full meaning of the struggle. Hence, he adopted the phrase 'civil resistance'.[24]

Thoreau did not believe in narrow sectarianism and felt that man is meant to experience God, not to theologize about him. Man, according to Thoreau, is a social being who is generally disposed to co-operation with fellow beings for social good. He felt that the moral institutions of the state supported by coercive authority hamper the individual's moral and spiritual freedom. He, therefore, visualized a society in which the government will disappear. 'That Government is best which governs not at all', or, which governs least. Like Thoreau, Gandhi also held that the democracy could be realized only in a stabiles society based on truth and non-violence. And Gandhi described it as *Sarvodaya*, which promotes not only social welfare but spiritual upliftment. Thus, Gandhi heard an echo of his own thoughts in Thoreau.[25]

The Bhagvad Gita

Gandhi drew his primary strength and inspiration from the *Bhagvad Gita.* To Gandhi, the *Gita* is the 'Eternal Mother'. According to him, the theme of the *Gita* is self-realization. He says: 'self-realization and its means is the theme of the Gita'.[26] Again, he affirms, 'to one who reads the spirit of the Gita, it teaches the secret of non-violence, the secret of realizing the self through the physical body'.[27]

The sole aim of the *Gita* is to suppress unrighteousness and to establish *dharma*. It wants to bring prosperity and peace to all. It presents in concise form the Hindu view of life, which in turn stands for the universal brotherhood of all beings. It also highlights the importance of all selfless service for the promotion of the welfare of the whole creation since God and the creation is one. Through *Svadharma*, the *Gita* aims at *Sarvabhutahita* or the good of all beings.[28] In this way, the *Gita* preaches the message of the welfare of all or *Sarvodaya*, which influenced Gandhi's thought, and action.

Isavayopanisad

The first verse of *Isavayopanisad* deals with the ideology of *Sarvodaya*. The first part of the verse contains the principles of equality and fraternity. And the second part reveals the ideas of renunciation, non-acquisitiveness, non-exploitation and service to the society. According to Gandhi, since the entire universe is pervaded by God, the verse preaches the philosophy of equality and fraternity, which are the fundamental principles of the welfare of all. He confirms, 'Universal brotherhood not only brotherhood of all human beings but of all living beings, I find in this mantra…'[29]

Buddhism

According to Lord Buddha, all life is suffering. Suffering has to be extirpated in order to enjoy the bliss of nirvana, which is the highest goal in Buddhism. Nirvana is both individualistic and universal or cosmic. It may be realized in his life, here and there. It may also be known as full and perfect enlightenment for the sake of all beings. All can obtain nirvana if they meticulously follow the Noble Eight-Fold Path of the Buddha. Gandhi was highly influenced and deeply impressed by the Buddhist philosophy, which preached universal love, non-injury to living beings, sacrifice and renunciation for the sake of promoting the welfare of all. The Buddha stressed on purity of means which, in turn, influenced Gandhi who constantly maintained that there is indissoluble relationship between pure means and noble end.[30] Buddha preached about the middle path. Similarly, in *Sarvodaya*, it is understood that no one should take any extreme step.

Jainism

The ideal of the welfare of all forms is the corner stone of Jainism. *Ahimsa* forms one of the five vows. The positive aspect of non-violence is the love for fellow beings, not only human but also all creatures. A Jain Tirthankara's duty is to devote his whole life for showering happiness on all the beings of the whole universe. Regarding the place of *Sarvodaya* in Jainism, Binudhar Pradhan states: 'The concept of welfare of all was so much an integral part of Jain philosophy that the term *Sarvodaya* was used by one Jain teacher Samantabhadra even before the Christian era.'[31] Further, Benudhar Pradhan argues that though the word *Sarvodaya* was used by the Jain Saint Samantabhadra for the first time, yet Gandhi's use of the word is completely his own. According to him, the term *Sarvodaya* came to Gandhi 'as if in a flash'.[32] Therefore, he maintains that 'the word *Sarvodaya* … was purely his own coinage.'[33]

Islam

Gandhi had a great respect for Islam. He learnt the message of universal brotherhood from it. As for Islam, Gandhi declares that in his view, 'the point of brotherhood is manifested in no other religion as clearly as in Islam'. The reading of the *Holy Quran* convinced Gandhi that the basis of Islam is not violence.[34] In fact, Gandhi shows remarkable catholicity and sympathetic and reverential attitude towards all religions of the world.

Apart from *Unto This Last, The Kingdom of God is within you*, the Upanishads, the *Gita*, Buddhism and Jainism, Gandhi's concept of *Sarvodaya* was also influenced by Vaishnavism, Zoroastrianism and Christianity. The revival of the ancient teachings by Gandhi and incorporating them in his philosophy of *Sarvodaya* is perhaps his greatest contribution to the world of thought. Gandhi attempted the synthesis of the ideas of Vedanta, Buddhism, Jainism, Christianity and the teaching of prophets like Tulsidas, Tolstoy, Thoreau, Ruskin and national leaders of the Indian Renaissance movement. The philosophy of *Sarvodaya* takes up the Gandhian synthesis and tries to work out the implication of their ideas at more critical and analytical levels.[35]

Ends and Means in Sarvodaya

Morality is the essential means to achieve spirituality and good society or good ends. But communists like Machiavelli maintain that the end justifies the means. This reveals that through any impure means like cunningness, hypocrisy, hatred or violence one can get one's own desired end. To them, ends and means are watertight compartment. End is everything, no matter what or how the means are. Means become good if they serve the end. Jayaprakash Narayan observed impartially: 'In Marxism, any means are good means provided they serve the ends of the social revolution.'[36]

For Gandhi, the m means determine the end. He says, 'As the means so the end'.[37] Means are as important as the ends. In a way, his unique contribution to the world lies in his maintaining that the means are more important than the ends.'[38] His emphasis on means rather than on the end is based on the doctrine of Niskamakarma which holds that a person can have control over actions and not on their fruit. Gandhi is fully convinced that man can only strive but cannot command results. He maintains that 'means are, after all, every thing. There is no wall of separation between means and ends. Indeed, the creator gives us control over means, none over the end. Realization of the goal is in exact proportion to that of the means. This is a proportion that admits of no exception.'[39] Gandhi's stress on the strength of the means is based on the following reasons:

- He believes in the progressive evolution of man.
- He fixes the end of man as self-perfection.
- He feels that the end is always out of man's grip till it is attained.

- He is convinced that if means are subordinated to ends, the ends to which means are subordinated are likely to be less effective. All the above convictions made Gandhi believe that man must have complete control over means, despite the fact that both means and ends are various and contradictory.[40]

According to Gandhi, the end justifying the means is dangerous in practice and unsound ethically. If it is accepted, it permits resources to violence, fraud, untruth and opportunism. Gandhi viewed human beings as supreme. They are ends in themselves. If the means are pure, so does the end. When we take care of the means, the end will take care of itself.[41] By emphasizing only the means, Gandhi does not intend to give a secondary place to the ends. To him, means and ends are inseparably connected just like seed and trees are connected.[42]

By considering means and ends as a continuous process, Gandhi dissolved the age-old opinion of viewing both as watertight compartments. The difference between them is imaginary.[43] Therefore, he takes them as an organic whole. In a way, he proposes that both means and ends must be homogeneous. He also holds that the extreme of means is itself the end. In other words, the end progressively realizes itself through the means. The end can never result all of a sudden out of the means. In fact, when it slowly progresses, it turns itself into the end. The means, apart from leading to an end, shape the end. In Gandhian philosophy, self-realization or spiritual freedom is the end of all human actions. Gandhi, throughout his life, tirelessly tried to use *Sarvodaya* social order as the means to achieve spiritual freedom. *Sarvodaya* society guarantees moral freedom to every individual. This moral freedom, in turn, progresses itself into spiritual freedom, when it is followed meticulously placing faith in the supremacy of God. Moral freedom as the means and spiritual freedom as the end forms a continuous process or organic wholes. They cannot be divided into watertight compartments. Their difference is only imaginary. Both are convertible terms. That is what Gandhi too reveals. What is needed is understanding and practicing ethics as god has given us. *Sarvodaya*, as it enjoys an ethico-spiritual basis, can also be equitable to both moral freedom and spiritual freedom. Thus, the problem of ends and means, as an organic whole, occupies a unique place in Gandhian thought, contributing to *Sarvodaya*, moral, spiritual, political, and spiritual economic freedom.

Sarvodaya *Social Order*

Gandhi, with his many-sided personality, had a clear vision and definite approach to the problems, which faced India of his time. Indian society was full with deep-rooted evils. It had totally degenerated itself socially, politically, economically and educationally. Penury had further ruined India's social conditions which were already corroded with caste conflicts, child marriages, untouchability, sati, purdah, negation of education to women, dowry, polygamy, corruption, exploitation and other social crimes. Gandhi tried to find immediate solutions to all these problems.[44]

In *Sarvodaya* society, there is no scope for exploitation, discrimination, inequality and violence. Gandhi[45] envisaged that *Sarvodaya* society should also be free from evils like 'politics without principle', 'wealth without work', 'knowledge without character', 'commerce without morals', 'science without mankind' and 'service without scarifies'. It should not be divided into watertight compartments called social, political and religious where all these act and react upon one another. His aim of *Sarvodaya* made him establish a close correlation among these problems. The *Sarvodaya* society is an indivisible whole. In order to establish a democratic and free society, Gandhi suggested every individual to imbibe the spirit of love, tolerance, kindness, fearlessness and non-violence. A non-violent society, however small it is, is the strongest one. Non-violence as the law of life includes individuals, societies and nations. To him, non-violence is both a personal and social virtue. A society built on the basis of complete *ahimsa* is the purest anarchy.[46]

For *Sarvodaya* mentality, certain attributes are essential. Gandhi offered the 'eleven vows' to discipline oneself so that a disciplined society could emerge. Self-sacrifice is the essence of *Sarvodaya* social order. Every individual is to be ready and willing to sacrifice his happiness for the sake of others. Every one is to follow the policy of giving and not taking. He is to work for others and not expect anything in return for the same. Through *Sarvodaya*, he wanted to rebuild the nation 'from the bottom up wards' and establish a new social order based on freedom, justice, equality and fraternity. Gandhi's ideal (*Sarvodaya*) society would be marked by following characteristics:[47]

- There should be no coercive state power in it and social cohesion should be maintained through the citizens' sense of social obligation like the obligations of *Varnashram dharma* in ancient India
- It should consist of villages or rural agricultural settlements in which wants are few and co-operation, conservation and decentralization are the governing norms of social, civil and economic activity
- Besides agriculture, other production should be based on cottage industries and handicraft. Even education should be handicraft-centred.
- The ruling principles of decentralized and handicraft-centred production, three other economic norms should be maintained or practiced, namely; village self-sufficiency, bread-labour (that is, winning one's bread through work done by one's own body labour), and non-possession (acquiring or using the minimum possible articles of consumption). Heavy machines and heavy transport will have no place in this society.
- In such a society, disputes or conflict (generally arising out of the craze for power, property or possession) will be few and for between. But in order to deal with such disputes, as may possibly or occasionally arise, village panchayats should be organized. In the unlikely event of the failure of panchayats, recourse may be had to *Satyagraha*.

Gandhi had set up his first *Sarvodaya* community in a farm near Durban and called it Phoenix Settlement (c. 1904), followed by another one (c. 1910) over Johannesburg, which was named after Leo Tolstoy. The idea behind these two settlements was that the inmates had to perform all chores of running the farms—whatever is their avocation—on living wages, so that they become self-reliant and self-sufficient. In fact, through the pursuit of *Sarvodaya* ideals, Gandhi wanted to chart out an alternative course. The ideas on *Sarvodaya* social order find their fullest expression in his constructive work programme that began to unfold itself on his arrival in India from South Africa. *Khadi*, communal amity, removal of untouchability, promotion of village industries, village sanitation and basic education came one after another and so did the supporting organizations. Some of these organizations were: All India Spinners Association, All India Harijan Sewak Sangh, Hindustani Prachar Sabha, Hindustan Talimi Sangh and Akhil Bharat Sewa Sangh. The *Sarvodaya* society is an ideal society and an ideal cannot be fully realized. Gandhi also believed that an ideal is never fully realized in life.'[48]

Sarvodaya Political Order

Sarvodaya as a political doctrine is mildly anarchist. In fact, the political ideal of *Sarvodaya* is an anarchism of its own variety. It concedes that a fully stateless society is beyond the reach of man, and the goal of human endeavour can only be to reduce the power and sphere of the state to the minimum. The politics of *Sarvodaya* is politics of *Lokniti* instead of *rajniti*. *Lokniti* is a comprehensive term, which denotes simultaneously a way of life, a form of social order and a method. As a way of life, it stands for the self-regulation of individual conduct and for a habit to act on one's own initiatives. As a form of social order, it envisages a society in which police and military will have little to do and the law will interfere, least with life. A man will have the utmost freedom of action. As a method, it stands for social change in a manner that would maintain men's freedom of action.[49] The *Sarvodaya* political order is based on certain fundamental political assumptions:

- All individuals are equally born.
- People are the custodians of the supreme power in the state.
- Political power should be decentralized both at individual and the village level.
- All must train themselves for self-rule.
- All should believe in the divinity of every individual and strive for the welfare of all people.[50]

The ultimate goal for Gandhi was the greatest good of all people. Good, to him, meant only the self-realization but not the material well being of the individuals or the society. A study on the nature of *Sarvodaya* political order demands a brief survey of his view on state, Swaraj, *Satyagraha*, democracy, nationalism, internationalism and *Ram Rajya*.[51]

According to Vinoba Bhave,[52] there are ten criteria of an ideal polity:

- International fraternity.
- The conscious, spontaneous (as far as possible) and hearty co-operation of all the inhabitants of the country.
- The identity of the good of the capable minority and the general majority.

- The orientation towards the universal and equal development of all.
- The widest dispersion of political sovereignty.
- The least amount of government.
- The easiest availability of *tantra* or justice (*Sulabhatama tantra*).
- The least possible expenditure.
- The lowest degree of external protection.
- One universal, uninterrupted, and neutral or objective spread of knowledge.

Sarvodaya Economic Order

Gandhi adopted an integral approach to human problems. His basic aim was to reduce economics to terms of religion and spirituality. For him, ethics and economics were not two different entities. Economics that hurt the moral well-being of an individual or a nation are immoral and, therefore, sinful.[53] True economics, according to Gandhi 'stands for social justice; it promotes the good of all equally including the weakest and is indispensable for decent life.'[54] He mainly wanted to formulate such an economic constitution to both India and the World that no one would suffer from want of food, clothing and shelter. All necessities of life 'should be freely available to all as God's air and water are or ought to be…'[55] He aimed at building such an economic constitution not on material wealth but on spirituality. This is only possible when every one shows more truth than gold, greater fearlessness than pomp of power and wealth, greater charity than love of self.

The Gandhian *Sarvodaya* economic order is based on simplicity, decentralization, self-sufficiency, co-operation, equality, non-violence, sanctity of labour, human values, self-sufficient village units, nationalization of basic industries, *swadeshi*, and the theory of trusteeship. These, in turn, will solve the problems pertaining to labour, capital, production, distribution and profit.

In the Gandhian economic order, dependence on others is slavery and self-sufficiency is freedom. Regional self-sufficiency is a must in *Sarvodaya* economic order. People should produce their own needs of life. Production must be in accordance with the need.

In the *Sarvodaya* economic order, man is totally free from material bondage. He never becomes a slave to material wants. He lives above his greed and amassing of riches. He views work as service. It is divine for him. He cherishes the principles of self-suffering, sacrifice, dedication and renunciation. His eating, clothing or dwelling shows no superiority or inferiority. He finds no difference between the rich and the poor. *Sarvodaya* economic system is practical, realistic and humane.

Socialism, Communism and *Sarvodaya*

Gandhi called himself a socialist and even a communist but for him socialism and communism were transcendental forms of an egalitarian social philosophy that find their fulfillment and culmination in *Sarvodaya*.[56] Although the situational background from which socialism and *Sarvodaya* have emerged is different, still their humanist idealism is almost similar.[57] According to Jayaprakash Narayan, *Sarvodaya* represents the highest socialist values. Socialism arose in the West as a philosophy of the industrial proletariat and challenged the pretensions of the contemporary state, which bolstered the interests of the capitalists.[58]

Socialism and communism are basically idealistic, ethical and humanitarian in nature. They are concerned with the illumination of the misery of the millions, elevation of the status of poor, unfortunate and downtrodden and founding a society based on the principle of economic equality and social justice. *Sarvodaya* stands for the just society free from all types of exploitation and human miseries. According to Rajendra Prasad,[59] *Sarvodaya* represents an aspiration 'towards a society based on truth and non-violence in which there will be no distinction of caste or creed, no opportunity for exploitation and full scope for development both for individuals as well as groups.' Jayaprakash Narayan[60] writes about *Sarvodaya* thus, 'What we desire is the establishment of a society in which there will be no exploitation, there will be perfect equality and each individual will have equal opportunities for development.'[61] *Sarvodaya* aims at a 'classless, casteless and non-exploitative society.'[62] Vinoba Bhave[63] said 'There is no permanent conflict between the two ideologies-Marxism and *Sarvodaya*. Whatever differences there might be between Gandhism and communism, there are also points of similarity between these and these too are important. The cause of the have-nots is the basic sentiment running through both. Both Gandhism and communism regard the well-being of the poor and the oppressed with the intensely loving regard of the mother.' K. G. Mashruwala, a prominent Gandhian observes, 'the common point between Gandhi and Marx is the extreme concern of both for the suppressed and the oppressed, the resource less and the ignorant, the dumb and starving section of humanity.' Similarly, Jayaprakash Narayan[64] said 'If we are true socialists, we would be true follower of *Sarvodaya* as well.'

In spite of some fundamental similarities between socialism and *Sarvodaya*, there are great differences between them on the question of means and methods. From the *Sarvodaya* stand point; there are two shortcomings in the socialist philosophy. First, the basic technique for effectuating socialism is supposed to be nationalization, but nationalization may entrench the control of the bureaucrats and may be another name for state capitalism. According to *Sarvodaya*, the socialist belief in positive state action as the sovereign remedy for human ills is unfounded. *Sarvodaya* pleads for villagization, while socialism believes in nationalization. *Sarvodaya* accepts village ownership. Secondly, socialism adheres, at least in some cases, to the concept of violent revolution. But *Sarvodaya* has no place for violence in its philosophy and technique.[65]

The difference between *Sarvodaya* and communism are far more basic and fundamental. Communism advocates a violent technique for a change over in favour of an egalitarian society, a society free form exploitation and privilege. *Sarvodaya*, on the contrary believes in persuasion and change of heart. Both Marx and Engels expressed their conviction that 'violent overthrow of the bourgeoisie lays the foundation for the sway of the proletariat'. Lenin and Mao used the technique of violence to bring about a change in the Soviet Union and China, respectively, while Gandhi taught the ethics of self-suffering to convert the opponent because violence can never be the foundation of a just and equal society.[66] Violence breeds counter-violence. And on the basis of violence it is not possible to establish a just social order. In fact, a new form of exploitation of man has come into existence and that is exploitation by the party bosses, bureaucrats and the state machine.

The *Sarvodaya* avoids the evils of legislative or legal coercion in democratic socialism and violence and physical coercion involved in communism. It relies on the techniques of conversion to bring about social transformation in the direction of a non-exploitative and egalitarian society. Gandhi was concerned with the welfare of all and, hence, rejected the view that the welfare of all can ever be attained by physical, intellectual and moral coercion perpetrated by a section of the people against the rest of the community. Gandhi believed that *Sarvodaya* could be realized only by the application of a moral and ethical method. He also believed that through the application of the technique of persuasion and appeal to the innate good sense of the rich and the privileged, they might be made to renounce their privileges and apply their superfluous wealth for the welfare of the community. Such renunciation of wealth and privilege was to be for the good of the poor and the rich. 'The essence of the revolution contemplated by *Sarvodaya* is that it plans its faith on human approach, at the root of which stands the concept of revolution by human beings for the proliferation of human values and human virtues, and through a method that is strictly humane.'[67]

The advocates of *Sarvodaya* also differ from the communists and socialists in respect of the role of the state. Both the communists and the socialists have their faith in the potency of the state to bring about equality in society. In the economic sphere, the communists and socialists advocate centralization and concentration of economic powers in the hands of the state and the proliferation of the economic activities of the state. To quote Jayaprakash Narayan,[68] 'Democratic socialists, communists as well as welfarists are all statists'. The concentration of both political and economic power in the hands of the state leads to too much of bureaucratization, dehumanization and loss of individual freedom. To quote Jayaprakash Narayan,[69] 'The democratic state remains a Leviathan that will sit heavily on the freedom of the people'. The state is still worse under communism. It is true that the communists talk about the withering away of the state in the long run, but during the transitional period, the state is not only tolerated but also becomes more and more powerful. It devours the lofty ideals of classless society-liberty, equality, fraternity and fellowship. Jayaprakash Narayan is of the belief that, 'The remedy is to create and develop forms of socialist living through the voluntary endeavor of the people rather than seek to establish socialism by the use of the power of the state. In other words, the remedy is to establish people's socialism, rather than state socialism.'[70]

Considered from all angles, *Sarvodaya* is a far nobler, subtler, loftier, broader, deeper and transcendental concept than socialism or communism. According to Vinoba Bhave, '*Sarvodaya* is a better word than "socialist"; it is also our own native word, born from our own soil and carrying a noble meaning. We do not use the word because we are a little doubtful if we can live up to it. So we prefer the world "socialist". But our goal is, in fact, *Sarvodaya* and our people are being prepared for absorption into the sea of *Sarvodaya*'. It is true that socialism and communism can realize their true meaning and fulfill their objective by merging their identity with *Sarvodaya*. Jayaprakash Narayan[71] writes, 'Socialism as we understand it today, cannot take mankind to the sublime goals of freedom, equality, brotherhood and peace. Socialism no doubt gives promise to bring mankind closer to those goals than any other competing social philosophy. But I am persuaded that unless socialism is transformed into *Sarvodaya*, those goals would remain beyond its reach. Vinoba writes, 'There is no permanent conflict between the two ideologies—Marxism and *Sarvodaya*. As the Ganges becomes wider and wider and moves on and finally merges in the ocean, I hope Marxism will merge in *Sarvodaya* one day.'[72]

Sarvodaya and Contemporary Crisis

The *Sarvodaya* principles are capable of meeting the greatest challenge of the age. The most urgent need of today is the abolition of human suffering as well as of war. Even *Sarvodaya* will be very important in 21st century due to complexity of human behaviour. *Sarvodaya*, by laying stress on the goodness of human nature, unity of mankind, service of man, application of moral principles considered valid for individuals to group life and inter-state relations, the non-violent process of change, social and economic equality, economic and political decentralization, tries to resolve the various kinds of tensions that disturb domestic and international harmony. *Sarvodaya* is capable of strengthening the forces of love, creativeness and joy of life. *Sarvodaya* takes the whole view of man and emphasizes his spiritual nature. In modern context the concept of *Sarvodaya* can be interpreted as the 'awakening of one and all'. Thus, in addition to the awakening of everyone, it refers to the awakening of the total human spirit and personality. *Sarvodaya* is also related to achieving the highest level of self-realization in which one sees one's manifestation in all others.

Our political, social and economic life has been sized with a malady. The malady of our times, perhaps of all times, is a mad quest for power, whether it is political, social or economic. Service is being given up in quest of personal aggrandizement. Humanity is undergoing almost a phase of moral collapse and ethical nihilism. In the era of the mad rush for power, the significance of *Sarvodaya* lies in stressing the permanent value of self-abnegation. *Sarvodaya* is giving expression to a moral principle of cardinal importance because it wants to enshrine the primacy of goodness and character in place of the skill of manipulation and self-assertion. *Sarvodaya* appeals to the mind and heart in terms of values and goals. The decadence and corruption which, in fact, organized institutional mechanism, can be removed only by the reassertion of moral and spiritual values and their ever-growing incorporation in social, political and economic life. *Sarvodaya* is the only way to solve the problems of unemployment, unequal distribution of wealth and growing corruption in public life. The moral collapse and prostration of our world needs the revitalizing notion of ethical idealism and stresses on the moral approach to social and economic problems, which *Sarvodaya* envisages.

Summing up

Sarvodaya philosophy, based on the insights and experiences of Gandhi, is a reassertion of the valuation and moral approach to the problems of mankind, which has been a part of ancient Indian culture for ages. Vinoba Bhave has rightly said '*Sarvodaya* stands for not only making all happy by eliminating suffering from all but also for bringing a world state based on equality.'[73] For Gandhi, *Sarvodaya* stands for the merger of one in all with self-sacrifice and a selfless service. His *Sarvodaya* ideal, apart from standing for the meaning of the welfare of all, implies the meaning of the universal welfare and integrated development of all. As a universal ideal, it aims at not only fulfilling the minimum material needs but also developing the ethico-spiritual aspects of all people. The great contribution of *Sarvodaya* in the present century lies in the reassertion of the Gandhian moral approach to the problems of mankind and a vision that looks forward to the creation of a welfare state and society.

Notes and References

1. Verma, V. P., *The Political Philosophy of Mahatma Gandhi and Sarvodaya*, Agra: Lakshmi Narayan Agarwal, 1980, 4th Edition, p. 279.
2. Mohanty, J. N., '*Sarvodaya* and Aurobindo: A Rapprochement', *Gandhi Marg*, Vol. 4, No. 30, July 1960, p. 211.
3. Pandey, B. P., *Gandhi, Sarvodaya and Organizations*, Allahabad: Chugh Publications, 1988, pp. 20–21.
4. Tandon, Vishwanath, *The Social and Political Philosophy of Sarvodaya After Gandhi,* Varanasi: Sarva Seva Sangh Prakashan, 1965, p. 2.
5. Mishra, Anil Dutta, *Fundamentals of Gandhism*, New Delhi: Mittal Publications, 1995, p. 5.
6. Mahajan, P. Mani and Bharathi, K. S., *Foundations of Gandhian Thought,* Nagpur: Dattsons, 1987, p. 68.
7. The Collected works of Mahatma Gandhi, Vol. 8, Publications Division, Government of India, New Delhi, 1962, pp. 239–41.
8. Rathnam Chetty, K. M., *Sarvodaya and Freedom: A Gandhian Appraisal*, New Delhi: Discovery Publishing House, 1991, p. 46.
9. Sharma, B. S., 'The Philosophical Basis of *Sarvodaya*', *Gandhi Marg*, Vol. 4, No. 3, July 1960, p. 259.
10. Ibid.
11. Rathnam Chetty, K. M., op. cit., p. 47.
12. *Harijan*, 13.2.1949.
13. Pandey, B. P., *Op. Cit.,* p. 14.
14. Dharmadhikari, Dada, *Sarvodaya Darshan*, Varanasi: Sarva Seva Sangh Prakashan, p. 18.
15. Rathnam Chetty, K. M., op. Cit., p. 48.
16. Ibid., p. 38.
17. Ibid.
18. Pradhan, Benudhar, *The Socialist Thought of Mahatma Gandhi,* Delhi: G. D. K. Publications, 1980, Vol. I, p. 284.
19. Gandhi, M. K., *An Autobiography or The Story of my Experiments with Truth*, Ahmedabad, Navjivan Publishing House, 1948, p. 365.
20. Pradhan, Benudhar, op. cit, p. 285.
21. Rathnam Chetty, K. M., op. cit., pp. 39–40.
22. Ibid., p. 40.
23. Ibid., pp. 40–41.
24. Ibid., p. 41.
25. Ibid.
26. Gandhi, M. K., *Young India*, 12-11-1925.

27. Ibid.
28. Rathnam Chetty, K. M., op. cit., pp. 42–43.
29. Mishra, Anil Dutta, op. cit., p. 11.
30. Ibid. p. 11
31. Pradhan, Benudhar, op. cit., p. 294.
32. Ibid., p. 301.
33. Ibid., p. 302
34. Rathnam Chetty, K. M., op. cit., p. 45.
35. Ibid.
36. Narayan, Jayaprakash, *Socialism, Sarvodaya and Communism*, Bombay: A. P. H. , 1964, p. 149.
37. Gandhi, M. K., *Young India*, p. 364.
38. Gopalan, S., Means and ends: The Gandhian view, *Gandhi Centenary Volume*, 1969, p. 70.
39. Gandhi, M. K., *Young India*, 17.7.1924.
40. Tendulkar, D. G., *Mahatma,* Vol. II, New Delhi: Publications Division, 1951, p. 299.
41. Gandhi, M. K., *Harijan,* 27.2.1949.
42. Gandhi, M. K., *Hind Swaraj or Indian Home Rule*, Ahmedabad: Navajivan Publishing House, 1946, p. 60.
43. *Harijan*, 27 February 1949.
44. Mishra, Anil Dutta, op. cit, p. 14.
45. Ibid.
46. Ibid., p. 15.
47. Gangal, S. C., *Gandhian Thought and Techniques in the Modern World,* New Delhi: Criterion Publications, 1988, pp. 158–59.
48. Ibid., p. 159.
49. Tandon, Vishwanath, op. cit., pp. 124–125.
50. Rathnam Chetty, K. M., op. cit., p. 66.
51. Mishra, Anil Dutta, op. cit., pp. 16–17.
52. Varma, V. P., *The Political Philosophy of Mahatma Gandhi and Sarvodaya*, Agra: Lakshmi Narayan Agarwal, 1980, p. 295.
53. Bose, N. K., *Selection From Gandhi*, Ahmedabad: Navjivan Publishing House, 1994, p. 40.
54. *Harijan,* 9 October, 1937.
55. *Young India*, 15 July 1928.
56. Mahajan V. D., *Modern Indian Political Thought*, Sultan Chand & Sons, New Delhi, 1987, p. 569.
57. Narayan, Jayaprakash, *From Socialism to Sarvodaya*, Madras: Socialist Book Centre, 1956, p. 96.
58. Varma, V. P. op. cit., p. 283.
59. Mahajan, V. D., op. cit., p. 569.
60. Ibid.
61. Ibid., pp. 569–70.
62. Ibid., p. 570.
63. Ibid.
64. Ibid.
65. Varma, V. P., op. cit., p. 285.
66. Bhave, Vinoba, *Swarajya Shastra*, New Delhi: Sasta Sahitya Mandal, 1953, pp. 58–68.
67. Majahan, V. D., op. cit, pp. 573–4.
68. Narayan, Jayaprakash, op. cit., p. 33.
69. Ibid., p. 34.

70. Ibid., p. 34.
71. Ibid., p. 21.
72. Majahan, V. D., op. cit., p. 574.
73. Mishra, Anil Dutta, op. cit., p. 17.

Summary

- Even before Gandhi, the idea of *Sarvodaya* was found in religious books: *Vedas*, *Upanishads*, the *Ramayana*, the *Gita, Quran* and many others.
- *Sarvodaya* is Sanskrit in origin which is comprised of *Sarva*, meaning all and *Udaya* meaning rising. The etymological meaning of *Sarvodaya* is the rising of all.
- After the death of Gandhi, the word *Sarvodaya* came into greater prominence, when his fellow-workers assembled at Sevagram (Wardha), in March 1948, and decided to form an organization named *Sarvodaya* Samaj.
- The prominent thinkers of *Sarvodaya* were Acharya Vinoba Bhave, Kishorlal Ghanshyam Mashruwala, J. C. Kumarappa, Kaka Kalelkar, Shankerrao Deo, Dhirendra Mazumdar, Loknayak Jayaprakash Narayan and Acharya J. B. Kripalani.
- *Sarvodaya* is essentially a spiritual activity, which has two meanings, namely negative and positive. As a negative concept, *Sarvodaya* is not limited to one person or to one group of persons. Nobody is excluded from enjoying anything from other. It is not something which one man or set of men can gain or enjoy to the exclusion of others. As a positive concept, *Sarvodaya* implies the participation of all kinds of people irrespective of class, caste, creed and religion.
- According to Acharya Vinoba Bhave, the term *Sarvodaya* commands a two-fold meaning. Firstly, *Sarvodaya* means making all happy by removing suffering and poverty with the help of scientific knowledge. Secondly, establishing a world state full with divinity, kindness and equality is called *Sarvodaya.*
- Ruskin's *Unto This Last*, Tolstoy's *The Kingdom of God is Within You*, Thoreau's *Civil Disobedience*, *The Bhagvad Gita*, *Isavasyopanisad,* Buddhism, Jainism, and Islam are main sources of *Sarvodaya.*
- Morality is the essential means to achieve spirituality and good society or good ends. But communists like Machiavelli maintain that end justifies the means. Jayaprakash Narayan observed impartially, 'In Marxism any means are good means provided they serve the ends of the social revolution.' For Gandhi means determine the end. He says, 'As the means so the end'.
- In *Sarvodaya* society, there is no scope for exploitation, discrimination, inequality, and violence.
- The politics of *Sarvodaya* is politics of *Lokniti* instead of *rajniti.*
- *Sarvodaya* economic order is based on simplicity, decentralization, self-sufficiency, co-operation, equality, non-violence, sanctity of labour, human values, self-sufficient village units, nationalization of basic industries, *swadeshi*, and the theory of trusteeship. Dependence on others is slavery and self-sufficiency is freedom. Regional self-

sufficiency is must in *Sarvodaya* economic order. People should produce their own needs of life. Production must be in accordance with the need.

- The *Sarvodaya* principles are capable of meeting the greatest challenge of the age. The most urgent need of today is the abolition of human suffering as well as of war. *Sarvodaya* philosophy, based on the insights and experiences of Gandhi, is a reassertion of the valuation and moral approach to the problems of mankind, which has been a part of ancient Indian culture for ages.

Further Readings

Bandyopadhyaya, J., *Social and Political Thought of Gandhi*, Calcutta: Allied Publishers, 1969.

Bhattacharyya, Buddhadeva, *Evolution of Political Thought of Gandhi*, Calcutta: Calcutta Book House, 1969.

Datta, D. M., *The Philosophy of Mahatma Gandhi*, Madison: University of Wisconsin Press, 1953.

Dhawan, Gopi Nath, *The Political Philosophy of Mahatma Gandhi,* Ahmedabad: Navajivan Publishing House, 1962.

Iyer, Raghavan, *The Moral and Political Thought of Mahatma Gandhi*, Chicago: Oxford University Press, 1973.

Lohia, Rammanohar, *Marx, Gandhi and Socialism,* Hyderabad: Rammanohar Lohia Samata Vidyalaya Nyasa, 1978.

Mishra,Anil Dutta, *Gandhism After Gandhi*, Delhi: Mittal Publications, 1999.

Radhakrishnan S. (ed.), *Mahatma Gandhi: Essays and Reflections on His Life and Thought*, Allahabad: Kitabistan, 1944.

Roy, Ramashray, *Contemporary Crisis and Gandhi*, New Delhi: Discovery Publishing House, 1986.

Verma, V. P., *The Political philosophy of Mahatma Gandhi and Sarvodaya*, Agra: Lakshmi Narain Aggarwal, 1981.

Vinobha, Bhave, *Swaraj Sastra*, Varanasi: Sarva Seva Sangh Prakashan, 1963.

7

An Alternative Modernity with Special Reference to Hardiman

Introduction

Euro-centric thinkers treat the period between Enlightenment (17th and 18th centuries) in Europe and the Second World War as modern and all that happened in that period as the product of modernism. Prior to modern was a long stretch of an era designated as pre-modern and the new thinking on progress that emerged in the West after the Second World War had been branded as post-modern.

Gandhi lived in the era called modern. It was the era which witnessed a major shift in values that charted the course of history from times immemorial. To distinguish the modern from the millennia bygone, the latter was designated as pre-modern. Europe and Anglo-America were declared modern; the rest of the world was pre-modern. Modern connoted and still connotes social, economic and technological advancement; a shift from agriculture to manufacturing, from rural to urban, and from experiential knowledge to scientific knowledge. The pre-modern was conceived to be archaic, backward looking and traditional. Each of these epithets convey hidden meanings. It would, therefore, be pertinent to go deeper into what these terms mean.

Pre-modernism, Modernism and Post-modernism

Pre-modern in the vocabulary of the modernists meant a social system that was collectively possessed by authority—all powerful kings, emperors, religious heads and village heads, wherein individuals were dominated by traditions and what the elders did. In pre-modern society, all had to conform to the time-honoured practices. Any questioning thereof is amounted to heresy. Thus, pre-modernism relied on the authority of scriptures, traditions and conventions. Everyone was assigned a place in the society, which was immanent and fixed. It is not that things did not change. They did, but very slowly. Even the traditions changed; old ones were rejected and new ones introduced but no one knew exactly when the old was out and the new was in. It was proclivity on the part of the people to adhere to what was customary and was more important than the customs themselves.

In pre-modern society, duties were more important than rights. Individuals were important but only as inseparable members of the family and community. The pre-modern society was essentially rural and agricultural; there were cities too but they served as centres of administration and business. Production, both agricultural and industrial, was village based.

In the wake of the 18th century, enlightenment came as a result of the discoveries of new lands. A series of scientific breakthroughs, a belief set in Europe that progress was essentially in a linear direction and material in content took place. Anything that did not liberate the man to do what he considered best for himself was rejected. Religion, faith and belief were branded as irrational and, therefore, unscientific. Given this paradigmatic shift, things that did not meet the standards of logic were rejected. And thus was born the concept of modernity.

As has been mentioned earlier, modernism is associated with European enlightenment (Renaissance); it represents the rejection of tradition and authority in favour of reason and natural sciences. It takes the autonomous individual as the sole source of truth—the Cartesian cogito. History is linear and so also progress. It was associated with the Protestant mode of consciousness, which rejected authority in all spheres of life. It is also associated with industrialization, scientific and technological discoveries and capitalism. The fundamental act of modernity is to question the foundation of past knowledge brought forward through traditions, rituals and conventions.

Modernity seeks order out of chaos and believes that rationality and rational behaviour alone can bring about order. It assumes that the more rational a society is, more ordered it would be and more ordered it is, the better it would function. Modern societies, therefore, reject things that generate disorder. Thus, they tend to label everything that does not fit into the paradigm of modernity as disorder which, in practical terms, means 'the other'; something that is foreign. Thus, anything non-white, non-male, non-heterosexual, non-hygienic, non-rational becomes part of the disorder, and has to be eliminated from the ordered, rational modern society.

Modernism is based on the belief that reason is the ultimate judge of what is true and, therefore, in a world governed by reason, truth, goodness and beauty (*satyam, shivam* and *sundaram*) would have no meaning if they do not conform to the standards set by logic. Modernism believes that there is stable, coherent knowable self, which is conscious, rational, autonomous and universal. The self knows itself and world through reason or rationality. The objective rational self knows the universal and eternal truth through science. The knowledge or truth produced by science would always lead to progress and perfection. Science is neutral and objective. Language or the mode of expression used in production and dissemination of knowledge must also be rational; it must represent the real or perceivable world, which the rational mind observes.

Modern societies, by distinguishing order from disorder, try to achieve stability and uniformity through grand or master narratives, which are a sort of meta-theories or meta-ideologies. For example, the grand narrative of the American culture is democracy as the most rational and enlightened form of government. Democracy backed by capitalism is the best form of governance and social order; it alone can bring happiness to the whole world. Anything undemocratic must be rejected and ousted. The grand narrative of the USSR was Marxism, which is based on the theory that capitalism will collapse and a utopian socialist world will evolve. Clash of interests of the capitalists and the labour class would ultimately lead to the victory of the latter and thus a more ordered society would come into being.

The products and byproducts of modernism has produced reactions in many a thinkers. The violence, destructions, and negative ecological consequences produced by modernism have given rise to a set of thinkers who challenge some of the very bases on which it is based. This reactive thinking became more pronounced after the Second World War, although its roots go back to some of the 19th and early 20th century thinkers. This paradigm is known as post-modernism.

According to the Oxford Dictionary, post-modernism is a philosophical stance, which claims that it is impossible to take grand statements—meta-narratives—about the structures of society or about historic causation, because everything we perceive, express and interpret, is influenced by our background in terms of let us say gender, class and culture. No one interpretation is, therefore, superior to other.

For example, the truth as perceived by a perpetrator of violence and the one who suffers the violence would be different. What is rational depends on the paradigm of our thinking and perceiving. As such, even the grand narratives like democracy can be perceived differently. The ideal world is, therefore, one which does not move linearly; which is not homogenous; and which protects the weaker sections of the society. Broadly speaking, post-modernism:

- Rejects the rationality of human actions.
- Respects heterogeneity and diversity.
- Shuns the postulations of theories and meta-narratives.
- Champions the cause of the poor, the weak, marginalized and downtrodden.
- Challenges the concept of development as structural transformation of the national economy and calls for transmogrification of a society, including sustainable development.
- Calls for integration of time and space to reach the truth.
- Believes in behavioural, experimental and participatory approaches rather than statistical and positivistic explanations;
- Lays stress on the micro as against the macro.
- Rejects the concept of sovereign, autonomous individual and lays emphasis on anarchic, collective, anonymous experience, collage, diversity, the mystically unrepresentable Dionysian passion.

- Refers to the incipient or actual dissolution of the social norms and forms associated with modernity.

To begin with, post-modernism rejects master narratives on which modernity relies because they serve to mask the contradictions and instabilities that are inherent to any social organization or practice. In other words, every attempt to create order always demands the creation of an equal amount of disorder. It favours mini-narratives, stories that explain small practices, local events, rather than large-scale universal or global concepts. These mini-narratives are situational, provisional, contingent and temporary, making no claim to universality. This is a sarcastic playful parody of Western modernity and John Wayne.

In post-modern societies, knowledge is functional—you learn things not for knowledge sake; you learn to use that knowledge. Education in schools and colleges, therefore, should stress on skills and training more than on vague humanist ideals of education in general. The question is not how to get a degree; it is what is the use of the degree? The modes of production, storage, distribution and arrangement of information are ICT based. Thus, the opposite of knowledge is not ignorance; it is the inability to convert the knowledge into digital formats.

There are lots of questions to be asked about post-modernism. Is the process of fragmentation, tentativeness and instability good for the man and his society? One of the consequences of post-modernism seems to be the rise of religious fundamentalism as a sort of reaction to the questioning of the grand narratives. Salman Rushdie's book the *Satanic Verses* was banned in Islamic countries and Taslima's novel was banned in Bangladesh because they deconstructed a grand Islamic narrative.

Gandhian Alternative

Gandhi lived and worked in the so-called modern age. When he wrote *Hind Swaraj* in 1909, modernism had swept all over Europe and America and had put the rest of the world in bondage. Gandhi challenged the notion of modernity on many counts. He blazed a trail that transcended even post-modernism and posed before humanity a challenge that it must meet squarely in order to survive and move towards its destiny.

Let me put before you some of the postulates of Gandhi, which would help us to understand him better vis-a-vis the paradigms of modernism and post-modernism.

- Gandhi did not subscribe to the dualism of man and nature; man is an inseparable part of nature. There is a Cosmic Law that keeps the universe in balance. This law is immanent and, hence, should be adhered to by all, including the humans.
- Gandhi rejected Darwin's theory of evolution of species based as it was on survival of the fittest. He saw cooperation among the species as more powerful a force than competition that determined the evolutionary processes. At the same time, he perceived cooperation and competition as two sides of the same coin. Modernism looks at the side of competition, ignoring cooperation on the reverse. Thus, it is the observer who differentiates between the two even if they together form a single whole.

- Human body is not an assemblage of cells, tissues and organs. It has body, mind and soul and the three are inseparably linked to form a cohesive whole. Humans without mind would be animals and those without soul would be worst than animals.
- Human progress is not the same thing as material progress. It means moral progress, leading humans to higher levels of consciousness. Material progress is essential only so long as it enhances moral progress. And hence the concept of progress or development centering on material and technological developments as has evolved in the West cannot be considered to be a goal towards which humanity must move. At best, it is a means and hence it must be moderated and tempered by the goal of real human progress. Further, it must be dispensed with when it comes in the way of moral progress.
- Human progress is not linear as perceived in the West; nor is it circular as perceived in the East. It is helixical—a combination of linear and circular. And hence its division into Pre-modern, Modern and Post-modern is arbitrary and unscientific.
- History as written in the West is not a true history of human progress. It records only the deviations from the main currents of progress that the humans have made through centuries and millennia. It is the history of wars and of kings and emperors; not the history of human society as such.
- For the progress and survival of humanity, its goal must be *swaraj*: *swaraj* of individuals, communities and societies, nation states included. *Swaraj* can be achieved only through *Sarvodaya*—the holistic development of all. Swaraj means self-control and *sarvodaya* means moral and material development of all: from each according to his ability to each according to his need.

To a question as to what Gandhi thought about modern civilization, he replied 'it is a good idea'. He considered modern civilization to be one, which had put human beings on a high moral pedestal. And since it had not happened that far, it could at best be called an idea.

Commenting on what was berated as modern civilization, Gandhi called it a disease that ought to be cured. He considered the pre-modern Indian civilization more modern than the 20th century because it had the cure for the disease of modernity. He did not subscribe to the view that body welfare was the main object of life. And hence material advancement, which formed the core of modernity, could not be treated as the end to all. At best, it could be a means to fulfill the far higher ends of life. Similarly, scientific and technological development—unmindful of its negative potentialities of destruction—must be treated as a dangerous proposition. To quote him:

> 'This civilization takes note neither of morality nor of religion. Its votaries calmly state that their business is not to teach religion. Some even consider it a superstitious growth. Others put on the clock of religion, and prate about morality. But after twenty years of experience, I have come to the conclusion that immorality is often taught in the name of morality... Civilization seeks to increase bodily comforts, and it fails miserably even in doing so.'[1]

> Gandhi further wrote, 'This civilization is such that one has only to be patient and it will be self-destroyed. According to the teachings of Mohammad, this would be considered a satanic civilization. Hinduism calls it the Black Age… It is eating into the vitals of the English nation… Civilization is not an incurable disease, but it should never be forgotten that the English people are at present afflicted by it.'[2]

Gandhi made a frontal attack on the institutions that go with modernity. He makes special mention of parliaments, railways, lawyers, doctors, machinery and the education system. He uses un-parliamentary language to describe the proceedings of the House of Commons. His remarks are apt to our parliament and state legislatures today. It is unfortunate indeed that despite Gandhi's forewarnings, we threw away the British but kept the British institutions close to our heart.

Railways symbolized speed; they increased our mobility; cities grew in number and size and became exploitative; villages were impoverished and human touch that once constituted the soul of Indian civilization was lost in the wonder world of modernity. Gandhi was not against railways as such nor against speed either. He wanted the ill-effects of both to be countered by a constructive programme that brought people together. If the living conditions of the people were improved; self-government was strengthened, and institutions, which could bind the people together for cooperative action were strengthened, the necessary base for *swaraj* would be established.

Gandhi's remarks on the judiciary, medical practitioners, education, technology and many other instrumentalities of the so-called modern civilization are as apt today as they were in 1909. His opinion of lawyers and doctors is quoted below:

> 'My firm opinion is that the lawyers have enslaved India… Those who want to perpetuate their power do so through the courts… Doctors have almost unhinged us. Sometimes, I think that quacks are better than highly qualified doctors… Hospitals are institutions for propagating sin.'[3]

Gandhi's views on education and machinery are equally unconventional, radical and relevant to this day. ' Character building has the first place in its education and that is primary education. A building erected on that foundation will last.' Gandhi approvingly quotes the definition of liberal education as given by Professor Aldous Huxley.[4]

> 'That man I think has had liberal education who has been so trained in youth that his body is the ready servant of his will and does with ease and pleasure all the work that as a mechanism it is capable of; whose intellect is clear, cold, logic engine with all its parts of equal strength and in smooth working order… whose mind is stored with knowledge of the fundamental truths of nature… whose passions are trained to come to heel by a vigorous will, the servant of a tender conscience… who has learnt to hate all vileness and to respect others as himself. Such a one and no other, I conceive, has had liberal education, for he is in harmony with nature. He will make the best of her and she the best of him.'

Gandhi defined true civilization in the following words: 'Civilization is that mode of conduct which points out to man the path of duty. Performance of duty and observance of morality are convertible terms. To observe morality is to attain mastery over our mind and passions. So doing we know ourselves[5]… the tendency of the Indian civilization is to elevate the moral being, that of the Western civilization is to propagate immorality. … it behooves every lover of India to cling to the old Indian civilization even as a child clings to the mother's breast.'[6]

Was Gandhi a Post-modernist?

During Gandhi's time, post-modernism had not emerged as a paradigm. Despite the dissenting voices here and there, the first half of the twentieth century marked the culmination of the final stage of modernism. The questions that Gandhi raised on the basic postulates of modernism were far more subtle than those raised by the post-modernists. His critique of modernity was devastating; he labelled it as retrogressive and unrepresentative of true modernity which, he thought, was yet to emerge. He considered modern civilization retrogressive for it came in the way of real human progress, which was none other than moral progress. The so-called modern civilization empowered man to subjugate both nature and man and to deprive others of dignity, life support and basic human rights. Modernity to Gandhi was a deviation that man has inadvertently taken from the road that led him to his ultimate destiny.

The world we are living in today is a world full of violence, hatred, greed and selfishness. True, it is a world where a lot of things are at the disposal of man, which his ancestors could only dream of but behind the facade of material prosperity lay a shattered humanity and an uncertain future. It is a runaway world: a world beyond man individually and collectively to manage. We admit that we have to adjust our lives to the new exigencies of the time as it moves from one crisis to the other. Gandhi challenged this helplessness and proved that post-modernism was nothing but an extension of modernism, a devise to save modernism from total eclipse. He showed the way to recover humanity in man and to take it towards a new future—a future without violence, hate, inequality and exploitation. He not only showed the way but also demonstrated how to traverse it.

It would be pertinent to mention here that Gandhi did not reject Western civilization. His attack centred on modern industrial civilization, which first emerged in the West (Europe) but it was not rooted in Western civilization. He was appreciative of many of the traits of Western civilization, such as liberalism, democracy and dignity of the individual. Gandhi was devastatingly critical of Western civilization because it deviated from its own principles when it was weighed against its relations with other civilizations and people. How else could it allow the wholesale destruction of many races, people and civilizations of what later became Latin America? How else could it sanction the subjugation of much of the world beyond Europe and Anglo-America and keep nations of rich cultural heritages under its feet for over two centuries? How else could it take away the rights of non-Europeans to govern themselves?

Post-modernism did not go far enough to undo the wrong perpetrated on much of humanity by the West. It was only a palliative; an apology; and an intellectual move in the face of the rise of the tormented people. It was not actualized to bring a semblance of equity, dignity and righteousness. Gandhi had no interest in intellectual movements, which did not liberate the marginalized, downtrodden and materially or spiritually poor. He went far beyond the post-modernist thinkers and gave a paradigm that could liberate not only the politically bonded non-Europeans but also the spiritually bonded Europeans.

Gandhi had two main complaints against Western civilization as represented by the industrial civilization of his time. It was not modern in the true sense of the term. It represented a deviation from the real progress or evolution, which was none other than moral progress. Human beings to be so-called must become better human beings morally and ethically. Secondly, it did not adhere to its own norms and principles while interacting with other peoples, races and cultures. In fact, it was known for the violations of its own norms more than for their adherence. Gandhi's paradigm of modernism, rooted as it was in nonviolence (*manasa-vacha-karmana*); *Sarvodaya*, that is, rise of all in all respects; and *swaraj*, that is, self-control, was not only an idea but also a practical proposition, which he put into practice. In act, his domain was action, not intellectual debate. He went beyond what is rational and logical to what is rational and logical within a moral frame of reference. Tit for tat philosophy may be logical as a sensual response but not as a response of an enlightened human being. For Gandhi, tit meant a moral, not physical, attack on tat. His was proactive philosophy designed to create a peaceful world order and to open up the route to real human progress.

In this connection let me refer to what David Hardiman in his book *Gandhi in His Time and Ours* (2003) has to say on the Gandhian critique of modernity.

> 'What is taken as Gandhi's "critique of modernity" generally refers to his critique of the doctrines of materialism and instrumental rationality, the belief in scientific and technological progress, practices such as large-scale methods of production, rapid transportation, allopathic medicine, adversarial parliamentary system of democracy and so on, and the accompanying conviction that it was the duty of those who subscribed to such values to impose them on the rest of the world. Against this, he counterpoised his own definition of what entailed a genuine civilization that had, he argued, to be rooted in an alternative morality. His position in this respect is set out most clearly in *Hind Swaraj*.'

We have now reached a stage in our discussion to reflect on some of the major challenges that modern civilization has posed before us and see how the Gandhian paradigm of alternate modernity can be used to face them successfully.

New Dimensions of Modernism: Globalization

Globalization is one of the most popular terms in the world today. Every language has coined an equivalent of it. No matter what aspect of life we take into account, the impacts and implications of globalization are very real. It is, however, most prominently visible in two fields, namely, information communication technology and international trade and associated financial transactions. Information Communication Technology (ICT) has converted the globe into a village. We are so close to each other, that distance does not matter. Unfortunately, this gift of modern technology has been harnessed more negatively than positively. We are so close to each other physically yet so far away from each other spiritually. Technology is neutral to its use; it can be used constructively or destructively. Much depends on how advanced we are as human beings.

Then let us take a look at the speed with which the electronic communication moves today. Morse invented his system of dots and dashes to send messages to ships on the high seas in 1849. This system beamed its last message on February 1, 1999: '*Calling all. This is our last cry before our eternal silence.*' The new communication system has changed our lives no matter where we live. The other day when people were trying to rescue whatever was left after the devastating Tsunami disaster, I saw on the TV screen a lady who had lost everything, including her family members, rescuing her television set and moving towards the relief camp with her two children. Electronic communication has become a part of our life. It brought down the closed regime of the USSR and is now threatening other regimes, democratic or undemocratic, which refuse to become transparent and people oriented. Globalization is not confined to economy; it has penetrated the innermost precincts of our houses and even hearts.

The level of world trade is much higher today than ever before, and so is the volume of global financial transactions. More than a trillion dollars are now exchanged daily on global currency market. To give an idea of what this means, let me say that a billion (million million) dollars in currency notes of 1000 dollars each, when stacked one on the other, would be over 192 km high, 20 times higher than Mount Everest. It is this exchange that determines the value of the money we have in our pockets or bank accounts.

Globalization has yet another effect, which many of us fail to perceive. It pushes the better off up and pulls the worse off down. This happens because the two do not have level laying fields. As the nations become too small to solve global problems, they also become too large to solve the local problems. At the same time, globalization produces lateral effects and creates pockets of excellence and deprivation, leading to widening of gaps between rich and poor individuals, groups and areas. While Bengaluru becomes the Silicon Valley of India, just a few kilometers away, peasants commit suicide because agriculture is no longer remunerative to help farmers make their ends meet. The share of poorest fifth of the world in global income has been secularly declining. It came down from 2.30 per cent in 1990 to 1.4 per cent in 2000. And it must be lower by a few points today.

According to the International Labour Organisation (ILO), 120 million people are unemployed and about 700 million people are underemployed. One thousand three hundred million people live in absolute poverty; they earn less than US $ 1 per day. More than half of the population of the world lives on less than US $ 2 per day. If we look at the data given in the recent Human Development Report, 46 countries of the world have become poorer since 1990. The poorest 20 per cent of people of the world account for only 1 per cent of the entire world's income, which was 1.4 per cent in 1990. At the same time, the total assets of 358 billionaires of the world were more than the combined GDP of 2300 million people, that is, more than 40 per cent of the world population.

In India too, the picture is highly disturbing. The number of distress suicides by farmers has gone up phenomenally. Rates of unemployment and underemployment have been increasing steadily and alarmingly as has been the number of people below the poverty line. At the same time, the number of billionaires had gone up from 71 in 1995 to 311 in 2005. On the social front, the situation is equally alarming. Half the population of India is functionally illiterate, the census data giving higher figures notwithstanding. In the land of world-class universities (IITs and IIMs), higher education in general is in shambles. It has little if any relevance to the problems of un- and underemployment that the country faces. The general state of the health of the people has deteriorated, as the number of doctors and hospitals has gone up. The control of major killers like plague, cholera and smallpox has brought the mortality rates down but not the morbidity rates.

To add to these negative outcomes, the ecological and environmental risks that the country faces have increased. It is not just the question of fast decreasing access to natural resources; even the resources that the country has in abundance are being misused. The meaning of nature, nation, tradition, marriage, family and work is changing, giving rise to many unexpected setbacks. The *Panchabhootas* or five elements (land, water, air, energy and open space) are in distress. As globalization gets de-centralized, the risks accompanying it are spreading out uniformly all through the society and economy. We cannot handle these risks by the very means that promote them. We do not have appropriate managerial instrumentalities to face them. The institutions that worked well in the past are now no longer able to handle the emergent problems. They have become shell institutions; the appearance is shining and strong but the interior is muddy and rotten.

Our world is more hazardous today than ever before. Risks that accompany natural hazards have been a part of life. If the recent tsunami that hit Japan is any indicator, the risk of nature revenge has increased. In the days gone by, people worked with nature; they adapted themselves to the natural principle of symbiosis. When the hazards occurred, their fury was less devastating. People were prepared to face such hazards both psychologically and physically. When calamities came, people joined hands to help each other. No one blamed the government nor waited for the government to come forward with help. And hence the risks were lowered and community solidarity cemented.

Modernization has changed much of old ways of handling crisis. Fate was ousted by an active engagement with the future. Man became the master of all he surveyed. He set upon to rule over nature. Armed as he was with science and technology, he tinkered with nature at will. A mad rush to tame the nature and to use it for industrialization, urbanization and locomotion was set in. Each step man took to control the nature enriched him materially in the short run but produced a series of unexpected setbacks in the long run. So, the apparent gains turned into real losses. Man spent billions of dollars to undo the ill effects of what was till some years ago considered a great step forward.

Now the future appears to rebound, forcing us to find new ways of handling it. We face a new type of risk—a risk that is self-inflicted; that is manufactured by us. These are ecological and environmental risks; and risks attendant to poverty, inequity and loss of dignity. We are less interested in what nature can do to us and for us, and more about what we can do to nature so that it behaves the way we dictate. We just do not know what will be the risk of tinkering with nature, modifying genes, consuming fossil fuels, promoting large-scale urbanization, and proliferating nuclear arsenals. We cannot depend on scientists because scientific findings are never final. Further, many a times, science has no answer for the problems we face.

The manufactured risks are not confined to ecology. We face equal or maybe greater threat when we do away with family ties, marriage customs, and other traditions. Think of what has emerged from promiscuity in sexual relations. Science never warned us that AIDS would spread like wildfire. We do not know, what else is there in store for our health. Many of the ancient traditions are based on experiential knowledge derived from thousands of years of real life experience. Modern scientific knowledge is derived from controlled experiments in the laboratories. Both are important; they must cross-check each other and help man move up to the higher level of consciousness.

Ours is a world where the manufactured hazards are as or even more threatening than those that come from nature. These manufactured risks are double edged; they affect us all no matter where we live in the form of ecological disasters like climatic change, nuclear hazards, terrorism and other forms of violence or even in the shape of widespread poverty and inequity in the midst of bourgeoning world economy. All these affect us individually also through the media of our diet or the medicines we consume, the education we get, and the work we do.

Loss of Human Values

We pride ourselves for being non-traditional. It is abusive to call anyone a traditional person for it means a person who unquestioningly follows a mysterious theology or ceremonies. Traditions provide a framework for action as also for life and living. There are people who guard traditions: wise men, elders, priests, sages and so on. It is they who had the privilege and also the power to interpret traditions. All traditions were invented to meet a particular challenge. When the situation changed, so did the traditions, albeit very slowly. Traditions are, thus, invented and reinvented. Our traditions provide a framework for human relations.

The 18th-century Enlightenment in Europe gave tradition a bad name. It succeeded in weakening its hold but not in uprooting it. Even in Europe and America, there are traditions that have persisted for centuries. It happened because modern civilization did not percolate down to the hearts of the people; it remained confined to various public institutions especially governments, economies and politics. Traditions pertaining to family, gender and sexuality remained more or less as they were until the advent of the post-modern era, that is, in recent years.

However, globalization has changed the situation drastically. It has created a society that is living not only at the end of nature but also at the end of tradition. A new global society, far more cosmopolitan than anything before, is on the rise. It is a society in which the old and the new as also tradition and the reason do co- exist. In India, many scientists are also devout Hindus. If we take a look at the academic world, we shall see that all disciplines work with a given tradition. But it is also part of the academic life to explore new frontiers.

It is being increasingly realized that no man can live and be happy without faith. Gandhi demonstrated the fact that faith and reason must co-exist. When his reason failed to give an answer to a problem he faced, he called upon his inner self to guide him. If traditions become reflective of the experiential knowledge, they should be discarded only when we are armed with new and dependable knowledge. Even rituals have social meaning; if they are discarded new rituals would have to be created to prepare grounds for new traditions. Once the tradition retreats, people live in a more open, reflective and autonomous way. But they find themselves lost in a world where nothing is fixed; there are no norms to go about. There is uncertainty all around.

The effect of this situation is anxiety and growth of addiction that is excessive attachment or inclination towards intoxicants, sex, work, food and violence. Tradition was maintained by the collectivity; the addiction by the individual. Anxiety, anomaly, and the need to reinvent oneself and find a place in a world where nothing is sure, produces a sickness of the mind and therefore the need arises for psychopathic treatment.

Two of the glaring consequences of the clash between science and tradition are rise of fundamentalism and terrorism. This conflict points at the limitations of science on the one hand and the acute sense of deprivation on the other. Fundamentalism need not be just religious; it could also be anti-religious. Think of the Red Guards of Mao's China. They were not religious zealots. I would assert that fundamentalism is a child of modernism and post-modernism. Look at the use of modern communication technology by Osama bin Laden. Violence is inbuilt in fundamentalism. And we know that violence cannot be contained by violence. It forces us to ask ourselves: Can we live in a world where nothing is sacred? Unless there are universal values which guide our lives and that form the basis of the new institutions that we have created, fundamentalism of one sort or the other will continue to raise its head.

It is here that Gandhi comes to the forefront as the emancipator. We have to rethink about traditions, science and technology, progress and development, civilization and the question of means and ends that Gandhi raised from time to time. 'All of us need moral commitments that stand above the petty concerns and squabbles of every day life. We should be prepared to mount an active defense of these values wherever they are poorly developed or threatened. None of us would have anything to live for, if we did not have something dying for.' Gandhi had a lot to die for and so he lives on despite his death.

Undemocratic Democracy

Let me now come to one of the most or perhaps the most powerful energizing idea of the 20th century, that is democracy. Leaving aside a few semi-feudal states such as Saudi Arabia, there is hardly a nation state that does not call itself democratic. Even the USSR called itself people's democracy, as does China today. Without going into the epistemological definitions, we can define democracy as a system of governance involving effective competition among political parties for position of power through regular and fair elections in which all adults can vote. This electoral process is accompanied by civil liberties like the right to vote irrespective of sex, religion, economic status; freedom of holding opinions and expressing the same without any hindrance; and freedom of forming and joining political parties. It should be noted that the freedom to these rights did not come easily; they were fiercely resisted by the elites who held power during the 19th century.

For a long time, very few of the countries had democratic governments. Strangely, it was the 'democratic' Europe which suppressed democracy in Asia, Africa and Latin America until the 1940s. But even in Europe, democracy was only partially developed. Before the First World War, women had the right to vote only in Finland, Norway, Australia and New Zealand. They got this right in Switzerland only in 1974. Some countries like Germany, Italy, Austria, Spain and Portugal moved back from democracy to authoritarian rule. Since the 1970s, democracy has spread all over the world, a few military dictatorships and semi-feudal monarchies notwithstanding.

This does give some hopes but there are disturbing signs emerging from even the so-called mature democracies. The people are getting disillusioned with their governments. In a world based on modern information and communication technology, power that comes from the top to the bottom loses its sharpness. The orthodox form of democracy confined to the top becomes insensitive to the change sweeping through people's lives at the bottom. People lose a good deal of trust they earlier reposed in politicians and political institutions. Yet they support democracy as the only means of governance acceptable to them. So, democracy continues to be the choice of the people but the politicians are becoming increasingly unpopular. Politics has now become a corrupt business and politicians self-interested rather than having the good of the citizens in their view. The younger generation is especially disillusioned with the way the governments are handling the global economic issues and local ecological, gender and human rights issues. The current wave of terrorism has further alienated the people from their governments.

The global sweep of ICT has both positive and negative effects on democracy. On the one hand it has made the government more porous than ever before; on the other, the hold on multinationals on information channels has given them greater control over the minds of the people than the politicians have. Countering these ill-effects needs democratization of democracy. The sovereign nation states have lost part of their sovereignty to global forces. Environmental risks, fluctuations in global economy and global technological changes do not respect national boundaries. At the same, a new space has been created between the global and national institutions, which needs to be filled up by multinational entities like the European Union, apart from transnational corporations. In the same way, the space between the individuals and the nation has to be filled by mini-democratic institutions. In popular parlance, it is known as decentralization. In the context of India, it would be Gandhi's Gram Swaraj. Then and then alone will democracy take deeper roots.

Breaking Down of Family Solidarity

Another institution that is under tremendous pressure of modernization is the family. There is hardly any country except, of course, the ones governed by fundamentalist and authoritarian governments, where the future of the family is not one of the major social concerns. The old family ties were based on certain emotional and economic interdependencies. As these dependencies weaken, the family structure falls apart. Marriage was earlier not a sexually driven contract. The inequality of men and women was built into the system. Women and children did not have many of the human rights that people demand today. Children were cared for because they would keep the family going till eternity. They had a role to play. Sexuality was, therefore, dominated by reproduction. Sexual promiscuity among the males was considered a sign of masculinity but the same trait among the females was treated as a crime. Homosexuality too was almost invariably considered as not only unnatural but also perverse, even if it was tolerated as an act of a small minority.

In the traditional family, the married couple was just one and often a minor part of the family. Whether it should continue to live together or not did not depend on its own decision; the decision had to be taken by the whole family. Today, a married couple is the core of the family. The family ties are based on emotional and sexual satisfaction, at least in the early stages and the decision as to whether they should live together or not depends on them and them alone.

In the new family culture, it is equality among the sexes and transparency that keeps it together. Conflicts are sorted out by discussion and dialogue. Thus, a good relationship depends on how equal the members are and how honest they are to each other—in other words, how democratic the family is. This applies to ties with children too. Parents must have some authority over their children but this authority must be based on certain democratic principles so that the child grows up understanding the logic behind how and why his parents treat him in a particular way.

The traditional family is on the way out but a family based on equality of sexes is still a far cry. The equality of sexes based on equality of promiscuity, violence and hatred is not the answer. As the family breaks and anomy grips the young and old alike, the result is demand for new policies on family life, check on divorce, and regulations on sexual expression. Family without love and sacrifice can never be enduring. And where there is love and sacrifice, there is democracy too. This is what Gandhi said as early as 1909.

David Hardman on 'An Alternative Modernity'[7]

Gandhi is believed to be against modernity in all its forms. His *Hind Swaraj* is quoted as an evidence of this. But, actually, a deeper analysis of Gandhi's thoughts and actions shows that he was not against all the aspects of modernity. In fact, several key aspects of modernity like equality, democratic representation, and governance through persuasion, were all acceptable to him.

Gandhi was not totally against modernity but was critical of some of its aspects. He was against the belief that only Western modernity was the best way of life and everyone wishing to become civilized must accept or follow it. He presented his own definition of a genuine civilization, based on a different kind of morality, in *Hind Swaraj*.

Hind Swaraj

This book by Gandhi was written in 1909 in Gujarati, then translated into English in 1910. Gandhi presented his views on the uselessness of violence here in a dialogue form. He was very critical of equating a civilization's progress with material achievements. He was of the opinion that railways, machines, printing press, weapons, new technology brought into India by the British have not benefited India but harmed it. It actually helped the British gain control over India.

Gandhi used a Gujarati term for civilization *sudharo*, meaning 'good way of life'. To him, civilizational progress should be seen in terms of moral achievements. Having control over our own desires and greed would be the best sign of a civilized life. He maintained that the pre-British Indian civilization was really civilized and each Indian must try to go back to those values.

The British government reacted by banning *Hind Swaraj*. Gandhi stuck to this view till 1914, when he changed the tone of his comments and made it clear that in *Hind Swaraj* he had not criticized the British as such but the present-day modern European civilization.

In his later years, Gandhi accepted quite practically that some aspects of modern civilization were indispensable like railways, hospitals, mills, and other similar necessities. What could be done, however, was to not let these elements rule us. These should be used as a utility and not as an object of enjoyment.

Gandhi was not against Western culture as such but was critical of the modern ways of life. He was equally against the British when they used it, as he was against the Indian nationalists who favoured violence as a means to the end.

Although Gandhi was severely criticized for his stand against modernity, later on it proved to be valid. His views were very strong but they left their mark and proved to be true as time went by.

A Gandhian Civilization

Gandhi's criticism of modern civilization was directed at its consumerism, competitiveness, slavery of desires and subjugation to technology.

Gandhi preferred a civilization that would use technology and science for the benefit of the human beings and not for satisfying the greed of a few rich capitalists.

Donald Worster has explained this divide in terms of two types of thinking prevalent in current times. One is an imperialist science and the other, an Arcadian sensibility. In simple words, the former stands for an aggressive control over nature, with a completely materialistic understanding of the world of life; the latter believes in a harmonious coexistence within nature, an ethical, spiritual understanding of nature, world and people.

Gandhi stood for the latter. His understanding of the concept of nature shows this attitude. His notion of nature was determined by the concept of *prakruti;* it is not just a material from but a manifestation of God. He did not, like others, see a divide between nature and culture. For him, *prakruti* or nature stood for 'the original, natural form of anything'.

So in this sense, no divide exists between material force and divine force, or between nature and culture.

Gandhi found the modernist scientific attitude misplaced when it showed an arrogance of having conquered nature. He believed that to think so is to challenge the unlimited powers of god and nature. He promoted a scientific attitude that would be humble, that would not dream of conquering nature, that would take from nature only as much as is required. He suggested that if human beings stopped exploiting nature for their greed, there would be enough for everyone on the earth.

Gandhi disliked modern cities with their noise, rush and smoke. His ideal was that of a small-scale agricultural community, cultivating common land in a sustainable, self-sufficient way. He tried to have this sort of life in his ashrams. He was in the favour of rational or scientific approaches so long as they stayed under the guidance of moral principles.

The Constructive Programme

This programme of incorporating technology in a people-friendly manner comprised of three principles—*Swadeshi* (home-based production); *sarvodaya* (aim of public welfare) and *aparigraha* (non-possessiveness). This programme was inaugurated during 1920–1921 and was very close to Gandhi's heart.

A technology appropriate for the majority of people's needs was to be encouraged. India required labour-intensive technology as there were many hands available which would be unemployed if labour-saving technology was used. Self-reliance through labour was also considered important for the Indians. The spinning wheel was a key example of this approach. This *charkha* campaign was launched in 1919. A small, portable design of the spinning wheel was popularized. People were encouraged to make *khadi* for themselves and for the markets. Economically, however, *khadi* did not prove to be a very profitable venture. It was expensive as compared to mill-produced cloth. It led to criticism of Gandhi's economic theory. He was accused of promoting time-consuming, back-breaking devices instead of labour-saving mechanisms. Actually, to an extent this criticism was not wrong because technology had made people's life easier in many ways and which had also proved to be beneficial. For example, improved *chulhas* (stoves), bio-gas plants, hand pumps, new designs of ploughs, new varieties of seeds, improved breeding programmes, and new techniques of water harvesting and water storage proved to be hugely beneficial for the people.

Even *khadi* could have been a success but the problem was that khadi weaving was put on a very high symbolic form while the equally important aspect of sustainable cotton-growing economy was neglected.

An open-minded, clear, investigative approach is equally important for a noble cause to survive and make an impact. Gandhi realized the importance of this method and, following the example of the great Victorian investigators of the British, he sought to learn about and understand the problems of the people through fieldwork, data and local investigation.

This interest in the problems of the local people of various districts indirectly popularized the nationalistic sentiment of Gandhi.

Gandhi's View on Socialism

Gandhi's picture of an ideal civilization did not give much significance to Marxian School of Socialism. It did support views like equality and eradication of poverty but the essential importance of struggle for it in Marxian theory was not appreciated by Gandhi.

More and more leaders in India's freedom struggle were getting influenced by socialism. Gandhi entered into a dialogue with them. He respected the basic aims of socialism like the right of everyone to a livelihood and elimination of poverty, but he claimed that the method of the socialists was flawed. It was a very political method that gave importance to violence and believed in destroying the capitalist for attaining its aims. Gandhi subscribed to an entirely different approach. His method was driven by compassion not just for the poor but also for the capitalist. He maintained that the enemy was not the capitalist but capitalism. Cooperation of the capitalists should be sought in order to eradicate the ills of modern capitalism.

Violence, he said, would only increase hatred. Instead of class struggle, he gave the solution in the form of *satyagraha*.

Both the capitalist and the worker should be made to realize that without each other's help, they would be destroyed. In fact, the capitalist should be encouraged to behave like a trustee of social property. Gandhi argued that it was possible to appeal to the good in every person, however oppressive they might appear to be.

Everyone should practice *aparigraha,* that is, an attitude of non-possessiveness. Each should hold whatever assets they have for the good of the society. Owners should not take more than what is required for a comfortable life. The workers should be treated as the members of a family.

This view of Gandhi's was criticized by socialists for downplaying the class struggle. But it is true that although Gandhi was against the use of violence, he was very deeply, strongly dedicated to the cause of the upliftment of the poor.

It is sad that except for a few industrialists (like Jamnalal Bajaj, J. R. D. Tata) none respected this spirit of social good.

Gandhi's views on class struggle are similar to those of Paul Ricoeur who maintains that there are various factors like language, culture and nationality that cut across the class boundaries and can act as integrating forces. The effort should not be towards destroying the enemy but towards integrating everyone, friend and foe alike.

Gandhi's Influence Beyond India

The Gandhian way of resolving socio-economic problems is being emulated outside India also. The trend was started by E. F. Schumacher (1911–1977), a German economist who had been an advisor to the British Government during the 1940s and the 50s. Schumacher felt that the so-called developing countries were moving on an economic strategy that would ruin their resources and economy. The local conditions in these regions were not compatible with the demands of the capital-intensive economic models. These regions needed a technology suited to their circumstances. In most cases, it meant labour-intensive, small-scale, low investment technology.

Schumacher stood for a Gandhian attitude favouring an appropriate technology, an intermediate technology, in the sense that it should be superior to primitive technology but at the same time, much simpler, cheaper and freer than the super technology of the modern times.

Schumacher differentiated—using Gandhi's views—between mass production and production by the masses. The system of mass production is highly capital intensive, consumes high energy, and is violent, ecologically damaging. The production by the masses, on the other hand, uses human resources like creativity and skillful hands. It encourages production activities that are compatible with local resources, is eco-friendly and frees the human beings from the servitude of machines. Technologies should not be copied or aped but should be tailor made for each socio-economic context. This requires much higher level of innovation and creativity.

Another propagator of an alternative economic order was Ivan Illich (1926), an Austrian who worked as a Catholic priest in the 50s. During the period 1970 to 1975 he wrote four books, one of which talked of decentralization and the importance of knowing the limits of growth. He was critical, like Gandhi, of the Western medicine. He found that the Western styled doctors did nothing to really cure the patients. They never advised any control over appetites or prescribed discipline over self.

Illich was also against rapid transport. He saw more ill in it than good. In his opinion, such a system not only consumed a lot of energy and caused severe pollution, but also enslaved human beings because in order to have them and use them, people needed to slog for hours.

Another international agency to be influenced by Gandhi's ideology on economics was Oxfam, a non-government organization working for the betterment of underdeveloped countries. In 1966-67, Oxfam's relief workers working in Bihar came in contact with some Gandhian workers. For the first time, it is commented, that a truly authentic and inspirational Indian ideology was seen at work. Through this interaction, the Oxfam directors realized that the Green Revolution which they thought was benefiting the poor countries was, in fact, not all that beneficial. It emphasized on the use of high-yielding plant hybrids developed by multinational agencies, which needed lots of water, fertilizers and pesticides, which increased the dependency of the farmers on the multinational companies. From a Gandhian perspective, the Green Revolution increased the gap between the rich farmers and the poor farmers. This could not be good for rural development.

During the 1970s, Oxfam became known for its criticism of such big plans that were unsuitable for the poor, developing countries. It started focusing on working with local people and tried to be sensitive to local methods and requirements. Appropriate technology was encouraged with emphasis on maximum village self-sufficiency.

Gandhi saw these problems basically rooted in lack of morality, lack of principles. He blamed materialism and consumerism for most of the ills of the present-day society.

Summing Up

We can say that Gandhi was a traditionalist as well as a modernist. He extolled traditions that took man on the path of morality seen in its broadest perspectives. He was a modernist because he stood for reason, rationality and search for truth. At the same time, he was not a modernist because all through his life he fought against all that modernity had created in his time: colonialism, inequality, exploitation of nature and man by man, gender inequality and war. Gandhi was a post-modernist, because he refused to take any scripture as the words of god and, therefore, final because he questioned the rationality of science and its power to solve all human problems, because he worked for gender equality, and because he worked for peace and harmony. But he was not post-modernist because he rejected the sovereignty of the individual; because he did not accept material progress as the goal of humanity and because he did not reject god even if it meant truth. His life was a personification of the *Brihadaranyaka Upanishad* verse chanted at his funeral pier:

Asato Ma Sadgamaya
Tamso Ma Jyotirgamaya
Mrityour Ma Amritamgamaya
[Lead me from Unreal to Real
From Darkness to Light
From Death to Immortality]

Gandhi became immortal. So who was Gandhi? Gandhi belonged to a genre of his own. He transcended all classifications of time and space based on scientific reasoning. His was a universe that was essentially human and spiritual and scientific at the same time. If the human spirit is one, Gandhi cannot be bound in any artificial division and classifications. Einstein was right indeed when he paid his homage to the Mahatma on his death in words that sum up his personality in totality. 'Generations to come will scarce believe that such a one as this ever in flesh and blood walked upon this earth.'

Notes and References

1. Gandhi, M. K., *Hind Swaraj or Indian Home Rule*, Ahmedabad: Navajiwan Publishing House, 1938, pp. 32–33.
2. Ibid., p. 33.
3. Ibid., pp. 47–50.
4. Ibid., p. 51.
5. Ibid., p. 53.
6. Ibid., p. 55.
7. Paraphrased version of David Hardiman's book, *Gandhi in His Time and Ours*, New Delhi: Permanent Black, 2003.

Summary

- Gandhi lived in the era called modern which witnessed a major shift in values that had charted the course of history from times immemorial.
- In pre-modern society, duties were more important than rights. Individuals were important but only as inseparable members of the family and community. The pre-modern society was essentially rural and agricultural. Production, both agricultural and industrial, was village based.
- Modernism represents the rejection of tradition and authority in favour of reason and natural sciences. It takes the autonomous individual as the sole source of truth—the Cartesian cogito. It is associated with industrialization, scientific and technological discoveries, and capitalism. The fundamental act of modernity is to question the foundation of past knowledge brought forward through traditions, rituals and conventions.
- Post-modernism is a philosophical stance. It rejects the rationality of the human action; respects heterogeneity and diversity; shuns the postulations of theories and meta-narratives; champions the cause of the poor, the weak, marginalized and downtrodden; challenges the concept of development as structural transformation of the national economy; calls for transmogrification of a society, including sustainable development; calls for integration of time and space to reach the truth; believes in behavioural, experimental and participatory approaches rather than statistical and positivistic explanations; lays stress on micro as against macro; rejects the concept of sovereign autonomous individual and lays emphasis on anarchic collective anonymous experience, collage, diversity, the mystically unrepresentable Dionysian passion; and refers to the incipient or actual dissolution of the social norms and forms associated with modernity.
- Gandhi considered the pre-modern Indian civilization more modern than the 20th century modern civilization because it had the cure for the disease of modernity. He did not subscribe to the view that body's welfare was the main object of life.
- Gandhi made a frontal attack on the institutions that go with modernity. He makes special mention of the parliament, railways, lawyers, doctors, machinery and the education system.
- For Gandhi, civilization is that mode of conduct which points out to man the path of duty. Performance of duty and observance of morality are convertible terms. To observe morality is to attain mastery over our mind and passions. So doing we know ourselves.
- The questions that Gandhi raised on the basic postulates of modernism were far more subtle than those raised by the post-modernists.
- Gandhi did not reject Western civilization. His attack centred on modern industrial civilization, which first emerged in the West (Europe) but it was not rooted in Western civilization.
- David Hardman said that Gandhi is believed to be against modernity in all its forms. His *Hind Swaraj* is quoted as an evidence of this. A deeper analysis of Gandhi's

thoughts and actions shows that he was not against all the aspects of modernity. In fact, several key aspects of modernity like equality, democratic representation and governance through persuasion were acceptable to him. He was not totally against the modernity but was critical of some aspects of it. He was against the belief that only Western modernity was the best way of life and everyone wishing to become civilized must accept or follow it. He presented his own definition of a genuine civilization, based on a different kind of morality. Gandhi saw these problems basically rooted in lack of morality and principles. He blamed materialism and consumerism for most of the ills of the present-day society.

Further Readings

Bandyopadhyaya, J., *Social and Political Thought of Gandhi*, Calcutta: Allied Publishers, 1969.

Brown, M. Judith, *Gandhi: Prisoner of Hope*, Delhi: Oxford University Press, 1992.

Chakrabarty, Bidyut, *Social and Political Thought of Mahatma Gandhi*, London: Rutledge, 2006.

Chatterjee, Partha, *Nationalist Thought and the Colonial World,* New Delhi: Oxford University Press, 1986.

Hardiman, David, *Gandhi In His Time and Ours*, New Delhi: Permanent Black, 2003.

Mishra, Anil Dutta, *Understanding Mahatma Gandhi:Speeches and Writings that Reveal his Mind Methods and Mission*, New Delhi: Concept, 2012.

Mishra Anil Dutta, *Revisiting Hind Swaraj*, New Delhi: Concept, 2010.

Parekh, Bhikhu, *Colonialism, Tradition and Reform: An Analysis of Gandhi's Political Discourse*, New Delhi: Sage Publications, 1989.

8

Trusteeship: A New Economic Concept

Introduction

Trusteeship is Gandhi's most revolutionary economic philosophy. It is true that of all Gandhi's ideas and concepts, trusteeship was the most original as it was also the most tentative since he did not have time to experiment with it on a scale that would have the grandeur of the concept. In reality, he was attempting to evolve something in the form of a very comprehensive system which would eliminate both capitalism and the bureaucratic system. Trusteeship is a new theory of property ownership. It is an answer to welfare activities and all kinds of philanthropies. In other words, trusteeship is a theory of need-based production, equitable distribution and social justice. It is a method of reducing disparities in the society from one point of time to another.

Gandhi perhaps used the term trustee and trusteeship for the first time in his *Hind Swaraj* or *Indian Home Rule* in 1909. The main thrust of trusteeship is very broad and deep and it is not easy to comprehend. There is no historical example of it to go on. Trusteeship is not absolute but relative in space and time and to the needs of the society.

Gandhi approached the concept of trusteeship at four different levels. First of all, trusteeship, as the sole universalizable means of continuously redistributing wealth, could be seen as a coronary of the principle of non-violence and simultaneously assure the generation and intelligent use of wealth[1]. Secondly, Gandhi's practical psychological intuition allowed him to see that fear would prevent other means of economic distribution from succeeding in the long run[2]. Thirdly, Gandhi contended that the idea of trusteeship could be put into practice non-violently, because it could be instituted by degrees.[3] Fourthly and finally, Gandhi believed that social conditions were ripe for imaginative applications of the principle of trusteeship[4].

Origin of Trusteeship

Gandhi was fed up with the high-handedness of power and violence in both capitalism and communalism and was looking for solutions to them. The result was the birth of trusteeship. Trusteeship is derived from three basic Gandhian concepts: non-violence, swaraj and equality, which are all interlinked with one another. Gandhi said that the more we are committed to non-violence, the easier it will be to achieve the goal of equal distribution. Trusteeship is both an ends as well as the means.

Sabina Saghvi[5] observes, 'At the time Gandhi was formulating his ideas on trusteeship, the world had two principal methods of economics: capitalism and communism.' Gandhi had seen the shortcomings in both capitalism as well as communism. Both had failed to provide a fuller life for everybody. Instead of rejecting them straightway, he tried to incorporate some of the positive features of both into his alternative plan of trusteeship. He propounded the valuable idea of trusteeship to make the Indian economy self-sufficient on the basis of truth, non-violence and co-operation. Trusteeship is a synthesis of both capitalism and communism through the elimination of violence. In other words, capitalism plus communism minus violence is equal to trusteeship.

The trusteeship formula was evolved by Kishorilal Mashruwala, Narahari Parikh and others. Professor Dantwala from Bombay had sent the draft of simple, practical trusteeship formula which he had prepared. It was placed before Gandhi, who made a few changes in it.[6]

The amended final six-point draft contains the basic ideals of trusteeship as follows:

- Trusteeship provides a means of transforming the present capitalist order of society into an egalitarian one. It gives no quarters to capitalism, but gives the present owning class a chance of reforming itself. It is based on the faith that human nature is never beyond redemption.
- It does not recognize any right of private ownership of property except so far as it may be permitted by society for its own welfare.
- It does not exclude legislative regulation of ownership and use of wealth.
- Thus, under state-regulated trusteeship, an individual will not be free to hold or use his wealth for selfish satisfaction or in disregard of the interest of society.
- Just as it is proposed to fix a decent minimum living wage, even so a limit should be fixed for the maximum income that could be allowed to any person in society. The difference between the minimum and maximum incomes should be reasonable and equitable and also variable from time to time so much so that the tendency would be towards obliteration of the difference.
- Under the Gandhian economic order, the character of production will be determined by social necessity and not by personal whim or greed.

Source of Trusteeship

The concept of trusteeship was not coined by Gandhi. It had been practiced by Indians since time immemorial in different forms. Gandhi's genius lay in digesting the spirit of trusteeship from our ancient people and trying to apply it as an alternative to capitalism as well as communism.

Gandhi was influenced both by Eastern and Western thoughts. Among the Indian sources, the *Upanishads*, the epics and the *Gita* influenced him to a great extent when he was formulating the concept of trusteeship. The *Gita* says that 'those who want salvation should act like the trustees', and the *Isopanisad* proclaims 'enjoyment through renunciation'. Gandhi liked the first verse in the *Isopanisad*, which deals with private property. The meaning of the verse runs as follows:

> 'God, the ruler, pervades all there is in the universe. Therefore, renounce and dedicate all to him and then enjoy or use the portion that may fall to the lot. Never covet anybody's possession.'

This verse totally transformed Gandhi's thoughts. Indian philosophy and religion contains that idea of trusteeship. The ancient kings were the real trustees.[7]

Among the Western thinkers, the work of Snell, Ruskin and Tolstoy influenced Gandhi. According to Snell's equity, the legal owner of property himself holds the property. He need not renounce his right over property, but he holds it for the benefit of others. This reflects the scheme of trusteeship. Gandhi, while studying British law—particularly Snell's discussion of equity—was able to understand the ownership system. In a brief about its influence, Gandhi wrote, 'My study of English law came to help. Snell's discussion of the maxims of equity came to my memory.'[8] Ruskin's *Unto This Last* left a profound influence upon Gandhi. This consists of the philosophy of social affection and social justice. It emphasizes the principles of sacrifice and renunciation. According to Tolstoy, the meaning and significance of human life lies in serving the whole world by establishing the greatest possible unity among all living beings. Everyone has to discharge one's duty to his family, to the state and to the universe. He accepts the fact that the source of an evil is property. He renounced his own property, the vast Yasnaya Polyana estate, in favour of the peasants, and lived the life of a trustee. This influenced Gandhi into thinking of bringing into implementation the ideas of non-possession, renunciation and trusteeship.

Basis of Trusteeship

According to J. D. Sethi, a well-known economist, the theory of trusteeship is based on three Gandhian concepts: non-violence, *swaraj* and equality, that are inter-linked with one another. On the other hand, according to Ravindra Varma, former Union Minister for Labour and Parliamentary Affairs, the concept of trusteeship flows from the ideals of *aparigraha* and *ahimsa*.

Broadly speaking, truth (*satya*), non-violence (*ahimsa*), bread labour and non-possession (*aparigraha*) led Gandhi to the concept of trusteeship. Let us discuss briefly their relationship vis-à-vis this concept.

Truth

To Gandhi, truth occupied the first place and *ahimsa* second. In the course of his pursuit of truth, he discovered *ahimsa*, But his goal was truth. He wanted to realize the truth through *ahimsa*. To him, truth was a harmony of thoughts with words and of words with actions. He viewed *ahimsa* and truth as the two sides of a single coin. They were not viewed as separate entities. One could not be understood without the other. Gandhi did not accept sacrificing the truth to save the life of a person. To him, truth was supreme to the individual.[9]

To Gandhi, the statement 'God is Truth' was only partial. The statement 'Truth is God' is all inclusive and pervasive. The social worker is in search of truth by way of his service; the craftsman is in search of truth by way of his craftsmanship; the philosopher searches for truth by way of the prime cause and the scientist is in quest of truth by way of empirical experimentation. Thus, each and every one would be serving god, according to Gandhi's definition that says Truth is God.[10] To him, truth stood above everything in this universe. He was ready to sacrifice everything, including man, to uphold the truth. Gandhi said, 'Wife, children, friends, and possessions should be held subservient to truth. Each one of these should be sacrificed in search of truth.'[11]

Non-violence

Gandhi saw that the idea of trusteeship was inherent in the ideology of *ahimsa*.[12] 'Non-violence is the law of the human race and is infinitely greater than and superior to brute force.'[13] For him, trusteeship was an inescapable stage in the methodology of a non-violent revolution. It was not transitional. It was a stage that yields the result that one was seeking. In that sense, therefore, it was both a means as well as an end. Hence, Gandhi claimed 'no other theory is compatible with non-violence'.[14] While acquisition stands for violence, non-violence stands for non-acquisition. A votary of non-violence keeps away from possessions. Every kind of possession is based on exploitation which is a form of violence. On the other hand, a non-violent society is a non-exploitative society. It can be non-violent only when it assures economic equality. The ideal here is equal distribution.

One has to understand trusteeship as part of the scenario of a non-violent revolution, as an instrument in the *satyagrahi's* struggle for economic equality and elimination of classes. Trusteeship is a solution for removing economic disparities first and later political as well as social, through non-violence.

Bread-labour

'The law, that to live man must work first came to me', Gandhi says, 'upon reading Tolstoy's writing on bread-labour'.[15] Man must earn his bread by labouring with his own hands. This law was first stressed by a Russian writer T. M. Boundaref and later popularized by Tolstoy.

Gandhi was deeply influenced by this concept. Further, he was greatly attracted by the *Gita's* view that 'he who eats without offering sacrificial fruit to others is a thief'.[16] Gandhi said that 'sacrifices may be of many forms, one of them may well be bread labour.' For Gandhi, labour is the root of the entire creation, and 'to people flourishing and idle, the only acceptable form in which God can dare appear is work and promise of food as wages.' Therefore, work is god. Everyone can see god through his own work. Gandhi believed that no body should eat his bread without performing sufficient labour. The idea is that every healthy individual must labour enough for his food. In a way, one's living is based upon one's labour. Gandhi clarified that whoever performs labour acquires the legitimate right to his bread. Nobody should acquire more than his absolute need. In other words, need-based acquisition is the root to establishing an egalitarian society. Gandhi has mentioned, 'If all laboured for their bread and no more, then there would be no cry of over population, no disease and no such misery as we see around'.[17] He accepted the fact that intellectual abilities and physical capacity differ from person to person. Some are efficient in earning more and more through their physical efforts. Some other people have to bring greater material prosperity through their best intellectual abilities.

No nation or society survives without work. Gandhi was against those people who believed that there was no need to work after fulfilling one's minimum needs. Every type of labour has its own value. No work or labour is low. He announced that 'under my system it is labour which is the current coin, and not metal.' But persons with universal abilities should contribute their might to the societal progress. Gandhi said, 'Men will no doubt do many other things whether through their bodies, or through their minds but all this will be labour of love for the common good'.[18] Adding clarity on intellectual labour, Gandhi opines, 'Mere mental, that is, intellectual labour is for the soul and has its own satisfaction. It should never demand payment. In the ideal state, doctors, lawyers, and the like will work solely for the benefit of society and not for self.'

A silent revolution in the structure of the society can be brought about by obeying the law of bread labour. Compulsory obedience to it only breeds poverty, disease and discontent. It is a state of slavery; willing obedience alone brings contentment, health and wealth. In fact, the Gandhian concept of bread-labour epitomizes, 'From each according to his ability, to each according to his need.' When everyone works and become trustees of their labour, there will not be either rich or poor.[19]

Aparigraha

Aparigraha is the ethical ideal of non-possession; of the renunciation of ownership; of liberation from the subtle as well as the coarse bonds that possessions forge for one. It is a hoary ideal sanctified by every religion.[20] In a pithy verse, the *Isopanisad* exhorts:

Tena Tyaktena Bhunjeethah: Ma Gridha Kasyaswiddhanam? (Enjoy by renouncing, do not covet, or cling or to possessions; for, whose is wealth?) [21]

According to Gandhi, 'Non-possession means non-dependence on material things. It implies total abolition of private property in all kinds of belongings.' This view is more radical that of extreme communists. To Gandhi, stealing lies in possessing something which is not at all needed now. Non-possession is the result of non-stealing. He says: 'I suggest that we are thieves in a way. If I take anything that I don't need for my own immediate use and keep it, I steal it from somebody else. I suggest it is the fundamental law of nature, without exception that nature produces enough for our wants from day to day and if only everyone took enough for himself and nothing more, there would be no pauperism in this world'.[22]

Absolute non-possession is an abstraction. It is unattainable in its fullness. Therefore, Gandhi considered that non-possession lies in not only taking our clothes off our body, but taking our flesh off our bones. Non-possession does not mean remaining satisfied with poverty. Already Indian masses are suffering with hunger and poverty. They need not practice voluntary poverty. They have to work and get sufficient food. What Gandhi wanted was to avoid unnecessary possession by which individual and society are deprived of legitimate enjoyment.[23]

Non-possession makes a man keep everything open. In trusteeship nothing is hidden. Everything that is excess from everyone, joins the trust and is readily available to every needy. It is by practicing non-possession that trusteeship can be strengthened. Possession of any kind goes against the spirit of trusteeship. Further, non-possession implies giving up ownership.[24]

Gandhi cited five reasons to explain why man should practice non-possession. These are as follows:[25]

- Possession is not present in nature. God creates everything in accordance with the need of the hour. So possessing more than the need reveals man's thief mentality.
- Right from birth, man depends upon the things created by both nature and society. Using these without replacing them makes him a thief. Moreover, he stands as a debtor both to nature and society. So, his duty lies in not indicating anything. Even when he uses anything, he should replace them through his labour—physical, mental and spiritual.
- Hoarding for future deprives the real needy.
- The attitude of possessing leads to the multiplication of wants. Consequently, it results in the lack of peace both in the individual and in the society.
- Possession implies all kinds of troubles. It is always accomplished by force. A man having faith in non-violence never resorts either to possession or to force; he prefers non-possession.

The concept of non-possession commands certain social implications which lead to trusteeship.

- In a society where non-possession is in practice, wealth is not the mark of respect.
- Multiplication of wants is not the measure of civilization.
- As every need can be fulfilled by work, work is the medium of self-expression and existence.
- A man of work possesses a right to honourable livelihood.

- As all work has equal value, all receive equal remuneration.
- The means adopted is always based on truth and non-violence.
- An ethical life leads everyone to attain self-realization.[26]

Non-possession, to Gandhi, was a noble idea. No doubt, practically he himself renounced his wealth. But possession grants a sense of satisfaction and security to man. So, Gandhi wisely offered a solution. Accordingly, he asked to shed possessiveness if not possession, and greed for wealth, if not wealth itself. The rich may keep their wealth by considering their excess of wealth as the property of the community. They become the trustees of such wealth and use it for the welfare of all. As total dispossession is a remote possibility, Gandhi suggested, 'I accept the proposition that it is better not to desire wealth than to acquire it and become its trustees. But what am I to advise those who are already wealthy or who would not shed their desire for wealth? I can only say to them, that they should use their wealth for service'.[27] In this way, Gandhi offered trusteeship as a realistic solution to set right the lopsided development of both individual and the society.

Meaning of Trusteeship

The concept of trusteeship is not Gandhi's creation; it is traced to *Isavasya Upanishad.* In the Indian context, the term trustee is used in connection with temples and *maths*. Trustee means any individual who manages the temple property without any self-interest. For Gandhi, trusteeship should be implemented step by step gradually. The life of a human being is a privilege. According to Devadatta Dabholkar, 'voluntary surrender of privileges, power and prestige without expecting anything in return (even by way of appreciation or recognition) is trusteeship'.[28] According to K. Arunachalam, 'trusteeship means confidence reposed in a person with respect to property of which he has possession and over which he can exercise power to the extent that he may hold the property or exercise the power for the benefit of some other person or object'.[29] In 1970, V. K. R. V. Rao found Gandhi's vision of trusteeship 'prophetic for the world' and, according to J. D. Sethi, 'in trusteeship, Gandhi produced a grand alternative to the prevailing economic organizations whether in the communist or capitalist countries'. Further, J. D. Sethi viewed trusteeship as the most original concept. He is right in saying that Gandhi did not have the time to experiment with it and define it with full implications.

The concept of trusteeship implies several meanings. A brief analysis of such meanings is given below.

Trusteeship as an Attitude

Trusteeship as an attitude involves everyone's identification with the entire humanity. G. S. Shroff, H. K. Paranjape and Arvind A. Deshpande regard trusteeship as an attitude. According to G. S. Shroff, 'trusteeship is an attitude. It has to come from within. It cannot be forced outside. It can never be imposed on people for long. It should not be done.'[30]

H. K. Paranjape believes, 'To say that trusteeship is a matter of an attitude of the mind is, in effect, to say that there are certain ethical values which have always been, at least formally, endorsed by humanity. Truth, non-exploitation of others, honesty and helpfulness—even generosity towards others have been such values'.[31]

In fact, as an attitude, trusteeship ensures a balanced relationship among different productive elements. The kind of relationship between those who work and those who direct the work is always dependent upon their attitude. Trusteeship involves a certain responsive attitude by different elements in the economic system towards each other. Through trusteeship, Gandhi was emphasizing a basic moral attitude on the part of all.[32]

Arvind A. Deshpande says, 'Trusteeship as perceived by Gandhi is all embracing. It is an attitude first, then a technique and finally a constitutional form'.[33] He further says, 'the Gandhian concept of trusteeship expresses enterprise to its workers, shareholders, consumers and the community and the mutual responsibilities of each to the other. This is the price of democracy. Without virtue in the individual and in the organ of society, democracy cannot survive.'[34]

Trusteeship as an attitude treats all as equal and trains a man to be service oriented. 'To be a trustee is different from to trust'. To trust oneself is to fulfill one's desires. This is not called service. When there is trust in others, there comes an attitude to attend other needs. Therefore, every individual is linked with another individual with this kind of attitude. Gandhi recognized that service to mankind is service to god.

Trusteeship as a Method

Trusteeship is a method for the socialization of wealth. Wealth belongs to all. As god is the supreme and only owner of everything, to hold it exclusively with love alone is a sin. It is the ownership that is a centre for all kinds of exploitation. As both the individual and, the society are expressions of divinity, all right over everything in this universe lies with God. Trusteeship as a method also stands for socializing everything. As a trustee, the capitalist, becomes a co-sharer. At that moment, all are joined as trustees for everything. There is no place for unnecessary personal claims.

Trusteeship becomes a method in checking every individual not to spoil himself by possessing excess talent or property. As a method, trusteeship reduces the burden of the individual by relieving him of his excesses. Actually, as a method, it increases man's activity for better results. Trusteeship as a method drives every individual to achieve *sarvodaya.*

Trusteeship as a Movement

Trusteeship is not a choice; either to a capitalist or to a selfish bureaucrat. It is a movement towards social self management of industry. As a movement, it aims at a socio-economic and political arrangement in the society. At the personal level, trusteeship as a movement makes man strengthen himself. At the inter-personal level, trusteeship as a movement always tries to establish cordial relationship. It streamlines and strengthens the relations between the individual. At the institutional level, trusteeship's role is laudable. As an institution, it stands for serving a common purpose. Trusteeship as a movement goes against every kind of authority—economic, political and social. It is against the monopoly of decision making. Every man has the power of decision making. In fact, trusteeship provides ample opportunities to human beings in all spheres.

Trusteeship as a Legal Institution

Gandhi was ready to make trusteeship a legalized institution. He wanted to give it a statutory form through the legislative channel. He mentioned the following series of measures to bring about the change in the heart of the rich:

- Appeal to the better instincts in the rich.
- Persuasion.
- Education regarding inevitability of change.
- The greater unattractiveness of the alternative of change by violence.
- Non-violent, non-cooperation by the exploited that would make the exploiters functioning impossible.
- Legislative action.

Trusteeship law[35] should guard against:

- Non-production if good or services are of anti-social character.
- Non-production of goods or services which contribute to the modern degeneration.
- Non-production of goods or services which prevent attempts at spiritual development.
- Non-production of goods or services which prevent the development of the best in the individual consumer.

Trusteeship law should provide scope for modern technology and methods of production. This should be in tune with natural harmony and ecological balance. Further, it should also safeguard the interests of coming generations.

Trusteeship law should be for promoting cultural and aesthetic values in production and distribution. Work should be a thing of joy and self-fulfillment. There should be no pain or frustration.

Trusteeship law should provide for the separate registration of all economic activities. Trusteeship system should be given privileges and incentives on par with co-operative institutions and philanthropic foundations.

Separate departments of trusteeship should be opened at both the centre and the state. Separate ministers should be allotted for the same.

The report of the ministers should be presented before the public and the legislations for free discussions and development.

Special recognition should be given to trustee enterprises which contribute to the growth of the individual and the spiritual awakening.

An enterprise need not be registered under the trusteeship law with compulsion. Without proper registration, no enterprise is entitled to special privileges. Gandhi's opinion was to see trusteeship as a legalized institution. Accordingly, the state has the following functions:

- It has to give a statutory recognition to the institution of trusteeship.
- It has to determine the rate of commission for the trusteeship.
- It has to supervise the fulfillment of conditions of trusteeship.
- Depending upon the end, it has to regulate and approve the appointment of a successor trustee.
- It has to disapprove a trustee who fails to act in accordance with the basic features of trusteeship.

The constitution of trusteeship need not be governed by laws, as every law carries with it some violence. But Gandhi accepted laws sanctioned by public opinion. U. N. Dhebar views the Gandhian approach as follows: 'The basic approach to the concept of the trusteeship which is a part and parcel of the law of property, is merely to ensure proper use of property for the benefit of its owner-subject to certain social obligations.' In fact, the purpose of Gandhian trusteeship is much wider and more fundamental than the narrow legal conception.[36]

Trusteeship as a Theory

Theory of trusteeship, no doubt, is present in our epics and was well practiced by our kings. In the modern world, life is becoming highly polluted as a result of man's greedy nature. Gandhi had no other alternative than to bring trusteeship into human life. Gandhi's trusteeship was accepted by one and all in theory. But nobody came forward to put it in practice. Everyone wants freedom but not the responsibility. As freedom is a responsibility, no one prefers it. Freedom lies in self-ruling. The whole tautology lies in the problems that no one likes to be a slave to anyone, but wishes to be a master. In every field, the problem of master-slave exists. The economic field is no exception.

Gandhi found a way out of this problem. It is trusteeship that relates labour or work directly to production but not to its price or to consumption. Every man has some talent. He has to go on producing the excess of his talents and pool it in the trust. His primary duty lies in production. At no time should he value it by attaching a rate. At the same time, he should not produce anything with the view of self consumption. This is well illustrated by the work done in our families. The mother prepares food for everyone in the family. It is produced not on the basis of equality, but according to the need of each person.[37]

Trusteeship as an Ideal

Every right thinking man has to put before him some goals or deals either as primary or secondary. Accordingly, he has to travel to fulfill them. Trusteeship as an ideal is there to perfect the human life of every individual here, on earth. It brings discipline, devotion and dedication of a man's body and mind. A well-trained personality is bound to realize himself which is the ultimate goal of every man. Thus, trusteeship is the best secondary ideal to push and place man as the fittest person for self-realization.

Nature of Trust

When a group of individuals join together and pour their excess of faith, a trust is born. The excess of either talent or property or wealth is put together for the proper utilization by the need in the society. The trust is a boon to the whole mankind. A trust contributor is above caste, creed, colour, age and sex. Trust belongs to no one. It is everybody's treasure. There is a need to look after the trust, which is a deposit of all the excess of the genuine needy. He who is called a 'trustee' is selfless service-oriented personality. Without trust, any human transaction on this earth is impossible. Gandhi said, 'the most practical, the most dignified way of going on in the world is to take people at their word when you have no positive reason to the contrary'.[38] He further said, 'I believe in trusting. Trust begets trust. Suspicion is foetid and only stinks. He who trusts has never yet lost in the world...'[39] A trustee is so cautious that he has never broken a promise. To him, a breach in promise is a serious issue because it happens to our trust in others. Gandhi had observed, 'To my knowledge throughout my public and private career, I have never broken a promise...'[40]

Qualities of a Trustee

A trustee is one who self-consciously assumes responsibility for upholding, protecting and putting to good use whatever he possesses, acquires or earns'.[41] He is always a moral giant. A trustee has no heir but the public.

Raghavan Iyer[42] describes the following as the essential characters of a trustee:

- He is self-governing.
- He is morally sensitive.
- He always knows the unmet needs of others.
- He has the capacity to control and transmit his own tendencies.
- He always improves his generous feelings and altruistic hopes for others.
- He consciously keeps away all exploitative attitudes and relationships.
- He always strives to become self-regulating, reliable and sacrificial.
- He learns to think altruistically.
- He behaves with utmost purity and solicitousness, in his speech, touch and act. He is always alert to all situations both inner and outer. He holds that everything belongs to God, mankind and to future generations.
- He never exhibits the fear of multiplying his possessions, talents and gifts.
- He never exhibits selfish indifference.
- He never hoards anything.
- He trains himself as a servant to the whole mankind.

- He enjoys inward moral balance.
- He lives with detachment.
- He reposes unshakable confidence in the ontological plenty of nature and in the inexhaustible resourcefulness of man.
- He has a benevolent and self-sustaining motive.

R. B. Upadhyaya also brilliantly enumerates twenty-four qualities of a trustee 'which may work as general directions for the trustees to mould their personality traits accordingly'.[43] These qualities are given below:

- A trustee should be a man of high character, and complete honesty on his part is presumed.
- He should always act in good faith with the best of intentions for the benefit of the party that has reposed confidence in him.
- His action should be taintless.
- If there is even the slightest doubt, he should always be ready to submit himself to the strictest of public scrutiny.
- He must maintain accurate and correct accounts of receipts and payments, assets and liabilities of the trust. He should be prepared to get them audited and examined by independent and impartial authority.
- He must practice utmost frugality in regard to trust money.
- He should never use trust money and property for his personal work.
- He should not believe in conspicuous consumption and vulgar display of wealth and must lead a simple life not very different from the living standards of the society.
- He should possess business acumen and managerial talent.
- By nature and conviction, he should believe in the dignity of physical labour and should put himself in some physical labour daily.
- He should try to eschew snobbery, high-brow and ivory tower mentality, and should not have false airs about himself. He should be attracted towards the ideal of self-effacement.
- He should know that he is a mere servant of the co-operation and not a boss.
- He should be straightforward, simple and considerate but firm in his manners and behaviour.
- He should behave like a leader of the group.
- He should be a firm believer in individual dignity and freedom and should abhor flattery.
- He should be committed to a sense of social responsibility and growth of his business within the bounds of fair trade practices.
- He should belong to a higher level of need-hierarchy so that he is motivated more by social and self-realization needs.
- He should believe in building upon egalitarian society and should possess a judicial bent of mind in his behaviour towards all, particularly towards his opponents.

- Though he may have material ambitions, he considers material prosperity as a means to an end rather than an end in itself. He should have a balanced view of life as a whole.
- He should take a philosophical view of life and avoid excessive greed in his behaviour.
- He should be a man of firm conviction in regard to basic and fundamental principles of life but, at the same time, he should know that in relation to the numbers of the society, a compromising temper in regard to details is a great asset.
- He should be a man of drive and dynamism, active and dedicated to work.
- Real understanding requires empathy, that is, an attempt by one person to put himself in the position of another and then viewing the situation accordingly.
- He should believe in the dictum, 'service first and profit second'.

Trusteeship is not a temporary technique. It should become a permanent feature to bring social revolution, leading to the establishment of an egalitarian society. It has eternal value and perennial significance. 'Although men are mortal and individual trustees are no exception to it, yet trusteeship system is a continuous process, ever operative but never a thing of the past'.[44] After renouncing his possessiveness, every individual trustee holds his wealth—earned by legitimate means—as trustee on behalf of the society. He has the right to fulfill his legitimate needs. The rest of the wealth shall be spent for the welfare of the society. Thus, a trustee, by sacrificing his self-interest, always strives to protect and promote the interests of the society and the nation. Hence, the successor of a trustee should have such spirit. Necessarily, a trustee's children need not be his successors. Thus, family inheritance is not strictly admitted as the principle to decide the succession to trusteeship. Gandhi observes, 'Their children would inherit the stewardship only if they proved their fitness for it'. If the children of the trustees are socially dedicated and ethically oriented, holding the interests of society superior to self-interest, they would be fit to be the successors; if not, they would forfeit it.

In this way, trusteeship provides an alternative to the four different contemporary systems to the running of economic enterprise, but as micro-units and a collective system: corporation; state capitalist or socialist bureaucracies; system of industrial democracy; and mixed economic models.

The political economy of trusteeship is widely different from that of the corporation-society relationship. Trusteeship rejects both consumer sovereignty and producer sovereignty. Trusteeship is against all types of concentration of economic power. It has rejected both state capitalists and socialist bureaucracies, because both systems are increasingly giving rise to a new powerful class which has been exploiting even the basic human values and economic objectivity. Trusteeship is very different from socialism. Trusteeship as an institution of business organization is not only a negation of the concept of private firm but also a negation of public sector undertakings run by the state bureaucracy. Trusteeship has also rejected industrial democracy. Although the trade union and social democratic parties in developed countries are increasingly emphasizing the importance of industrial democracy, their conditions seem to be going against that demand. The narrowness of the trade unions—their being confined largely to wages and collective bargaining—has reduced the whole question of industrialism to bilateral competition between the workers and the capitalists. The trade unions have emerged as very undemocratic. Above all, the tripartite elite arrangement between state bureaucracy, trade unions and capitalists has erected a serious barrier in the way of developing a system of industrial democracy. In contrast, trusteeship satisfies the requirements of industrial participatory democracy. Trusteeship, being divorced from the entire profit motive, introduces the element of fraternity. Its area of participation is wide; it is more equalitarian than all other systems.

In India today, we have a mixed economy in the industrial and commercial sectors, whereas the agriculture sector is totally privately owned. But the distribution of resources is highly skewed in both the sectors. The degree of concentration of economic power in the one hundred largest industrial firms is enormous. The process of nationalization has resulted in the creation of a new bureaucratic class in whose hands all kinds of power get compounded. The workers are losing their elementary rights to struggle for higher wages, status and unions.

Trusteeship provides an alternative system for reducing the concentration of economic power. In India's case, this scheme will require three steps:

Firstly, a certain percentage of the assets of large houses will have to be transformed to a set of trustees.

Secondly, all other new industries and firms will have to follow the principle of trusteeship.

Thirdly, some basic principles with respect to prices, distribution, wages and profits will have to be laid down for trusteeship firms.

There may be some objections but as all other systems of economic organization are coming into dispute and becoming increasingly exploitative, the search of trusteeship will be a suitable answer. The struggle for establishing trusteeship cannot be isolated from the overall struggle for transforming society and for the emancipation of the masses. This is how and why the Gandhian approach becomes revolutionary.

Gandhi was well aware of nation-building. He also pointed out that a nation cannot be built on the basis of greed. Hence, he suggested that by adopting trusteeship, we can bring total equality and integration.

Trusteeship Bills

The late Dr. Ram Manohar Lohia gave notice of his intention to move an 'Indian Trusteeship Bill' in the Lok Sabha in March 1967. The bill made detailed provisions for efficient management of trust corporations in the light of Gandhi's views on trusteeship. The President of India withheld sanction to the introduction of this bill in Lok Sabha on the grounds that the aforesaid provision made it a Money Bill. Dr. Lohia had appealed to the President for reconsideration, but death snatched him away before he could pursue the matter.

On November 21, 1969 George Fernandes introduced the same 'The Indian Trusteeship Bill' in the Lok Sabha but it lapsed without discussion.

Atal Behari Vajpayee introduced the same on April 18, 1975 but it also lapsed with the dissolution of the Lok Sabha in 1977.

The Janta Trusteeship Bill of April 20, 1978 also met the same fate.

Criticism of the Concept of Trusteeship

The principle of trusteeship has been subjected to much misconceived criticism. It has been described as make-shift, an eye wash, a shelter for the rich and as merely appealing to the more fortunate ones to show a little more charity. It has been generally objected to, on the grounds that as a means of affecting social transformation, this theory—its ethical content notwithstanding—is ineffective. Professor M. L. Dantwala in *Gandhism Reconsidered,* quotes a Marxist appraisal of the doctrine.

> 'The division of the society into the property owning and the property-less classes, which is the characteristics of capitalism, is sought to be retained in Gandhism also. The only difference in Gandhism is that the erstwhile capitalist property owning classes will consider itself as a trustee on behalf of the proletariat. The change is purely on the subjective sphere. The objective conditions of production will continue by remaining as they were in capitalism. Production will continue by unplanned private competition among the individual trustees. These conditions of production have a compelling logic of their own which will lead to the same contradictions as are witnessed under capitalism today. The class appropriation of surplus value, which trusts that production will continue in a pious guise, will mean larger and larger accumulations of capital on one hand and pauperization of the masses on the other... These evils cannot be banished by wishing a change in the hearts and minds of the owners of property.'

E. M. S. Namboodiripad has attacked not only Gandhi's philosophy but also his intentions. In his own words, 'Not only in relation to the rural poor, but also in relation to the working class and other sections of the working people his was an approach which, in actual practice, helped the bourgeoisie. His theory of trusteeship, his insistence on certain moral values as the guiding line for any political activity, the skillful way in which he combined his own extra-parliamentary activities (constructive programme and *satyagraha*) with the parliamentary activities of his lieutenants, the characteristically Gandhian way of combining negotiations with the enemy even while carrying on mass direct action against him—all these proved in actual practice to be of enormous help to the bourgeoisie in rousing the masses in action against imperialism; and in preventing them from resorting to revolutionary mass action. This ability of his to rouse the masses and yet to check them, to launch anti-imperialist direct action and yet to go on negotiating with the imperialist rulers, made him the undisputed leader of the bourgeoisie'.

The criticism of the trusteeship theory has not been levelled only from the Marxist quarters. Even a sympathetic reviewer of Gandhian economics like Professor J. J. Anjaria doubts its validity as a long-term solution, 'as a short-term measure, this is excellent; coercion is ethically bad. On any large scale, it is also not expedient. But to run away from the problem by merely appealing to the more fortunate ones to show a little more charity—awful word—is no solution.'

Even Jawaharlal Nehru, Gandhi's political heir and most trusted disciple, wrote in his autobiography, 'Again, I think of the paradox that is Gandhiji. With all his keen intellect and passion for bettering the downtrodden and oppressed, why does he support a system which is obviously decaying, which creates this misery and the wastes? He seeks a way out, it is true, but is not that way to the past barred and bolted? And meanwhile he blesses all the relics of the old order which stand as obstacles in the way of advance—the feudal states, the big *zamindaris* and *taluqdaris*, the present capitalist system. Is it reasonable to believe in the theory of trusteeship to give unchecked power and wealth to an individual and to expect him to use it entirely for the public good? Are the best of us so perfect to be trusted in this way? …And is it good for the others to have even these benevolent supermen over them.'

The main thrust of trusteeship is very broad and deep and is thus not easy to comprehend. There is no historical example of it to go by. Besides full trusteeship cases have not been experimented anywhere. The problem with this doctrine is that either it has been bitterly criticized or eulogized but not experimented with. Gandhi had a way of prescribing sugar-coated quinine for the maladies of the society. He would administer the bitterest of truth under a thick coating of *ahimsa*. But his followers have developed a way of lapping up the sugar and spitting out the quinine. The theory of trusteeship has been dealt in the same manner. That is why the country has not yet been able to enact a statue on trusteeship through several efforts have been done for this.

Summing Up

Gandhi had hoped that statutory trusteeship would be India's gift to the world but up till now we have not yet been able to fulfill this moral responsibility. 'The mantra of trusteeship,' writes Gadre, 'can influx life into the skeleton of Gandhism which, if revived, will swallow us along with our comfortable armchairs. Because of this fear we always try to find out some scapegoat here or there in its implementation. It will snatch away from our rulers, leaders, industrialists, bureaucrats and other elites their luxuries and comforts and will distribute them into the masses. We will be able to realize Gandhi's dream only if in the pursuit of truth, we prefer self-sacrifice to self-preservation.' It is heartening to note that recently some eminent social scientists have shown some renewed interest in the theory of trusteeship. Dr. J. D. Sethi has shown particular interest in this field. In his *Gandhi Today,* he has termed Trusteeship as 'The Grand Alternative'.

Critics may view that trusteeship is utopian in nature. It is true that every idea looks utopian in the beginning. But given a proper attention and careful practice, nothing is beyond the human capacities. Gandhi has studied the grave situation in human societies, where there is an increasing gulf between the 'haves' and 'have-nots' aimed at establishing a classless society. As a great psychologist, Gandhi thought that every solution which is based on faith alone can serve and save mankind. He realized that human faith, tied with truth and non-violence alone, is the most powerful one to bind the whole humanity into one, despite its dissensions and disparities. In this respect, Gandhi is a great visionary in trying to establish 'Vasudhaiva Kutumbakam' (the world is one family).

Thus, every individual—by becoming a trustee for himself and for others—can cater to the needs of the society. This may dispel all the disparities both in the individual and social levels and contribute to the welfare of all. Except for this solution, there is no other alternative to the modern melodies of the mankind. This noble cause of saving the whole mankind made Gandhi choose trusteeship. Here lies the greatness of Gandhi.

Notes and References

1. Iyer, Raghavan, 'Gandhian Trusteeship in Theory and Practice', *Gandhi Marg*, Vol. 7, Nos 8 and 9, November-December 1985, p. 466.
2. Ibid., p. 467.
3. Ibid., p. 468.
4. Ibid., p. 471.
5. Deshmukh, S. K., (ed.), *Trusteeship, Concepts, Precepts and Practice,* Pune: Link Pulishers, p. 279.
6. Dantwala, M. L., 'Trusteeship: Its value and implications', *Gandhi Marg*, Vol. 7, Nos 8 and 9, November-December 1985, p. 504.
7. Singh, Ramjee, *Gandhi and the Modern World*, New Delhi: Classical Publishing Company, 1988, p. 188.
8. Gandhi, M. K., *The Story of My Experiments with Truth*, p. 198.
9. Rathnam Chetty, K. M., *Sarvodaya and Freedom: A Gandhian Appraisal*, New Delhi: Discovery, 1991, p. 18.
10. Ibid., p. 19.
11. *Harijan*, 22. 2. 1942.
12. *Young India*, 20. 10. 1946.
13. *Harijan*, 5. 9. 1936.
14. Varma, Ravindra, 'Gandhi's Theory of Trusteeship: An Essay in Understanding', *Gandhi Marg*, Vol. 7, Nos 8 and 9, November-December, 1985, p. 518.
15. Gandhi, M. K., *From Yeravada Mandir*, Ahmedabad: Navajivan, 1935, p. 50.
16. *Bhagvad Gita*, Chapter 3, verse 12.
17. *Harijan*, 29.6.1935.
18. Ibid.
19. Surineni, Indira, *Gandhian Doctrine of Trusteeship*, New Delhi: Discovery, 1991, p. 47.
20. Ravindra, Varma, op. cit., p. 510.
21. Ibid.
22. Surineni, Indira, op. cit., pp. 47–48.
23. Ibid., p. 48.
24. Ibid.

25. Ibid. pp. 50–51.
26. Ibid., p. 51.
27. Ibid., p. 59.
28. Dobhalkar, Devdatta, 'Trustees: A Blind Alley or Break Through,' *Gandhi Marg*, Vol. 7, No.8 & 9, p. 588.
29. Arunachalam, K., 'Applied Trusteeship', *Gandhi Marg*, Vol. 7, Nos 8 and 9, p. 621.
30. Deshmukh, S. K., (ed.), op. cit., p. 230.
31. Ibid., p. 239.
32. Surineni, Indira, op. cit., p. 259.
33. Deshmukh, S. K., (ed.), op. cit., p. 259.
34. Ibid., p. 269.
35. Surineni, Indira, op. cit., p. 73.
36. Ibid., p. 75.
37. Ibid., pp. 76–77.
38. Ibid., pp. 77–78.
39. *Young India*, 26.12.1924.
40. Ibid., 4.6.1925
41. *Harijan*, 22.4.1939
42. Iyer, Raghavan, 'Gandhian Trusteeship in Theory and Practice', in J. D. Sethi (ed.), *Trusteeship: The Gandhian Alternative*, New Delhi: Gandhi Peace Foundation, 1986, p. 8.
43. Upadhyaya, R. B., Social *Responsibility of Business and the Trusteeship Theory of Mahatma Gandhi*, New Delhi: Sterling, 1976, p. 252.
44. *Harijan*, 1.2.1942.

Summary

- Gandhi formulated his economic ideas and principles in the context of his design of an ideal social order, a non-violent, non-exploitative humanistic and egalitarian society.
- Gandhi rejected the Marxist solution to the most important and controversial issue of economic philosophy, that is, the right to private property, because he believed it was based on violence and tyranny.
- Gandhi also rejected the capitalistic solution because he considered it to be based on exploitation, competition and tyranny.
- Trusteeship was not just an economic expedient for Gandhi. It was a way of life.
- Indian philosophy, religion and morals are replete with trusteeship. The ancient Indian concept of rulers or kings was that of a real trustee.
- The trusteeship formula was evolved by Kishorilal Mashruwala, Narahari Parikh and others. Professor Dantwala from Bombay sent the draft of simple, practical trusteeship formula which he had prepared. It was placed before Gandhiji, who made a few changes in it. The amended final six-point draft contained the basic ideals of trusteeship as follows:
  - Trusteeship provides a means of transforming the present capitalist order of society into an egalitarian one. It gives no quarters to capitalism, but gives the

present owning class a chance of reforming itself. It is based on the faith that human nature is never beyond redemption.
- It does not recognize any right of private ownership of property except so far as it may be permitted by society for its own welfare.
- It does not exclude legislative regulation of ownership and use of wealth.
- Thus, under state-regulated trusteeship, an individual will not be free to hold or use his wealth for selfish satisfaction or in disregard of the interest of society.
- Just as it is proposed to fix a decent minimum living wage, even so a limit should be fixed for the maximum income that could be allowed to any person in society. The difference between such minimum and maximum incomes should be reasonable, equitable and variable from time to time so much so that the tendency would be towards obliteration of the difference.
- Under the Gandhian economic order, the character of production will be determined by social necessity and not by personal whim or greed.

- Trusteeship is based on three Gandhian concepts: non-violence, *swaraj* and equality, which are inter-linked with one another.
- Truth (*satya*), non-violence (*ahimsa*), bread labour and non-profession (*aparigraha*) led Gandhi to the concept of trusteeship.

Present Economic Theory versus Trusteeship

Present Economic Theory	**Trusteeship**
Alienation—man, society and nation	Integration—man, society and nation
Materialistic approach	Humanistic approach
Market centric	Man centric
Capitalism	*Sarvodaya*
Domination and conquest	Cooperation and change
Structural violence	Structural nonviolence
Development	Sustainable development
Freedom	*Swaraj*
Dichotomy—man and nature	Harmony—man and nature

- In the present-day India, the theory has become more relevant. Here we have a mixed economy model with a large public sector and very large private sectors. But the distribution of resources is highly skewed in both, much more sharply in industry than in agriculture.
- Trusteeship provides an alternative mechanism for reducing the concentration of economic power.

Further Readings

Anjaria, J. J., *An Essay on Gandhian Economics,* Bombay: Vora and Co., 1944.

Biswas, S. C. (ed.), *Gandhi: Theory and Practice, social Impact and Contemporary Relevance,* Shimla: Indian Institute of Advanced Study, 1969.

Gandhi, M. K., From *Yeravade Mandir*, Ahmedabad: Navajivan, 1935.

Namboodiripad, E. M. S., *The Mahatma and the I & M.* New Delhi: People Publishing House, 1959.

Surineni, Indira, *Gandhian Doctrine of Trusteeship*, New Delhi: Discovery, 1991.

Upadhyaya, R. B., *Social Responsibility of Business and the Trusteeship* Theory of *Mahatma Gandhi*, New Delhi: Starling, 1976.

9

Swaraj

Introduction

Swaraj is the one of the basic concepts of Gandhi's political philosophy. According to Gandhi, '*Swaraj* is a state of being of individuals and nations'.[1] *Swaraj*, a Sanskrit word, comprising of *swa* and *raj,* means self rule. A Vedic term, it frequently appears in ancient *shastras* and other literatures. It indicates the highest spiritual state of mind. *Swarajya* means 'independent domain' or 'sovereignty'. The ancient Indian political thought laid the concept of *Swaraj* or self-rule connected with the notion of *Swarajya,* which referred to a particular mode of securing self-determination in a polity comprised of several distinct sectors. In modern India, the term *Swaraj* was exclusively identified by Dadabhai Naoroji, B. G. Tilak and Sri Aurobindo with the goal of national independence. The emphasis was wholly shifted from the positive to the negative connotation of the term and its application entirely transferred from its individual to collective scope. Towards the end of the 19th century—even before the term *Swaraj*, in its new sense, acquired common currency in the nationalist movement—the Bengali militants sought to justify their doctrine of boycott of British goods in the name of *swadeshi* or patriotism.[2] It was the political goal of militant nationalists. Liberals regarded *Swaraj* as the progressive association of Indians with a process of governance. On the contrary, for the militants, it was not self-progressive. They took *Swaraj* as political independence from the British. It was not sovereignty but it was a whole thing and not a part.

Gandhi employed the term *Swaraj* in its specific and generic sense, to borrow an expression of Green. While he organized the Indian masses for *Swaraj* conceived as a constitutional, democratic, political order, he at the same time stressed on its economic, mass 'organic' content. *Swaraj* which first acquired its political meaning (of independence) through its use in that sense by Naoroji and later through its popularization by Tilak is closely allied with the meaning of *tapas* or renunciation. *Swaraj* literally means 'self-rule' and in its original connotation meant autonomy of the moral self (as in the *Brhadaranayaka Upanisad*) where strict control is exercised over the senses. In another words, it means self-rule and self-restraint, and not freedom from all restraint, which 'independence' often means.

Meaning

The concept of *Swaraj* is pre-Gandhian, but it was Mahatma Gandhi who defined it in its fullness. It is rather difficult to find a meaning of *Swaraj*. In a way, *Swaraj* is non-subjection to anyone. Non-subjection and self-subjection together will make a better sense of *Swaraj*. It may also mean freedom from bondage of any kind. Political *Swaraj* means to be able to manage one's affair. This was the visible nature of *Swaraj*. Tilak confined himself to the visible concept of *Swaraj*. He considered that political freedom should precede social reform, whereas Gokhale and Agarkar believed that social reform was equally, if not more, necessary than political reform. Tilak apprehended that the masses may be estranged from the Congress if it supported social reform. Tilak's contemporary, Aurobindo Ghose, appreciatively said that Tilak did not want the nation to 'Split itself up into warring factions by a premature association of the social reform question with politics.' Tilak did not consider social and political reforms to be interlinked. He referred to Ireland which had progressed in social matters but did not have political freedom, as also to Ceylon and Burma which enjoyed a considerable degree of social freedom but were politically backward. He felt that excessive emphasis on social reform would divide the nationalist and anti-imperialist forces. And so far as the reformers are concerned, he asked them first to reform themselves and to practice what they preached by participating in widow remarriage before preaching its virtues.

In 1908, Tilak was charged with sedition, sentenced to six years of rigorous imprisonment and was sent to Mandalay prison. While in prison he wrote *The Asiatic Home of the Vedas* and the *Gita Rahasya*. He considered that the real message of the *Gita* was more a call to action, as was propagated in its opening parts than renunciation as stated in its later parts. He claimed that the *Gita* had preached a gospel of incessant activity. A similar interpretation was later given by Aurobindo Ghose. Tilak said that 'from begging to open rebellion choose any one according to your ability and do it but remember the supremacy of *swadharma*'. For Tilak, *Swaraj* was the birthright of every Indian. In Tilak's value system, *Swaraj* was a moral necessity; it was *Swaraj* not only a right but also the exercise of one's *dharma* and one's *karma*. He gave a word and spiritual meaning also to *Swaraj*. Politically, *Swaraj* meant home rule. Morally, it meant the attainment of the perfection of self-control which is essential for performing one's duty. It was 'a life centered in self and dependent upon the self.' It meant self-control and inner spiritual freedom. But such spiritual freedom was possible only if there was political freedom in India.

Similarly, Bipin Chandra Pal said that the term *Swaraj* was used in the Vedanta to indicate the highest spiritual state ,wherein the individual, having realized his identity with the universal, was not merely freed from bondage, but was established in perfect harmony with everyone else in the world. To Bipin Chandra Pal, self-subjection meant subjection to the universal.

According to Tilak, the moderates and extremists had a specific relation to time, for the extremists of today would become the moderates of tomorrow, just as the moderates of today were the extremists of yesterday. In fact, Tilak began as a moderate. As moderate he had said that he did not desire to weaken the government, but 'to render it impregnable to all assaults, whether from Russian or any other foe.' To ensure this, he asked for greater association of Indians in the administration, but his expectations were not fulfilled. But even then, Tilak advocated only strong constitutional methods and not passive resistance. But by the middle of the first decade of the previous century , Tilak's attitude changed altogether and he advocated the adoption of the fourfold programme of *Swaraj*, *swadeshi*, *national education and boycott.* He then asserted that the political salvation of India lay not in supplication but in self-assertion, not in submission but in direct action. He said, 'Political rights will have to be fought for the moderates think these can be won by persuasion; we think that they can only be got by strong pressure.'

Analyzing the differences between the moderate Gokhale and the extremist Tilak, Pattabhi Sitaramayya, wrote:

> 'Gokhale's plan was to improve the existing constitution; Tilak's was to reconstruct it. Gokhale had necessarily to work with the bureaucracy; Tilak had necessarily to fight it. Gokhale stood for cooperation wherever possible and opposition whenever necessary; Tilak inclined towards a policy of obstruction. Gokhale's prime concern was with the admin and its improvement; Tilak's supreme consideration was with the nation and it's upbuilding. Gokhale's idea was love and sacrifice, Tilak's was service and suffering. Gokhale's method sought to win the foreigner, Tilak's to replace him. Gokhale depended upon other's help, Tilak upon self-help. Gokhale looked to the classes and the intelligentsia, Tilak to the masses and the millions. Gokhale's arena was the Council Chamber; Tilak's forum was the Village Mandap. Gokhale's medium of expression was English; Tilak's was Marathi. Gokhale's objective was self-government for which the people had to fit themselves by answering the tests preserved by the England; Tilak's objective was *Swaraj* which is the birthright of every Indian and which he shall have without it or hindrance from the foreigner. Gokhale was on a level with his age, Tilak was in advance of his time.'

Tilak, who advocated a policy of non-cooperation with the British government, poured ridicule on the moderates saying that their policy of three Ps—pray, please and protest—would never be effective . He said, 'Look to the example of Ireland, Japan, Russia, and follow their methods.' Though Tilak referred to the methods of Irish and Russian terrorists, he did not openly or unequivocally advocate violence. He used to say that if there was even a fifty per cent chance of the success of an armed rebellion, he would resort to it, but he was afraid that there was no such chance.

B. C. Pal said that in the disarmed and disorganized condition of the people, any violent uprising could easily be suppressed by the government. Similarly, Aurobindo admitted that the physical strength of the country belonged largely to the established authority, and he warned the people not to come into any physical conflict with it. In January 1907, Tilak declared, 'We are not armed and there is no necessity of arms either. We have stronger weapon, a political weapon in boycott.'

Tilak said, 'When you prefer to accept *swadeshi*, you must boycott *videshi* goods. Without boycott, *swadeshi* cannot flourish'. For Tilak, boycott was not so much an economic weapon as a weapon of political warfare and a substitute for the bullet.

According to Tilak, the agitation of the moderates based on the so-called constitutional method was a sheer waste of time, for Indians had no democratic constitution through which they could effect real changes. Tilak claimed that if Indians did not cooperate with the administration, then they could make their power felt and become free. Tilak observed that at one time Indians thought that everything that the rulers did was for their good that the government had descended from the clouds to save them from the invasions of Tamerlane and Chengiz Khan. But it soon become apparent that the peace which was established in the country did this; that Indians were prevented from going at each other's throats so that foreigners might go at the throat of every Indian, as Dadabhai Naoroji said. The Indians believed in the benevolent intentions of the government, but in politics there was no benevolence. Benevolence was used to sugarcoat and conceal rampant self-interest. But English education, growing poverty and better familiarity with the rulers opened the eyes of the Indian leaders, and even Dadabhai Naoroji had to tell the people about the drain of India's wealth to Britain.

There is no empire lost, Tilak claimed, by free grant of concession by the rulers to the ruled. Empires were lost by luxury, by being too bureaucratic or overconfident or from other reasons. But no empire had ever come to an end by the rulers voluntarily and from a sense of justice conceding power to the ruled. In 1914, in a letter in *The Maratha*, Tilak exhorted his countrymen to rush to the defense of Britain which had 'been compelled to take up arms in defense of weaker states.' Tilak hoped that the government would reciprocate the gesture. The government did not. This changed Tilak's mood. In 1916, he formed a league to fight for home rule. At this stage, however, Tilak's attitude to colonial self-governance was radically different from his earlier attributes. He said, 'Indians did want English people, institutions, English liberty and empire.' The meaning of *Swarajya*,' he declared in 1916, 'is the retention of our Emperor and the rule of the English people, and the full possession by the people of the authority to manage the remaining affairs. To put it more simply, 'the *Swaraj* of today is within the empire and not independent of it.' Tilak explained that he did not want to change the immutable government of the king, but what he demanded was that the management of the country affair should not be, as it was then, 'in the hands of the invisible government or the bureaucracy, but should be transferred to our hands.' This approach of Tilak was shared by other home rule leaders such as Annie Besant and C. R. Das.

The Congress met in December 1918 and claimed self government on the basis of the principle of national self-determination which the allied statesmen had repeatedly proclaimed during the war. It also claimed that, like the self-governing British Dominions, India should be represented at any conference that might be held to decide the terms of peace and reconstruction, and it selected Tilak and two other leaders to represent India at such conferences. At a session in Bombay in August 1918, the Congress considered the

Montague-Chelmsford Reform scheme. It felt that the reforms were disappointing and suggested modifications. Tilak's view was 'We asked for eight annas of self government. The report gives us one anna of responsible government.' Tilak was in favour of giving the reforms a trial. Indeed, he had formed the Congress Democratic Party with the objective of contesting the elections under the reform scheme.

But Tilak passed away in August 1920 and by the time the next Congress met in Calcutta in September 1920, the spirit of Congressmen had undergone a profound change, particularly because of the agitation against the Rowlett Bills, the Khilafat question and the tragedy of Amritsar. The Calcutta Congress, at the instance of Gandhi, approved of a policy of progressive non-violent non-cooperation with the government for obtaining redress for the Punjab tragedy and the Khilafat grievances as well as for the attainment of *Swaraj*.

After Tilak's death, the leadership of Congress passed to Gandhi, who continued and perfected the method of boycott which the extremists such as Tilak had originally adopted. The mantle of Tilak fell on Gandhi. But Gandhi also believed in non-violence as a creed, which Tilak did not. Tilak did not believe that *satyagraha* and fasting would have the least effect upon the minds of the British rulers. Further, he feared that even the method of *hartal*, which Gandhi advocated, may lead to violence.

Gandhi, on the other hand, had inward as well as outward focus regarding *Swaraj*. In the *Hind Swaraj* (1909), he appears as a devastating critic of Western civilization. He said, 'Our *Swaraj* is not the copy of England, nor we want a self-government of the type of South Africa, Canada or Australia. I was thinking of *Swaraj* which was truly Indian, but that *Swaraj* can be built on the destruction of much of the modern civilization.' He said that he had pictured a *Swarajist* society. My *Swaraj* is not dependent upon the British leaving the country. A true *Swaraj* is related to the social reform. There should be a movement towards total *Swaraj*.

A *swaraj* is what Gandhi worked out as representative of political institutions. *Swaraj* could be better achieved with the help of indirect election by an electoral collage consisting of five lakh people. To Gandhi, in 1947 we did not achieve *Swaraj*. The end of British rule was not the beginning of *Swaraj*. *Swaraj* is self-control, self-regulation and self-restraint. It is both a means as well as the end. It's a kind of struggle within one's self as well as without one's self.

In modern civilization, there are various obstacles in the attainment of *Swaraj*. *Swaraj* should be gained with the help of non-violent and truthful means. It must aim at the creation of the capacity of all the people. Gandhi was thinking in terms of capacity, self-restraint and self-denial. Richs are the obstacles in the attainment of *Swaraj*. Nehru wanted to develop the features of a modern civilized society, whereas Gandhi doubted the modern civilization as a whole. Nehru's concept of *Swaraj* was parliamentary institution and political independence in which there is fair play of democracy.

To the leftist thinker, the Gandhian *Swaraj* is difficult to understand. All these things are an indefinable spiritual mystery. To R. P. Dutt, A. R. Desai and others, *Swaraj* meant freedom from economic wants, and economic freedom. The first way to gain economic freedom is to get freedom from imperialism. Capitalism should be abolished. In Gandhian

Swaraj, one reaches the stage of *Swaraj* when we do not need governmental support and become self-sufficient. In order to achieve this type of *Swaraj*, there are some important requirements:

- **One needs to cultivate the spirit of bread-labour:** Try to earn your bread with the help of one's own labour. It will create a sense of self- sufficiency. This self-sufficiency can be attained by doing one's own work. Consumerism is an obstacle to the attainment of *Swaraj*. In order to overcome consumerism, Gandhi recommends khadi and indigenous products.
- **Gandhi was opposed to drinking and favored prohibition:** He said, 'If I will be a dictator, I will close down all the liquor shops without compensation.' Drinking is worse than stealing. It knocks down the cells of the brain and man's potential is so damaged that he cannot contribute to creative activities. It, in fact, hampers clear thinking. He said that India is a poor country and men folk spend most of their income in drinking and because of this no one can think of *Swaraj* and self-sufficiency. Prohibition is way to this self-sufficiency.

Gandhi on Swaraj

Mahatma Gandhi restored to the term *Swaraj* in its older meaning while retaining its newer sense to interpret the term *swadeshi* and also considerably extended its application. He restored the close connection between *Swaraj* and *swadeshi*, between individual self-rule and individual self-reliance, between self government and national self-dependence. Instead of assimilating the concept of freedom to that of community by merging the individual into an organic conception of society, he derived the very notion of communal self-reliance from his doctrine of individual self-rule and showed how the pursuit of *Swaraj* must necessarily involve the acceptance of *swadeshi*.

The concept of *Swaraj*, or self-rule, was developed during the Indian freedom struggle. In his book *Hind Swaraj* or *Indian Home Rule* (1909), Gandhi was emphatic that *Swaraj* 'much more than anything simply meant system of English rule without the Englishman; the tiger's nature but not the tiger.'[3] His argument centered on the belief that the socio-spiritual underpinnings of British political, economic, bureaucratic, legal, military and educational institutions were inherently unjust, exploitative and alienating. As Vivek Pinto in his book *Gandhi's Vision and Values* explicates, 'The principal theme of *Hind Swaraj* is the moral inadequacy of Western civilization, especially its industrialism, as a model for free India.'[4] On another level, the call for *Swaraj* represents a genuine attempt to regain control of the self—our self-respect, self-responsibility and capacities for self-realization—from institutions of dehumanization. As Gandhi states, 'It is S*waraj* when we learn to rule ourselves.' The real goal of the freedom struggle was not only to secure political *azadi* (independence) from Britain, but rather to gain true *Swaraj* (liberation and self-rule). Self-rule is the term used to describe a people or group being able to exercise all of the necessary functions of power without intervention from any authority which they cannot themselves alter. Self rule is associated in contexts where there is end of colonial rule, absolute government or monarchy, as well as demands for autonomy by religious, ethnic or geographic regions which perceive themselves as being un- or under-represented in a national government. Self-rule is, therefore, a fundamental tenet of republican government and democracy as well as nationalism.' Furthermore, Gandhi said, 'The *Swaraj* of my dreams is the poor man. The necessaries of life should be enjoyed by you in common with those enjoyed by the princes and the moneyed men. But that does not mean that you should have palaces like theirs. They are not necessary for happiness. You or I would be lost in them. But you ought to get all the ordinary amenities of life that a rich man enjoys. I have not the slightest doubt that *Swaraj* is not *Poorna Swaraj* until these amenities are guaranteed to you under it'.[5]

Gandhi's concept of *Swaraj* emerged out of what he said in *India of My Dreams*. It follows: 'I shall strive for a constitution, which will release India from all thralldom and patronage and give her, if need be, the right to sin. I shall work for an India, in which the poorest shall feel that it is their country in whose making they have an effective voice; an India in which there shall be no high class and low class of people; an India in which all communities shall live in perfect harmony. There can be no room in such an India for the curse of untouchability or the curse of intoxicating drinks and drugs. Women will enjoy the same rights as men. Since we shall be at peace with all the rest of the world, neither exploiting, nor being exploited, we should have the smallest army imaginable. All interests not in conflict with the interests of the dumb millions will be scrupulously respected, whether foreign or indigenous. Personally, I hate distinction between foreign and indigenous. This is the India of my dreams …I shall be satisfied with nothing less.'[6]

In 1924, Gandhi wrote 'Freedom for the meanest of our countrymen... I am not interested in freeing India merely from the English yoke. I am bent upon freeing India from any yoke whatsoever. I have no desire to exchange king log for king stork.'[7] Further, Gandhi wrote in 1925: 'By *Swaraj* I meant the government of India by the consent of the people as ascertained by the largest number of the adult population, male or female, native-born or domiciled, who have contributed by manual labour to the service of the state and who have taken the trouble of having their names registered as voters... Real *Swaraj* will come, not by the acquisition of authority by a few, but by the acquisition of the capacity by all to resist authority when it is abused. In other words, *Swaraj* is to be attained by educating the masses to a sense of their capacity to regulate and control authority.'[8] Self-government means continuous effort to be independent of government control, whether it is foreign government or whether it is national.

Gandhi elaborated the concept and said, 'The *Swaraj* of my…our…dream recognizes no race or religious distinctions. Nor is it to be the monopoly of the lettered persons or yet of moneyed men. *Swaraj* is before all, including the former, but emphatically including the maimed, the blind, and the starving, toiling millions.'[9]

'What we mean and want through *Poorna Swaraj* is an awakening among the masses, knowledge among them of their true interest and ability to serve that interest against the whole world, harmony, and freedom from aggression from within or without, and a progressive improvement in the economic condition of the masses…'[10] Further, Gandhi said, 'Real *Swaraj* must be felt by all—man, woman and child. To labour for that consummation is true resolution. India has become a pattern for all exploited races of the earth, because India's has been an open, unarmed, effort which demands sacrifice from all without inflicting injury on the usurper. The millions in India would not have been awakened but for the open, unarmed struggle. Every deviation from the straight path has meant a temporary arrest of the evolutionary revolution.[11] It has been said that Indian *Swaraj* will be the rule of the majority community, that is, the Hindus. There could not be a greater mistake than that. If it were to be true, I for one would refuse to call it *Swaraj* and would fight it with all the strength at my command, for to me *Hind Swaraj* is the rule of all people, the rule of justice. Whether, under that rule, the ministers were Hindus or Mussalmans or Sikhs and whether legislatures were exclusively filled by the Hindus or Mussalmans or any other community, they would have to do even-handed justice.[12]

'Today, our minds are clouded by delusion. In our ignorance, we quarrel with one another and indulge in violence against our own brethren. For such as these, there is neither salvation nor *Swaraj*. Self-discipline or rule over the self is the first condition of self-rule or *Swaraj*.' [13]

'In a vast country like this, there must be room for all schools of honest thought. And the least, therefore, that we owe to ourselves, as to others, is to try to understand the opponent's view-point and, if we cannot accept it, respect is as fully as we expect him to respect ours. It is one of the indispensable tests of a healthy public life and, therefore, fitness for *Swaraj*.[14]

Freedom of speech and pen is the foundation of *Swaraj*. If the foundation stone is in danger, you have to exert the whole of your might in order to defend that single stone.

Gandhi's scheme of comprehensive freedom as elucidated in the *Hind Swaraj* can be thus represented:

- True *Swaraj* = kingdom of the soul (spiritual and moral freedom).
- *Satyagraha* as the key to it (political freedom).
    - (*Satyagraha* = *Dayabala* or *Atmabala*)
- *Swadeshi* = (Economic freedom)
    - (Necessary for putting *satyagraha* into practice).

Spiritual and Moral Freedom

According to Gandhi, moral and spiritual freedom depends on the effective cultivation of the ancient virtues of truth and non-violence. Moral freedom means the conquest of the demands of the senses and the appetites, for the realization of the highest self. Thus, the self-subsistence of the particular will has to be purified by the devoted adherence to truth and non-violence. Self-indulgence eventually leads to destruction. The conquest of empirical desires alone is the path to immortality. Gandhi wrote: 'Freedom is a fruit of suffering, license is born of violence. What we are all pining for freedom that imposes restraints upon itself for the sake of society? License imposes suffering upon society so that it may enjoy exclusive privileges.'[15] Therefore, Gandhi never accepted the view of freedom as arbitrariness or license. Genuine freedom results in self-denial for the sake of society. Thus, genuine *Swaraj* is a function of the development of the moral sources of power.

Spiritual freedom for Gandhi was identification with the Supreme Being. At the Belgaum Congress in 1924, Gandhi said that *Swaraj* is part of truth. This view amounts almost to a sanctification, even spiritualization of the work of national emancipation or freedom. Freedom is the essence of man's spiritual personality. Like Rousseau in the *Social Contract*, Gandhi also considers freedom as the essence of man. If freedom is renounced, man becomes an 'automaton'. Any attempt to build society by the denial of liberty is 'contrary to the very nature of man.' [16] The renunciation of freedom would be the repudiation of human conscience. If truth is god, and if the constructive programme and *satyagraha*, which are the bases and techniques for the realization of *Swaraj* are, by implication, part of the truth, then it implies a conception of god as concrete real unity, an organic universal manifold, including different entities and not an undifferentiated abstract—a universal fact that is absolutely removed from human struggle. He said: 'On the principle that the greater includes the less, national independence or material freedom is included in the spiritual.' Gandhi laid down two stringent prerequisites for the enshrinement of moral and spiritual freedom. First, his conception of moral and spiritual freedom postulates the cultivation of *Anasakti*, or disinterestedness. As a follower of the *Bhagavad Gita*, he stressed on absolute disinterestedness, complete imperturbability and a resignation to the will of God as the essence of *Karmayoga*. Disinterestedness (*Anasakti*) is linked up with spontaneous devotion to the cause of the good of all living beings. Secondly, requirement for moral and spiritual freedom is fearlessness. Fearlessness can be acquired by surrendering to god whose implication and consequence is the absolute refusal to be bound by mundane temptations and threats. A man who realizes his spiritual humanity is not afraid of any law except the law of God. In a speech given at the anniversary of the Gurukul Kangri, on March 30, 1916 Gandhi said: 'In my humble opinion, fearlessness is the first thing indispensable before we could achieve anything permanent and real. This quality is unattainable without religious consciousness. Let us fear God and we shall cease to fear man. If we grasp the fact that there is a divinity within us who witnessed everything we think or do and which protects us and guides us along the true path, it is clear that we shall cease to have any other fear on the face of the earth save the fear of god. Loyalty to the governor of governors supersedes all other loyalties and gives an intelligent basis to the latter.'[17] Gandhi was a spiritual and ethical idealist but also an optimist. Despite being the critical of the mechanical and technological aspects of modern Western civilization, he had abiding faith in the realization of freedom in the future. He was, hence, more optimistic than Max Weber, according to whom there are slender prospects of genuine human freedom because of the accentuated technological rationality of the modern age. Gandhi rightly said, on the other hand, 'It is possible to have freedom in the modern age if there is a moral renaissance of man. Hence, against the immense and engulfing power of the technological and political structure, he stood for the purification of motives and conduct as the sure way to freedom. There is no genuine freedom without practice of moral obedience. The perfection of the value of liberty, equality, social justice and fearlessness will act as foundations for the kingdom of God on earth. Gandhi's life was dedicated to this end this was his message.

Political Freedom

Gandhi's devotion to the concept of individual rights made him a fighter for democratic freedom. In South Africa, as earlier pointed out, he launched the Satyagraha Movement for safeguarding the civil rights of Indians. He stood up for the rights of the poor, suppressed indigo planters in Champaran in 1917. He effectively sponsored the cause of the labourers in the spinning factories in Ahmedabad in February-March 1918. He also championed the rights of the peasants of the Khaira district in Gujarat in March-May 1918. He advised the peasants of Khaira not to pay rent because crops had failed and the government reluctantly acceded to the demands of the peasants.

Gandhi accepted the truth of the famous mantra given by Tilak that *Swaraj* is the birthright of Indians. In an article entitled '*Tampering with Loyalty*', he wrote that spreading disaffection against the British Government in India was the *dharma* of the Indians. He condemned British imperialism because it resulted in the political and economic prostration of India. In his famous Trial Speech on March 19, 1922, before Mr. C. N. Broomfield, District and Session Judge, Ahmedabad, he said:

> 'I came reluctantly to the conclusion that the British connection had made India more helpless than she ever was before, politically and economically. A disarmed India has no power of resistance against any aggressor if she wanted to engage in an armed conflict with him. So much is this the case that some of our best men consider that India must take generations before she can achieve the Dominion Status. She has become so poor that she has little power of resisting famines.'[18]

From 1920 onwards, Gandhi dedicated his life's aim to secure India's freedom from imperialistic bondage. He wrote, 'We are challenging the might of this Government because we consider its activity to be wholly foul. We want to overthrow the Government. We want to compel its submission to the people's will. We desire to show that the government exists to serve the people, not the people to serve the Government. Free life under the Government has become intolerable, for the price exacted for the retention of freedom is unconsciously great. Whether we are one or many, we must refuse to purchase freedom at the cost of our self-respect or our cherished convictions.'

Gandhi prescribed rigorous self-control, discipline, moral exercise and patient suffering in order to win *Swaraj*. Even in his early writings, for example, he categorically stated that freedom does not mean license. One may enjoy what is his but should never attempt to rob others of what is theirs. He said: 'Humility, earnestness, thoughtfulness—these are the foundations of *Swarajya*.'[19]

Gandhi wrote: 'Voluntary discipline was the first requisite of corporate freedom. If the people were well-behaved, the Government officials would become their true servants.' Only a *Swaraj* won by patient suffering and sacrifice could be lasting and stable. Political freedom or *Swaraj* could be obtained only by intense suffering and struggle. It would be chimerical to believe that it could come as a gift. In 1929, Gandhi said: 'A man who is made for freedom has got to take tremendous risks and stake everything.' He said at the Second

Round Table Conference in 1931: '…the page of history is soiled red with the blood of those who have fought for freedom.'[20] He believed that Indians were entitled to freedom, because of the immense sufferings they had undergone for it.

Political freedom also postulated social cohesiveness apart from disciplined suffering. It is essential to combine the quest for political individuality with the voluntary acceptance of social and political discipline which is the basis of social solidarity and cohesiveness. A divided and disrupted social structure could not wage successful political struggle. Only a community constituted by persons imbued with a sense of deep social cohesiveness can attain the benefits of *Swaraj*. Hence, Gandhi stressed upon communal unity and the absolute elimination of unsociability among the foundations of political freedom.

Economic Freedom

Gandhi stressed the economic prerequisites and foundations of freedom since he was able to accept that economic resources act as an effective apparatus for the realization of man's will. He felt that freedom was bound to remain a mere philosophical abstraction unless the vast masses had some gainful employment. Unemployment snatches the morsel from the mouth of the poor villagers and completely damages the personality of the victims. Hence, Gandhi wrote: 'Political freedom has no meaning for the millions if they do not know how to employ their enforced idleness.' As a moral prophet of *Ram Rajya*, Gandhi accepted the doctrine of equal distribution. A fundamental item in actualizing genuine equality, as discussed earlier, would be the revolutionary step of the acceptance and practice of equality of wages for the lawyer, the doctor or the teacher who are entitled to no more than the *bhangi*. This would provide the key to true civilization and be the basis of the reconstruction of an ideal humanity.

Thus, Gandhi pleaded that all useful labour should bring the same and adequate wages to the worker. But until that rather remote ideal of equal distribution was realized, he prescribed a more realistic formula of equitable distribution for the immediate present. The proposal was that every labourer should get enough remuneration to feed and clothe himself as well as his family. It was the imperative duty of the government to ensure this to all. 'A government that does not ensure this much is no government. It is anarchy. Such a state should be resisted peacefully.'[21]

Characteristic of Swaraj

Noted Gandhian scholar J. Bandyopadhyaya beautifully mentioned the essential characteristics of *Swaraj* as follows:

- *Swaraj* is based on inward freedom
- *Swaraj* belongs to the individual alone
- *Swaraj* means freedom for all or *sarvodaya*
- *Swaraj* is eternal vigilance on the part of the individual
- *Swaraj* involves equality
- *Swaraj* involves non-violence

Firstly, *Swaraj* is based on inward freedom. Since freedom of action comes through acquired virtue, it follows that *Swaraj* or the external freedom enjoyed by an individual would depict directly on the degree of his self-perfection through acquired virtue. His external *Swaraj* cannot exceed his internal moral evolution. 'The outward freedom that we shall attain,' says Gandhi, 'will only be in exact proportion to the inward freedom to which we may have grown at a given moment. And if this is the correct view of freedom, our chief energy must be concentrated upon achieving reform from within.' *Swaraj* is, thus, fearlessness born out of self perfection, as in the case of Socrates or Jesus Christ—a fearlessness that defies not only all external authority, including the authority of the mightiest state or empire, but even death itself. As Gandhi observes: 'If *Swaraj* is delayed (in the case of India), it is because we are not prepared calmly to meet death and inconveniences less than death.' And this applies not only to the individual, but also to the entire nation. 'That nation is great,' he says, 'which rests its head upon death as its pillow. Those who defy death are free from all fear. An individual of a nation that has developed this inner freedom cannot be controlled by any external authority.' Tolstoy said, Gandhi understood the nature of such inward freedom. What Tolstoy preached, like all world teachers, he says, is that every man has to 'obey the voice or his own conscience, and be his own master, and seek the Kingdom of God from within'. For him there is no government that controls him without his sanction.

Secondly, *Swaraj* belongs to the individual alone. A corollary of the inwardness of freedom and of personal moral responsibility is that *Swaraj* is essentially a matter of individual attainment. Gandhi challenges the very basis of all totalitarian political thought by his insistence that freedom necessarily belongs only to the individual, and freedom can, according to Gandhi, exist only as a corollary of individual freedom, not in opposition to it. 'The individual is the one supreme consideration', he declares. Therefore, any conception of freedom must begin with the individual. As Gandhi observes, 'The first step to *Swaraj* lies in the individual. The truth: As with the individual, so with the universe, is applicable here as elsewhere.'[2] Hence, freedom for a society or a nation only is the result of the freedom of all the individuals comprising it. He insists that '*Swaraj* of people means the sum total of the *Swaraj* of the individuals. 'Political self-government of the people, therefore, cannot be external, but can only be the result of the inward moral freedom of all the individuals as explained by Gandhi in the following words: 'I have, therefore, endeavoured to show both in word and deed that political self-government, or self-government—for it constitutes a large number or men and women—is no better than individual self-government, and, therefore, it is to be attained by precisely the same means that are required for individual self-government or self-rule.'

Thirdly, *Swaraj* means freedom for all or *sarvodaya*: An essential concomitant of such absolutist individualism is the rejection of the utilitarian view of democracy as representing the greatest good of the greatest number. Fundamental to the Gandhian social and political thought is the contention that true freedom can be ensured in human society only by the greatest good of all. Freedom is not a numerical phenomenon and cannot be quantitatively expressed. Every individual represents an end in itself, and the curtailment of the freedom of a minority of individuals leads to a qualitative deterioration of the freedom of the whole society. To such a concept of universal freedom, Gandhi gives the name of *sarvodaya* (the equal development of all), a Sanskrit word used by Gandhi also as the title for his Gujarati translation of Ruskin's *Unto This Last* (written by him when he was in South Africa).

In a *sarvodaya* society, naturally, freedom would mean simply a majority rule: 'Unlike democracy,' says Gandhi, 'individual liberty of opinion and action is jealously guarded. I, therefore, believe that the minority has a perfect right to act differently from the majority…' In matters of conscience, moreover,' he argues, 'the law of majority has no place'.'

But such universal freedom would also necessarily limit the autonomy of each individual in such a way that it does not interfere with the freedom of others. In other words, by his own value commitments the individual is also committing the whole society, and it is therefore, his moral responsibility to see it that his actions do not interfere with the values of other individuals. 'There is not a single virtue,' says Gandhi, 'which aims at, or is consistent with, the welfare of the individual alone. Conversely, there is not a single offence which does not, directly or indirectly, affect many others besides the actual offender. Hence, whether an individual is good or bad is not merely his own concern, but really the concern of the entire community, and, of the whole world.

Fourthly, *Swaraj* is eternal vigilance on the part of the individual. Freedom of this kind would naturally transient the mere political independence of a country from foreign rule. Although Gandhi's immediate objective was the ending of the British rule in India, he never regarded India's freedom as identical with the achievement of political independence. On the other hand, he regarded independence from foreign rule as a mere prelude to the achievement of freedom by the Indian people. To him, there was no distinction—as he had said many times in his life—between British tyranny and actual or potential Indian tyranny. Nor was there any distinction between an American Rockefeller and a potential Indian Rockefeller, as he said in *Hind Swaraj*. Where there is no freedom, there is no liberty, whether the country is ruled by its own people or by foreigners. And so Gandhi declared: 'I am not interested in freeing India merely from the English yoke. I am bent upon freeing India from any yoke whatsoever.'

It follows that the kind of freedom envisaged by Gandhi exists only in a society in which the people do not depend heavily on the state for the protection of their rights. 'Self-government means', he says, '…continuous effort to be independent of government control, whether it is foreign government or whether it is national. A *Swarajjist* government will be a sorry affair if people look up to it for the regulation of every detail of life.'

As a matter of fact, fundamental to the Gandhian concept of political freedom is the idea of it, as there is a basic contradiction between the autonomy of an individual and the authority of the state. The free society visualized by Gandhi is, therefore, 'an exploitation-free society in which the supreme instrument of defending just rights lay within the grasp of the unarmed individual.' Awakening a consciousness of this fact in Indian society and even outside was regarded by Gandhi as one of his primary tasks in life. 'My work will be finished,' he said three-and-a-half years before his death, 'if I succeed in carrying conviction to the human family, that every man or woman, however weak in body, is the guardian of his or her self-respect and liberty. This defense avails, though the whole world may be against the individual register.'

Fifthly, *Swaraj* involves equality. 'The freedom of the individual cannot obviously be regarded as fundamental to the concept of liberty unless there is a prior acceptance of the hypothesis that all men are equal. The Gandhian conception of freedom, therefore, necessarily includes the notion of equality. Freedom and the equal development of all, which Gandhi calls *sarvodaya*, are, interchangeable terms. Without equality—social, political and economic egalitarianism—there can be no true freedom. Inequality in any sphere vitiates ab initio the possibility of universal freedom. Economic equality, Gandhi said, is the master key to *Swaraj*. Without the elimination of the disparities between the rich and the poor, between labour and capital, there can be no real freedom for anyone in society. The contrast between the palaces of India's major cities and the hovels of the poorer classes which existed in India will have to be lessened if India was ever to achieve freedom in the real sense. He demanded that in India that was truly free sweepers, doctors, lawyers, teachers and merchants must all get the same wages for an honest day's work.

Sixthly, *Swaraj* involves non-violence. The *sarvodaya* society representing universal freedom must be necessarily based on non-violence, for non-violence alone, Gandhi insists, can preserve and promote freedom. The path of violence will inevitably lead to dictatorship, he argues, while the non-violent way shall guide to democracy. The reason was obvious to him: 'True democracy or the *Swaraj* of the masses can never come through untruthful and violent means, for the simple reason that the natural corollary to their use would be to remove all opposition through the suppression or extermination of the antagonists. That does not make for individual freedom. Individual autonomy can have the fullest play only under a regime of unadulterated *ahimsa*.' Moreover, it is necessary for the growth of this universal freedom that every individual, including women and children, should participate actively in it, for the very participation in the process of freedom widens the horizons of individual liberty. Such a universal development of freedom would not be possible, argues Gandhi, in a society where freedom is protected by the violent power of the state; it would emerge inevitably only in a non-violent society. As he puts it, 'Granted that India produced sufficient arms and ammunition and men who know the art of war, what part or lot will those who cannot bear arms have in the attainment of *Swaraj*? I want *Swaraj* in the winning of which even women and children would contribute an equal share with physically those who are the strongest. That can be under *ahimsa* only.'

Summing Up

To conclude, it can be said that Tilak was one of the dominant political figures in the early years of the 20th century who gave to the people of India the first lesion in the consciousness of the right of *Swaraj*. He enlightened the population of India into a political recognition of the general will of the nation. At a time when apathy prostration and frustration were rampant in the country, Tilak appeared as the prophet of *Swaraj*. He taught the people of the country to hate slavery. Hence, he appeared before the Indian people as a link in the chain of the great Indian heroes, who have championed the cause of liberty against injustice and subjugation. After Tilak's death, Gandhi further enriched the concept of *Swaraj* and popularized in mass and ultimately India won its independence. But for real *Swaraj* the fight is still going on. The goals of actual *Swaraj* will be achieved by fulfilling the dream of the father of the nation. It is high time for both our policy makers and the people to turn the torch within so that they may be inspired to adopt the Gandhian way, if not for any other consideration, but for its pragmatic strength to solve our present-day maladies of rural India. There is need to reiterate Gandhian values, and instead of merely garlanding the portraits of Gandhi, India must translate his ideals into real life and make rural India free from hunger, poverty and exploitation.

Notes and References

1. *The Collected Works of Mahatma Gandhi*, New Delhi: The Publications Division, Vol. 20, p. 90.
2. Iyer, Raghavan, *The Moral and Political Thought of Mahatma Gandhi*, Delhi: Oxford University Press, 1973, p. 347.
3. Gandhi, M. K., *Hind Swaraj* or *Indian Home Rule*, Ahmedabad: Navjivan Publishing House, 1938, p.26
4. Pinto, Vivek, *Gandhi's Vision and Values: The Moral Quest for Change in Indian Agriculture*, New Delhi: Sage Publications, 1998, p. 15.
5. *Young India*, 26-3-1931.
6. *Young India*, 10-9-1931.
7. *Young India*, 12-6-1924.
8. *Young India*, 29-1-1925.
9. *Young India*, 26-3-1931.
10. *Young India*, 18-6-1931.
11. *Harijan*, 3-3-1946.
12. *Young India*, 16-4-1931.
13. *Harijan*, 28-4-1946.
14. *Young India*, 17-4-1924.
15. *Young India*, 1-5-1930.
16. Gandhi, M. K., *In Search of Supreme*, Vol. I, p. 267.
17. Mishra, Anil Dutta, Understanding Gandhi, New Delhi: Concept Publishing Company, 2012, (Under Publication).
18. Ibid.
19. *The Collected Works of Mahatma Gandhi*, New Delhi: The Publications Division, Vol. IX, p. 451.
20. Mishra, Anil Dutta, op. cit.
21. *Harijan*, 9-6-1946.

Summary

Swaraj is the one of the basic concepts of Gandhi's political *Swaraj* philosophy. Swaraj, a Sanskrit word, comprising of *swa* and *raj,* means self rule. Swaraj is a Vedic term. It literally means 'self-rule' and in its original connotation meant autonomy of the moral self (as in the *Brhadaranayaka Upanishad*), where strict control is exercised over the senses.

In modern India, the term *Swaraj* was exclusively identified by Dadabhai Naoroji, B. G. Tilak and Sri Aurobindo with the goal of national independence. Gandhi employed the term *Swaraj* in its specific and generic sense, to borrow an expression of Green.

Tilak confined himself to the visible concept of *Swaraj*. He considered that political freedom should precede social reform, whereas Gokhale and Agarkar believed that social reform was equally, if not more, necessary than political reform. Similarly, Bipin Chandra Pal said that the term *Swaraj* was used in the Vedanta to indicate the highest spiritual state ,wherein the individual, having realized his identity with the universal, was not merely freed from bondage, but was established in perfect harmony with everyone else in the world. To Bipin Chandra Pal, self-subjection meant subjection to the universal.

Gandhi had inward as well as outward focus regarding *Swaraj*. He said: 'Our *Swaraj* is not the copy of England, nor we want self-government of the type of South Africa, Canada or Australia. I was thinking of *Swaraj* which was truly Indian, but that *Swaraj* can be built on the destruction of much of the modern civilization.'

To R. P. Dutt, A. R. Desai and others, *Swaraj* meant freedom from economic wants, primarily economic freedom. The first way to gain economic freedom is to get freedom from imperialism.

Gandhi's scheme of comprehensive freedom as elucidated in the *Hind Swaraj* can thus be represented as::

- True *Swaraj* = Kingdom of the soul (Spiritual and moral freedom).
- *Satyagraha* as the key to it (Political freedom)
- *Satyagraha* = *Dayabala* or *Atmabala*)
- *Swadeshi* = (Economic freedom)

(Necessary for putting satyagraha into practice)

Bandyopadhyaya beautifully mentioned the essential characteristics of *Swaraj* as follows:

- *Swaraj* is based on inward freedom
- *Swaraj* belongs to the individual alone
- *Swaraj* means freedom for all or *sarvodaya*
- *Swaraj* is eternal vigilance on the part of the individual
- *Swaraj* involves equality
- *Swaraj* involves non-violence

The goals of real *Swaraj* will be achieved by fulfilling the dream of the father of the nation. It is high time for both our policy makers and the people to turn the torch within so that they may be inspired to adopt the Gandhian way, if not for any other consideration, but for its pragmatic strength to solve our present-day maladies of rural India. There is need to reiterate Gandhian values, and instead of merely garlanding the portraits of

Gandhi. India must translate his ideals into real life and make rural India free from hunger, poverty and exploitation.

Further Readings

Bandyopadhyaya, J., *Social and Political Thought of Gandhi*, Calcutta: Allied Publishers, 1969.

Bhattacharyya, Buddhadeva, *Evolution of Political Thought of Gandhi*, Calcutta: Calcutta Book House, 1969.

Datta, D. M., *The Philosophy of Mahatma Gandhi*, Madison: University of Wisconsin Press, 1953.

Dhawan, Gopi Nath, *The Political Philosophy of Mahatma Gandhi*, Ahmedabad: Navjivan Publishing House, 1962.

Parekh, Bhikhu, *Colonialism, Tradition and Reform : An Analysis of Gandhi's Political Discourse*, New Delhi: Sage Publications, 1989.

Parel, Anthony J., *Gandhi, Freedom, and Self-Rule*, New Delhi: Vistaar Publications, 2000.

10

Swadeshi

Introduction

The acute poverty of the Indian masses during the British rule in India was caused by the destruction of its village industries. As early as 1909, Mahatma Gandhi gave vent to his feelings about 'the ancient and sacred handlooms' in *Hind Swaraj.* He advised the people to take up the spinning wheel, and asked the wealthy persons of the society to devote their money to its progress and development. He defined *swadeshi* as 'the spirit in us which restricts us to the use and service of our immediate surroundings to the exclusion of the more remote'.[1] He would apply this principle to religion, politics and everything else. *Swadeshi* is both a political and an economic agenda for providing immediate benefit to the people. It is the Gandhian programme of a decentralized economy, economic revival of villages and communities, mass employment and self-reliance. During India's freedom movement, *swadeshi* became an important form of resistance to the British colonial rule.

Swadeshi is a dynamic concept of Gandhian philosophy. It is a doctrine having both economic and political implications. Unfortunately, most of us think that the *swadeshi* spirit has no meaning at present. This is due to the misunderstanding of the concept of the term. *Swadeshi* means to serve the needs of the next door neighbour.

Concept of *Swadeshi*

The idea of *swadeshi* came into the Indian Freedom Movement well before Gandhi, in mid-19th century itself as a reaction to the ruination of artisan-based Indian industry and rural economy and the resultant poverty and famines under the British rule. However, *swadeshi* as a mass movement first arose in protest against the Bengal Partition, which remained in force from 1905 to 1911. Its scope included political resistance, setting up cottage and rural industries and Indian enterprises, boycott of imported goods, reviving national education, arts, science and literature, and giving up government jobs and social reforms. Sister Nivedita's message: 'Believe in your organic relatedness. Imagine a life in which all have common interests, common needs and mutual complementary duties' summed up that sprit of *swadeshi.*

After 1915, under the dynamic leadership of Gandhi, the concept of *swadeshi* acquired newer dimensions. Gandhi defined it as an ideology under which the first care one owes is to one's neighbours, the area of concern gradually growing in 'ever-widening never-ascending' circles till it covers the entire world.

Gandhi was the originator of the concept of *swadeshi*. According to him, the purpose of the Swadeshi Movement was to foster the manufacture of useful articles in India through small-scale industries. He defined the concept of *swadeshi* in the following words: 'After much thinking I have arrived at a definition of *swadeshi* that, perhaps, best illustrates my meaning. *Swadeshi* is that spirit in us which restricts us to the use and service of our immediate surroundings to the exclusion of the more remote. Thus, as for religion, in order to satisfy the requirements of the definition, I must restrict myself to my ancestral religion. That is the use of my immediate religious surrounding. If I find it defective, I should serve it by purging it of its defects. In the domain of politics, I should make use of the indigenous institutions and serve them by curing them of their proved defects. In that of economics, I should use only things that are produced by my immediate neighbours and serve those industries by making them efficient and complete where they might be found wanting.'[2]

Swadeshi provides an ethical direction to economic choices and under it sharing and self-provisioning become the basis of a humane and egalitarian social order. It engenders brotherhood and cooperation. In the meeting of village workers at Nagpur on February 23, 1935 Gandhi said that 'if you love your neighbour as thyself, he will do likewise with you'. Further, Gandhi rightly said, '*Swadeshi* is the only doctrine consistent with the law of humanity and love.'[3] In fact, the concept of *swadeshi* involving love and service of motherland is not different in essence from that of our obligation to serve mankind, since our capacity to serve is conditioned by our knowledge of the world in which we live. It means that we can do our best only to those who are immediately known to us and our neighbours and countrymen must be the first to receive our service. This, in fact, is nothing but humanism or love of mankind. However, it should not be read in between lines as it would communicate the idea of narrow nationalism.[4]

Purity of service is the very essence of *swadeshi*. Gandhi regards *swadeshi* as 'the acme of universal service[5].' According to him, our capacity for service is limited by our knowledge of the world in which we live. Hence, we must dedicate ourselves to the service of our immediate neighbours—the nearest and the best known to us.[6]He further adds, 'he is guilty of culpable neglect of his neighbour who has a claim on his service. His attempt would also be an unintended disservice to the people of distant places for, in his ignorance, he would very likely disturb the atmosphere of new place.'[7] In fact, it is arrogant to think of serving the distant places when one is hardly able to serve even his immediate neighbor.[8] *Swadeshi* recognizes 'the scientific limitations of human capability for service'.[9]

The broad definition of *swadeshi*, 'is the use of all homemade things to the exclusion of foreign things, insofar as such use is necessary for the protection of home industry, more especially those industries without which India will become pauperized'.[10] In his presidential address delivered at the first Gujarat Provincial Political Conference held at Godhra in October 1917, Gandhi complained that the people of India did not realize the fact that *swaraj* was almost wholly obtainable through *swadeshi*. 'If we have no regard for our respective vernaculars, if we dislike our clothes, if our dress repels us, if we are ashamed to wear the sacred *shikha*, if our food is distasteful to us, our climate is not good enough, our people uncouth and unfit for our company, our civilization faulty and the foreign alternative, in short, if everything native is bad and everything foreign pleasing to us, I should not know what *swaraj* can mean for us. If everything foreign is to be adopted, surely it will be necessary for us to continue long under foreign tutelage, because foreign civilization has not permeated the masses. It seems to me that before we can appreciate *swaraj* we should have not only love but passion for *swadeshi*... Every one of our acts should bear the *swadeshi* stamp. *Swaraj* can only be built upon the assumption that most of what is national is on the whole sound... Every country that has carried on the *swaraj* movement has fully appreciated the *swadeshi* spirit. The Scot Highlanders hold on to their kilts even at the risk of their lives. We humorously call the Highlanders the petticoat brigade. But the whole world testifies to the strength that lies behind that petticoat, and the Highlanders of Scotland will not abandon it even though it is an inconvenient dress and an easy target for the enemy. The object in developing the foregoing argument is not that we should treasure our faults, but that what is national, even though comparatively less agreeable, should be adhered to, and that what is foreign should be avoided, though it may be more agreeable than our own. That which is wanting in our civilization can be supplied by proper effort on our part. I do hope that the *swadeshi* spirit will possess every member in this assembly, and we would carry out the *swadeshi* vow in spite of great difficulties and inconvenience. Then *swaraj* will be easy for attainment.'[11]

Swadeshi and Cottage Industries

Gandhi had selected propagation of khadi on sound economic considerations as no other alternative could give productive part- time work to the idle rural masses. Now, obviously, the principal of *swadeshi* must operate on today's economic realities. Under *swadeshi*, a consumer tends to limit his wants as he depends largely on local produce. *Swadeshi* helps in improving the range and quality of local goods and the costs go down due to the use of indigenous skills, resources, manpower and technology, and lesser need for marketing, transport and storage.

Gandhi desired a speedy development of cottage industries concurrently with the establishment of the bigger ones. He was convinced that true *swadeshi* exists in encouraging and reviving home industries, and handicrafts which alone can help the villages of India. He said, 'Without cottage industries India can never prosper or give jobs to all the people.

Spinning is the easiest, cheapest and the best of these industries. It will make us self-reliant, and if people use khadi instead of mill cloth, sixty crores of rupees will be saved every year. Above all, there will be a change in the outlook of the people. *Swaraj* can come only through *swadeshi*.'

Gandhi fully agreed with the philosophy of the *Gita*. The *Gita* says: 'It is better to die performing one's duty or *swadharma*, but *paradharma*, or another's duty, is fraught with danger'. Interpreted in terms of one's physical environment, this gives us the law of *swadeshi*. What the *Gita* says with regard to *swadharma* equally applies to *swadeshi* also, for *swadeshi* is *swadharma* applied to one's immediate environment.[12]

Gandhi contradicted the view that the *swadeshi* movement was harmful to foreign mill owner. In his words, '*Swadeshi* in its purest form is the acme of universal service... Let no one suppose that the practice of *swadeshi* through khadi would harm the foreign mill owners. A thief, who is weaned from his vice, is not harmed thereby. On the contrary, he is the gainer, consciously in the one case, unconsciously in the other.'[13] He also held that, 'It is the greatest delusion to suppose that the duty of the *swadeshi* begins and ends with merely spinning some yarn anyhow and wearing khadi made from it. Khadi is the first indispensable step ...A votary of *swadeshi* will carefully study his environment and try to help his neighbours wherever possible, by giving preference to local manufactures, even if they are of an inferior grade or dearer in price than things manufactured elsewhere.'[14]

Gandhi's clarification in this context is very relevant. He said, '*Swadeshi* is not a cult of hatred. It is a doctrine of self-less service that has its roots in the purest *ahimsa*, that is love.'[15] Further he adds, 'my nationalism is as broad as my *swadeshi*. I want India's rise so that the whole world may benefit,'[16] He detested narrowness, selfishness and exclusiveness. It is important to note that he considered nationalism as a step towards internationalism.

Swadeshi does not mean boycott of all things foreign. It only means 'the use of local resources to the extent practicable for the protection of home industry, more especially those industries without which India will become pauperized'.[17] But wasteful efforts to make in one's own area items for which it is not suited would be a 'negation of the *swadeshi* sprit.'[18]

Swadeshi and Globalization

Swadeshi is not a chauvinistic or exclusive concept of self- sufficiency but one of decentralized and need-based economics and full employment through production by masses. It harmonizes the individual and social concerns. *Swadeshi* provides an alternative and solution in the present era of globalization. *Swadeshi* means self-reliance in every field. In other words, *swadeshi* is service and if we understand it, we will simultaneously benefit ourselves, our families, our country and the world. Gandhi delimited the modus operandi of *swadeshi* in terms of limited wants and the capacity of social surroundings and resources to meet the need of the people. In his famous sentence, Gandhi laid down his dictum: 'Nature produces enough to meet the needs of all the people but not enough to satisfy the greed of anyone.'[19] Our motto in present situation should be simple living and high thinking so that we can stop the evils of the society. In fact, the Swadeshi movement may become part of renaissance in the present situation, because it conveys the idea of returning to one's own country—to its culture, heritage and tradition and screen the mud of the next door neighbour. This is an appropriate time for us to understand the concept of *swadeshi* and implement it in every possible manner. We will be ensuring this progress by making ourselves self-reliant and self-suffocate in every field and we would be free from moral degradation, economic exploitation and political subjugation.

Swadeshi is not opposed to a rational and need-based trade among nations. But, 'what is equality of rights between a giant and a dwarf?' Before one can think of equality between unequals, the dwarf must be raised to the height of the giant. The conventional economic theory of international trade is based on 'comparative advantage'. It is preoccupied with reciprocal demands and profit maximization rather than mutual need, cooperation, employment and equitable distribution of gains. It means free trade among rank unequals and in the interest of those having purchasing power for unending wants and luxuries. International free trade would, as foreseen by Gandhi, mean exploitation of weaker economics by the stronger and of the rural poor by urban elites. Gandhian doctrine of international trade would pursue non-exploitation and fulfillment of mutual needs and protect the poor in developing countries from any adverse terms of trade. It would be guided by the ethics of 'unto this last' through trade.

Gandhi set the tone of globalization as early as in *Young India* on June 1, 1921, when he said that 'I do not want my house to be walled in an all sides and my window to be stuffed. I want the cultures of all lands to be blown about my house as freely as possible. But I refuse to be blown off my feet.' This must not be misunderstood while analyzing the concept of globalization.

Globalization is not something new but the present era has some distinctive features such as shrinking space, shrinking time and disappearing borders that are linking people's lives more deeply, more intensively and more immediately than ever before. Globalization is a process integrating not just the economy but culture, technology and governance. Globalization is considered to be neo-liberal. Its normative base is the celebration of the market. In other words, it is a triumph, not only over so-called global 'historic alternatives' [F. Fukuyama (92) *The End of History and the Last Man*] but also over unions and Keynesian states.

Globalization has become the current mantra or even panacea to solve all human problems. It is believed that the achievements of globalization would make the people all over the globe happy, prosperous and contended and that there would be no conflicts, no poverty and inequality, no violation of human rights, no malnutrition, no illiteracy, and no disease. Each individual and community would be so integrated with the world that the benefits would flow both laterally and vertically so smoothly that no one would remain untouched by prosperity. There would be nation states without boundary. It is said that global markets, global technologies, global ideas and global solidarity can enrich the lives of people everywhere, greatly expanding their choices. The growing interdependence of people's lives calls for shared values and a shared commitment to the human development of all people.

This era of globalization is opening many opportunities for millions of people around the world. Increased trade, new technologies, foreign investments, expanding media and internet connections are fuelling economic growth and human advance. All these opportunities offer enormous potential to eradicate poverty in the present century. Today, we have more wealth and technology—and more commitment to a global community—than ever before.

In the present scenario, globalization is irreversible and unstoppable. Most of the countries of the world, willingly or unwillingly, have already accepted it and others may have to acknowledge it. However, it is mostly agreed that globalization should be introduced with a human face for the benefit of the poor and the needy.

Summing Up

In fact, *swadeshi* movement was a part of the renaissance in India. It conveys the idea of returning to one's own country, to its culture and heritage, its own genius and tradition. Thus, *swadeshi* is like a swing of the pendulum motivated by the new kind of patriotism. In its economic sense, it means economic self-reliance, economic independence, and reconstruction of the rural economy by laying the foundation of a new approach to Indian economy and organizing them to fight the evils of poverty and economic backwardness.

This is the appropriate time for us to understand the concept of *swadeshi* and implement it in every possible manner and we will be marching ahead on the road to progress by making ourselves self-reliant and self-sufficient in every field.

Notes and References

1. Tendulkar, D. G., *Mahatma*: The Life of M. K. Gandhi, Delhi, Ministry of Information and Broadcasting, 1961, Vol. I, p. 226.
2. *Speeches and Writings of Mahatma Gandhi*, p. 336.
3. Prabhu, R. K and U. R. Rao, *The Mind of Mahatma Gandhi*, Ahmedabad: Navjivan, Publishing House, 1968.
4. Rolland, Romain, *Mahatma Gandhi*, London: George Allen and Unwin, 1930, p. 110.
5. Gandhi, M. K., *Yerawada Mandir*, Ahmedabad: Navjivan Publishing House, 1933, p. 93.
6. *Harijan*, 22.8.1936.
7. Gandhi, M. K., *Yerawada Mandir*, pp. 89–91.
8. *Speeches and Writings of Mahatma Gandhi*, p. 281.
9. *Harijan*, 23.3.1947, p. 79.
10. *Young India*, 17.2.1926, p. 218.
11. Gandhi, M. K., *Economics of Khadi*, Ahmedabad: Navjivan Publishing House, 1941, pp. 12–13.
12. Gandhi, M. K., *Yerawada Mandir*, p. 91.
13. Gandhi, M. K., op. cit., pp. 93–94.
14. Ibid., pp. 95–96.

15. *Mind of Mahatma Gandhi*, p. 415.
16. *The Collected Works of Mahatma Gandhi*, Vol. 26, Publication Division, Delhi, p. 279.
17. *Young India*, June 17, 1926.
18. *Young India*, June 18, 1931.
19. Mishra, Anil Dutta and Rani Gupta, *Inspiring Thought of Mahatma Gandhi (Gandhi in Daily Life)*, Delhi, Concept Publishing Company, 2008.

Summary

- *Swadeshi* is both a political and an economic agenda for providing immediate benefit to the people. It is the Gandhian programme of decentralized economy, economic revival of villages and communities, mass employment and self-reliance.
- *Swadeshi* is a dynamic concept of Gandhian philosophy. It is a doctrine having both economic and political implications. *Swadeshi* means to serve the needs of the next-door neighbour.
- *Swadeshi* provides an ethical direction to economic choices and under it, sharing and self-provisioning become the basis of a humane and egalitarian social order. It engenders brotherhood and cooperation.
- The broad definition of *swadeshi*, 'is the use of all homemade things to the exclusion of foreign things, in so far as such use is necessary for the protection of home industry, more especially those industries without which India will become pauperized.'
- *Swadeshi* helps in improving the range and quality of local goods and prices go down as a result of the use of indigenous skills, resources, manpower and technology, and lesser need for marketing, transport and storage.
- True *swadeshi* exists in encouraging and reviving home industries, and handicrafts which alone can help the villages of India.
- *Swadeshi* in its purest form is the acme of universal service.
- *Swadeshi* is not a cult of hatred. It is a doctrine of self-less service that has its roots in purest *ahimsa*, that is, love.
- *Swadeshi* does not mean boycott of all things foreign. It only means the use of local resources to the extent practicable 'for the protection of native industries, especially those industries without which India will become pauperized'.
- *Swadeshi* is not a chauvinistic or exclusive concept of self-sufficiency but one of decentralized and need-based economics and full employment through mass production. It harmonizes the individual and social concerns. *Swadeshi* provides an alternative and solution in the present era of globalization. *Swadeshi* means self-reliance in every field.
- *Swadeshi* is not opposed to a rational and need-based trade among nations.

Further Readings

Bandyopadhyaya, J., *Social and Political Thought of Gandhi*, Calcutta: Allied Publishers, 1969.

Bhattacharyya, Buddhadeva, *Evolution of Political Thought of Gandhi*, Calcutta: Calcutta Book House, 1969.

Chatterjee, Partha, *Nationalist Thought and the Colonial World,* New Delhi: Oxford University Press, 1986.

Dhawan, Gopi Nath, *The Political Philosophy of Mahatma Gandhi*, Ahmedabad: Navjivan Publishing House, 1962.

Mishra, Anil Dutta, *Understanding Mahatma Gandhi: Speeches and Writings that Reveal his Mind Methods and Mission*, New Delhi: Concept, 2012.

Parekh, Bhikhu, *Colonialism, Tradition and Reform: An Analysis of Gandhi's Political Discourse*, New Delhi: Sage Publications, 1989.

11

Non-violence

Introduction

Non-violence is not a new concept; it is as old as the hills and Indian civilization. Gandhi used non-violence very beautifully in practical, day to day life and demonstrated its power and utility in socio-economic transformation as well as political liberation of mankind. For Gandhi, it was indeed a critical stage when humanity had to decide and distinguish between truth and untruth, good and bad, love and hate, violence and non-violence. It was an opportunity for Gandhi to turn a new leaf in the history of mankind. And to that end, Gandhi accepted the challenge of the situation, and put forward the age-old principle of non-violence as a good worth trying for. He was then trying to pull back non-violence on earth and place it among his fellow beings to be accepted and practised.

Gandhi's greatness as a leader and thinker lay in his transformation of the individualistic message of non-violence into a success technique for direct mass action. Mahavira, Buddha, Nagesena and Santideva have conceived of *ahimsa* as a tenet of personal action and motivation. But Gandhi transformed it into a social and political technique. He, thus, attempted to apply the theory of *ahimsa* enunciated by the ancient Indian teachers and prophets on a social and political plane. The supreme concept, according to him, which is necessary for the reformation of politics, is non-violence.

Concept of Non-violence

Non-violence is not a cloistered virtue to be practised by the individuals for peace or final salvation, but it is a rule of conduct for the society if it is to live consistently with human dignity and progress towards the attainment of peace it has been yearning for ages past. Gandhi's concept of non-violence was not a superimposition upon his ethico-political outlook of society. He did not add it simply to serve as a mere political expedient in the national struggle. Non-violence is the basic premise of Gandhi's thought and is very comprehensive in its nature and scope. It is concerned not merely with the overt actions of people but also with their characters. It has cultural connotation in the sense that one of its aim is to cultivate the inner springs of human behaviour pattern.

Ahimsa is not merely the negative act of refraining from doing offence, injury and harm to others but represents the ancient law of positive self-sacrifice and constructive suffering. Gandhi interpreted it as signifying utter selflessness and universal love. The ultimate aim of *ahimsa* is even to love the so-called enemies or opponents. In 1930, Gandhi said that he would suck the poison out of a dying enemy of his if he was a victim of snake-bite. '*Ahimsa,* thus, is equivalent to positive compassion and love.' It even implies the cultivation of gladness and felicity involved in suffering for others. *Ahimsa* is implicitly latent in all human beings because all are sharers in the divine spiritual reality and its culmination is the negation of self-subsistence, particularity and a realization of the feeling of love and substantive unity with the whole of creation. It is the substitution of arrogance, antagonism and alienation by love. Hence, Gandhi wrote in his Autobiography, 'I must reduce myself to zero. *Ahimsa* is the farthest limit of humility.' The supreme vocation or man is the purposive evolution, of *ahimsa* as universal positive love. *Ahimsa,* as conceived by Gandhi, is a profound social import. Aristotle said that friendship is the cohesive bond of communities. Gandhi also pleaded for brotherly ethics and believed that *ahimsa* has almost an obligatory and compelling power to bring peace and unity to the world.

Gandhi also interpreted human history in terms of the slow evolution of *ahimsa.* Like some Western anthropologists, he said 'our remote ancestors were cannibals.' That was succeeded by stage of chase—the life of wandering hunters. The third stage was of agriculture which marked the growth of civilized stable life. Man 'founded villages and towns, and from member of a family he became member of a community and a nation. All these are signs of progressive *ahimsa* and diminishing *himsa.* Had it been otherwise, the human species should have been extinct by now, even as many of the lower species have disappeared.'

It may appear surprising to several students of Gandhism to find him speaking here as an adherent of the school of evolutionary anthropology rather than one deriving his theory of social origins from the *Purusha Sukta* or the Puranas. He regarded the process of human evolution as a vindication of the superiority of *ahimsa as love.* 'It is my firm faith that man is by nature going higher,' he wrote. The social application of *ahimsa,* according to Gandhi, is upon the acceptance of spiritual metaphysics and the necessity of the growth of social charity. He laid stress on the fact that the universe is permeated with a divine spirit and all life is sacred. *Ahimsa* is vitally integrated with truth or god. All men, according to Gandhi, are children of god. Hence, to slight a single being is really to inflict injury upon the divine spirit in man and, thus, it amounts to an injury upon the whole world. 'The Bible rightly taught that vengeance belonged to God.'

The tyrannical group leaders and governments that are the repositories of violence are proved to be in the wrong. Non-violence is only the replacement of retaliation and is no surrender to wickedness. But resistance does not imply hatred for the adversary. Gandhi held the view that it is possible and advisable to resist a perverse system but 'to resist and attack its author is tantamount to resisting and attacking oneself'. Hence, *ahimsa* is the attitude of harmlessness even to the wrong-doer. Gandhi went a step further and said that it implied positive love even to the wrong-doer. But this does not mean rendering any help to the wrong-doer in the prolongation of his wrong.

The spiritual overtones in Gandhian non-violence—exceedingly though it is when non-violence is practiced primarily spiritual ends and only secondarily for the achievement of the secular goal of social change—nevertheless led to certain inner compulsions which have reduced its acceptability to modern societies. This is unfortunate, for the importance of the Gandhian orientation lies precisely in the successful manner in which he showed how the heavenly Ganga of non-violence can be brought down to earth and tamed for worldly ends. Among these inner compulsions, probably the most serious was the need he felt (no doubt genuinely) to make sweeping generalizations about non-violence and, in the process, to ignore the essentially finite nature of all human instruments.

Violence is a comprehensive category and is manifested both at the personal and the institutional levels. Evil thoughts, sentiments of revenge and brutality, verbal pugnacity, and even accumulation of unnecessary things represent examples of personal violence. Falsehood, trickery, intrigues, chicanery and deceitfulness are also forms of violence, according to the comprehensive connotation given to the term by Gandhi. Physical punishments, imprisonment, capital punishment and wars represent examples of violence committed by government. Economic exploitation and strangulation of others are also manifestations of violence. Even excess of emulation and competition can become species of violence. Non-violence or *ahimsa* is, hence, necessarily, equally comprehensive and represents the total neutralization of violence in all forms.

The practice of *ahimsa* requires faith in the reality and compassion of God and deep self introspection. 'The votary of non-violence has to cultivate the acquisition of freedom from envy, hatred, malice, lust, cupidity and uncharitableness.' This leads to the acceptance of an elevated standard of virtues. The code of vows or *vrata* has to be followed by the non-violent *satyagrahi* and has to become the standard for cultivation by others. The acceptance of the norms of non-violence would thus almost amount to a moral transvaluation of values. The law of love, if courageously practiced, is bound to lead to the elevation of the accent, quality and character of politics and civilization.

As a Vedantist and a Vaishnavite, Gandhi regarded all life as sacred and precious. Hence, he had deep faith in the sanctity of the right to life. He would not kill even a snake. He said: 'God alone can take life, because He gives it.' The believer in *ahimsa* would regard even the lives of the opponents as worthy of reverence. In an article in the *Harijan,* Gandhi wrote: 'You are no *satyagrahi* if you remain silent or passive spectators while your enemy is being done to death. You must protect him even at the cost of your life.' He accepted the supremacy of the right to life merely because man as an individual is not just the subject of social and political rights but because in his inmost essence man is a soul. Hence, like Tolstoy, Gandhi accepted the immutability and obligatory character of the law of love. For himself, he regarded the law of *ahimsa* as absolute, although he had acquired it after a long struggle. He considered it an infallible weapon, mightier than the force of arms, and believed in it as a categorical imperative.

Non-violence is not merely non-killing or non-injury, but is an attitude of mind that recognizes the unity and dignity of human life. Non-violence, ultimately, is humanism. This conception of non-violence was based upon the corresponding integral view that Gandhi took of violence. He recognized that overt violence was the consequence of deep-seated social imbalances and implicit violence. Non-violence, then, implied equal opportunity for all, weak and strong, for participation in a truly human society.

Gandhi's view of human nature is fundamentally different from the Hobbes. Gandhi was peace loving. By nature, man is good, whereas, Hobbes' man is by nature quarrelsome, nasty, greedy and what not. For Gandhi, moral perfection of man is the prime and ultimate concern; one has to go beyond the common ideas about non-violence to assess its true meaning and place in Gandhi's thought. In his book *An Autobiography* or *The Story of My Experiments with Truth*, Gandhi declared that a brute by nature knows no self-restraint, and man is man because he is capable of and only in so far as he exercises self-restraint. Gandhi wrote 'Non-violence is the law of our species as violence is the law of brute. The spirit lies dormant in the brute and he knows no law but that of physical might. The dignity of man requires obedience to a higher law, to the strength of the spirit'.[1] The essential difference between man and brute is that the former can respond to the call of the spirit in him, can rise superior to the passions he has in common with the brute, and, therefore, superior to selfishness and violence, which belongs to the brute nature and not the immortal spirit of man. The *Bhagvad Gita* says 'He who controls the organs of sense and action by the mind, and remaining unattached undertakes the yoga of action through these organs, he excels.'[2] The moral perfection of man, which is instrumental in drawing him away from purely brute instincts, is the dominant motive of Gandhian thought and of his concept of non-violence as well.

T. K. Mahadevan rightly points out 'when Gandhi spoke of non-violence, he spoke of it in tandem with truth and not as a separate entity. In fact, Gandhi spoke of truth and non-violence, as a two-legged concept.'[3] Gandhi, being the 'practical idealist' that he was, always spoke of truth and non-violence, never of non-violence alone. Within the meaning of his 'practical idealism', the practice of non-violence became, in other words, an exercise in the art of the possible.

Non-violence and truth were one interpenetrated whole—a mosaic in which each patch of colour lent meaning to the other. Gandhi never spoke of non-violence in the abstract but only as it related to some concrete situation. Of course, like all human beings, he did at times, especially in his later years, indulge in the luxury of generalizing from particular events. But, as a rule, his awareness of reality, painfully acute at all times, tended to over-master the natural human gravitation towards romanticism.

Gandhi said, 'As I proceed in my quest for truth, it grows upon me that truth comprehends everything. I often feel that *ahimsa* is in truth and not vice versa. Out of truth emerges love and tenderness.' Gandhi's idea of truth is much akin to the traditional Hindu view. Hinduism is a relentless pursuit after truth. Gandhi's own pursuit, as that of Hinduism, was for truth, which was also simultaneously the existential truth of the moment. Yet it was the realization of wholeness, the truth, which gave any meaning and sanction to the latter. In Hindu tradition, *dharma* or moral duty is associated with and sanctioned by this wholeness, which is conveniently put under the word god. Since the realization of truth, or absolute reality, or god, is an inner experience at the most, Gandhi's concept of truth and non-violence are primarily inner experiences. 'Truth, in Gandhi's sense, points to the next stop in man's realization of man as one human species, and thus to our only chance to transcend whatever we are.' From Gandhi himself the most revealing statement, I believe, on truth came in a letter to an atheist friend. 'Truth means existence of that we know and that we do not know. The sum total of all existence is absolute truth... that truth I call God. Thus, existence, of life on earth is truth. And whatever upholds the same and perpetuates it is the existential truth of the moment. Existential truth may or may not be, though it ought to be, truthfulness or veracity. The distinguishing criterion would be its association with the truth, which is existence. Hence, truth is that which relegates the forces of destruction and chaos to the background, and untruth that which will help the same. Destruction implied in untruth is not a total and immediate set, but the inevitable consequence to destructive tendencies. Whatever is destructive of the principle of life and creation that is untruth? Truth then is a comprehensive principle that upholds life and existence, known and unknown. In that sense, it is a dynamic concept. Truth of the moment has to be defined then and there. *Dharma* or moral duty is identified with truth in Hindu scriptures, and no clearer definition of *dharma* may be found than in *Mahabharata*, where Vyas writes 'It is to serve the ends of human advancement that the concept of *dharma* has been enunciated.

From the Gandhian perspective, absolute truth implies the entire existence that transcends this earth. This total existence, of what we call universe, is incomprehensible and something that fails our perception. It is associated with god, a convenient word for complete obscurity. God is the word for 'unfathomable multiformity' that surrounds the earth. Absolute truth comprehends the existence on earth and transcends it. Truth, as men see it, is only a realization of subsidiary levels of existence. For men, truth is defined by their own existence as a fact. Yet at this level too, man cannot easily comprehend, the fact of his existence in the perspective of total human existence on earth. He does begin by forming his own conception of existence around him and derives from it guidelines of his own behaviour, defining truth for himself. Various factors influence him in that conception. But in the realization of truth what is more important is that the moment he employs his distinguishing quality, that is, mind, to determine truth for himself, he draws away from untruth. Absolute truth, truth and faith in truth form—in that order—the successive stages of an inner realization of the entire existence. A true faith is thus the first step, the partial realization of truth.

Non-violence is the means and truth the end. Absolute non-violence would coincide with absolute truth. Only a relative non-violence is a means to truth as seen by man. Absolute non-violence—like absolute truth—cannot be realized by man. Gandhi then, was striving for relative truth and non-violence. Apart from this necessity of non-violence in the initial faiths in truth, there is another important implication in truth and non-violence. Truth in action is non-violence, *ahimsa*. This would be clear from the very definition of truth. Since truth is existence and all that promotes and preserves existence, violence can only be untruth. Violence, which implies force and injury, is violence for all times and places, since it is destructive of existence and creation. A man indulging in violence would be drawing away from truth back to the realm of his brute nature. A man cannot know what upholds human existence by indulging in destruction. Getting away from destruction is truth. Thus, non-violence itself is one aspect of truth and a means to higher truth. 'A man cannot reach truth by untruthfulness.'

Gandhi did not offer any simplistic definition of non-violence. He was the first person who used non-violence as a means of change and liberation. Gandhi himself used the terms inter-changeably, non-violence being his own translation into English of the Hindu concept of *ahimsa.* Having clarified its liberal meaning, we shall retain the term non-violence. Non-violence then, has two aspects: not to do harm to any living thing; and to give proof of the most distinguished love towards every living creature.[4] Non-violence to Gandhi could not be just mere non-killing or a happy renunciation of all fight. Rather, a fighting spirit and indomitable courage is the essence of it, and so-called violence often the truest form of non-violence. Gandhi wrote, 'I accept that interpretation of *ahimsa*, namely, that it is not merely a negative state of harmlessness, but a positive state of love of doing good even to the evil door. But, it does not mean helping the evil doer to continue doing wrong or tolerating it by passive acquiescence. On the contrary love, the active state of *ahimsa*, requires you to dissociate yourself from the evil doer even though it may offend him or injure him physically'.[5] So, when good is pitted against evil, physical injury to him who personifies either has to be taken in the stride, though it is essential that a fighter for good must stick to it and not stray into evil. On the question of injury, Gandhi was more explicit elsewhere 'Each time I inflict injury on a life under whatever form it may be, I must carefully examine if this action is inevitable or not. In any action, I should never go beyond the indispensable even for matters indifferent in appearance. To confuse non-violence with physical impotence or passive acquiescence would be nothing short of a complete caricature of the concept. It is farther away from cowardice than violence is in terms of manliness.' As Gandhi said, 'My creed of non-violence is an extremely active force. It has no room for cowardice or even for weakness. There is hope for a violent man to be some day non-violent, but non for a coward. If we do not know how to defend ourselves, our women and our places of worship by the force of suffering, that is, non-violence we must, if we are men, be at least able to defend all these by fighting.' Further Gandhi wrote, 'Non-violence—peacefulness—does not mean cowardice; it means the spirit of manliness in its perfection. Non-violence does not mean submission to others, does not mean weakness. He alone can forgive who is brave.' Non-violence pre-supposes the ability to strike. It is a conscious deliberate restraint put upon one's desire of vengeance. But vengeance is any way superior to passive effeminate and helpless submission. Forgiveness is higher still. Therefore, non-violence is, in its active form, goodwill towards all life, a positive virtue. 'Non-violence is complete innocence. Complete non-violence is complete absence of ill-will against all that lives. It is pure love.' Non-violence does not ask one to abstain from force at all times; rather, it tells us that our spirit must be pure. Complete non-violence is complete abstention from ill-will towards any creature in this world. It implies control of passions and appetites.

Characteristics of Non-violence

Gandhi gave a new dimension and interpretation to non-violence. The fundamental characteristics of Gandhi's concept of non-violence are as follows:

Firstly, non-violence is primarily an inner realization.

Secondly, non-violence is inter-penetrated with truth. The pursuit of truth gives a man the humility to accept the need for non-violence in his relationship with fellow beings who are also truth seekers in their own ways. Thus, non-violence pre-supposes a search for truth. Unless a man has faith in truth, he cannot appreciate the value of non-violence in his behaviour.

Thirdly, non-violence is not an alternative to violence or conflict. An acceptance of the principle of non-violence does not imply a total rout for overt violence. The more important aspect of this principle is that it defines what is good, and thus, desirable. Non-violence is important because it stigmatizes violence. K. M. Munshi has observed, 'Non-violence is absolute in principle; but on occasions, as the one which presented itself to Arjun in the *Bhagvad Gita*, it has to be a mental attitude, not an absolute refusal to resist violence by violent methods'.

And fourthly, non-violence is not a negative concept, since violence is that which is destructive of life and creation, non-violence is that which upholds the same. It is positive benevolence towards all life. Thus, the meaning of non-violence should not be narrowed down in terms of violence. Non-violence is not zero violence.

As Gandhi said, 'the only means for the realization of truth is *ahimsa*.'[6] Non-violence is the law of our species as violence is the law of the brute,'[7] as otherwise human society would not have survived. Only non-violence can resist violence, otherwise superior violence will prevail. Non-violence also means the capacity to suffer and sacrifice. It means fearlessness and forbearance. Non-violence is 'not a weapon of the weak. It is a weapon of the strongest and the bravest'.[8] But, 'where there is only a choice between cowardice and non-violence', Gandhi would advice violence.[9] That a weak man can hardly have the opportunity to preach non-violence, much less to practice it, is thus clear enough from the evidence of Gandhi's individual experience. Gandhi was a perfect devotee of civility and humility, but he explicitly, unconditionally and categorically stated that if the only actives were cowardice and violence he would choose the latter. He was not tired of repeating that fear or cowardice should have no place in the national dictionary. He wrote: 'The truth is that cowardice itself is violence of a subtle and, therefore, dangerous type, and far more difficult to eradicate than the habit of physical violence. A coward never risks his life. A man who would kill often risks it. A non-violent person's life is always at the disposal of him who would take it.'

Non-violence, hence, is to be regarded as the summit of bravery. Gandhi pointed out that he could no more preach non-violence to a cowardly man than he could tempt a blind man to enjoy healthy scenes. He insisted on the development of that moral courage and strength which proceeds from an indomitable will. He said in Noakhali on November

27, 1946: 'The only real guarantee is to be sought in the personal courage of individuals. Everything else depends on it.'[11] The operation of *ahimsa* is the exercise of soul-force and it is a gospel of strength, according to Gandhi. It proceeds from moral and spiritual strength. It is the strongest force known and it is a force of the subtlest kind. It is a demonstration of the resolute strength of the heroic soul which refuses to hurt any body because every living creature is essentially a spirit and fundamentally one with himself. *Ahimsa* is farthest removed from a false masquerade for one's weakness.

Non-violence: An Analysis

Gandhi wanted India to follow the doctrine of non-violence but not because she was prostrate due to political subjection. He affirmed that India had an imperishable 'soul' which could rise above all weaknesses. But after independence, nevertheless, Gandhi, a little pessimistically and with some amount of mortification, said that India had adopted only the non-violence of the weak because once the British power was out of the picture, the people engaged in unrestrained and intensely violent slaughter and internecine struggles. He confessed, 'I have to hang down my head in shame.' Gandhi wrote: 'I have already said that the non-violence that was offered during the past thirty years was that of the weak ... India has no experience of the non-violence of the strong.'[13] He stuck, however, to his faith in the moralization and spiritualization of politics and remained thoroughly devoted to the principle that increasing adherence to *ahimsa* alone would emancipate mankind from all kinds of conflict and evil.

Gandhi applied non-violence into the field of politics and pathways to liberation of India. In his attempt to make politics non-violent and non-violence practical, Gandhi based himself upon a path of Karmayoga or spiritual realization through social action. Gandhi treated spiritual realization as part of life and dedicated his life to the propagation of non-violence. While discussing his beliefs with a group of missionaries in 1938 he said, 'I could not be leading a religious life unless I identified myself with the whole of mankind and that I could not do so unless I took part in politics. The whole gamut of man's activities today constitutes an indivisible whole... I do not know of any religion apart from activity.'

Gandhi's approach to politics was the turning point of his thought into action. It is also the turning point in the sense that his contribution to the concept of non-violence began here. In a correspondence with Satyanand Babu, Gandhi wrote that whereas it was not very important to trace the origin of the concept of non-violence, its use on the political platform could be said to have begun with him. While Gandhi's realization of the concept of non-violence, in all its effulgence, was in itself a remarkable achievement, his signal contribution to India, and mankind at large was his serious attempt to inject the ideal into the mundane affairs of human society. He visualized the dream of non-violent revolution and converted this dream into reality.

Gandhi, who had himself subjectively realized the utility of non-violence to mankind, would admit to no failings in the principle. The principle of non-violence was absolute and good, he firmly believed. He wrote 'it is much better for me to say I have not sufficient non-violence in me rather than admit exceptions to an eternal principle. Moreover, my refusal to admit exceptions spurs me to perfect myself in the technique of non-violence.' Thus, fully conscious of his limitations, Gandhi went ahead with his attempt to make non-violence practical and, thus, intelligible to the masses.

Coming back to the policy of non-violence that Gandhi sought to put forward before the people, as distinguished from his own creed of non-violence, he did not leave his position ambiguous. Gandhi explained the difference between creed and policy, 'I have not put before India the final form of non-violence. The non-violence that I have preached from the Congress platform is non-violence as a policy. As a policy it means that it can upon due notice be given up when it proves unsuccessful or ineffective. But simple morality demands that when a particular policy is pursued, it must be pursued with all one's heart'.[10] Further, he wrote 'Non-violence may succeed, even if it is adopted as a matter of policy rather than a creed, if it is combined with courage and real love for the country or the cause.' Realizing that he was preaching non-violence to weak and helpless people, Gandhi was under no illusions about the results he might expect. But he was confident that success of non-violence as a policy would establish people's faith in its efficacy in human relationships, and hence serve as a stepping stone to its final acceptance as a creed. Gandhi rightly said, 'I am not preaching the final law through the Congress or the Khilafat Organization. I know my own limitations only too well. I know that any such attempt is foredoomed to failure. To expect a whole mass of men and women to obey that law all at once is not to know its working. But I do preach from Congress platform deductions of that law. Given true workers, the limited measure of its application can be realized in respect of the vast masses of people within a short time.' He further said, 'being a practical man, I do not wait till India recognizes the practicability of spiritual life in political world… She takes up non co-operation out of her weakness. It must still serve the same purpose; namely, bring her delivery from the crushing weight of British injustice, if a sufficient number of people practise it.' In a nutshell, non-violence as a technique of political action was thus evolved by Gandhi in response to the pressure of circumstances. And to him, this was a step in the direction of final inner realization of truth and non-violence by the general masses.

Gandhi himself wrote that 'means and ends are convertible terms in my philosophy of life.' As the means, so is the end. There is no wall of separation between means and ends.' Gandhi was more concerned about the simultaneous progress of practical non-violence, 'if non-violence has to fight people's violence in addition to the violence of the government, it must still perform its task at any cost.' He [Gandhi] declared that if the people who followed him did not fulfil the basic conditions, he himself would practise *satyagraha* against them. In general, however, the non-violent registers did not succumb to provocations and implicitly obeyed Gandhi's directions.

For Gandhi, in practical non-violence there was an umbilical relationship between constructive programme and non-violent direct action. In 1942, Gandhi wrote, 'if we wish to achieve *swaraj* through truth and non-violence, gradual but steady building up from the bottom upwards by constructive effort is the only way.'

For Gandhi, non-violence was not only a means of conflict resolution, but as a social value, denoting respect for the dignity of man. The economic system that Gandhi witnessed under the British was thoroughly gripped with violence, both overt and implicit; it subjected a vast majority to lead a life worse than death. 'There may be for more *himsa* (violence) in slow torture of man and animals, the starvation and exploitation to which they are subjected out of selfish greed, the wanton humiliation and oppression and the killing of their self-respect that we witness all around us today than in the more benevolent taking of life.' Thus, Gandhi argued that greed, exploitation and violence are linked in a chain of social causation in the capitalist system of economy.

Non-violence is humanism, it takes man as an end in itself and not as a means to an end that transcends him. With Gandhi, 'the supreme consideration is man'. He often used to say 'with me man comes first'. Also, 'My life is an indivisible whole, and all my activities run into one another and they all have their rise in my insatiable love for mankind.' His meeting with the peasants of Champaran, and the account he gave of it in his *Autobiography* is the best instance of whatever Gandhi and his non-violence stood for. I cannot help repeating his own words, 'it is no exaggeration but the literal truth to say that in this meeting with the peasants, I was face to face with god, *ahimsa*, and truth.' This represents the core of Gandhi's thought and work, the poor, half clad, innocent, calm and hopeful peasant was his God. Non-violence is a concept that would fulfil the hopes of such men and enrich humanity in true terms.

Non-violence of Gandhi is a revolt against de-humanization of man. He rejected as violent anything that denied the value of human personality, or sought to subjugate it and exploit it. As we have seen in his concepts of civilization, human nature and truth, Gandhi integrated humanism. A man dominated by the machine, by his fleeting desires and passions, or by the sheer complexity of his immediate surroundings was an anathema to him. In so far as this elemental and integral humanism is concerned, Gandhi was at one with Karl Marx in turning Hegel's cultural idealism upside down. Hegel sought to construct a complete philosophy, yet he saw the earthly world with its social systems as insignificant moments embedded in a sea of multiformity. Gandhi, like Marx, instead saw it as significant moments and attached great importance to them. He realized the unity between spirit and man, and yet gave primacy to man rather than the spirit. And that makes all the difference for his concept of non-violence. Addressing a prayer meeting at Sodepur on November 1, 1946, Gandhi said that 'any peace to be substantial must be honourable, never at the cost of honour'. He, therefore, pointed out that he could never agree to any settlement which amounted to the humiliation or loss of self-respect for any one.

Mass non-violent resistance, then, may not be regarded as an essential part of Gandhi's non-violence. It was more of a situational accretion to his concept. His willing acceptance of this method initially was influenced, if not dictated by the traditional conditional complex in which he lived and worked. It was a technique of political action that served its purpose of creating a mass upsurge quite well in the circumstances. Yet by itself, it could not help in the practicability of non-violence as such. So, when it had served its political purpose, non-violent resistance had to be replaced by constructive non-violence which is a pre condition to the reshaping of attitudes non-violently.

Constructive non-violence is indeed the essence of practical as well as conceptual non-violence. Overt non-violence cannot be its essence for where constructive non-violence has not been practised, nothing can prevent violence from erupting; where construction work is lacking, societal violence in its manifold manifestation is bound to emerge; and corruption in public life is one aspect of this violence. In late 1930s, which was perhaps the most significant period of Gandhi's practical non-violence, the Indian National Congress went through a rehearsal of what was to happen on much larger scale after independence. This is what happened and continues to happen to Gandhi's non-violence.

Gandhi preached the gospel of *ahimsa* both for the East and the West. But in their different situational contexts, *ahimsa* implied somewhat different things for them. For India, *ahimsa* as a social and political technique meant pooling together of the energies of the people for the work of national liberation. It implied the elimination of petty local jealousies and group, caste and communal discriminations and persecutions and notions of regional superiority. It also signified the notion of the realization of a national community based on suffering, tolerance, self-abnegation and the neutralizations of fissiparous trends. For the Western world, the Gandhian philosophy of *ahimsa* mainly appeared as a gospel of renunciation Machtpolitik. In 1947, Gandhi wrote that if Europe was to save itself from suicide something along the lines of non-violence had to be adopted. Non-violence applied to international politics, signified a spiritual substitute for struggle and war and the consequent repudiation of 'blood and iron' and 'the mailed fist'. It, thus, meant the negation of the cults of power, stratagems, exploitation, enslavement, economic imperialism and war. But it was to be only a moral substitute for war and not the tame acceptance of status quo. In the face of the advancements in nuclear energy, Gandhi, stood for the resort to techniques of love because he was deeply concerned with the survival of man.

Summing Up

Non-violence is not merely intellectual conviction but intuitive faith. It is way of life. Non-violence is not 'irrelevant', 'out-dated', or 'obscure and mystical'; rather, it is becoming more relevant in contemporary times. Essentially, Gandhi's non-violence is of people, by the people and for the people. This has been proved in case of the Arab world where the people have overthrown the despotic regimes in Egypt and other countries. In fact, non-violence is the correct path in all situations, and lack of success could never be blamed on non-violence but only on the insufficient or inadequate use of it.

One thing is certain: either Gandhi's spirit will triumph, or it will manifest itself again, as was manifested, centuries before, by the Messiah and Buddha, till there finally is manifested, in a mortal half god, the perfect incarnation of the principle of life that will lead a new humanity on to a new path.

Notes and References

1. *Young India*, August 11, 1920.
2. The *Bhagvad Gita*: 3:7.
3. Mahadevan, T. K. 'An Approach to the Study of Gandhi' *Gandhi Marg*, New Delhi, No. 49, p. 31.
4. Gandhi, M. K., *From Yeravada Mandir*, Ahmedabad: Navjivan Publishing House, 1935, p. 22.
5. *Young India*, August 25, 1920.
6. Gandhi, M. K, *An Autobiography* or *The Story of My Experiment with Truth, The Collected Works of Mahatma Gandhi,* New Delhi: Publications Division, Vol. 39, p. 401.
7. *Young India*, November 8, 1920.
8. *Harijan*, April 14, 1938.
9. *Young India*, August 8, 1920.
10. *Young India*, March 2, 1922.

Summary

- Gandhi's greatness as a leader and thinker lay in his transformation of the individualistic message of non-violence into a success technique for direct mass action.
- Non-violence is the basic premise of Gandhi's thought and action.
- Non-violence is not merely non-killing or non-injury, but is an attitude of mind that recognizes the unity and dignity of human life. Non-violence, ultimately, is humanism.
- Non-violence is means and truth the end. Absolute non-violence would coincide with absolute truth. Only a relative non-violence is a means to truth as seen by man. Absolute non-violence, like absolute truth, cannot be realized by man.
- Gandhi did not offer any simplistic definition of non-violence. Gandhi was the first person who used non-violence as a means of change and liberation. Non-violence has two aspects: not to do harm to a living thing; and to give proof of the most distinguished love towards every living creature.
- Non-violence does not mean submission to others, does not mean weakness.
- The fundamental characteristics of Gandhi's concept of non-violence are:

  Non-violence is primarily an inner realization
  Non-violence is inter-penetrated with truth
  Non-violence is not an alternative to violence or conflict
  Non-violence is not a negative concept
- Non-violence is 'not a weapon of the weak. It is a weapon of the strongest and the bravest.' But, 'where there is only a choice between cowardice and non-violence', Gandhi would advice violence.
- Gandhi applied non-violence into the field of politics and pathways to liberation of India. Gandhi's approach to politics was the turning point of his thought into

action. It is also the turning point in the sense that his contribution to the concept of non-violence begins.

- Non-violence is humanism, it takes man as an end in itself and not as a means to an end that transcends him. Non-violence of Gandhi is a revolt against de-humanization of man.
- Non-violence is not merely intellectual conviction but intuitive faith. It is way of life.

Further Readings

Bondurant, Joan, *Conquest of Violence: The Gandhian Philosophy of Conflict*, Bombay: Oxford University Press, 1959.

Gregg, Richard B., *The Power of Non-Violence*, Ahmedabad: Navjivan Publishing House, 1960.

Ostergaard, Geoffrey, *Non-violent Revolution in India,* New Delhi: Gandhi Peace Foundation, 1985.

Parekh, Bhikhu, *Colonialism, Tradition and Reform: An Analysis of Gandhi's Political Discourse*, New Delhi: Sage Publications, 1989.

Sharp, Gene, *Gandhi Wields the Weapon of Moral Power Three Case Histories*, Ahmedabad: Navjivan Publishing House, 1960.

Sharp, Gene, *The Politics of Non-Violent Action: Power and Struggle, Part 1*, Boston: Porter Sarget Publishers, 1973.

12

Gandhi and Nationalism

Introduction

Nationalism is a modern phenomenon. Two major dimensions need to be considered when analyzing the concept of nationalism. We must look at the ways in which nationalism shapes and attempts to cope with the rise of the modern state; and because the study of nationalism cannot be limited to its political character, we have to fully acknowledge the role of nationalism as one of the major sources of identity for contemporary individuals.[1] Nationalism originated from the assumption that nations are the primary focus of political allegiance. The spread of nationalism has been the result of Europeanization and modernization of non-Western and pre-modern societies. Its rise is linked to numerous phenomena, important among these are: 'origins of popular sovereignty; the theory of government by the active "consent" of the governed; the growth of secularism; the lessening of the older religious, tribal, clannish, or feudal loyalties; and, the spread of urbanization, industrialization and improved communications'.[2]

A *Dictionary of Political Thought*[3] defines nationalism as 'The sentiment and ideology of attachment to a nation and to its interests'. The *Dictionary of Contemporary English* defines nationalism as 'desire by a group of people of the same race, origin and language to form an independent country'.[4] In other words, nationalism means love for your own country and the belief that it is better than any other country.

Nationalism is also defined as 'a political creed that underlies the cohesion of modern societies and legitimizes their claim to authority. Nationalism binds the supreme loyalty of the overwhelming majority of the people upon the nation-state, either existing or desired. The nation-state is regarded not only as the ideal, 'natural', or 'normal' form of political organization but also as the indispensable framework for all social cultural and economic activities'.[5] By nationalism, Montserrat Guibernau[6] means the sentiment of belonging to a community whose members identify with a set of symbols, beliefs and ways of life, and have the will to decide upon their common political destiny.

In fact, nationalism is a political ideology that involves a strong identification of a group of individuals with a political entity defined in national terms as a nation. In the 'modernist' image of the nation, it is nationalism that creates national identity. There are various definitions for what constitutes a nation. However, this leads to several different strands of nationalism. Nationalism is sometimes reactionary, calling for a return to a national past, and sometimes demanding the expulsion of foreigners. Other forms of nationalism are revolutionary, calling for the establishment of an independent state as a homeland for an ethnic underclass. Nationalism emphasizes collective identity—the 'people' must be autonomous and united, and express a single national culture. Integral nationalism is a belief that a nation is an organic unit, with a social hierarchy, co-operation between the different social classes and common political goals. However, liberal nationalists stress individualism as an important part of their own national identity.

In the context of European nationalism, it is generally considered that this concept encompasses certain specific characteristics such as organic unity in terms of population, distinct territory, a single economy, common language, common psychological orientation and a common culture. E. H. Carr[7] has described the major traits of nationalism as under:

- The idea of a common government, whether as a reality in the present or past, or as an as aspiration of the future.
- A certain size and closeness of contact between all its individual members.
- A more or less defined territory.
- Certain characteristics (of which the most frequent is language) clearly distinguishing the nation from other nations and non-national groups.
- Certain interests common to the individual members.
- A certain degree of common feeling or will associated with a picture of the nation in the mind of the individual members.

R. S. Yadav has rightly pointed out that these traits are not available in the later kind of nationalism that spread in the Third World countries. Moreover, nationalism is sometimes associated with those states whose identity as a political unit is already established. Simultaneously, it can also spring up in ethnic, social or cultural communities that do not exist as independent political units but are under the domination of other states. Gandhi wrote in *Young India*, June 18, 1925 that, 'It is no nationalism that is evil; it is the narrowness, selfishness, exclusiveness which is the bane of modern nations which is evil'. Again, explaining in detail in *Young India* dated September 10, 1925 Gandhi wrote that 'Illustrations are taken from recent wars and administration of law in civilized societies to prove that hatred seems to be of the essence of nationalism. Nevertheless, it is the grossest of delusions.' Nationalism is the dominant feature of Gandhi's political ideology.

Indian Nationalism

According to Wikipedia, Indian nationalism refers to the many underlying forces that molded the Indian independence movement, and strongly continue to influence the politics of India, as well as being the heart of many contrasting ideologies that have caused ethnic and religious conflict in Indian society. Indian nationalism often imbibes the consciousness of Indians that—prior to 1947—India embodied the broader Indian subcontinent and influenced a part of Asia, known as greater India.

Nationalism in India can, thus, be described as the consciousness and the recognition of the socio-cultural unity in the past. But it was more than a spiritual imperative because it had to operate as a device to letting out the aspiration and the hopes of the educated middle class.

The development of Indian nationalism was not always coherent and consistent. This liberal nationalism was primarily secular. The confluence of religion and politics in extremist nationalism succeeded in broadening the base of the nationalist movement. Religion and nationalism became almost convertible terms in the speeches and the writings of the extremists. This is true of both Hindu and Muslim extremism. Gandhi was impressed by the extremists but was more influenced by the liberals. Gandhi's nationalism can be described as quasi-liberal and quasi-extremist.

Gandhi's attempt to formulate the theory of nationalism on the basis of certain liberal and extremist principles was deliberate. He was half-liberal, half-extremist. He surely succeeded in striking a new track. It is interesting to note that Gandhi described himself as the true disciple of Tilak but, at the same time, declared Gokhale as his political guru. What Gandhi borrowed from Tilak was 'the love of country and the steady pursuit of *swaraj*.'

Indian nationalism has its own features. Firstly, it must be admitted that Indian nationalism has not developed in the format and stages of nationalism as it has developed in Europe. The nature and context of Indian nationalism has been quite different from that of the European nationalism, where, generally, a nation is considered to be composed of certain specific characteristics such as organic unity in population, district territory, a single economy, common languages, common psychological orientation and a common culture. In contrast, Indian nationalism has grown and developed in a peculiar complex socio-economic and political background. Hence, it is different from that of the classical tradition of European nationalism.

Secondly, Indian nationalism is the by-product of struggle for freedom. The changing contours in the way of achieving the goal to free the country from colonial yoke have also changed the very nature and scope of Indian nationalism. In other words, Indian nationalism is also not the by-product of a certain revolutionary ideology or product of certain social transformation due to different stages of growth in the economic system. Rather, it is based on certain unorthodox experiences linked to the growth of the anti-imperialistic thrust of the movement. The challenges of the colonial period, along with the sufferings caused to its people due to colonial rules, made its leaders devise strategies to handle that crisis. Moreover, as a result of the prevailing foreign rule, the main objective of this struggle has been towards the independence of India.

Western sociologist G. Aloysius[8] argues that Indian nationalism is 'nationalism without a nation'. Whereas Cambridge historians like Percival Spear, Duncan Forbes, John Gallagher, C.A. Bayly, Judith Brown, Francis Robinson, Anil Seal, Richard Gordon, David Wash Brook, C. J. Baker and Sir Valentine Chirol view Indian nationalism to have emerged more as the by-product of a skilful game to be played for fame, status, survival, self-interest and advancement of personal interests, rather than giving importance to certain ideals, ideas and ideological thinking. John Breuilly[9] pointed out that like other Third World countries, Indian nationalism is considered 'primarily a form of politics' manifested in the form of anti-colonial struggle. Gandhi wrote in *Young India*, dated October 13, 1921 that 'Indian nationalism is not exclusive, nor aggressive, or destructive. It is health-giving, religious and, therefore, humanitarian'. Further, he wrote in *Young India*, dated March 12, 1925, 'My nationalism is as broad as my *swadeshi*. I want India's rise so that the whole world may benefit. I do not want India to rise on the ruin of other nations.'

India's concept of nationhood is based not just on territorial extent of its sovereignty. Nationalistic sentiments and expression encompass India's ancient history, as the birthplace of the Indus Valley Civilization and Vedic Civilization, as well as four major world religions—Hinduism, Buddhism, Jainism and Sikhism. Indian nationalists see India stretching along these lines across the Indian subcontinent.

Indian nationalism is as much a diverse blend of nationalistic sentiments as its people are ethnically and religiously diverse. Thus, the most influential undercurrents are more than just *Indian* in nature. The most controversial and emotionally-charged fibre in the fabric of Indian nationalism is religion. Religion forms a major—and in many cases—the central element of Indian life. Ethnic communities are diverse in terms of linguistics, social traditions and history across India.

Gandhian Perspective

Gandhi's idea of nationalism was part of his overall philosophy from which interpretation of nationalism could be discerned. It was linked to his struggle for the freedom of India. Gandhi wrote 'My idea of nationalism is that my country may become free, that if need be the whole of the country may die, so that the human race may live. There is no room for racial hatred there. Let that be our nationalism.'[10] Further, he wrote that 'nationalism, like virtue, is its own reward. A nationalist will ever think of service, never of power or riches'.[11]

It was in South Africa that Gandhi first acquired his vision of Indian nationalism, a fact which differentiates his nationalism from those of the other Indian nationalists. In other words, it was in the politics of the Transvaal that Gandhi first developed his unique political philosophy and political techniques. Gandhi has not explained his views on nationalism at one place; rather, his ideas could be understood by his total readings and his personal experiences and evolved along with him. Genuine difficulties do arise in defining Gandhian nationalism in terms of traditional academic formats, from the fact that Gandhi was not a theoretician in the accepted sense. He had written: 'I am not built for academic writings. Action is my domain.'[12] His political thought was an integral part of his total philosophy of human social order, which itself evolved over a half century of his relentless 'Experiments with Truth'. Application of his ideas, though flowing from a set of universal principles, was also rooted in the issues and the Indian situation of his period.

Gandhi discussed the idea of nationalism for the first time at great length in the seminal work *Hind Swaraj* or *Indian Home Rule* in 1909. However, he seldom used the term nation. He used the terms *swaraj, swadeshi* or Indian civilization. Gandhi used the word *praja* for nation. He felt that the traditional notion of *praja* offers a basis upon which new edifice of a modern, composite Indian nation-state could be built. In *Hind Swaraj* he pleaded for the development of moderate, liberal nationalism based on the concept of *praja*. Gandhi referred that India was not a motley collection of groups but consisted of people sharing common aspiration and interests and a vague but nonetheless real commitment to the kind of spiritual civilization. In this context, Bhikhu Parekh has rightly observed that when Gandhi occasionally used the term 'nationalism', he largely meant 'love of one's country'. For the most part he preferred ideas of collective pride, ancestral loyalty, mutual responsibility and intellectual and moral openness.

Gandhi was of the opinion that despite its multifarious castes, religions and cultures, India has always been a nation though the West never recognized it as such. Gandhi asserted that, 'The English have taught us that we were not one nation before and that it will require centuries before we become one nation. This is without foundation. We were one nation before they came to India. One thought inspired us. Our mode of life was the same. It was because we were one nation that they were able to establish one kingdom. Subsequently, they divided us'.[13] In *Hind Swaraj*, Gandhi expounded the broad view of the Indian nation. India has been unified under many emperors and governments in history. Ancient texts mention India under Emperor Bharata and Akhand Bharat; these regions roughly form the entities of modern-day greater India. The Mauryan Empire was the first to unite all of India, South Asia, and much of Persia. In addition, much of India has also been unified under a central government by empires, such as the Gupta Empire, Rashtrakuta Empire, Pala Empire, Mughal Empire and the Indian Empire.

Gandhi's vision of nationalism is composed of three major ingredients: *swaraj*, communal harmony and non-violence. *Swaraj* is the first. *Swaraj* signified self-rule and self-restraint. *Swaraj* would not mean a change of rulers but it would provide an opportunity for the establishment of justice, liberty and equality for one and all in the country. Justice and slavery could not co-exist. *Swaraj* would, therefore, ensure the regulation and control of authority by the people. It would be a 'healthy and dignified independence'. The second ingredient of Gandhi nationalism was communal harmony. According to him, it amounted to the active participation of all the communities in the freedom struggle. It also meant the unity of the people which should come through religion. Gandhi subscribed to composite nationalism. He did not countenance nationalism based on religion, especially in the Indian context of multiplicity as it would divide the people on artificial lines. So, *swaraj* and strong self-government is not possible without communal harmony. Non-violence is the third ingredient of Gandhi's nationalism. For Gandhi, non-violence was the first and the last article of faith. 'My marriage to non-violence is such an absolute thing that I would rather commit suicide than be deflected from my position,' said Gandhi. He thought that non-violence would prevent a bloody revolution and anarchy in the country. It would lead to democracy and not to despotism. It is the law of the human race and is infinitely greater than the brute force. It is not 'the weapon of the weak' but 'presupposes the ability to strike'. It is an active force free from weakness. It exercises a sane pressure of love and good-will.

From the study of *Gandhian Thought and Action* and available literature, the following features of nationalism emerge: Firstly, Gandhi's nationalism was 'incorporative', forging a nationalist harmony between different kinds of groups in India.[14] His ideas of composite nationalism included not only religious groups but also castes and communities in general. Secondly, Gandhian nationalism was pursuit of emancipation from the colonial yoke. He was against the use of any sort of violent and aggressive means for this objective as had been the case in the West. He emphatically rejected a nationalism that sought freedom through violence. He was in favour of use of the method of *ahimsa* or non-violence in thought, action and deed for this end. Thirdly, Gandhi's nationalism has been the collective assertion of all communities, including the deprived strata of the society. He was always for a nation based on the plurality of population from different strata of the society. Fourthly, Gandhian nationalism has secular outlook, despite his being attached to religion. Fifthly, Gandhian nationalism had internationalist overtones. Gandhi wrote: 'It is impossible for one to be internationalist without being a nationalist. Internationalism is possible only when nationalism becomes a fact, that is, when people belonging to different countries have organized themselves and are able to act as one man. It is not nationalism that is evil; it is the narrowness, selfishness, exclusiveness which is the bane of modern nations which is evil. Each wants to profit at the expense of, and rise on the ruin of the other. Indian nationalism has struck a different path. It wants to organize itself or to find a complete self-expression for the benefit and service of humanity at large'.[15] Sixthly, Gandhi was also not in favour of the communitarian approach; rather, he used the context of civilization in terms of plurality and synthesis. This becomes all the more evident during the time of Jinnah's demand for separate nationhood on the basis of Muslims as separate community. Gandhi viewed that unlike the European countries, India was not a nation but a civilization which had over the centuries been benefited from the contributions of different races and religions and was distinguished by its plurality, diversity and tolerance. It was 'community of communities', each enjoying considerable autonomy within a larger and shared framework. Gandhi added further that Indian Muslims are Indian not merely in a territorial but also in cultural sense, and co-heirs with the Hindus to Indian civilization. Though they did have several distinct customs and social practices, yet this was equally true of every other community and could not prevent them from living peacefully within a single state. Seventhly, his nationalistic thrust was based on the total mobilization of the masses. That is why, the arrival of Gandhi on the scene of Indian freedom movement brought about a qualitative difference in the emergence of nationalism.

Summing Up

R. S. Yadav put it beautifully when he wrote that 'Gandhian nationalism was beyond a sectarian and narrow outlook coordinating all castes and classes together. It even pleaded for the upliftment of downtrodden and backward classes so that an egalitarian and harmonious social system could be evolved. His nationalism was secular and above the narrow and petty confines of religion. It was not dogmatic and ritualistic; rather, it imbibed the larger framework of civilizational context preserving Hindu-Muslim unity. Gandhi was not a conservative nationalist but more of an internationalist in his approach. His nationalism was woven in the all-embracing concerns for humanity. He did not approve of the "communitarian" nationalistic frame, but he was in favour of "civic humanism". In India, nationalism is closely linked with its struggle against the colonial yoke. So Gandhi made this feeling of nationalism a movement for the masses. To mobilize the huge masses, he not only preached and practiced non-violent movements but also introduced constructive programmes for the national unity and integrity. Therefore, Gandhian nationalism could be well understood by understanding his philosophy and broad ideological moorings which not only worked towards the independence of India but also integrated it in the form of a nation.'

One may conclude with what Simone Panter Brick in his book 'Gandhi and Nationalism: The Path to Indian Independence' wrote: Gandhi's nationalism seems simple and straightforward: he wanted an independent Indian nation state and freedom from British colonial rule. But in reality, his nationalism rested on a complex and sophisticated moral philosophy. His Indian state and nation were not based on any shallow ethnic or religious communalism—despite his claim to be Hindu to his very core—but were grounded on his concept of swaraj. Gandhi preached and practiced enlightened self-control and self-development leading to harmony and tolerance among all communities in the new India. He aimed at moral regeneration, and not just the ending of colonial rule. Any perceptive and original portrayal of Gandhi's nationalism analyses his spiritual and political programme. Gandhi's nationalism was, in Roger Louis's phrase, 'larger than the struggle for independence'. He sought a tolerant and unified state that included all communities within a 'Mother India'.

Notes and References

1. Guibernau, Montserrant, *Nationalisms: The Nation-State and Nationalism in the Twentieth Century*, Cambridge: Polity Press, 1996, p. 46.
2. Kohn, Hans, 'Nationalism', *International Encyclopaedia of Social Sciences*, Chicago, 1976, Vol. 11, p. 64.
3. Scruton, Roger, *A Dictionary of Political Thought,* London: Pan Books, 1982, p. 315.
4. Longman's Dictionary of Contemporary English, Harlow: Pearson, 2009, p. 1159.
5. *The New Encyclopaedia Britannica*, Chicago, 1987, Vol. 8, p. 552.
6. Guibernau, Montserrant, *Nationalisms: The Nation-State and Nationalism in the Twentieth Century*, Cambridge: Polity Press, 1996, p. 46.
7. Carr, E. H., *Nationalism*, 1939, p. xx.
8. Aloysius, G., *Nationalism Without a Nation in India*, Delhi: Oxford, 1997.
9. Breuilly, John, *Nationalism and the State,* Chicago: University of Chicago Press, 1982, p. 1.
10. *Young India*, September 10, 1925.

11. *Harijan*, September 7, 1947.
12. *Harijan*, March 3, 1946.
13. Gandhi, M. K., *Hind Swaraj* or *Indian Home Rule*, Ahmedabad: Navjivan Publishing House, 1938, p. 40.
14. Hardiman, David, Gandhi in His times and Ours, New Delhi: Permanent Black, 2003, pp. 12–38.
15. Gandhi, M. K., *India of My Dreams*, Ahmedabad: Navjivan Publishing House, 1947, p.14. For detail also see, *Young India*, 18-6-1925.

Summary

- Two major dimensions need to be considered when analyzing nationalism. Firstly, we must look at the ways in which nationalism both shapes and attempts to cope with the rise of the modern state. Secondly, the study of nationalism cannot be limited to its political character.
- Nationalism is defined as 'The sentiment and ideology of attachment to a nation and to its interests'. In fact, nationalism is a political ideology that involves a strong identification of a group of individuals with a political entity defined in national terms, i.e., a nation.
- In the context of European nationalism, it is generally considered to encompass certain specific characteristics such as organic unity in terms of population, distinct territory, a single economy, common language, common psychological orientation and a common culture.
- E. H. Carr has described the major traits of nationalism as under:
    - The idea of a common government whether as a reality in the present or past, or as an as aspiration of the future
    - A certain size and closeness of contact between all its individual members
    - A more or less defined territory
    - Certain characteristics (of which the most frequent is language) clearly distinguishing the nation from the other nations and non-national groups
    - Certain interests common to the individual members
    - A certain degree of common feeling or will associated with a picture of the nation in the mind of the individual members
- Nationalism is the dominant feature of the political thinking of Gandhi.
- Nationalism in India can, thus, be described as the consciousness and the recognition of the socio-cultural unity in the past.
- Gandhi's nationalism can be described as quasi-liberal and quasi-extremist.
- Indian nationalism has its own features. Firstly, Indian nationalism has not developed in the format and stages of nationalism as that has been developed in Europe. Secondly, Indian nationalism is the by-product of the struggle for freedom.
- Gandhi's idea of nationalism was part of his overall philosophy from which inter-

pretation of nationalism could be discerned.

- It was in South Africa that Gandhi first acquired his vision of Indian nationalism, a fact which differentiates his nationalism from those of the other Indian nationalists.
- Gandhi discussed the idea of nationalism for the first time at great length in the seminal work *Hind Swaraj* or *Indian Home Rule* in 1909. He, however, seldom used the term nation. He used the terms *swaraj, swadeshi* or Indian civilization. Gandhi used the word *praja* for nation.
- Nationalism of Gandhi is composed of three major ingredients: *swaraj*, communal harmony and non-violence.
- Features of Gandhi's nationalism are: Firstly, Gandhi's nationalism was 'incorporative', forging a nationalist harmony between different kinds of groups in India. Secondly, Gandhian nationalism was pursuit of emancipation from the colonial yoke. Thirdly, Gandhi's nationalism has been the collective assertion of all communities, including the deprived strata of the society. Fourthly, Gandhian nationalism has a secular outlook, despite his being attached to religion. Fifthly, Gandhian nationalism had internationalist overtones. Sixthly, Gandhi was not in favour of the communitarian approach; rather, he used the civilizational context in terms of plurality and synthesis. Seventhly, his nationalistic thrust was based on the total mobilization of the masses.
- Gandhian nationalism was beyond sectarian and narrow outlook coordinating all castes and classes together.
- Gandhi's nationalism seems simple and straightforward: he wanted an independent Indian nation state and freedom from British colonial rule. But, in reality, his nationalism rested on complex and sophisticated moral philosophy.

Further Readings

Chandra, Bipan, *Indian National Movement: The Long Term Dynamics*, New Delhi: Vikas, 1988.

Guha, Ramachandra, *India After Gandhi: The History of the World's Largest Democracy*, New Delhi: Picador, 2008.

Hardiman, David *Gandhi in His times and Ours*, New Delhi, Permanent Black, 2003.

Mishra, Anil Dutta, *Understanding Mahatma Gandhi: Speeches and Writings that Reveal his Mind, Methods and Mission*, New Delhi: Concept, 2012.

Mishra, Anil Dutta, *Revisiting Hind Swaraj*, New Delhi: Concept, 2010.

Parekh, Bhikhu, *Gandhi's Political Philosophy: A Critical Examination*, Delhi: Ajanta, 1995.

Gandhi, M. K., *India of My Dream*, Ahmedabad: Navjivan Publishing House,1947.

13

Constructive Programme

Introduction

In 1909, in *Hind Swaraj,* Gandhi outlined a new philosophy of individual freedom and development for the full appreciation of which political freedom was also essential. Gandhi was, however, not a barren philosopher—one of his greatest qualities was that he never expressed or publicized an idea unless he was aware of the key to open the door to its practical application. He, therefore, proceeded to inspire the country to put into effect various items of constructive work which, in a free country, it would be the prime duty of the government to put into effect. All those items were closely inter-related and calculated to lead to the full development of the individual and to develop his powers of self-reliance and self-confidence which, after freedom, could be used to influence the government to fulfil its duties in an efficient manner.

The constructive programme may otherwise and more fittingly be called construction of Poorna Swaraj or complete independence by truthful and non-violent means.[1]

Effort for construction of independence so called through violent and, therefore, necessarily untruthful means we know only too painfully. Look at the daily destruction of property, life and truth in the present war (second world war)[2]. The primary aim of the constructive programme should be to secure for the worker his due share in production.[3]

The best preparation for—and even the expression of—non-violence lies in the determined pursuit of the constructive programme. Anyone who believes that, without the backing of the constructive programme he will show non-violent strength when the testing time comes he will fail miserably. It will be like the attempt of a starving, unarmed man to match his physical strength against a fully fed and panoplied soldier, foredoomed to failure.[4] He who has no belief in the constructive programme has, in my opinion, no concrete feeling for the starved millions. He, who is devoid of the feeling, cannot fight non-violently.[5] The execution of the constructive programme in its entirety means more than swaraj: it means Ramrajya, Khudai Sultana or the Divine Kingdom. I am thirsting after such a place. My God does not reside up above. He has to be realized on earth. He is here, within you, within me. He is omnipotent and omnipresent. You need not think of the world beyond. If we can do our duty here, the beyond will take care of itself.[6]

Constructive programme will lead to the reconstruction of both men and society by correcting the faults of private and public life. It differs from what is generally termed as social service in the sense that its object is not only to give relief to the afflicted, but also to eliminate the very need of that relief by removing the causes that give rise to it. It is performed of one's own accord. It is purely a moral action, which builds up morality in men. It is not actuated by any temptation or fear. Itself an expression of non-violence, it further aids in its growth. Gandhi regarded constructive work to be 'the fulfillment of swaraj'.[7]

Gandhi launched a movement of constructive programme for economic betterment and for improving the tenor of social life for generation after generations. The constructive programme is the long-term pre-requisite of a system of non-violent self-rule, without which political power or formal independence would prove to be a sham. The constructive programme includes individual and collective efforts on behalf of the unity between diverse religious communities, the removal of social abuses such as untouchability, programmes of rural education and reconstruction, the decentralization of production and distributions, schemes for the improvement of health, sanitation and diet, the promotion of local handicrafts, and in general, concrete work by all to promote the common good.

Constructive programme was an integral and positive aspect of Gandhi's post-1920 Satyagraha movement. It was adopted for the achievement of economic self-sufficiency and inculcation of the swadeshi spirit amongst the masses. It was employed for the promotion of communal harmony and removal of social evils like untouchability, unemployment and illiteracy. As a way of total non-co-operation with the alien British rule in India, constructive programme was also adopted to replace the government institutions with voluntary public (national) institutions.

Constructive programme as a method of satyagraha was adopted by Gandhi for the first time during his non-violent non-cooperation Movement of 1920. In the course of this movement, national schools and institutions were started, arbitration courts and panchayats were established, and spinning on charkha began with the sole object of replacing government schools and colleges, law courts, and foreign goods which were to be completely boycotted.

Spinning and social welfare activities were continued throughout the Bardoli Satyagraha of 1928, with an emphasis upon the entire khadi programme. Even during his Salt Satyagraha of 1930, the wearing of handspun cloth was imperative for all satyagrahis. Welfare and self-sufficiency work was undertaken as a way of achieving swaraj.

However, the constructive programme as a definite method of achieving complete independence found its clear and full exposition only in the post-individual satyagraha period of December 1941. It was during this period that Gandhi expounded his entire philosophy of constructive programme and published a 25-page booklet entitled 'Constructive Programme'. This was written by him in the train from Sevagram to Bardoli. On February 15, 1945, Gandhi addressed the Kasturba Nidhi workers. The booklet on constructive work was revised with some more items added to the already existing thirteen.

Constructive Programme, according to Gandhi, is designed to build up the nation from the very bottom. It must mean complete independence in every sense of the expression. Indeed, his claim was that civil disobedience is not absolutely necessary to win freedom through purely non-violent effort if the co-operation of the whole nation is secured within the constructive programme. This does not mean that constructive work was merely a tactical instrument in a non-violent struggle against colonial regime. For Gandhi, constructive work was the heart of a matter.

In 1931 Gandhiji wrote, 'My work of social reform was no way less than or subordinate to political work. The fact is that when I saw that to a certain extent my social work would be impossible without the help of political work, I took to the latter and only to the extent that it helped the former. I must, therefore, confess that the work of social reform or self-purification of this nature is hundred times dearer to me than what is called purely political work.' The constructive programme is, therefore, central to the understanding of Gandhi's concept of swaraj, which was for him a step towards the ultimate goal of 'Ramrajya'.

Principles of Constructive Programme

- Performed on its own accord, it is purely a moral action which strengthens morality in man.
- Co-operation and mutual aid are important for constructive work. Voluntariness and sharing comprise the core of constructive activities.
- Self-reliance and self-help is another important principle of constructive programme.
- The fourth principle of constructive programme is building from below.
- Constructive programme is the concrete expression of the spirit of non-violence
- Decentralization is another important principle of constructive programme.

To quote Professor K. Arunachalam:

> 'In a centralized institution, one man is accountable for operational as well as managerial work. Through the delegation of authority and duties, it is possible for a top executive to secure the willing services of several competent managers. Decentralization promotes development of initiative, responsibility and morality among workers. When carried out in a proper way, it fosters personalities and improves working relationship. Four things are very necessary for the successful working of decentralization: the availability of trained, capable and devoted managers who can undertake responsibility and are willing to take decisions at their own levels; an arrangement for overall supervision and guidance so that the decentralized units can be controlled by fixed and predetermined standards of performance; provision of necessary service facilities which are not ordinarily available to basic units of any big organization; and an animating idea that can bind the decentralized units and keep them together in spite of their autonomous functioning.'

The Framework of Constructive Programme

Framework is a structure for supporting anything. constructive programme consists of several apparently unconnected, independent activities. But all these activities are united together by a framework which supports the idea of a novel revolution. Gandhiji believed in the dual revolution, in the minds of men as well as in the structure of society which brought power to local communities. He was confident that his constructive programme will lead on to this happy consumption.

Gandhiji wrote in Young India in 1924, 'I am a humble seeker after truth. I am impatient to realize myself, to attain moksha in this very existence. My national service is part of my training for freeing my soul from the bondage of flesh. Thus considered, my service may be regarded as purely selfish. For me, the road to salvation lies through incessant toil in the service of my country and through that of the humanity, I want to identify myself with everything that lives. So, my patriotism for me is a state in my journey to the Land of Eternal Freedom and Peace.'

Thus, the framework of constructive programme is made up of truth and non-violence supported by determination and dedication, vairagya and tyaga. Truth is the goal and non-violence is the means. The path to the goal on either side is guarded by the virtue of vairagya and tyaga.

The Content

Constructive programme was not conceived by Gandhi in a single day. It took several years to give shape and form to the programme.

In 1941, Gandhi had listed the following thirteen items:

- Communal unity
- Removal of untouchability
- Prohibition
- Khadi
- Other village industries
- Village sanitation
- New or basic education
- Adult education
- Women
- Education in health and hygiene
- Provincial languages
- Propagation of Rashtra Bhasa
- Promotion of economic equality.

In 1945, Gandhi added the following items:

- Kisans (farmers)
- Labour

- Adivasis
- Lepers
- Students

After Gandhi's death, the following items were added by his followers to strengthen the movement:

- Cow protection
- Nature cure
- Bhoodan
- Gramdan
- Shanti Sena

The goal of constructive programme is not to provide economic relief to the unemployment or to distribute some wages to the poor but to build up a non-violent social order. In this endeavour we have not made much headway; what was needed was a superior, more advanced type of worker, who would have a full understanding of the scientific basis of constructive work and effortlessly in its implications in terms of non-violence. Success would depend on uttermost purity; impatience would be fatal. Gandhi also desired that more and more workers in the future should be drawn from the villages themselves so that they can get under the skin of the village and instinctively think in terms of their thoughts.

Let us examine the items briefly.

Communal Unity

Unity does not mean political unity alone. It means an unbreakable heart-unity. The first thing essential for achieving such a unity is for every Congressman—whatever his religion may be—to represent in his own person Hindu, Muslim, Christian, Zoroastrian, Jew, and all other religions. The belief that unity is strength is not merely a copybook maxim, but a rule of life.[8] True unity comes of itself. No attempt has to be made for achieving it.[9] Unity is made of sterner stuff. It is not a showy nothing, to be merely named on a paper resolution. Unity to be achieved means solid action.[10]

'What does unity consist in and how can it be best promoted? The answer is simple. It consists on our having a common purpose, a common goal and common sorrows. It is best promoted by co-operating to reach the common goal, by sharing one another's sorrows and by mutual toleration. I believe in absolute oneness of God and, therefore, also of humanity. What though we may have many bodies? We have but one soul. The rays of the sun are many through refraction. But they have the same source.'[11]

Gandhi believed in the essential unity of man and, for that matter, of all that lives. If one man gains spiritually, the whole world gains with him; and if one man falls, the whole world falls to that extent.[12] Seeking to realize oneness of life in practice, I cannot be happy if I see communities quarrelling with one another or men suppressing fellowmen.[13] Gandhi said that 'we have to find unity in diversity… We are all children of one and the same God and, therefore, absolutely equal.'[14] Gandhi further said that 'Hindu-Muslim unity consists in our having common purpose, a common goal and common sorrows. It is best promoted by co-operating to reach the common goal, by sharing one another's sorrows and by mutual toleration.'[15] This unity cannot be a mere policy to be discarded it only when we are tired of swaraj. Hindu-Muslim unity must be our creed to last for all time and under all circumstances.[16] Without unity between Hindus and Muslims, no certain progress can be made by the nation. Hindu-Muslim unity means not unity only between Hindus and Muslims, but between all those who believe India to be their home, no matter to what faith they belong.

Gandhi wrote in Harijan, in October 29, 1938 that, 'For good or for ill, the two communities are wedded to India; they are neighbours, sons of the soil. They are destined to die here, as they are born here. Nature will force them to live in peace, if they do not come together voluntarily.'

Removal of Untouchability

Gandhi wrote in the Harijan: 'There is an ineffaceable blot that Hinduism today carries with it. I have declined to believe that it has been handed to us from immemorial times. I think that this miserable, wretched, enslaving spirit of untouchability must have come to us when we were in the cycle of our lives at our lowest ebb… That any person should be considered untouchable in this sacred land passes one's comprehension. Untouchability is a sin against God and man. There is no warrant in the Shastras for untouchability as we practice it today.'[17] 'Untouchability is a heinous crime against humanity. And why do I say that untouchability is a curse, a blot and a powerful poison that will destroy Hinduism? It is repugnant to our sense of humanity to consider a single human being as untouchable by birth. If you were to examine the scriptures of the world and the conduct of peoples other than Hindus, you do not find any parallel to the untouchability.'[18]

Gandhi believed that if untouchability could be really rooted out, it would not only purge Hinduism of a terrible blot, but its repercussion will be worldwide. In his words, 'My fight against untouchability is a fight against the impure in humanity. Removal of untouchability means love for, and service of the whole world, and thus merges into ahimsa. Removal of untouchability spells the breaking down of barriers between man and man, and between the various orders of being.[19]

Prohibition

On the issue of prohibition, Gandhi had very stringent views. He opined thus: 'We may not leave to the future government the fate of lakhs of men and women, who are labouring under the course of intoxicants and narcotics. We have to discuss ways of weaning the drunkard and the opium addict from this course. India has the capacity and the opportunity to lead the world in the matter of prohibition. Can she forego the revenue derived from this degrading traffic? She must, if she is to live.'[20] The positive side of prohibition must run side by side with the negative. The positive consists in providing the drinker with counter-attractions, giving him health and innocent amusement. [21]

We shall not be able to combat drinking successfully till prohibition comes… without prohibition it is impossible to bring about sober habits among the labouring population in India.[22] India is a country in which total prohibition can succeed. People are not habitually given to drink. It is not a fashionable vice. The climate does not demand its use.[23]

Total prohibition is prohibition against sales of intoxicating drinks and drugs, except under medical prescription by a practitioner licensed for the purpose and to be purchasable only at government depots maintained therefore.

Khadi

Khadi connotes the beginning of economic freedom and equality for all in the country. It must be taken with all its implications. It means a wholesale swadeshi mentality, a determination to find all the necessities of life in India, and that too, through the labour and intellect of villages. 'Khadi, to me [Gandhi], is the symbol of unity of Indian humanity, of its economic freedom and equality and, therefore, ultimately, in the poetic expression of Jawaharlal Nehru, 'the livery of India's freedom.'[24]

Habitual use of Khadi is a sign that the wearer identifies himself with the poorest in the land, and has patriotism and self-sacrifice enough in him to wear khadi, even though it may not be so soft or elegant in appearance as foreign fineries, nor so cheap. Khadi is the breath of national life, just like swaraj. It cannot be given up. To give up khadi would be to sell the masses—the soul of India.[25] In Young India, June 17, 1926, Gandhi said that 'khaddar (khadi) is the concrete and central fact of swadeshi. Swadeshi without khadder is like the body without life, fit only to receive a decent burial or cremation. Khadi is the central sun, round which the other village industries resolve like so many planets.

Khadi economics is wholly different from the ordinary. The latter takes no note of the human factor. The former wholly concerns itself with the human. The latter is frankly selfish, the former necessary scarily unselfish. Competition and, therefore, prices are eliminated from the conception of khadder.[26]

Village Industries

Village economy cannot be complete without the essential industries such as hand grinding, hand pounding, soap making, paper making, match making, tanning, oil pressing, and other small-scale industries. All should make it a point of honour to use only village articles, whenever and wherever available. Given the demand, there is no doubt that most of our wants can be supplied from our villages. When we have become village-minded, we will not want limitations of the West or machine-made products, but we will develop a true national taste in keeping with the vision of a New India, in which pauperism, starvation and idleness will be unknown.[27]

The idea behind the village industries scheme is that we should look to the villages for the supply of our daily needs, and that when we find that some needs are not so supplied, we should see whether, with a little trouble and organization, they couldn't be profitably supplied by the villagers. In estimating the profit, we should think of the villager, not of ourselves.

In a nutshell, of the things we use, we should restrict our purchases to those articles that villages manufacture. Their manufactures may be crude. We must try to induce them to improve their workmanship, and not dismiss them because foreign articles or even produced in cities, that is, big factories, are superior.[28]

Village Sanitation

Instead of having graceful hamlets dotting the land, we have villages, looking like dung-heaps. It is the duty of everyone to make our village turn into models of cleanliness in every sense of the word. Some foreign observers have testified that of all the nations of the earth, India comes, perhaps, to the top in the observance of personal cleanliness. But I fear that it is not possible to say the same of corporate, in other words, village, and cleanliness. To put it in yet other words, we have not made much advance beyond the family interest. We would sacrifice everything for the family as distinguished from the village, i.e., in a sense, the nation. Members of a family will keep their own home clean, but they will not be interested in the neighbour's. They will keep their courtyard clean of dirt, insects and reptiles, but will not hesitate to shove all into the neighbour's yard. As a result of this want of corporate responsibility, our villages are dung heaps.[29] We must keep our village clean. It is duty of everyone.

Basic Education

Basic Education links the children, whether of the cities or the villages, to all that is best and lasting in India. It develops both the body and mind of the child. This education is meant to transform village children into model villagers. It is principally designed for them. The inspiration for it has to come from the villages.

'The object of basic education is the physical, intellectual and moral development of the children through the medium of handicrafts... The emphasis laid on the principle of spending every minute of one's life usefully is the best education for citizenship, and incidentally makes basic education self-sufficient.'[30]

Basic education must become literally education for life. All educational activity of the government should be along basic education lines. If I had my way, I would conduct adult education drives also through a basic craft. By education I mean an all-round drawing out of the best in child and man—body, mind and spirit. Man is neither mere intellect, nor the gross animal body, nor the heart or soul alone. A proper and harmonious combination of all the three is required for the making of the whole man and constitutes the true economics of education.[31]

Adult Education

Adult education means, first, true political education of the adult by word of mouth. Side by side with the education by the mouth will be literary education. This is itself a specialty. One should begin with opening the greatness and vastness of this country. The villager's Indian is contained in his village.

The goal is character building—an all round drawing out of the best in the child and the man. The common central feature of both will be the imparting of education through village crafts. Agriculture will play a very important part in adult education under the basic scheme. Literary instruction must also be a part of it. A lot of the information will be given orally. There will be books, more for the teachers than for the taught. We must teach the majority how to behave towards the minority and vice-versa. The right type of adult education should teach neighbourliness and cut at the very root of untouchability and the communal problem.[32]

Regarding adult education, Gandhi observed that it had become clear to him that the scope of basic education had to be extended. It would have to include the education of every body at every stage of life.[33]

Women

Woman is the incarnation of ahimsa. Ahimsa means infinite love, which again signifies an infinite capacity for suffering. Who but woman, the mother of man, possesses this capacity in the largest measure? Let her forget that she ever was or can be the object of man's lust. And she will occupy her proud position by the side of man as his mother, maker and silent leader.[34]

A woman, I hold, is the personification of self-sacrifice, but unfortunately, today, she does not realize what a tremendous advantage she has over man. As Tolstoy used to say, women are labouring under the hypnotic influence of man. If they would realize the strength of non-violence, they would not consent to be called the weaker sex.

To call the women the weaker sex is a libel; it is man's injustice to woman. If by strength is meant brute strength, then indeed a woman is less of a brute than man. If by strength is meant moral power, than woman is immeasurably man's superior. Has she not greater intuition, is she not more self-sacrificing, has she not greater courage? Without her, man could not be. If non-violence is the law of our being, the future is with the woman.[35] Woman is not helpless. She must never regard herself as weaker than man. She should not, therefore, beg for any man's mercy nor depend upon him. Woman will not regard herself as dependent, weak or helpless. She is not really pure. Her purity makes her conscious of her strength. I have always held that it is physically impossible to violate a woman against her will. The outrage takes place only when she gives way to fear or does not realize her moral strength. Women need not look for protection to men. They must rely on their own strength and purity of character and on god.

'Woman is the companion of man, gifted with equal mental capacities. She has the right to participate in the very minutest detail in the activities of man, and she has an equal right of freedom and liberty with him. Would that woman will realize the power that she has latent in her for good, if she has also for mischief. It is in her power to make the world more livable both for her and her partner, whether as father, son, or husband, if she would cease to think of herself as weak, and fit only to serve as a doll for man to play with.'[36]

'If you women would only realize your dignity and privilege, and make full use of it for mankind, you will make it much better than it is. But man has delighted in enslaving you and you have proved willing slaves till the slaves and the slaveholders have become one in the crime of degrading humanity. My special function from childhood has been to make woman realize her dignity. I was once a slaveholder myself, but Ba proved an unwilling slave and thus opened my eyes to my mission. Her task was finished. Now I am in search of a woman who would realize her mission.'[37]

Education in Health and Hygiene

'The very high death rate among us is, no doubt, due largely to our growing poverty, but it could be mitigated if the people were properly educated about health and hygiene. Observance of the fundamental laws of health and hygiene is necessary to cure any illness. Resort to nature cure according to your resources. It is health, which is the real wealth, not pieces of silver and gold.[38] Perfect health can be attained only by living in obedience to the laws of God, and defying the power of Satan. Only that man can be said to be really healthy, who has sound mind in a sound body. The relation between the body and the mind is so intimate, that if either of them got out of order, the whole system would suffer. The remedy of the mind lies in the mind itself. In other words, it means that by meditating upon God alone, all our sorrows come to an end.'[39]

'A pure character is the foundation of health in the real sense of the term, and we say that all evil thoughts and evil passions are but different forms of disease. Mens sana in corpore sano is perhaps the first law for humanity. A healthy mind in a healthy body is a self-evident truth. There is an inevitable connection between mind and body. If we were in possession of healthy minds, we would shed all violence and, naturally obeying the laws of health, we would have healthy bodies without an effort.'

Oliver Wendal Holmes rightly said about the modern system of medicines that, 'If all the medicines in the world were thrown into the bottom of the sea, the health of mankind would improve; it would, of course, harm the fish'.

Provincial Languages

The neglect of our mother tongue had led to disastrous results. The disservice caused to India by this neglect of its great languages cannot be measured. How can the masses make their contribution to the independence movement, unless they are explained every step in all its implications in their own languages?

Our love of the English language in preference to our own mother tongue has caused a deep chasm between the educated and the politically minded classes and the masses. The languages of India have suffered impoverishment. We flounder when we make the vain attempt to express abstruse thoughts in our mother tongue. There are no equipments for scientific terms. The result has been disastrous. The masses remain cut off from the modern mind. We are too near our own times correctly to measure the disservice caused to India by this neglect of its great languages. It is easy enough to understand that, unless we undo the mischief, the mass mind will remain imprisoned. The masses can make no solid contribution to the construction of swaraj. It is inherent in swaraj based on non-violence that every individual makes his own direct contribution to the independence movement. The masses cannot do this fully, unless they understand every step with all its implications.

College education provides an individual with a career. It is a passport for entrance to the charmed circle. Pardonable hunger for knowledge cannot be satisfied otherwise than by going through the usual rut.

People do not mind the waste of precious years in acquiring knowledge of an utterly foreign language, which takes the place of the mother tongue. The sin of it is never felt. They and the teachers have both made up their minds that the indigenous languages are useless for gaining access to modern thought and the modern sciences.

The medium of instruction must always be the mother tongue.

National Language

For all-India intercourse we need from the Indian stock, a language which the majority of the masses already know and which the others can easily pick up. That language is indisputably Hindi (Hindustani). Equally important is the question of the national or all-India language. (It can never be English, which is undoubtedly the language of foreigners and international commerce, but Hindustani alone can be the national language.) At present, Hindustani has two forms. In order to understand both the forms of the national language, Hindu and Urdu, and for their natural synthesis, we must learn the Devanagari and the Persian scripts. I find it lacking even in my immediate surroundings. All our signboards must be written in both the scripts and there should be none amongst us who cannot easily read and write either.

We are slaves who have hugged the language of those who have kept us enslaved. It has become a fashion to blame the Englishman for all our ills. I have not hesitated to blame them for many things they have done. I have never charged them with compelling us to adopt precious years of our lives to learning the English language, our ambition being to be able to speak English as Englishman, and our breast swells with pride when an Englishman pats us on our back for speaking flawless English. Think of the time and energy of our youth expended on learning English language, as if it was our mother tongue, and calculate by simple multiplication the energy that is lost to the nation. National languages should enable one to understand and speak both forms of speech and write in both the scripts.[40]

In 1920, a deliberate attempt was begun to recognize the importance of Indian languages for the political education of the masses, as also of an all-India common speech which politically minded, India could easily speak and which congressmen from the different provinces could understand at all India gatherings of the congress. Such National languages should enable one to understand and speak both forms of speech and write in both scripts.[41]

Economic Equality

Working for economic equality means abolishing the eternal conflict between capital and labour. A violent and bloody revolution is a certainly one day unless there is a voluntary abdication by the rich of riches, and the power that riches give, and sharing them for the common good.

Economic equality of my [Gandhi's] conception does not mean that everyone would literally have the same amount. It simply means that everybody should have enough for his or her needs.[42] Further, Gandhi said in Harijan, October 6, 1946 that 'I do not believe in dead uniformity. 'All men are born equal and free' is not nature's law in the literal sense. All men are not born equal in intellect, for instance; but the doctrine of equality will be vindicated if those who have superior intellect will use it not for self-advancement at the expense of others, but for the service of those who are less favoured in that respect than they.'

While explaining to the ashram sisters, Gandhi wrote that the real meaning of economic equality is: 'To each according to his need'. That is the definition of Marx. If a single man demands as much as a man with wife and four children, it would be violation of economic equality.

We are all absolutely equal. But equality is of souls and not bodies. Hence, it is a mental state. We need to think of and to asset equality because we see great inequalities in the physical world. We have to realize equality in the midst of this apparent external by any person over any other, is a sin against God and man.[43] While we are born equal—meaning that we have a right to equal opportunity—all do not have the same capacity. It is in the nature of things impossible. For instance, all cannot have the same height, or colour or degree of intelligence; therefore, in the nature of things, some will have ability to earn more and others less.[44] If we wish to develop in us the capacity to look on all as equals, we should aim at getting only what the rest of the world gets. Thus, if the whole world gets milk, we may also have it. We may pray to God and say: 'O God, if you wish me to have milk, give it first to the rest of the world'.

Kisans

'Swaraj is a mighty structure. Eighty crores of hands have to work at building it. Of these kisans, i.e., the peasantries are the largest part. In fact, being the bulk of them (probably over 80 per cent) the kisans should be the Congress. The kisan or the peasant—whether as a landless labourer or a labouring proprietor—comes first. He is the salt of the earth, which rightly belongs or should belong to him, not to the absentee landlord or Zamindar. But in the non-violent way, the labourer cannot forcibly eject the absentee landlord. He has so to work as to make it impossible for the landlord to exploit him.'[45]

In Gandhi's opinion, the kisan must not be used for power politics. He considers it contrary to the nonviolent method. Kisans must be properly organized. To this end, special organizing bodies or committees should be formed where there are none, and those already in existence should be reformed and strengthened.

Labourers

The Ahmedabad Labour Union is a model for all India to copy. Its basis is non-violence, pure and simple. Gandhi stated, 'If I had my way, I would regulate all the labour organizations of India after the Ahmedabad model.' Labour is more than money. When labour is intelligent enough to organize itself and learn to act as one man, it will have the same weight as money, if not much greater. Labour is far superior to capital. Without labour, gold, silver and copper are a useless burden. It is labour, which extracts precious ore from the bowels of the earth.

Capital controls labour because it knows the art of combination. Drops in separation can only fade away. Drops in seperation could only fade away; drops in co-operation made the ocean, which carried on its broad bosom ocean greyhounds. A true and non-violent combination of labour would act like a magnet, attracting to it all the needed capital.[46]

Labour should be made conscious of its duty, from whose performance rights follow as a matte of course. Like a ship without direction or destination, labour without an ideal, is fruitless. Labour, in Gandhi's opinion, must not become a power in the hands of the politicians on the political chessboard. It must, by its sheer strength, dominate the chessboard. A nation may do without its millionaires and without its capitalists, but a nation can never do without its labour.

Adivasis

Service of the adivasis is also a part of the constructive programme. The adivasis or the tribals are not an inconsiderable group as you say. There are over two crores or 23 million of them spread all over India—from Assam in the North-East, through Bihar, Madhya Pradesh, Rajasthan, Gujarat and Maharashtra in the west, and from north to south. Little work was done among them during the period of the British rule except by Christian missionaries who, with a few exceptions like Elwyn Verrier, actually alienated them from the stream of Indian nationalism, and were mainly interested in their conversion to Christianity. Of the Congressmen, Thakkar Bapa did some work among the Bhils in Gujarat and Balasahib Kher threw himself with his usual zeal into this much-needed service in Thana in the 1940s. But, by and large, this difficult work was completely ignored.

It should have received a fillip after political independence was gained, but this did not happen. Congressmen, as the other parties, never took to constructive work, and the constructive programme was given a complete go-by. Congressmen and the Congress Government became wholly engrossed in the exercise of power and the fruits that power brings. They failed to realize that it was difficult to make good their claim to be one nation, unless every group acquired a living consciousness of being one with all others. They also forgot that service of the tribals was not only humanitarian but also solidly national and designed to bring them close to true independence.

If a sizable section of our people has to be brought into the national stream, both the ruling and the other parties should stop using the Adivasis for their own ulterior ends, as they have been recently doing in Assam and elsewhere, and begin in all earnestness constructive work among them.[47]

Leprosy

'Leper is a word of bad odour. India is perhaps a home of lepers, next only to Central Africa. Yet, they are as much a part of society as the tallest among us. But the tall absorb our attention, though they are the least in need of it. The lot of the lepers, who are much more in need of attention, is steeped in neglect. I am tempted to call it heartless, which it certainly is, in terms of non-violence.'[48]

Why should there be a stigma about leprosy any more than about other infectious diseases? Real leprosy is attached to an unclean mind. To look down upon fellow human beings, to condemn any community or class of men, is a sign of a diseased mind far worse than physical leprosy. Such men are real lepers of society. [49]

Students

Students are the hope of the future. It is from these young men and women that the future leaders of the nation will rise. Students must not take part in party politics. They may not resort to political strikes. They must do all sacrificial spinning in a scientific manner. They should be khadi users all through and use village products. A student's life has been rightly likened to the life of a sanyasi. He must be the embodiment of simple living and high thinking. He must be discipline incarnate. His pleasure is derived from his studies. Education provides real pleasure; when study ceases to be a tax the student has to pay. What can be a greater pleasure than that a student marches from knowledge?[50]

The life of a student is to correspond to the life of a sanyasi up to the time his studies end. He is to be under the strictest discipline.

'How can we understand the duty of students today? We have fallen so much from the ideal. The parents take the lead in misleading their children. They feel that their children should be educated only in order that they may earn wealth and position. Education and knowledge are thus being prostituted and we look in vain for the peace, innocence and bliss that the life of a student ought to be.'[51]

Students have to become nation builders. The base imitation of the West, and the ability to speak and write correct and polished English will not add one brick to the temple of Freedom. Students must become pioneers in conservation and reform, conserving all that is good in the nation and fearlessly ridding society of the innumerable abuses that have crept into it Students have to react for the dumb millions. They have to learn to think, not in terms of a province, or a town, or a class, or a caste, but in terms of a continent and of the millions who include among them the untouchables, drunkards, hooligans and even prostitutes, for whose existence in our midst every one of us is responsible.[52] Students have to search within and look into their personal character. Purity of personal life is the one indispensable condition for building a sound education. No man or women with an impure heart can possibly appear before the Great White Throne. All our learning or recitation of the Vedas, correct knowledge of Sanskrit, Latin, Greek and what not, will avail us nothing, if they do not enable us to cultivate absolute purity of heart. The end of all knowledge must be building up of character.

An individual's education is absolutely worthless, if it is not built on a solid foundation of truth and purity. 'If you, boys, are careful about the personal purity of your lives, and if you are not careful about being pure in thought, speech and deed, then I tell you that you are lost, although you may become perfect, finished scholars.

'I do not care what you learn or what you do not learn in your school, if you will observe two conditions. One condition is that you must be fearlessly truthful against the heaviest odds, under every circumstance imaginable. A truthful boy, a brave boy, will never a think of hurting even a fly. He will defend all the weak boys in his own school and help—whether inside school or outside the school—all those who need his help. A boy who does not observe personal purity of mind and body and action, is a boy who should be driven out of any school.

Students should have the greatest freedom of expression and of opinion. But, in my opinion, they may not have freedom of action whilst they are studying. Students cannot afford to have party politics. They may listen to all the political parties, as they read all sorts of books, but their business is to assimilate the truth of all and reject the balance. That is the only worthy attitude that they can take. The students should know that the cultivation of nationalism is not a crime but a virtue.

Gandhi advised what the students should do and what they should not do:

- Students must not take part in party politics. They are students and researchers, not politicians.
- They should not resort to political strikes. All differences with the teaching staff and management should be settled peacefully and amicably.
- The students must all do either sacrificial spinning in a scientific manner or perform other bread or body labour in addition to their studies.
- They will be khadi wearers all through and use village products to the exclusion of all analogues things, either foreign or machine-made.
- They should honour the national flag and harbour neither communalism nor untouchability in their hearts.
- They will make it a point to give first-aid to their injured neighbours and do scavenging and cleaning in the neighbouring villages and instruct the village children and adults.
- They will learn and teach the national language, in one or both scripts—Devanagari or Persian.
- They will translate into Hindustani or the mother tongue everything new they may learn, and transmit it to the villagers.
- They will do nothing in secret, will be above board in all their dealings, will lead a life of self-restraint, shed all fear, be always ready to protect all their weak fellow students, and be ready to quell riots by non-violent conduct at the risk of their lives.
- They will be scrupulously correct and chivalrous in their behaviour towards their girl fellow students.

Gandhi said. 'For working out the programme I have sketched for them, the students must find time. I know that they waste a great deal of time in idleness. By strict economy of time, they can save many hours. I would, therefore, advise patriotic students to lose some period, not at a stretch but spread over their period of study. They will find that a year or more, so given, will not be a waste of time. The effort will add to their equipment—mental, moral, and physical—and they will have made, even during their studies, a substantial contribution to the social and economic freedom movement.[53]

Cow Protection

Cow protection is one of the most wonderful phenomena in human evolution. It takes the human being beyond his species. The cow to Gandhi meant the entire subhuman world. Man, through the cow, is enjoyed to realize his identity with all that lives. Why the cow was selected for apotheosis is obvious to me. In India, the cow was the best companion. She was the giver of plenty. Not only did she give milk but she also made agriculture possible. The cow is a poem of pity. One reads pity in the gentle animal. She is the mother to millions of Indian mankind. Protection of the cow means protection of all the whole dumb creations of God. The ancient seer, whoever he was, began with the cow. The appeal of the lower orders of creation is all the more forcible because it is speechless.'

A Hindu who protects the cow should protect every animal. But taking all things into consideration, we may not cavil at his protecting the cow because he fails to protect the other animals. The only question, therefore, to consider is whether he is right in protecting the cow. And he cannot be wrong in doing so if non-killing of animals generally may be regarded as a duty for one who believes in ahimsa. And every Hindu and, for that matter, every man of religion, does so. The duty of non-killing animals—generally and therefore of protecting them—must be accepted as an indisputable fact. It is then so much to the credit of Hinduism that it has taken up cow protection as a duty. And he is a poor specimen of Hinduism who stops merely at cow protection, when he can extend the arm of protection to other animals as well. The cow merely stands as a symbol, and the protection of the cow is the least that a man is expected to undertake.'[54]

Nature Cure

The laws of nature are changeless, unchangeable, and there are no miracles in the sense of infringement or interruption of nature's laws. The essence of nature cure is that we learn the principles of hygiene and sanitation, and abide by those laws as well as the laws relating to proper nutrition. Thus, every one becomes his own doctor. Nature cure connects a way of life which has to be learnt; it is not drug cure as we understand it. Nature cure is not like a doctor giving medicine in a bottle. It is really the natural way of keeping health and happiness.

'Whether you get or not, what does it matter? The more reliance we place on God, the more peace of mind we shall have. Vaidyas and doctors are there, of course, but they take us farther away from God. Nature cure treatment takes us nearer to God. I will have no objection whatever if we could do even without it. But why be afraid of fast or avoid pure air? The meaning of nature cure is to go nearer to nature, that is, God.'[55]

The human body, the living temple of god, and a living miraculous machine, is self-relevant in maintaining health, as well as curing ill health .Nature cure is an art as well a science of healthy living and a drugless system of healing based on well-founded philosophy. It has its own concept of health and disease and the principles of treatment.

Nature cure is a system of man building in harmony with the constructive principles of nature on physical, mental, moral and spiritual planes of living. It is a great way of promoting good health, and also has curative and rehabilitative potential. In fact, nature cure is an ancient method of living and curing diseases. The main concepts of nature cure are morbid matter theory and the concept of vital force. The fundamental difference between nature cure and other systems is that its theory and practice are purely based on a holistic view point, unlike the latter's approach, which is specific. Nature cure does not believe in the specific cause of disease and its specific treatment but takes into account the totality of factors responsible for the disease, such as one's unnatural habits, thinking, working, sleeping, relaxation, sexual indulgence, and other physical needs. It also considers the environmental factors involved that disturb the normal functioning of the body and lead it to a morbid, weak and toxic state. For treatment purposes, nature cure primarily tries to correct all the factors responsible for the diseases and allows the body to recover itself. A nature cure physician simply helps in nature's effort to overcome any disease by applying correct natural modalities and controlling the natural forces to work under safe limits. The five main modalities of treatment in nature are air, water, heat, mud and space.

Naturopaths believe that the human body is composed of five great elements (or Pancha Maha Bhootas). Imbalances of these create diseases. These five elements include air, water, earth, heat and space. Treatment through these elements is what is called nature cure.

Bhoodan

Pochampalli is the village where the first bhoodan took place, wherein, for the first time in India, 100 acres of land was offered from the hands of Shri Ram Chandra Reddy to Acharya Vinoba Bhave on April 18, 1951 in Andhra Pradesh, in an area affected by Marxist violence. After this land gift, Vinoba Bhave started his marathon Bhoodan Yatra of 80 thousand kilometers, which took him 13 years to complete. Vinoba calculated that India had 10 million landless families and they required 50 million acres of land, which was one-sixth of the country's cultivable, land—namely, 300 million acres. The assumption was that each landless family would need about 5 acres of land for its support.

Vinoba Bhave walked on foot from state to state and asked every landlord for one-sixth of his land. Thousands of acres poured in as free gifts. The Bhoodan Movement attracted national and international attention. It then led to Gramdan. Now the village community could redistribute the available land and start a new programme of cooperative farming or group and individual farming along with allied programmes like animal husbandry, rural industry and village health. In a new social climate the village as a whole could plan sanitation, village education and other developmental measures.

Gramdan

Gramdan grew as a natural offshoot of Bhoodan as a consequence of all, or almost all, the landowners in a village donating all their land in the village. This occurred first, as early as May 1952, at Mangroth in Uttar Pradesh where the donated land was vested in the village community and subsequently distributed among the villagers in pieces, which varied according to each family's capacity and needs. Some of the families then formed a cooperative farm, the others continuing to farm as family units. The radical implications of Gramdan when compared with Bhoodan soon became apparent. Whereas Bhoodan involved donations from individuals, Gramdan also involved community action. Under Bhoodan, individual ownership of land was retained but under Gramdan it was abolished and the land 'villagized'. Thirdly, whereas the beneficiary of Bhoodan was an individual or group of individuals, the beneficiary of Gramdan was the entire village community. In short, the move from Bhoodan to Gramdan represented a move from a basically individualist programme (and one which could be criticized for increasing the fragmentation of landholdings) to a basically socialist programme. Despite the more radical character of Gramdan, the number of villages opting for it increased until nearly 2,000 had done so by the end of 1956. In 1957, therefore, instead of the movement ruefully lamenting the failure to meet its Bhoodan target, it announced that its sights were now set on ending private ownership of land altogether. The original target was absorbed in this new resolve; the target, henceforth, was Gramdan as the basis for establishing Gramswarajya.

Shanti Sena

Gandhi thought of 'Peace Brigades' or 'Shanti Senani' as early as 1938 in the context of communal riots in India. He wrote in the Harijan on June 18 1938.

'Some time ago I suggested the formation of a Peace Brigade whose members would risk their lives in dealing with riots, especially communal. The idea was that this brigade should substitute the police and even the military. This needs ambition. The achievement may prove impossible. Yet, if the Congress is to succeed in its non violent struggle, it must develop the power to deal peacefully with such situations'.

In that article, Gandhi listed the qualifications and attributes of a member of the peace brigade:

- He or she must have a living faith in nonviolence. This is impossible without a living faith in god.
- The messenger of peace must have equal regard for all the principal religions of the earth.
- Peace work can be done either singly or in groups.
- The messenger of peace will cultivate through personal service, contacts with the people in his locality.
- A peace bringer must have a character beyond reproach and must be known for his strict impartiality.
- A peace brigade will not wait till the conflagration breaks out, but will try to handle the situation in anticipation.
- There should be a distinctive dress worn by the members of the peace brigade so that they can be recognized without difficulty.

This list of qualifications and attributes gives an idea of the way Gandhi's mind was working at that time regarding the Shanti Sena.

Gandhi's life and death gave a brilliant demonstration of what a Shanti Sainik (Peace Soldier) should be like. In his last years, he functioned as a shining embodiment of the ideal of Shanti Sena. His own wonderful performance at Calcutta is part of history. Gandhi's lonely trek in the village of riot-torn Noakhali is also part of history. Lord Mountbatten called Gandhi 'the One man Boundary Force'.

Summing Up

The future lies in India, its path of democracy as well as the spiritualism that lies at its core, through constructive work programme. India achieved political independence on August 15, 1947, but it still has to attain economic and social freedom. This is possible by adopting Gandhi's constructive programme. Gandhi himself came to believe that his constructive programme or constructive work was generally even more important. He realized in 1939 that the origin of satyagraha was constructive work, and he believed that the future of India 'for thousand years was constructive work'.

The Gandhian constructive programme never failed to furnish a vital, moral and spiritual background to the secular activities contained in it. All those engaged in the constructive programme developed in a larger or smaller measure a missionary zeal. At whatever point they worked, they felt the inspiration that their work is necessary in a great programme of national reconstruction.

Gandhi felt the constructive programme in its entirely is to enable masses to emerge out of bondage into freedom and out of economic and social deprivation into self-reliance and out of state of alienation into cooperative living. Through this programme, he explored the possibility of building up a power-free, non-authoritarian, non-exploitative society by changing the present set up. This is not purely administrative or managerial task. Crucial to the successful realization of Gandhi's original objective is the urgency of two-fold action. Firstly, it is reiterating and reaffirming the essential purpose of constructive work, viz., to bring about socio-economic changes and reconstruct the social and human relations based on freedom, equality and respect for the individual personality and ultimately building a non-violent, non-exploitative social and economic order—a society based on the ideals of sarvodaya. Secondly, it is evolving such practical ways as will enable us all to ensure that the principles and fundamental revolutionary intention which lay behind Gandhi's programme get woven into our routines of work and this his ideals remain in command.

There are increasing problems. With courage and conviction and with abiding faith in the teachings of Gandhi, we have to tackle the problems of poverty, ignorance, malnutrition, insanitary conditions, population explosion, and the caste system. In every village, there should be a body of workers (not servants) of the nation engaged in constructive work to achieve social, moral and economic freedom. It should be organized democratically from the bottom upwards. Five adult workers should form a unit. Two contiguous panchayats should elect a leader. Fifty first grade elders should elect a second grade leader and so on till they cover the entire country.

Salvation of the present and future crisis can be resolved by fully adopting the constructive programme as evolved by Gandhi. It would help us to lead from darkness to light. Constructive work should become both a lamp and a mirror. As a lamp it will guide us, and as a mirror it will show us what we are. Both lamp and mirror will enable us to consciously introspect our behaviour and conduct so that we will not become a notoriously divisive lot.

Notes and References

1. Gandhi, M. K., *Constructive Programme: Its Meaning and Place*, Ahmedabad: Navjivan Mudranalaya, 1941, p.5.
2. Ibid.
3. Gujral, M. L., *Thus Spake Bapu, or Dialogues Between Gandhi's Spirit and the Scribe*, New Delhi: Gandhi Peace Foundation, 1985, p. 119.
4. *Harijan*, April 12, 1942.
5. Ibid.
6. *Harijan*, Jan. 4, 1946.
7. Tandon, Vishwanath, *The Social and political Philosophy of Sarvodaya after Gandhi*, Varanasi: Sarva Seva Sangh, Rajghat, 1965, pp.163–164.
8. *Young India*, May 11, 1921.
9. *Young India*, October 21, 1926.
10. *Young India*, January 15, 1925.
11. *Young India*, September 25, 1925.
12. *Young India*, December 4, 1924.
13. *Harijan*, March 2, 1934.
14. *Harijan*, Febuary 2, 1934.
15. Ibid.
16. *Young India*, December 2, 1920.
17. *Harijan*, March 2, 1934.
18. *Harijan*, June 20, 1936.
19. *From Yeravada Mandir*, p. 33.
20. *Harijan*, September 15, 1946.
21. Ibid.
22. *Harijan*, January 19, 1934.
23. Ibid.
24. Tendulkar, *D. G., Mahatma*, Vol. VI, p. 20.
25. *Harijan*, January 20, 1927.
26. *Young India*, July 16, 1931.
27. Gandhi, M. K., *Constructive Programme: Its Meaning and Place*, Ahmedabad: Navjivan *Mudranalaya*, 1941, p. 11.
28. *Harijan*, November 30, 1934.
29. *Harijan*, February 8, 1935.
30. Harijan, April 6, 1940.
31. Harijan, December 19, 1938.

32. Tendulkar, D. G., Mahatma, V. 6. p. 290.
33. Ibid., p. 289.
34. Young India, October 17, 1929.
35. Young India, April 10, 1930.
36. Harijan, November 14, 1936.
37. Letters to Rajkumari Amrit Kaur.
38. Harijan, June 29, 1935.
39. From a Letter to Vidya Hingorani, March 3, 1932.
40. Gandhi, M. K., Constructive Programme: Its Meaning and Place, Ahmedabad: Navjivan Mudranalaya, 1941, p. 21.
41. Ibid.
42. Harijan, October 6, 1946.
43. Young India, June 4, 1931.
44. Young India, November 26, 1931.
45. Press Report, October 26, 1944.
46. Harijan, September 7, 1947.
47. Gujral, M. L., Thus Spake Bapu, or Dialogues Between Gandhi's Spirit and the Scribe, GPF, New Delhi, 1985, p. 120.
48. Harijan, November 2, 1947.
49. Ibid.
50. Harijan, August 17, 1947.
51. Young India, January 29, 1925.
52. Young India, June 9, 1927.
53. Gujral, M. L., op. cit., pp.133–134.
54. Ibid., pp. 121–122.
55. From a Letter to Anand T. Hingorani, January 9, 1945.

Summary

Constructive programme will lead to the reconstruction of both men and society by correcting the faults of private and public life. Gandhi regarded constructive work to be 'the fulfillment of swaraj'.

Gandhi launched a movement of constructive programme for economic betterment and for improving the tenor of social life for generation after generations.

The constructive programme is the long-term pre-requisite of a system of non-violent self-rule, without which political power or formal independence would prove to be a shame.

The constructive programme includes individual and collective efforts on behalf of unity between diverse religious communities, the removal of social abuses such as untouchability, programmes of rural education and reconstruction, the decentralization of production and distributions, schemes for the improvement of health, sanitation and diet, the promotion of local handicrafts, and in general, concreted work by all to promote the common good.

Constructive programme is designed to build up the nation from the very bottom. It must mean complete independence in every sense of the expression.

In 1931 Gandhi wrote, 'My work of social reform was no way less than or subordinate to political work. The fact is that when I saw that to a certain extent my social work would be impossible without the help of political work, I took to the latter and only to the extent that it helped the former. I must, therefore, confess that the work of social reform or self-purification of this nature is hundred times dearer to me than what is called purely political work.'

Constructive programme consists of several apparently unconnected, independent activities. But all these are united together by a framework which supports the idea of a novel revolution. Gandhi believed in the dual revolution, in the minds of men as well as in the structure of society which brought power to the local community.

In 1941, Gandhi had listed the following thirteen items:

> Communal unity, removal of untouchability, prohibition, khadi, other village industries, village sanitation, new or basic education, adult education, women, education in health and hygiene, provincial languages, propagation of Rashtra Bhasa, and promotion of economic equality.
>
> In 1945, Gandhi added the following items:
>
> Kisans, labour, adivasis, lepers and students.
>
> After Gandhi's death, the following items were added:
>
> Cow protection, nature cure, Bhoodan, Gramdan and Shanti Sena.

The future lies in India, its path of democracy as well as the spiritualism that lies at its core through constructive work programme. India achieved political independence, but it still has to attain economic and social freedom. This is possible by adopting Gandhi's constructive programme.

Gandhi felt the constructive programme in its entirely is to enable masses to emerge out of bondage into freedom and out of economic and social deprivation into self-reliance and out of state of alienation into cooperative living. Through this programme, he explored the possibility of building up a power-free, non-authoritarian, non-exploitative society by changing the present set up.

Further Reading

Dhawan, Gopinath, The Political Philosophy of Mahatma Gandhi, Delhi: Gandhi Peace Foundation, 1990.

Gandhi, M. K., Non-violence in Peace and War, Ahmedabad: Navjivan Publishing House, 1949.

Mehta, Ved, Mahatma Gandhi and His Apostles, New Haven: Yale University Press, 1993.

Parekh, Bhikhu, Colonialism, Tradition, and Reform: An Analysis of Gandhi's Political Discourse, New Delhi: Sage Publications, New Delhi, 1989.

14

Communal Unity

Introduction

India is a land of diversity, populated by heterogeneous people of multifarious languages, religions, castes and creeds. In spite of all such diversities of character, there is an underlying unity among them since time immemorial. The fact also remains that there is always a threat of narrow communal feelings.

There are different categories of community—racial, lingual and religious. The racial communities generally comprise Aryans, Dravidians, Anglo Indians and aborigines. The lingual communities are generally those who speak Bengali, Punjabi, Gujarati, Marathi, Oriya, Assamia, Tamil, Telegu, Kannada and Malayalam. The religious communities are generally Hindus, Muslims, Sikhs, Christians and Parsis, along with some more minorities. Within the religious communities also, there is a division. People of these communities fall easy prey to narrow communal sentiments. Some anti-social elements and political self-seekers fan narrow communal feelings for their own selfish interests and create narrow communal feelings in people. They appeal to their communal emotions, leading to riots, discord and disharmony, all in the name of communality. Such activities will, no doubt, weaken our national unity.

In modern India, Gandhi was one of the greatest champions of communal unity. He lived his whole life striving for it, ensuring it, stood firmly by it, and finally sacrificed his life in the pursuit of communal unity. For Gandhi, the issue of communal unity was greater than even *swaraj*. None of the political leaders or religious priests were as devotedly concerned about communal unity as Gandhi was.

Communal unity was the first and foremost concern for Gandhi. Gandhi said that '*Swaraj* was impossible without Hindu-Muslim Unity'.[1] Mahatma Gandhi devoted his entire life in propounding communal harmony. When speaking of the India of his dream, he wished, 'I shall wish for an India, in which the poorest shall feel that it is their country in whose making they have an effective voice; an India in which there shall be no high class and low class of people; [and above all] an India in which all communities shall live in perfect harmony.'

Gandhi left no stone unturned in his efforts to bring about Hindu-Muslim unity. He preached, he wrote, he negotiated, fasted and prayed for communal unity. In his constructive programme, he gave the first place to communal harmony among the people of different faiths.

Gandhi pleaded for the cause of better understanding among individuals and communities. Everywhere in the world, individuals and groups are divided because of fear, suspicion and hatred towards each other, which further depends on whether the division is expressed along the lines of religion, economy, politics, caste, or colour. Whatever is the form, insecurity is perhaps the major cause of individual or social dissensions. A person who is integrated and sure of himself fears none and, consequently, provokes no fear. We have examples of such heroic individuals. But till date, we do not have any instances of societies or communities that are fully integrated and, therefore, fearless.

Gandhi felt the need of community unity during his stay in South Africa. The principal question before him was harmony between Hindus and Muslims who inhabited the country. Gandhi felt that if Hindu-Muslim unity was established, unity with other communities could be easily strengthened. He never found serious differences between the Hindus and Muslims and other minority communities like the Christians and the Sikhs, not to speak of the small community of Parsis. Naturally, therefore, he turned to the question of Hindu-Muslim unity.

Gandhi insisted that the Hindus who are in a majority in the country should help the Muslims and should never entertain any idea of enforcing their rights but try to win the hearts of the minority community. He wrote: 'I am striving to become the best cement between the two communities. My longing is to be able to cement the two with my blood, if necessary. There is nothing in either religion to keep the two communities apart. In nature, there is a fundamental unity running through the diversity. Religions are no exception to the natural law. They are given to mankind so as to accelerate the process of realization of fundamental unity. The need of the moment is not an establishment of a universal religion but to develop mutual respect towards the different religions.'

In *Young India*, February 25, 1920 Gandhi wrote that 'Hindu-Muslim unity consists in our having a common purpose, a common goal and common sorrows. It is best promoted by co-operating to reach the common goal, by sharing one another's sorrows and by mutual tolerance.' Further, in December 2, 1920 in *Young India*, he writes that, 'This unity cannot be a mere policy to be discarded when we are tired of *swaraj*. Hindu-Muslim unity must be our creed to last for all time and under all circumstances.'

Communalism Defined

Communalism is one of the most serious problems that India has to face before and after her freedom from colonial rule. This problem, which has existed among the followers of two principal religious communities, Hindus and Muslims, has often raised a great challenge before the secular structure of India.

Not only in India but also all over the world, scholars and subject-specialists have defined communalism in different manners. And, all these definitions, unfortunately, do not reveal the complete meaning or sense of communalism in clear-cut terms. However, Richard C. Lambert, who has given the definition of community according to the conditions prevailing in the country, provides us with a correct picture regarding the position of communalism in India. According to Lambert, 'The word community is used in India for the unequal social units.' It may be said that communalism is the negative aspect of the community. That is to say, when the people of a particular community care only for their own narrowly concerned interests, through the means of their religious faiths, old customs and conservative practices, disregarding the interests of whole society, then it may be termed as communalism.

Noted historian Bipan Chandra in his book *India's Struggle for Independence* wrote that communalism consists of three basic elements. First, it is a belief that people who follow the same religion have common secular interests, i.e., common political, economic, social and cultural interests. Second, in a multi religious society like India, secular interests such as social, cultural, economic and political of one religion are dissimilar with that of other religions. Third, communalism arises when the interests of different religions are seen as mutually in compatible, antagonistic and hostile.

Communal ideology starts when persons or groups believe that people of the same religion have the same socio-economic interests. The second stage is reached when a person or a group believes and practices communal politics, i.e., while holding that different religion-based communities have their own special interests. These interests can be reconciled and accommodated. The third stage is reached when the religious differences are converted into secular differences and are seen to be incompatible with each other.

K. P. Karunakaran[2] wrote that, 'communalism in India meant that philosophy which stood for the promotion of the interests of a particular religious community or the members of a particular caste'. The first Prime Minister of India, Pandit Jawahar Lal Nehru,[3] a historian of repute, wrote that 'one must never forget that communalism in India is a later-day phenomenon which has grown up before our eyes'.

Hindu-Muslim Communalism: The Context

Before the coming of the British in India, the Hindu and Muslim masses on the whole lived together without antipathy or bitterness, though there existed certain religious trends which were exclusive and antagonistic. Even in the 1857 revolt, Hindus and Muslims fought together side by side and their anger was directed against the common enemy, the foreign rulers at whose hands all of India suffered alike. But during this early phase of Indian nationalism, Muslims lagged behind. Nationalist ideas spread among the Hindu middle and lower middle classes but not to an equal extent among the Muslims.

As the national movement spread and grew, there was the threat that it might unify the people and pose serious problems for the empire. 'A united people cannot be kept under subjugation for a long time.' The British decided to do all they could to keep the people disunited and quarrel and compete among themselves. They decided to divide the people in the name of their different religions and to encourage communal and separatist tendencies in Indian politics.

The rise of Muslim communalism is associated with the name of Sayyid Ahmed Khan. He began as a great educationist and social reformer. Initially, he believed in the close co-operation of the Hindus and the Muslims. For the establishment of the Mohammedan Anglo Oriental College at Aligarh, he received donations from both Hindus and Muslims. In 1884 he said 'Do you not inhabit the same land? Are you not burned and buried on the same soil? Remember that the words Hindus and Mohammedan are only meant for religious distinction; otherwise all persons, whether Hindu or Mohammedan, even the Christians who reside in this country, are all in this aspect belonging to one and the same nation.'[4]

However, with the rise of the Indian National Congress, Sayyid Ahmed became apprehensive about the position of the Muslims. The British also pulled strings behind the scenes. Sayyid Ahmed declared that 'the interests of Hindus and Muslims were different and even opposite'. He told his followers that 'if the British withdrew, the Hindu majority would dominate over and be unfair to the Muslim minority.'[5] He advised the Muslims not to join the Indian National Congress. He also declared that if the educated Muslims remained loyal to the British, they would reward them with government jobs and other special favours.

Then came the Bengal Partition in 1905. It was ostensibly for better administration of an unwieldy province but the actual reason was to curb the radical Bengali nationalists. Administrative convenience and development of Assam were the avowed objects of the plan. But politics had already crept in. 'It was a measure whose object was to break the growing solidarity of the political community which led India in opposition to government.'[6] Risley wrote, 'Bengal united is a power, Bengal divided will pull several different ways … one of our main objects is to split up and thereby weaken a solid body of opponents to our rule.'[7]

Curzon knew very well that 'Calcutta is the centre from which the Congress party is manipulated throughout the whole of Bengal and indeed the whole of India. Its best wire-pullers and its most frothy orators all reside here; they dominate public opinion in Calcutta. The whole of their activity is directed to creating an agency so powerful that they may one day to able to force a weak government to give them what they desire.'[8]

The partition was came into being because the British rulers were alarmed at the growth of national solidarity in India and were anxious to thwart it. October 16, 1905, the day when the partition was made effective, was called a day of national mourning. Hindus and Muslims tied *rakhis* to one another's wrists as a symbol of fraternity. Gokhale referred to the partition as 'a cruel wrong'.

A concrete shape and setting to the communal theory was given in 1906 when the All India Muslim League was set up under the leadership of Aga Khan, Nawab Salimullah of Dacca and Nawab Mohsin-ul-Mulk. The league supported the partition of Bengal and demanded special and separate electorates. The British were waiting for just such an opportunity. They made full use of it and announced that they would protect the 'special-interests' of the Muslims. The League said that 'the interests of the Muslims were different and divergent from those of the rest of the nation'.[9] One major objectives of the league was to keep the Muslims from joining the Congress. Its activities were directed against the Congress and not against the British government.

Viceroy Minto decided to play the game of 'divide and rule' once again. The Morley-Minto Reforms introduced a system of separate electorate and representation for the Indian Muslims. It provided for separate constituencies from which only a Muslim could stand as candidate and for which only Muslims would vote. The main feature of this reform was its emphasis upon the principle of community and group interests. It encouraged separatist tendencies. The real purpose of this move was to divide the nationalist movement and to check the growing unity among the Indians by encouraging the growth of Muslim communalism.

The communal view of politics was unscientific and irrational but it played upon the fears from which any minority tends to suffer. Under these circumstances, it was very important to tie the loose knot of unity strongly and tightly. Gandhi's understanding of the communal problem was of momentous consequence. His main concern was not only to free the country from British rule but also to establish communal harmony.

Indian National Movement and the Question of Communal Unity

Gandhi emerged as an undisputed leader of the Indian national movement. He returned to India in January 1915 from South Africa. In the course of his struggle against racialism in South Africa, he had developed his unique philosophy of action—*satyagraha.* Its two major elements were truth and non-violence. Gandhi said, 'If *satyagraha* was successful in Africa, why not try it in India? I have no doubt that the British government is a powerful government but I have no doubt also that *satyagraha* is a sovereign remedy.'[10] He experimented with his plan of action in Champaran, Kheda and Ahmedabad.

The First World War ended in November 1918. Indians were expecting substantial constitutional concessions in return for their whole hearted support to the British government during the war. But Rowlatt Bills were passed (measures of arbitrary arrests without trial and restrictions on the movement of persons suspected of anti-government activities). Gandhi's patience came to an end. 'This was the beginning of the transformation from a loyal citizen of the empire to an extreme rebel.'[11] He again said that, 'The British Empire today represents Satanism and those who love God can afford to have no love for Satan.'[12] *Amrita Bazar Patrika* called this act a 'gigantic blunder which would arouse the worst passions of peaceful law abiding people.'[13]

In Delhi, Satyagraha Diwas was observed on March 30, 1919. Hindus and Muslims together joined the demonstration. Swami Shraddhanand, an eminent Arya Samaj leader was invited to address the Muslims at Jama Masjid. Gandhi and Sarojini Naidu made speeches in a mosque. The fraternization of the Hindus and Muslims and the excitement in the masses were portents of danger in the eyes of authorities. Then occurred the massacre of Jallianwala Bagh on April 13, 1919. This tragedy brought Gandhi into the forefront of Indian politics. Now there was no other way except non-cooperation with British government.

Khilafat Movement and Communal Unity

The First World War ended (November 1918) with the victory of the Allies. Germany surrendered on November 11 and Turkey had capitulated on October 31. The Ottoman Empire lay shattered. The Sultan of Turkey was to recognized as the Caliph, i.e., religious head of the Muslims and had to perform certain duties towards the holy places of Islam. But the harsh terms imposed upon Turkey by the Treaty of Sevres reduced her to utter ruin. The Muslim community was stirred to its depths. The war created a serious religious dilemma for them. As subjects of Britain, they owed loyalty to the government which had allowed them freedom of belief and worship, but in deference to their tradition, they were bound to obey the Caliph, who was the religious head of the entire Muslim community.

Gandhi, who had been an ardent advocate of Hindu Muslim unity since the days in South Africa, got an opportunity with the issue of the Khilafat question. He spoke extensively on the subject and cultivated influential Muslims like the Ali brothers, Hakim Ajmal Khan, Shuaib Qureshi and Dr. Ansari, in order to understand their fears and aspirations. Gandhi felt that their Khilafat demand was just. For him, 'It was a golden opportunity to cement that unity for good, an opportunity which might perhaps never again recur.'[14] Gandhi also realized the depth of their feelings over the issue and decided to champion their cause.

Gandhi stated, 'I am bound as an Indian to share the sufferings and trials of fellow Indians. If I deem the Mohammedan to be my brother, it is my duty to help him in this hour of trial to the best of my ability if his cause commends itself to me as just.'[15] On July 20, 1920, Gandhi attended the Khilafat committee and called upon 'The 23 crore Hindus to help seven crore Muslims and to desist from helping the government'.[16] Gandhi wrote, 'To my amazement and dismay I have discovered that the present representatives of the empire have become dishonest and unscrupulous. I can no longer retain affection for a government so evilly manned as it is now a days.'[17]

The non-cooperation movement started. Gandhi wrote to the viceroy, 'The Imperial government has acted in the Khilafat matter in an unjust and immoral manner.' Along with the letter, Gandhi returned all the medals which the government had bestowed on him as mark of appreciation for his service to the nation.

Gandhi, Shaukat Ali, Muhammad Ali and other leaders toured extensively through India, rousing the people's enthusiasm and laying stress upon Hindu-Muslim unity. Gandhi said, 'It is just my sense of moral responsibilities which has made me take up the Khilafat question and to identify myself entirely with the Mohammedans. It is perfectly true that I am assisting and countenancing the union between Hindus and Muslims.'[18] It was recognized that the Hindu-Muslim unity was the key to *swaraj*.

Even Mohammed Ali Jinnah held identical views at that time. Jinnah said in a Muslim League meeting, 'We must not forget that one essential requisite condition to achieve *swaraj* is the political unity between the Hindus and the Mohammedans. I am almost inclined to say that India will get Dominion Responsible government the day the Hindus and Muslims are united.'[19] Gokhale called Gandhi 'the Ambassador of Hindu-Muslim unity.'[20] Gandhi also held the same views. He wrote, '*Swaraj* for India must be an impossible dream without an indissoluble union between the Hindus and the Muslims.'[21]

Gandhi felt the distrust between the two communities. 'The cement binding the two is yet loose and wet,' he wrote. 'I know there is much distrust of one another …The Hindus believe that *swaraj* means Muslim Raj... Muslims, on the other hand, fear that the Hindus being in overwhelming majority will smother them.'[22]

While both sides were in a jittery state, Hindu-Muslim quarrels began raising their head in Bengal, Punjab and other provinces. The worst case was that of Kerala where the Moplah riot of August 1921 took place. The Moplahs perpetrated inhuman atrocities upon the Hindus and forcibly converted some of them to Islam. One result of all these happenings was to accentuate the community consciousness of the Muslims and the Hindus as well as their political apprehensions. Both of them began to regard themselves as separate political entities with diverse political interests. 'Hindu-Muslim unity, the firm rock on which Gandhi hoped to build a united free India, had been all but submerged in an angry tide of hostility between the two communities.'[23]

The Khilafat Movement was dead, killed not by Britain, but by Kemal Pasha, the master of Muslim Turkey, who created a secular republic. So, left without a cause, the Khilafat Movement disintegrated. Hindu-Muslim collaboration came to an end. Gandhi dedicated the entire May 29, 1924 issue of *Young India* to his 6000-word article on 'Hindu Muslim Tension, Its Causes and Cure'. Gandhi was blamed for this situation. He was criticized for bringing the Muslims into the anti-imperialist struggle on a religious issue. But Gandhi defended his participation in Khilafat. 'To bring Muslim masses into the national movement as many Muslims did not regard themselves as Indians. In spite of the present strained relations between the two communities, both have gained. The awakening of the masses ….is itself a tremendous gain.'[24]

On September 18, 1924, Gandhi started a 21-day fast for Hindu-Muslim unity. 'The fast was dictated by duty to the highest cause …the universal brotherhood of man.'[25] The fast was an adventure in goodness. The stake was one man's life. The prize was a nation's freedom. 'If Indians were united as brothers, no outsider could long be their master.'[26] But the Hindu-Muslim problem defied Gandhi's efforts. 'I am helpless' he admitted. 'I have now washed my hands. But I am a believer in god …something within tell me that Hindu-Muslim unity will come sooner than we might care to hope, that god will one day force it on us.'[27]

Partition of India

The Hindu-Muslim unity, which was build up during the last few years, gave way to communal hostility and division. From 1930 onwards, a section of the Muslim intelligentsia began nourishing the idea of a separate independent Muslim state in India. Bipan Chandra wrote,

'The previous theory was that India which consisted of distinct religious communities with their separate socio-economic and political interests could still form a single nation and the methods for this could be a separate electorate, communal rights, reservations and other similar measures within a single country. Now, the idea of living together as a single nation began to be replaced by the politics of hatred, fear, enmity towards the other communities and separation. The interests of Hindus and Muslims were declared to be contradictory and permanent in conflict. The move towards Pakistan seemed inevitable since separation was the only part of the communal programme that was left unfulfilled.'[28]

Jinnah had once stood so firmly for Hindu-Muslim unity that Gokhale had called him 'the ambassador of Hindu-Muslim unity'. Now, he too changed his tone. He gave new slogans to the community: 'Protection of the integrity of Islam', 'Equality in political power with Hindus' and 'Complete national independence'. Jinnah expanded his 'Two nations' theory' and declared that, 'It was a common mistake to assume that the Muslims were a minority. They were not; they were a nation by any definition.'[29] He claimed that 'Islam and Hinduism were not religions in the strict sense but were different and distinct social orders and that it was futile to expect that India would ever be able to evolve a common nationality. Hindus and Muslims belong to two different religious philosophies, social customs, and literatures. They neither inter-marry nor inter dine and indeed they belong to two different civilizations which are based mainly on conflicting ideas and conceptions. Hindus and Muslims derive their inspiration from different sources of history. They have different epics and different heroes. To yoke together two such nations under a single state—one as a numerical minority and the other as majority—must lead to growing discontent and destruction.'[30] The only solution to this problem was to allow the major nations separate homelands by dividing India into autonomous national states.

Meanwhile, Hindu communalism also began to take an extreme form. The Hindu Maha Sabha which was originally founded as a social, cultural and religious organization, became a communal party for the Hindus, just as the Muslim League was for the Muslims. It came under the direction of V. D. Savarkar who gave the concept of nationality based on Hindus alone, and not on all the people of diverse faiths inhabiting India. He rejected the idea of a secular state. Savarkar formulated 'Two nations theory' long before Jinnah had and said, 'There are two antagonistic nations living side by side in India'. The Rashtriya Swayam Sevak Sangh, founded by K. B. Hedgrwar, also believed in the revival and purification of Hindu culture. His successor, M. S. Golvalker adopted the same lines as that of Savarkar. He stood for the assimilation or merger of the minorities within the Hindu nation. If the Muslim League raised the bogey of 'Islam in danger', the Hindu communalists also raised the cries of 'Hinduism in danger'.

The country was partitioned on August 15, 1947. According to Bipan Chandra, 'Gandhi's helplessness in accepting the Partition was neither Jinnah's intransigence nor the lust of power of Nehru and Patel but the communalization of his people. The Congress accepted the Partition because the people wanted it. It was the desire of Hindus and Sikhs for Partition that rendered him ineffective, blind and impotent. The Muslims already considered him their enemy. In such circumstances what a mass leader, without the masses could do. But Gandhi accepted the Partition as an "unavoidable necessity" in the given circumstances.'[31]

On August 15, 1947, India got independence but Gandhi considered partition 'a spiritual tragedy'.[32] He stated, 'thirty-two years of work have come to an inglorious end'.[33] India would become independent. But the victory was a cold, political arrangement. It was the hollow husk of freedom. It was victory with tragedy, a victory that found the army defeating its own general. Independence brought sadness to the architect of independence. He did not take part in the independence celebrations. He issued no message to the nation. He was sad. He wrote to Raj Kumari Amrit Kaur, 'There is disturbance within'.

Instead of participating in the celebration of independence, Gandhi walked bare-footed from village to village in Noakhali to restore pace and harmony in that area. Then he proceeded to Bihar and Calcutta to establish amity and peace. It was his fast for 72 hours that brought about the change of atmosphere in Calcutta. In the words of Lord Mountbatten, 'What fifty thousand well-equipped soldiers could not do, the Mahatma has done. He has brought peace. He is a one-man boundary force.' After Calcutta, Gandhi came to Delhi where the Hindus were determined to turn the Muslims out of the capital of India. He went on a fast and demanded that the Hindus must allow the Muslims to live in Delhi. He made a vibrant appeal for Hindu-Muslim unity, restoration of mosques converted into temples, and the payment of Rupees 55 crore which was due to Pakistan by way of division of assets. All this infuriated the orthodox and narrow-minded Hindus and Gandhi was shot dead by Nathuram Godse, a Hindu fanatic on January 30, 1948. It is indeed an irony of fate that the apostle of non-violence had a violent death.

Gandhi's visit to Noakhali was more than a call for mercy and empathy. It was his resolve to do or die. Gandhi stated that 'he would not be at peace unless he visited the disturbed areas'.[34] Gandhi's appeal for peace in Bengal was totally self abnegating. He went there as a servant of the people and he met the Hindus and Muslims alike and appealed for unity. Gandhi's presence eased the tension, assuaged the mass anger and softened tempers. He cautioned the public that if they repeated violence it would mean that they were killing him. Gandhi's fast was more than penance and self purification. It was the totality of commitment for human values. He was committed to die so that communal amity could survive and get consolidated.

Gandhi on Communal Unity

Gandhi saw truth, love, compassion and service enshrined in all religions, which led him to accord equal respect to all faiths. All religions insist on equality of human race and developing a harmonious relationship with the entirety of creation. Any violation of the principle of equality gives way to conflict and violation.

Gandhi regarded Islam as a religion of peace in the same sense as Christianity, Buddhism and Hinduism. No doubt, there are differences in the degree. He said in this regard that he knew the passages that could be quoted from the Holy *Quran* to the contrary. But it is also possible to quote from the Vedas to the contrary. 'My reading of the *Quran* has convinced me that the basis of Islam is not violence but is unadulterated peace. It regards forbearance as superior to vengeance. The very word Islam means peace, which is non-violence. My experience of India tells me that the Hindus and the Muslims know how to live at peace among themselves. I decline to believe that the people have said good-bye to their senses, so as to make it impossible to live at peace with each other, as they have done for generations. The enmity cannot last forever.'

Gandhi had never accepted in principle the theory of the Hindus and the Muslims were two distinct nations and he tried to convince both of them of the pernicious character of this principle. It is remarkable that how, by his honest and fearless advocacy of communal unity, he had enraged many of the Muslims and a negligible few among the Hindus. The Muslims looked upon him as an enemy, while some Hindus felt that by showing humility, respect, regard and partiality for the Muslims, he was jeopardizing the cause of the Hindus.

The theme of communal harmony was central to Gandhi's order of priorities. The core of communal harmony was Hindu-Muslim unity. Gandhi was very right in saying that 'Hindu-Muslim unity means unity not only between Hindus and Mussalmans but between all those who believe India to be their home no matter to what faith they belong.'[35] In South Africa, he spread the message of hope for Hindus and Muslims to be together to strive for integral outlook. He had claimed to be 'a good Mussalman simultaneously with being a good member of other religions in the world'. He had accepted that 'Hindu-Muslim unity must be the cardinal creed for all times and under all circumstances'.[36] Gandhi's concept of harmony and conciliation among the communities was not idealistic, as it was motivated, inspired and fashioned by genuine urge for unity and integration. He believed that if Hindus and Muslims removed the causes of discord, peace would prevail. Communal harmony is a social necessity and this can be achieved through non-violence, love and faith.

The question of Hindu-Muslim unity was raised in *Hind Swaraj* (1909) also. The 'reader' raised the question to the 'editor' that 'The Hindus and Mohammedans are old enemies. How can they be one nation?' Our very proverbs prove it. Mohammedans turn to the west for worship, whilst Hindus turn to the East. The former look down on the Hindus as idolaters. The Hindu worship the cow, the Mohammedans kill her. The Hindus believe in the doctrine of non-killing, the Mohammedans do not. We thus meet with differences at every step. How can India be one nation?[37] Gandhi (Editor) clarified that 'In no part of the world are one nationality and one religion synonymous terms; nor has it ever been so in India.'[38] India cannot cease to be one nation because the people belonging to different religions live in it. The introduction of foreigners does not necessarily destroy the nation; they merge in it. If the Hindus believe that India should be peopled only by Hindus, they are living in a dreamland. The Hindus, the Mohammedans, the Parsis and the Christians who have made India their country are fellow country men and they will have to live in unity.

Our history is witness that 'The Hindus flourished under Moslem sovereigns and Moslems under the Hindus. Each party had recognized that mutual fighting was suicidal.

Therefore, they decided to live in peace. With the advent of the English, quarrels recommenced. We should not forget that many Hindus and Mohammedans own the same ancestors and the same blood runs through their veins. Do people become enemies because they change their religion? Is the God of Mohammedan different from the God of Hindu? Religions are different roads converging to the same point. What does it matter that we take different roads so long as we reach the same goal.' [39]

Gandhi again said, 'I do not say that the Hindus and Mohammedans will never fight. Two brothers living together often do so.'[40] But if the brothers want to live in peace, is it possible for a third party to separate them? 'A clay pot will break through impact if not with one stone, then with another. The way to save the pot is not to keep it away from the danger point out but to bake it so that no stone would break it.'[41] This can be easily done by the Hindus, as they are more in numbers. If Mohammedans ask for certain concessions, the Hindus should not oppose this and brotherliness would be the outcome.

In *Constructive Programme*, Gandhi wrote that 'Every body is agreed about the necessity of communal unity. But every body does not know that unity does not mean political unity which may be imposed. It means an unbreakable heart unity. The first thing essential for achieving such unity is for every congress men whatever his religion may be, to represent in his own person Hindu, Muslim, Christian, Zoroastrian and Jew, shortly, every one of the millions of the inhabitants of Hindustan. In order to realize this, every Congressman will cultivate personal friendship with persons representing faiths other than his own. He should have the same regard for the other faith as he has for his own.' [42]

Gandhi wrote, 'I do not expect India of my dreams to develop one religion, i.e., to be wholly Hindu or wholly Christian, or wholly Mussalman but I want it to be wholly tolerant, with its religious working side by side with one another.'[43]

In *India of My Dreams,* which is the compilation of the immortal pages of *Young India, Harijan* and other speeches and writings of Gandhi, it has been said: 'My whole soul rebels against the idea that Hinduism and Islam represent two antagonistic cultures and doctrines. To assent to such a doctrine is for me a denial of God.'[44] Gandhi said, 'Hindus and Mussalmans prate about no compulsion in religion. What is it but compulsion, if Hindus will kill a Mussalman for slaying a cow? It is like wanting to convert a Mussalman to Hinduism by force. And, similarly, what is it but compulsion if Mussalmans seek to prevent by force Hindus from playing music before mosques? Virtue lies in being absorbed in one's prayers in the presence of din and noise.'[45]

There are two constant causes of friction between Hindus and Muslims. One is cow slaughter and the other is the question of music before the mosques. On the issue of cow slaughter, Gandhi said, 'I have never been able to understand the antipathy towards the Mussalmans on that score. We say nothing about the slaughter that daily takes place on behalf of Englishmen. Our anger becomes red hot when a Mussalman slaughters a cow.'[46] Then, on the other issue he has stated that, 'music before mosques is a sore point with the Mussalmans. And just as Hindus cannot compel Mussalmans to refrain from killing cows, so can Mussalmans not compel Hindus to stop music or *arti* at the point of the sword.'[47] What is needed in these circumstances is religious tolerance. 'I have not a shadow of doubt that the iceberg of communal differences will melt under the warmth of the sun of freedom.'[48]

Summing Up

Without unity between Hindus and Mussalmans, no certain progress can be made by the nation.[49] The tenet that 'unity is strength' is not merely a copybook maxim but a rule of life. In no case is it so clearly illustrated as in the problem of Hindu-Muslim unity. Divided, we will fall.[50] Hindu-Muslim unity means not only unity between Hindus and Mussalmans, but between all those who believe India to be their home, no matter to what faith they belong.[51] Hindu-Muslim unity is nothing, if it is not a partnership between brave men and women. We must trust each other always, but, at the last resort, we must trust ourselves and our God.[52] We Indians, of whatever religion, have to live together. We are of the same soil, we are nursed by the self-same Mother and we cannot go on killing each other if India is to live.[53]

Gandhi did not fully succeed in Hindu-Muslim unity. To go into the reason for this, one has to understand the various factors which contributed to the failure of Gandhi in solving the communal problem. Some writers felt that Gandhi lacked a historical perspective. He did not take into account the hold that religion—with its dogma, tradition, custom, ritual and historical memories—has on the minds of men in the pre-modern society. Gandhi assigned only a derivative role to the cultural factor. He did not grasp the deeper social and cultural roots of the Hindu-Muslim conflict. Gandhi placed the entire blame for the communal problem on the British and overlooked the other facts. Gandhi thought that the Hindu-Muslim problem was essentially religious and missed the social aspect of the problem.

Gandhi always emphasized upon the necessity of openness of mind for the unity and harmony of society. It was not a question of failure or success. Gandhi realized that the only alternative to violence, coercion, retribution, distrust and chaos, was restoration of sanity among the misguided individuals. To counter frenzy and vindictiveness, Gandhi sought rehabilitation of balanced social interaction among the masses and the resolve to put the cause of the nation above all denominational prejudices.

Today, India is a secular nation. Democracy is mature. Muslims have got equal rights and opportunities and are more secure in India than any other country. The credit goes to the founding fathers of the Indian Constitution and Mahatma Gandhi.

Notes and References

1. *The Collected Works of Mahatma Gandhi*, Delhi: Publications Division, 1962, Vol. 43, p. 306.
2. Karunakaran, K. P., 'Political Philosophy and practice of the Hindu Mahasabha', paper presented at the seminar 'The communal problem in India 1919–1947,' Nehru Memorial Museum and Library, New Delhi, March 1971, p. 2.

3. Nehru, J. L., *Selected Works*, Vol. 7, p. 69.
4. Chandra, Bipan, *Freedom Struggle*, New Delhi: National Book Trust, 1972, p. 104.
5. *Ibid.*, p. 103.
6. Tarachand, *History of the Freedom Movement in India*, Vol. III, Publication Division, Ministry of Information and Broadcasting, Government of India, New Delhi, 2005, pp. 252–253.
7. Chandra, Bipan, *op. cit.*, p. 86.
8. Tarachand, *op. cit.*, p. 257.
9. Chandra, Bipan *op. cit.*, p. 111.
10. *Ibid.*, p. 127.
11. Tarachand, *op. cit.*, p. 400.
12. *Ibid.*
13. *Amrita Bazar Patrika*, January 13, 1919.
14. *CWMG*, Vol. 17, pp. 309–310.
15. *Young India*, June 2, 1920, p. 43.
16. Tarachand, *op. cit.*, p. 410.
17. Tendulkar, D. G., *Mahatma*, Vol. I, New Delhi: Publication Division, 1951, p. 365.
18. Tarachand, *op. cit.*, p. 413.
19. Tarachand, *History of the Freedom Movement in India*, Vol. IV, p. 9.
20. *Ibid.*, p. 17.
21. *Young India*, October 6, 1920, p. 404.
22. *Young India*, May 11, 1921, pp. 406–407.
23. Fischer, Louis, *The Life of Mahatma Gandhi*, London: Harper Collins Publishers, 1997, p. 275.
24. *CWMG*, Vol. 24, 137.
25. Fischer, Louis, *op. cit.*, p. 280.
26. *Ibid.*, p. 282.
27. *Ibid.*, p. 311.
28. Chandra, Bipan, *India's Struggle for Independence*, pp. 428–29.
29. *Speeches and Writings of Mr. Jinnah*, quoted in R. C. Vermani, chapter on 'Rise and growth of communalism,' p. 327.
30. *Ibid.*, pp. 327–328.
31. Chandra, Bipan, *op. cit.*, pp. 503–504.
32. Fischer, Louis, *op. cit.*, p. 587.
33. *Ibid.*
34. Pyarelal, *Mahatma Gandhi: The Last Phase*, Vol. I, Ahmedabad: Navjivan Publishing House, 1956.
35. Gandhi, M. K., *The Way to Communal Harmony*, Ahmedabad Navjivan Publishing House, p. 137.
36. *CWMG*, Vol. 23, p. 88.
37. Gandhi, M. K., *Hind Swaraj or Indian Home Rule*, Ahmedabad: Navjivan Publishing House, 2004, p. 41.
38. *Ibid.*, p. 43.
39. *Ibid.*, pp. 43–4.
40. *Ibid.*, p. 47.

41. *Ibid.*, p. 46.
42. Gandhi, M. K., *Constructive Programme*, p. 8.
43. Gandhi, M. K., *India of My Dreams*, *Ahmedabad*: Navjivan Publishing House, September 2004, p. 257.
44. *Ibid.*, p. v.
45. *Ibid.*, p. 244.
46. *Ibid.*, p. 245.
47. *Ibid.*, p. 246.
48. *Young India*, October 29, 1931, p. 93.
49. *Young India*, July 28, 1921.
50. *Young India*, May 11, 1921.
51. *Young India*, May 11, 1921.
52. *Young India*, September 29, 1921.
53. *Harijan*, April 27, 1947.

Summary

- In modern India, Gandhi was one of the greatest champions of communal unity. He lived his whole life striving for it, ensuring it, stood firm for it, and finally sacrificed his life in the pursuit of communal unity.
- For Gandhi, the issue of communal unity was greater than that of *swaraj*. Gandhi said that '*Swaraj* was impossible without Hindu-Muslim Unity'.
- Gandhi pleaded for the cause of better understanding among individuals and communities.
- Gandhi insisted that the Hindus who are in a majority in the country should help the Muslims and should never entertain any idea of enforcing their rights but try to win the hearts of the minority communities. Gandhi wrote that, 'Hindu-Muslim unity consists in our having a common purpose, a common goal and common sorrows. It is best promoted by co-operating to reach the common goal, by sharing one another's sorrows and by mutual toleration.'
- As the national movement spread and grew, there was the threat that it might unify the people and pose serious problems for the empire. 'A united people cannot be kept under subjugation for a long time.' The British decided to do all they could to keep the people disunited and quarrelling and competing among themselves. They decided to divide the people in the name of their different religions and to encourage communal and separatist tendencies in Indian Politics.
- A concrete shape and setting to the communal theory was given in 1906 when the All India Muslim League was set up under the leadership of Aga Khan, Nawab Salimullah of Dacca and Nawab Mohsin-ul-Mulk. The league supported the partition of Bengal and demanded special and separate electorates. The British were waiting for just such an opportunity. They made full use of it and announced that

they would protect the special interests of the Muslims. The League said that 'the interests of the Muslims were different and divergent from those of the rest of the nation'.

- Gandhi, who had been an ardent advocate of Hindu-Muslim unity since the days in South Africa got an opportunity with the Khilafat question. He spoke extensively on the subject and cultivated influential Muslims like Ali brothers, Hakim Ajmal Khan, Shuaib Qureshi and Dr. Ansari in order to understand their fears and aspirations. Gandhi felt that the Khilafat demand was just. For him, 'It was a golden opportunity to cement that unity for good, an opportunity which might perhaps never again recur.' Gandhi also realized the depth of their feelings over the issue and decided to champion their cause.
- Jinnah, who had stood firmly for Hindu-Muslim unity and Gokhale once called him 'the ambassador of Hindu-Muslim unity', changed his tone. He gave new slogans to the community: 'Protection of the integrity of Islam', 'Equality in political power with Hindus' and 'Complete national independence'. Jinnah expanded his 'Two-nations theory' and declared that 'It was a common mistake to assume that the Muslims were a minority. They were not; they were a nation by any definition.'
- Instead of participating in the celebration of independence Gandhi walked barefooted from village to village in Noakhali to restore pace and harmony in that area.
- Gandhi saw truth, love, compassion and service enshrined in all religions, which led him to accord equal respect to all faiths. All religions insist on equality of the human race and on developing a harmonious relationship with the entirety of creation. Any violation of the principle of equality gives way to conflict and violation.
- Gandhi had never accepted in principle the theory of the Hindus and the Muslims being two distinct nations and he tried to convince both of them of the pernicious character of this principle.
- Gandhi said that 'Hindu-Muslim unity means unity not only between Hindus and Mussalmans but between all those who believe India to be their home no matter to what faith they belong.'
- Without unity between Hindus and Mussalmans, no certain progress can be made by the nation. The belief that 'unity is strength' is not merely a copybook maxim but a rule of life. in no case has it been so clearly illustrated as in the problem of Hindu-Muslim unity. Divided, we will fall.
- Hindu-Muslim unity means not only unity between Hindus and Mussalmans, but also between all those who believe India to be their home, no matter to what faith they belong. Hindu-Muslim unity is nothing, if it is not a partnership between brave men and women. We must trust each other always, but, in the last resort, we must trust ourselves and our God.
- Gandhi did not fully succeed in bringing about Hindu-Muslim unity. To go into the reason for this, one has to understand various factors which contributed to the

failure of Gandhi in solving the communal problem. Some writers felt that Gandhi lacked a historical perspective.

Further Readings

Gandhi, M. K., *Hind Swaraj* or *Indian Home Rule*, Ahmedabad: Navjivan Publishing House, 1975.
Gandhi, M. K, *The Way to Communal Harmony*, Ahmedabad: Navjivan Publishing House, 1963.
Husain, S. Abid, *Gandhiji and Communal Unity*, Delhi: Orient Longmans, 1969.

15

Gandhi on Women's Question

Introduction

Mahatma Gandhi was unambiguous in his recognition of the fact that women had a clearly positive role to offer in the reconstruction of society. He declared himself uncompromising in the matter of women's rights because in order to bring about social justice, the recognition of the equality of women was imperative. He believed that many of his contemporary movements stopped half-way because of the condition of 'our women' and much of the work did not yield appropriate results because women power had not been used. In this understanding of the essence of the dilemma of women, Gandhi was far in advance of his time. The 19th-century consciousness of the women's issue was limited to their position within the traditional family structure. Very few people thought about the basic inequality and social justice that were a woman's lot politically, economically and socially. There was no awareness of the woman's role as the equal partner of man, nor was there any recognition of the identity of the woman as a person in her own right. Interestingly, the rulers of the day, a Western power, entirely disbelieved that women in India could ever be equal partners of men. In sharp contrast to this, Gandhi's consciousness of the problem stands out for its sensitivity and insightfulness. As early as 1921, writing in *Young India*, Gandhi said, 'Of all the evils for which man has made himself responsible, none is so degrading, so shocking or so brutal as his abuse of the better half of humanity to me, the female sex, not the weaker sex'.[1] He discerned the cause of the inequalities and injustice to women in general and in his relationship to them, squarely held that the opinion that 'if I were born a woman, I would rise in rebellion against any pretension on the part of man'.[2] Pragmatic as he was, Gandhi related his own relationship with Ba and stated simply that he found the true relationship when he 'decided to threat her (Kasturba) differently than I used to do... restored to her all her rights'.[4].

Own Identity

Gandhi had the unique thought and understanding that a woman is also a person in her own right. In a plan of life, he maintained that woman has as much right to 'shape her own destiny'[5] as man. Gandhi recognized very early that 'to the impartial outsider, the legal and customary status of woman is bad enough throughout and demands radical alteration'.

Following up his belief in the individuality of woman in her own right, Gandhi held the view point that fundamentally, man and woman are one, characteristically declaring that 'the soul in both is the same. The two live the same life, have the same feelings.' However, he believed that while both are fundamentally one, differences in their vocations and roles are to be expected and accepted. But it must be continually kept in mind that 'woman... is gifted with equal mental capacities. She has the right to participate in the minutest detail in the activities of man, and she has the same right of freedom and liberty as he..[5] Gandhi looked upon women as naturally entitled to the same rights as men. As a result of his insightfulness, he discerned that many unworthy men enjoyed superiority over women which they neither deserved nor should have been allowed by society, because of the 'sheer force of a vicious custom'. He regretted that many of the movements stopped half way because of the condition of our women, or did not yield appropriate results because woman power and the source of its strength were neglected.

Discussing the difference in woman's role and her vocations, Gandhi emphasized that although men and women are equal in status, they are not identical. Considering how long ago he said it, one marvels at his wisdom. Many people—both in the East and the West—are now saying the same thing in another language; that men and women do not have to be 'identical' in order to claim equality and justice in any sphere. They have been saying this in the sixth, seventh and eighth decades of the 20th century. On these issues, Gandhi had said nearly fifty years ago: 'They (man and woman) are a peerless pair being supplementary to one another; each helps the other so that without the one the existence of the other cannot be conceived; and therefore, it follows as a necessary corollary from these facts, that anything that will impair the status of either of them will involve the equal ruin of them both.'[6] He recognized that being members of the same humanity, the problems of man and woman 'must be one in essence', i.e., human problems. Gandhi held the view that women would not make their contribution to society and community by running a race with men. They could 'choose' to run the race but they could not rise to the great heights which Gandhi believed women were capable of achieving. He firmly believed in the complementing factor in the interpersonal relationship between man and woman. He believed, however, in the division of 'spheres of work'. 'As I have watched millions of peasants in their natural surroundings, and as I watch them daily in little Segaon, the natural division of spheres of work has forced itself on my attention'.[7] But he hastens to underscore that 'the general qualities required are practically the same for both the sexes'. Because Gandhi had basic respect for all work, any kind of labour, and because there was no hierarchy either in the kind of work or the worker as far as he was concerned, in the division of spheres of work he did not see any inferiority or superiority. As a matter of fact, Gandhi emphasized the concept of 'bread labour' for all members of the society. In other words, he saw in his experiences at Segaon a harmony in the midst of hard facts of living life in its grim reality.

Within Family

It is a well-known fact that Gandhi placed great emphasis on the family, its wholesomeness and function in human society. Hence, he was never tired of calling the attention of the Indians to the continuity and well being of the family as such. He showed his understanding of this joint responsibility, especially that of the husband and the wife, in the maintenance and strengthening of the home. He seemed to have depended more on women for this strengthening and expected greater things from them because 'woman is essentially the mistress of the house... she is the keeper and distributor of the bread... The art of bringing up the infants of the race is her special and sole prerogative. Without her care, the race will become extinct.'[8] Gandhi was not sentimental about motherhood; nor did he indulge in clichés. Rather, he viewed the responsibility of becoming a mother as 'no easy task. The procreation of children has to be undertaken with a full sense of responsibility ...She who gives intelligent, healthy and well brought up children to the country is surely rendering a service.'[9] It might be mentioned here that Gandhi was not against women working outside the home if they chose to do so and if that were within their capacity: 'In the new order of my imagination', he said, 'all will work according to their capacity for an adequate return for their labour.' However, with the practical sense that marked his insights, Gandhi believed that women in the new order will be part-time workers, their primary function being to maintain and continue the home. In other words, Gandhi did not believe in the superiority of 'jobs' outside the home because it fetched a salary in terms of money. By the same token, he did not believe that a woman should be discriminated against in any sphere of life—like jobs, property rights or marriage rights—by means of law. In today's world, many may not agree with the emphasis that Gandhi laid on women's role in the home, stressing the fact that in domestic affairs, in the upbringing of children and also in their education, woman must play the major role. In fact, the trend today is to hold the belief that both the parents must be equally responsible and share all the domestic affairs which include the upbringing of children, their education, and attending to their needs. But one cannot but agree with him when he says perceptively, that a woman, by virtue of being the leader in the home, is 'the maker and silent leader of men'. Therefore, she ought to have more knowledge in order to be equipped for this role within her family and also posses a discriminating appreciation of the basic values inherent in this important family responsibility.

Not Weaker Sex

Gandhi declared indignantly that it is a libel to call woman the weaker sex. Gandhi was pained and humiliated by the custom of purdah. He asked a very pertinent question: 'why do our women not enjoy the same freedom that men do? Why should they not be able to walk out and have fresh air?' He did not accept purdah as an Indian tradition. He pointed out logically that when the women of ancient India held public discourses and participated in them, they certainly did not do so from behind the purdah. It is not known among the peasantry even now, although many in our society, then and now, upheld, and continue to uphold purdah as an ancient custom. Gandhi asserted that 'we must list on the anvil of reason everything that is capable of being listed by it and reject that which does not satisfy it even though it may appear in an ancient garb.' Speaking in as early as 1927, he emphasized that humanity will remain diminished as long as the women are 'caged and confined in their houses and little courtyards'.

The phrases that Gandhi used for the dowry system are revealing. He called it 'the hateful system of dowry,' 'marriage by purchase', 'a degrading practice,' and so on. He saw inherent evil in the dowry system, both for the giver and the receiver because it creates a bondage, because it is like buying and selling, bargaining, and because this system turns human beings into 'things'. This system subdues human relationships and distorts and cripples them. It degrades men for putting themselves in the market and dishonours women because they become the silent observers in a matter of life-long relationship that should be uplifting and honourable. He believed the remedy of this degrading custom lay in the hands of the youth of the country. So, he said: 'There are many youth movements in the country. I wish that these movements would deal with question of these characters.' Gandhi called for the creation of a strong public opinion so that no one would want to dirty their fingers with the giving and receiving of dowry. He even advocated 'excommunication' for the young men who received dowry and urged that the parents of girls should ignore the criteria of castes and provincial differences to counter this evil custom. In 1929, he shocked many by declaring: 'If I had a girl under my charge, I would rather keep her a maiden all her life than give her away to one who expected a single pie for taking her for his wife'. He called upon men and women, parents, sons and the daughters—in short, all human beings involved in the perpetuation of this custom and being crippled by the shackles it inevitably forges—to bring about a radically new approach. Gandhi never tired of saying: 'No reform has ever been brought about except through intrepid individuals breaking down human customs'.

In 1936, Gandhi raised a very pertinent issue which is relevant even today: 'How is that so many boys and girls who have even passed through colleges, are found unable or unwilling to resist this manifestly evil custom (Compulsory marriage with dowry paid and received), which affects their future as intimately as does marriage?' He questioned the value of education if this did not dare defy a custom which was wholly indefensible and highly immoral. He further maintained that there was something radically lacking in the system of education that made the educated so insensitive to evil customs and ready to yield to them. He challenged the girls 'to remain spinsters if need be'. He did not subscribe to the practice that every girl has to get married. He discussed this while in Ceylon and maintained that 'it is an excellent thing for girls to remain unmarried' for the sake of an objective, for serving others in society. Addressing the Ashram sisters in one of his talks at a prayer meeting, Maniben writes, Gandhi had said that if one does not find a person who is compatible mentally, she should resolve to remain unmarried, but be 'wedded to independence. A girl dependent upon others can never remain unmarried.' Clearly, he did not see marriage either as a status-giving act; nor did he miss the implications in the acts of the parents getting their daughters married at any cost. He was tireless in his condemnation of this attitude and held the parents, the social mores and the men more than the women directly responsible for this ignoble situation.

When Gandhi spoke about widow remarriage and advocated the same, he was not merely expressing his compassion for the child widows who were victims of an evil custom and blind superstitions; he was also upholding the basic principle based on his sense of equity and justice that 'widows should have the same freedom that widowers have'. If Gandhi were to state what the rule should be, he affirmed more than once that the same rule should apply to women as to men. He was against two standards in this matter, especially in India, where a slave mentality in this regard is assiduously cultivated from childhood. As long as the Indians did not think freely, he did not know how they could even act freely. It is no wonder that as early as 1927, Gandhi was provoked to write that: 'chastity is not a hot-house growth. It cannot be superimposed.' This kind of attitude, according to him, interfered with the free growth of person whether it related to women or to the Harijans, and contributed to India's weakness.

The Indian society's indifference to the causes and condition of women forced some of them to take to the prostitute's profession which made him shudder. He was practical enough to recognize that the men would be as 'fallen' as the women if this profession spread and flourished as it did in India. He did not believe that the solution lay in merely finding for these women an honourable means of living. With his deep insight into human character, he maintained that: it is a social disease—'a moral leprosy', he called it—promoted by men of no moral or ethical standard. It is accepted by society as a necessary evil with the dual standard it allows. Women themselves will have to rise to the task of eradicating it. He hoped that a woman leader will emerge to take active leadership in abolishing this degrading profession. Laws alone could never be effective.' His whole being rebelled against the custom of devadasis, which insulted god. He said: 'in the name of religion, we commit a double crime' by degrading women and involving the worship of god along with it. We have this moral leprosy in today's India also, and along with it we have the responsibility of indirectly encouraging it through our indifference and perhaps lack of interest.

Gandhi wanted both men and women to use reason and so mould social and public opinion that would go a long way in rejecting these customs and social compulsions sanctified by time, which are unreasonable, inhuman, degrading and crippling, even though they might be ancient and time honoured.

Gandhi, challenged the young girls and warned them against, 'copying the modern girls' because the term 'modern girl' had a special meaning for Gandhi as he wrote in *Harijan* dated February 4, 1939 when some students complained to him about the misbehaviour of students toward the women students. 'I invite (you) to initiate a crusade against the rude behaviour of students. God helps only those who help themselves.' The phrases Gandhi uses are revealing—'crusading' and 'God helping those who help themselves'. Steadfastness, faith in one's own self, spiritual strength and tending dignity to a cause were basic, and continue to be basic, to the Gandhian way.

Mahadev Desai lists some of the clichés India helped to grow in his time, and they are by no means absolute in our time. To quote a few: the husband is like a god; son is preferable because he continues the family name and must inherit; the wife must remain faithful even if the husband is unjust because that attitude is her *dharma.*

The Gandhian response to these was that if the husband is a god, the wife is also a goddess. A daughter's share must be equal to that of a son. If a husband is unjust to his wife, she has the right to live separately. Both husband and wife have the onus to be responsible parents and each would forfeit their right if any one of them were found to be unfit. Gandhi was not making laws, nor was he preaching theoretically. He was merely saying that which he practiced, that which he believed to be true, just and equitable. He also confirmed through such statements the importance of a humane approach and of values for recognizing the ills and making a determined effort to remove them by seeing the truth as it is, and accepting it with courage and mental preparation. If society has treated woman as man's tool, she had found it easy to be so; she never resisted being one.

True to his ideal of *satyagraha,* Gandhi called upon the women of India to resort to it against all undesirable and unworthy restraints. He believed only in voluntary restraints, in self-disciplining. But he reminded everyone in the true Gandhian spirit, that if *satyagraha* is undertaken in order to remedy social ills, women must remember the presupposition on which true *satyagraha* rests, namely, the purity of the motive, not expediency and reasoned resistance.

Gandhi sometimes made categorical statements about women, always giving them a superior grade. One almost feels that either he was partial to women, or that he expected too much from them. For example, let me quote some of his statements: 'woman, the noblest of God's creation', 'personification of self-sacrifice', 'she is any way superior to man in her religious devotion,' 'woman, an incarnation of *ahimsa.*' There are many more such statements strewn around in his writings. Perhaps some of these claims about women in general will not stand today's psychological and scientific analysis. Perhaps, some women themselves in the East, and certainly in the West, would not take these statements as complimentary, imagining them to be motivated, rejecting them as unscientific, or a means to get something out of them. I see in these statements Gandhi's influence of the women in his life—his mother, his sister, his wife—in a word, the women he lived with and whom he knew intimately. Reference should also be made here of the respect, understanding and affection he received from the women who were his close followers right from the time he led India's movement against an alien rule. His letters to Maniben, Miraben, Amrit Kaur and the Ashram sisters amply prove the dedication and loyalty and effective work that they offered totally and unstintingly to the leader who was their Bapu. But these tributes that Gandhi paid to women in general may create a dilemma if today's women either become smug or hold themselves as being in no need of self-improvement and introspection. In some parts of the world, the liberation of women has become a battle between the two sexes. One has to watch lest there be a sense of superiority of women. This will not help the liberation movement, either for the women or the men. Only one group's superiority will be replaced by that of another. It falls on the women then to remain sensitive to the possibility of this dilemma.

In fact, Gandhi was far in advance of his time in recognizing that men and women were equal. He said many a times, 'I admit no distinction between man and woman except such as has been made by nature and can be seen with human eyes.' He stood squarely for women's education and believed that in proportion to the education they receive, they will become more sensitive and alert about the glaring inequalities to which they were, and are subjected. They would then naturally resent them. In his own life he never underestimated 'Stree Shakti'. As a matter of fact, the major force which acted as a catalyst in the achievement of political equality of women in India was Gandhi's preaching and practicing this faith of his in the equality and ability of women. As is well-known and also well-accepted historically, the massive participation of women in the national movement under Gandhi's leadership had a direct impact on the then social and political India. It is significant that when the government rejected women's demand of equal franchise, at the Karachi session, the Indian National Congress in 1931, under Gandhi's guidance, unconditionally accepted women's right to vote without any discrimination based on sex. The country redeemed this pledge politically after independence. The Constitution of India pledges the principles and equality of dignity of the individual, and proclaims the fundamental right of women to political, economic and legal equality.

Summing Up

But what of the reality today? Are we not far from translating those pledges in our own time, both economically and socially? Have we moved appreciably from where we were in Gandhi's times? Our present was Gandhi's future. History will judge us not by what we pledged in the past but how we perform in the present; not by promises made but by the promises kept.

One may say that women in India have to go a long way to attain the empowerment in political, economic, social and cultural fields. The need of the hour comprises not welfare, but development; not charity, but entitlement; not assistance, but empowerment; not structural adjustment, but structural change; not even social security but social and gender justice, if the women are to survive and flourish in the given situation.

Notes and References

1. *Young India*, September 15, 1921.
2. *Young India*, December 9, 1927.
3. *Young India*, December 8, 1927.
4. Gandhi, M. K., *Constructive Programme, Its Meaning and Place*, Ahmedabad: Navjivan Publishing House, 1941, p. 17.
5. Gandhi, M. K., *Women and Social Injustice*, Ahmedabad: Navjivan Publishing House, 1954, pp.4–5.
6. *Harijan*, February 24, 1940.
7. Ibid.

8. Ibid.
9. Gandhi, M. K., *Women and Social Injustice*, Ahmedabad: Navjivan Publishing House, 1954, p. 180.
10. *Young India*, February 14, 1929.

Summary

- Mahatma Gandhi was unambiguous in his recognition of the fact that women clearly had a positive role to offer in the reconstruction of society.
- Gandhi had the unique thought and understanding that a woman is also a person in her own right. In a plan of life, he maintained that woman has as much right to "shape her own destiny" as man.
- Gandhi held the view that fundamentally, man and woman are one, characteristically declaring that "the soul in both is the same. The two live the same life, and have the same feelings." However, he believed that while both are fundamentally one, difference in their vocations and roles are to be expected and accepted.
- Gandhi wanted both men and women to use reason.
- A daughter's share must be equal to that of a son.
- Gandhi during the freedom struggle, empowered women in socio-economic and political fields. He never thought of women as the weaker sex.

Further Readings

Bandyopadhyaya, J., *Social and Political Thought of Gandhi,* Calcutta: Allied Publishers, 1969.

Hardiman, David, *Gandhi In His Time and Ours,* New Delhi: Permanent Black, 2003.

Iyer, Raghavan, *The Moral and Political Thought of Mahatma Gandhi,* Chicago: Oxford University Press, 1973.

16

Gandhi and Untouchability

Introduction

Gandhi was the pioneer leader who made the removal of untouchability his life's mission. Gandhi made untouchability a national issue. He fought for the removal of untouchability, which is a blot on Indian humanity. His fight was unique and unparalleled. He stressed, in the main, that the conscience of the so-called 'higher' castes in Hindu society had to be roused against the crime or the practice of untouchability, which has tarnished their image. Gandhi desired to deliver the untouchables—whom he called Harijans—from the slavery of centuries by means of changing the hearts of the Hindus. This desire was as strong as Gandhi's desire for freedom and independence. He had said that freedom would be meaningless if untouchability was not removed. He also said that attainment of *swaraj* was a must, but that would not be complete unless a social order based on equality and fraternity was established. Through non-violence, Gandhi wanted to remove the untouchability from its very roots. In attacking untouchability, Gandhi had gone to the very root of the matter and, therefore, it was an issue of transcendental value, far surpassing *swaraj* in terms of political constitutions. Gandhi said that such a constitution would be a dead-weight if it was not backed by a moral basis in the shape of the present hope engendered in the hearts of the downtrodden millions that the weight is going to be lifted from their shoulders

Gandhi and Untouchability

Gandhi's ultimate search was for righteous conduct. For Gandhi, the means were more important than the end, and he believed that with the right means, desired ends were bound to follow. Gandhi showed India as well as the world the path of truth and non-violence.

He believed that it was truth alone that prevailed in the end. According to him, India's real emancipation depended on the abolition of untouchability. He worked hard for the upliftment of the Harijans, the name he had given to the untouchables. Besides, Gandhi regarded untouchability a sin against god and man.

Gandhi's influence over the masses was tremendous. The people of India had unflinching faith in him. The most remarkable feature of his leadership was that he was able to lead and direct the movement without holding any position of power of any high office. He was able to command the respectful obedience of millions though there was nothing divine about him as a person. However, he was also accepted as a great emancipated saviour and Messiah for the socially downtrodden and the victims of socio-economic exploitation. Gandhi had spoken and written more on untouchability than any other leader in India. He had publicly put the abolition of untouchability as the essential prerequisite for India's independence.

Varna-ashram and Purusharthas are both unique features of the Indian social order. At the same time, untouchability is the worst feature of the degraded caste system which is so deeply embedded in the minds of the Indian society that our entire outlook on life and politics is coloured by it. Caste is a reality and it has seeped into every aspect of human activities in Indian society. It has erected a powerful barrier against the emotional integration of the people of India. It has divided them into high-born and low-born caste compartments. The caste system has always exercised a predominant hold on the public and social life of Indian society. Untouchability has also remained a social concern for all those who have occupied any significant space in the Indian public domain.

Gandhi always held the high caste Hindus responsible for the plight of the untouchables and he also asserted that the Hindus would have no right to claim *swaraj* as long as freedom was not restored to the exploited classes. He believed that the political bondage of Indians was a well-deserved punishment meted out to them for observing untouchability. Therefore, at times, it is alleged what Gandhi categorically proclaimed that his Harijan Seva (upliftment) movement was not intended for the upliftment of Harijans, but for the salvation of high caste Hindus as penance for the crimes they had perpetrated against the Harijans.[1]

Gandhi aroused the people's attention more widely than anyone had done before in history, to the evils of untouchability. Gandhi took it upon himself to awaken the conscience of the human race. He sought to fight against the horrors of untouchability and the other social wrongs, which he found humiliating and shameful for Indian society. In 1925, Gandhi wrote, 'untouchability is our greatest shame; the humiliation of it is sinking deeper'.

In 1931, Gandhi named untouchables, the Shudras, and Chandalas as 'Harijan', i.e., men of god. Gandhi wrote; 'the 'untouchable: to me, is, compared to us, really a Harijan (a man of God), and we are Durjan (men of evil). For while the untouchable has toiled and moiled and dirties his hands so that we may live in comfort and cleanliness, we have delighted in suppressing him. We are solely responsible for all the shortcomings and faults that we lay at the door of these 'untouchables': it is still open to us to be Harijan ourselves but we can only do so by heartily repenting for our sin against them.'[2]

Gandhi argued that, 'Untouchability is a snake with a thousand mouths through each of which it shows its poisonous fangs. It needs no sanction from Manu or the other ancient law-givers. It has its own local Smriti. Thus, in Almora, a whole class of people, whose occupation is, even according to the Sanatana dharma so-called, innocent, are untouchables. They are all cultivators owning their own holdings. They are called Shilpi, i.e., farmers. Another similar class of people called Boras suffers in the same manner although they do not even eat carrion or take liquor and observe all the rules of sanitation as well as any others. Tradition has condemned them as untouchables'.[3]

Gandhi further proclaimed that, 'Hinduism that refuses to think and accepts the tradition unquestioningly exposes itself to merited ridicule and worse. Reformers are trying to cope with the evil. I feel, however, that much more drastic methods are needed than are employed to rid Hinduism of the blot. We are needlessly afraid to wound the susceptibilities of orthodoxy. We have to shed the fear, if we expect to end the evil in our own generation. This untouchability naturally recoils on the heads of those who are responsible for it'.[4]

The difference, therefore, between the caste system and untouchability is not one of degree, but of kind. An 'untouchable' is outside the pale of respectable society. He is hardly treated as a human being. He is an outcaste hurled into an abyss by his fellow beings occupying the same platform. The difference, therefore, is somewhat analogous to the difference between heaven and hell.

Gandhi was of the view that untouchability, as it was practiced in Hinduism, was a sin against God and man and was, therefore, like a poison slowly eating into the very vitals of Hinduism. He wrote, 'In my opinion, it has no sanction whatsoever in the Hindu *Shastras* taken as a whole. Untouchability of a healthy kind is undoubtedly to be found in the *Shastras* and it is universal in all religions. It is a rule of sanitation. That will exist to the end of time; but untouchability as we are observing today in India is a hideous thing and wears various forms in various provinces, even in districts. It has degraded both the untouchables and the touchable. It has stunted the growth of nearly 40 million human beings. They are denied even the ordinary amenities of life. The sooner, therefore, it is ended, the better for Hinduism, the better for India, and perhaps better for mankind in general'.[5]

Gandhi further elaborated his views, saying that it may not be denied that untouchability is an old institution. But if it is an evil, it cannot be defended on the ground of its antiquity. If the untouchables are outcastes of the Aryan society, so much the worse for that society. And if the Aryans at some stage in their progress regarded a certain class of people as outcastes by way of punishment, there is no reason why that punishment should descend upon their progeny, irrespective of the causes for which their ancestors were punished. It merely demonstrates that the evil cannot be confined and that its deadening effect is all pervading. He also felt that the existence of untouchability amongst the untouchables is an additional reason for the cultured Hindu society to rid itself of the curse with the quickest dispatch.

However, Gandhi did not believe in the caste system, even as distinguished from varnaashram, to be an odious and vicious dogma. It has its limitations and its defects but there is nothing sinful about it, as there is about untouchability, and if it is a by-product of the caste system, it is only in the same sense that an ugly growth is of a body, or weeds of a crop. It is as wrong to destroy caste because of the outcaste, as it would be to destroy a body because of an ugly growth in it or a crop because of the weeds. The outcasteness—in the sense we understand it—has therefore to be destroyed altogether. It is an abscess to be removed, if the whole system is not to perish. Untouchability is the product, therefore, not of the caste system, but of the distinction of high and low that has crept into Hinduism and is corroding it. The attack on untouchability is, thus, an attack upon this 'high' and 'low'-ness. The moment untouchability goes, the caste system itself will be purified, that is to say, according to Gandhi's dream, it will resolve itself into true Varna dharma, the four divisions of society, each complementary of the other and none inferior or superior to the rest.

Gandhi regarded untouchability as the greatest blot on Hinduism. The idea was not brought home to him by bitter experiences during the South African struggle. It is equally wrong to think-as some people do—that he had taken his view from his study of Christian religious literature. His views date as far back as the time when he was neither enamoured of, nor was acquainted with the Bible or the followers of the Bible.

Gandhi was of the firm view that the removal of untouchability was much more than building a temple of brick and mortar. Hindus must bleed for it, must pay for it. They must be prepared to forsake wife, children and all for the sake of removing the curse. [6]

Gandhi also believed that to remove untouchability is a penance that high caste Hindus owe to Hinduism as also to themselves. 'The purification required is not of "untouchables" but of the so-called superior castes. There is no vice that is special to the "untouchables", not even dirt and insanitation. It is our arrogance which blinds us, superior Hindus, to our own blemishes and magnifies those of our down-trodden brethren whom we have suppressed and whom we keep under suppression. Religions, like nations, are being weighed in balance.' Gandhi further emphasized, 'God's grace and revelation are the monopoly of no race or nation. They descend equally upon all who wait upon God. That religion and that nation will be blotted out of the face of the earth, which pins its faith to injustice, untruth or violence. God is light, not darkness, God is Love, not hate, God is Truth, not untruth. God alone is great. We, His creatures, are but dust. Let us be humble and recognize the place of the lowliest of His creatures. Krishna honoured Sudama in his rags as he honoured no one else. Love is the root of religion'[7].

Gandhi told the Congressmen that 'by 'making the removal of untouchability a plank in our platform, we assert our belief that untouchability is not only a part and parcel of Hinduism but also a corroding and sinful superstition, which has infected Hinduism, and that it is the bounden duty of every Hindu to strive for its abolition. Every Hindu, therefore, who considers it a sin, should atone for it by fraternizing with untouchables, touching them in a spirit of love and service, deeming himself purified by that touch, redressing their grievances, helping them patiently to overcome ignorance and other evils due to the slavery of ages and inspiring other Hindus to do likewise. When one visualizes the removal of untouchability from this spiritual standpoint, its material and political results sink into insignificance in his eyes, and one befriends the so-called untouchables regardless of such results.'[8] Seekers after truth will never waste a thought on the material consequences of their quest, which is not a matter of policy with them but something interwoven with the very texture of their lives. This is equally true of the removal of untouchability which spelt for Gandhi the breaking down of barriers between man and man and between the various orders of being. Such barriers can be found erected everywhere in the world, but Gandhi was mainly concerned with untouchability, which had received religious sanction in India and reduced lakhs and crores of human beings to a state bordering on slavery.[9]

Gandhi also believed that the cause of Harijans and Hinduism will not be served by the methods of rabble. He found the exercise to be perhaps the biggest religious reform movement in India, if not in the world, involving as it did the well-being of nearly forty million human beings living in serfdom. One had to win them by love, by self-sacrifice, by perfect self-restraint, by letting the purity of one's life produce its own silent effect upon their hearts. It could be done by having faith in truth and love converting the opponents to one's own way.

Untouchability, Gandhi was convinced, could not be removed even by the force of law. It could only be removed when the majority of Hindus realized that this is a crime against God and man and they would feel ashamed of it. In other words, it was to be a process of conversion, i.e., purification, of the Hindu heart. Gandhi felt that the aid of law has to be invoked when it hinders or interferes with the progress of the reform as when—in spite of the willingness of the trustees and the temple-going public—the law prohibits the opening of a particular temple.

Gandhi maintained that the spirit of untouchability must have been a product of our lowest ebb. He called it a curse for society. So long as this curse prevails in the society, people will continue to commit crimes. Further, one finds that according to Gandhi, the idea of untouchability does not have any religious sanction. Religion did not provide any room for this. He reinforced and emphasized, 'Untouchability is not a sanction of religion; it is a device of Satan'. He often said and wrote, 'I regard untouchability as the greatest blot of Hinduism'.[10] He further emphasized, 'It is against the *shastras*'.

Gandhi tried to preach the gospel of love to the whole world. According to him, all men—irrespective of their caste affiliations—belong to one God. He said and believed that removal of this great sin of untouchability meant, 'love for, and service of, the whole world, and thus merges into *ahimsa.* Removal of untouchability spells the breaking down of barriers between man and man and between the various orders of being. We find such barriers erected everywhere in the world.'

Gandhi was an honest follower of non-violence. So, Gandhi sought to change the hearts of the high-caste Hindus by moral pressure. He strived hard to force on the Indian conscience the problem of untouchability as an issue of national concern. Although the measures of legally abolishing untouchability were adopted in the Constituent Assembly, Gandhi never advocated legal measures. He always felt that all changes must come voluntarily from the heart. Gandhi, no doubt, anathematized 'untouchability' with all the force of his spirit. His crystal earnestness was proved by the life he lived and the works he did. Work was worship for him 'I am an 'untouchable' by adoption,' Gandhi said to Ambedkar during the crucial talks before the Poona Pact of 1932 over the representation of

Scheduled Castes and Scheduled Tribes in the legislatures then to come under the Government of India Act, 1935. 'My greatest worry', he said then, as he had said repeatedly before and since, 'is the ignorance and poverty of the masses of India and the way in which they have been neglected by the classes, especially the neglect of the Harijans by the Hindus. We are custodians of a great religion and yet have been guilty of a crime which constitutes our greatest shame. Had I not been a believer in the inscrutable ways of providence, a sensitive man like me would have been a raving maniac.'[11] It was with this conviction that Gandhi could say unconventional things like: a 'Bhangi does for society what a mother does for a baby'. He could also match such words with action, as he did when he adopted an 'untouchable' girl as his daughter. From time to time, he used to express his desire that independent India should have on 'untouchable' woman as its President—a desire that is yet to be fulfilled.

Gandhi was strongly committed to a social philosophy which consolidated his faith in persuasion and he opposed what he called 'reform by compulsion'. He insisted that the '*satyagrahis* must stoop to conquer' and wanted 'to set even the most orthodox and the most bigoted at ease' during the Travancore Movement of 1924–25 for the unfettered use of roads to the temple by the 'untouchables', it was Gandhi's idea of 'the beauty of compromise' that led to a settlement, hailed by Gandhi himself as a 'miracle', adding only eight furlongs or so to roads free for all (including untouchables) which led to the creation of a new and more promising atmosphere for social change.

Gandhi believed in the traditional concept of *Varna* system cleansed of untouchability, in which untouchables would be Harijans and their unclean work would be accepted as honourable. That is why, though an ardent champion for removing untouchability, he sought to do so within the Hindu Chaturvarna framework. Gandhi said time and again that 'untouchability is the sin of the Hindus and they must purify themselves by paying the debt they owe to their suppressed brothers and sister. Hinduism has sinned in giving sanction to untouchability. It has degraded us, made us pariahs. Even the Mussalmans have caught the sinful contagion from us.'

Gandhi sought to emphasize that in Hinduism there is no sanction for treating a single human being as untouchable. In the estimation of a Brahmin, knowing and living his religion, a Shudra is as good as himself. The *Bhagavad Gita* has nowhere taught that a Chandala is in any way inferior to a Brahmin. A Brahmin ceases to be a Brahmin the moment he becomes insolent and considers himself as a superior being. India owes a deep debt to the Brahmins who voluntarily sacrificed themselves for the betterment of all. It was the Brahmins who have called god the 'Servant of Servants', the 'Purifier of the Fallen'. It was the Brahmins who taught that the prostitute and the Chandala could attain *moksha* if she or he only purified her or his heart.[12].

It was, therefore, Gandhi believed, the moral duty of all Hindus to see that the 'untouchables' did not feel that they were despised or looked down upon. Let them not be offered leavings from our plates for their subsistence, he exhorted the Hindus and questioned them as to how could one accord differential treatment to any person, be he a Brahmin or Bhangi, who worships the same god and keeps his body and soul pure and clean? He warned them that one would have to regard himself as having sinned if one gave to a Bhangi unclean food from the leavings from the kitchen or failed to render him personal assistance when he was in need.

The British Prime Minister, MacDonald proposed separate electorate for the untouchables at the Round Table Conference. Gandhi put a firm resistance. He argued endlessly that Muslims, Sikhs or Christians will remain so for all times, but why would the untouchables remain untouchables in the future too? His suggestion was to grant them adequate concessions to ameliorate their condition and even reservations to ensure their representation in the Councils and other elected bodies but no separation from the general electorate, which if decided, he would oppose with his life, Gandhi had warned.

In a few months when the proposal for separate electorate for the untouchable Scheduled Castes was moved in MacDonald's Communal Award, Gandhi announced his decision to undertake a fast till death, unless this provision was changed. He explained that his primary concern was not merely to oppose this particular administrative cum constitutional measure that the British Government was going to introduce in India.[13] His principal concern was the inhuman practice of untouchability which cried for its immediate abolition, together with other reforms in Hindu society, on the one hand, and the excuse and the justification it provided to the colonial power to play its game of disrupting and fragmenting Hindu society, on the other.

Gandhi was for granting whatever concessions the Depressed Classes leaders wanted, provided they strengthened the integration of Hindu society in general rather than weakening it. With the fast continuing and the Mahatma's life at stake, there was a tidal wave of public opinion, which battered against hardcore Hindu conservatism. Hundreds of temples were opened to the untouchables and a large number of Hindu leaders pledged to do away with the centuries-old discriminations practiced against the untouchables.[14]. In the bargain, the Scheduled Castes were offered almost double the number of reserved seats than what had been promised in the British White Paper. In the event the agreement was clinched; the British Government agreed to make the necessary amendments in the White Paper if the Scheduled Castes and the Hindu sides were mutually satisfied on their agreement. It was then that the Mahatma broke his fast on September 25, the seventh day of his fast unto death. Of all the large number of Indian leaders who had expressed their anguish at the impending threat to the Mahatma's life, it was Rabindranath Tagore who said that untouchability was a serious enough blemish on the face of Hinduism which justified even putting to risk the Mahatma's precious life for its removal.[15]

Parallel with the signing of the accord on the issue of representation of the Scheduled Castes and modalities of elections (popularly known as the Poona Pact), Gandhi insisted from his Yeravada prison that the Congress, the Liberals, and the Hindu Maha Sabha leaders also publicly announce their acceptance of another declaration, the text of which he drafted himself. This was adopted on September 25, 1932 at a joint public meeting held in Bombay. The text was as follows:

'This Conference resolves that henceforth, amongst Hindus, no one shall be regarded as an untouchable by reason of his birth, and that those who have been so regarded hitherto will have the same right as other Hindus in regard to the use of public wells, public schools, roads and all other public institutions. This right shall have statutory recognition at the first opportunity and shall be one of the earliest Acts of the Swaraj Parliament, if it shall not have received such recognition before that time.

It is further agreed that it shall be the duty of all Hindu leaders to secure, by every legitimate and peaceful means, an early removal of all social disabilities now imposed by custom upon the so-called untouchable classes, including the bar in respect of admission to temples'.

It is to be noted that Gandhi himself considered this declaration of historic significance and on several occasions in the course of the following decade and a half (till the transfer of power, that is), he reminded his fellow Hindus that this was a standing commitment.[17] Regrettably, however, neither any broad convention of Hindu society nor the Congress-led Ministries that were in office from 1937 to 1939 took any formal or legal step to implement the essence of this declaration.

Although the British Government, honouring the compromise agreement, withdrew its original proposal and accepted what came to be commonly known as the Poona Accord, there were all-round murmurings of perceived grievances on a large scale. In Bengal especially, the grumbling against the Communal Award generally as also against those aspects that emerged as a result of the Poona Accord, was particularly vociferous and organized. It was at this stage that the orthodox Hindu campaign went on a general offensive on the need to preserve the traditional customs of Hindu society on the one hand, and on the other, in its fight to ensure that the Hindus received their hitherto unquestioned lion's share of the concessions the British were about to grant in India.

Gandhi sought to evolve a new strategy and a new slogan that would enable him to mobilize the people, first of all the Hindu majority in their entirety. Gandhi believed that doing so would not only fully overcome the Savarna-Avarna divide but, having done so, would so integrate them, breaking down the hierarchical division of high and low in the Hindu society, that it would clear the path for communal unity too. He watched the situation: the depressed classes' movement was making very slow progress, but the orthodox camp's propaganda was becoming increasingly bold and offensive.

More than a year passed (14 months) between the Poona Pact and the start of the campaign during which Gandhi, apart from speaking at some meetings and talking to innumerable colleagues and other leaders, wrote very frequently on the question of untouchability. In fact, he declared several times that this was the one issue that was then commanding all his attention. He started new journals reflective of the new campaign: *Harijan*, first in English (February 1993) followed by other editions in Gujarati, Hindi, Bengali, Tamil, and other languages, all at short intervals.

During Gandhi's intense and passionate campaign against untouchability—he engaged himself from November 1933 to August 1934 on this burning issue—took him not only to almost all parts of British India but also to a large number of the adjoining Princely states. The Gandhi campaign was a great social-historical event in India. It represented a great social turmoil. This campaign, therefore, revealed and manifested all the contradictions of our social reality.

In a nutshell, Gandhi's strategy for tackling the evil of untouchability was as follows:

- He called untouchables as Harijans, that is, 'the children of God'.
- He tried to spread awareness against the evils of untouchability by actively involving the upper castes in order to change their mindset through awareness. In his efforts to do so, Gandhi started newspapers: *Harijan* in English, *Harijan Sewak* in Hindi and *Harijanbandhu* in Gujarati.
- He established the Harijan Sewak Sangh devoted to the upliftment of Harijans. Even in his ashram, Harijans were given due respect and they were at par with rest of the other inmates.
- He conducted 'Harijan Tours' throughout India to spread the message against untouchability and collected money for their betterment.
- Gandhi supported the movement for throwing open places of worship and temples for Harijans.
- Gandhi lent his support to the Vaikom Satyagraha in Kerala, which was organized for allowing the use of the road near temple for untouchables.
- Being a non-violent person, Gandhi was not averse to taking the help of law and constitutional means. Some of the inspired legislators introduced Bills aimed at removing the disabilities placed on Harijans by some Provincial Governments and in some provisions of law, from entering temples. In the 1930s, two Bills were awaiting the Viceroy's sanction, one for introduction in the Central Legislative Assembly by Ranga Iyer and other for introduction in Madras Council by Subbaroyan. Gandhi gave wide publicity to these Bills and requested the legislators to give their full support to them.
- Gandhi entered into dialogue with Narayan Guru of Kerala and the Self Respect Movement led by E. V. Ramaswamy.
- Gandhi's entire life was dedicated to the cause of Harijans. His efforts were unique. He struck at the very root of untouchability.

Gandhi on Untouchability

So far as the Harijans are concerned, every Hindu should make a common cause with them and befriend them in their awful isolation.

Untouchability means pollution by the touch of certain persons by reason of their birth in a particular state or family. It is an excrescence. In the guise of religion, it is always in the way, and corrupts religion.[16]

There is an ineffaceable blot that Hinduism today carries with it. I have declined to believe that it has been handed to us from immemorial times. I think that this miserable, wretched, enslaving spirit of untouchability must have come to us when we were in the cycle of our lives at our lowest ebb… That any person should be considered untouchable in this sacred land passes one's comprehension.[17]

Untouchability is a sin against God and man. There is no warrant in the *Shastras* for untouchability as we practice it today.[18]

I consider untouchability to be a heinous crime against humanity. It is not a sign of self-restraint, but an arrogant assumption of superiority.[19]

Untouchability is a snake with a thousand mouths, through each of which it shows its poisonous fangs. It defies definition. It needs no sanction from Manu or the other ancient lawgivers.[20]

Untouchability is a blot upon Hinduism and must be removed at any cost. Untouchability is a poison, which, if we do not get rid of it in time, will destroy Hinduism.[21]

And why do I say that untouchability is a curse, a blot and a powerful poison that will destroy Hinduism? It is repugnant to our sense of humanity to consider a single human being as untouchable by birth. If you were to examine the scriptures of the world and the conduct of peoples other than Hindus, you do not find any parallel to the untouchability.[22]

I believe that if untouchability is really rooted out, it will not only purge Hinduism of a terrible blot, but its repercussion will be worldwide. My fight against untouchability is a fight against the impure in humanity.[23]

What I want, what I am living for and what I should delight in dying for is the eradication of untouchability, root and branch.[24]

Removal of untouchability means love for, and service of the whole world, and thus merges into *ahimsa.* Removal of untouchability spells the breaking down of barriers between man and man, and between the various orders of being.[25]

Removal of untouchability means not merely touching the Harijans (untouchables), but also looking upon them as our own kith and kin; in other words, treating them in the same way as we would our own brothers and sisters. None is high, none low.[26]

They are not untouchables, we are untouchables. They eat and drink and think and feel even as we do. If a sum total of their virtues and vices and the privileges they are denied were to be made and compared with our virtues and vices and the privileges we enjoy and deny to them, I am sure in God's books we should find our debit side far heavier than theirs.[27]

Untouchability is repugnant to reason and to the instinct of mercy, pity and love. No man can consider another man inferior to himself. He must consider every man as his blood brother. It is the cardinal principle of every religion.[28]

It is a sin to believe that anyone else is inferior or superior to ourselves. We are all equals. It is the touch of sin that pollutes us, and never that of a human being. None are high and none are low for who would devote his life to service. The distinction between high and low is a blot on Hinduism, which we must obliterate.[29]

The distinction of high and low is at the bottom of untouchability. So long as the idea of high and low is not abolished, untouchability cannot be said to have been abolished.[30]

In battling against untouchability and in dedicating myself to that battle, I have no less an ambition than to see a complete regeneration of humanity. It may be mere dream, as unreal as the silver in the seashell. It is not so to me while the dream lasts, and, in the words of Romain Rolland: 'Victory lies not in realization of the goal, but in a relentless pursuit after it.[31]

In dealing with the monster of untouchability, my own innermost desire is not that the brotherhood of Hindus only may be achieved, but it essentially is that the brotherhood of man—be he Hindu, Mussalman, Christian, Parsi or Jew—may be realized.[32]

I do want *moksha*. I do not want to be reborn. But if I have to be reborn, I should be born as an untouchable, so that I may share their sorrows, sufferings, and the affronts leveled at them, in order that I may endeavour to free myself and them from that miserable condition... If I should die with any of my desires unfulfilled, with my service of the untouchables unfinished, with my Hinduism unfulfilled, I may be born again amongst the untouchables to bring my Hinduism to fulfillment.[33]

Summing Up

Gandhi is believed to have advocated that people should continue in their ancestral occupations and it is also alleged that he advised the Dalits to nurture a relationship with the upper castes analogous to that of the black Uncle Tom towards the latter's former white masters.[34] Nothing could be farther from truth and from what Gandhi really stood and campaigned for.

What is remarkable about Gandhi is that instead of falsely glorifying the past he, in fact, infused the past with his very modern ideas of truth, justice, fearlessness, fraternity, absence of hierarchy, and dignity of the individual values which he thought were essential for the revival of our ancient but also decadent society. Thus, he was most unsparing in condemning all that was reactionary, oppressive and exploitative in our traditional customs, characterizing them as the excretions of the historical process, and called for their absolute elimination.

Notes and References

1. *Young India*, 26-12-1924, and also *Harijan*, 28.9.1934.
2. *Ibid.*, 6.8.1931.
3. Tendulkar, D. G., *The Mahatma*, Vol. IV, pp. 125–26.
4. *Speeches and Writings of Mahatma Gandhi*, Vol. II, pp. 336–44.
5. *Harijan*, 9.10.1937, p. 292.
6. Iyer, Raghavan, *Political and Moral Thoughts of Mahatma Gandhi*, New York: Oxford University, 1973.
7. See for details, *Speeches and Writings of Mahatma Gandhi,* Vol. II, pp. 340–54.
8. *Young India,* April 27, 1921.
9. *Young India,* September 18, 1930.
10. *Young India,* January 21, 1926.

11. Tendulkar, D. G, The Mahatma, Vol. IV, pp. 125–26.
12. *Young India,* May 11, 1921.
13. *Speeches and Writings of Mahatma Gandhi,* Vol. II, pp. 336–44.
14. *Harijan*, 9. 10. 1937.
15. Iyer, Raghvan, *Political and Moral Thoughts of Mahatma 'Gandhi'* , New York : Oxford University Press, 1973.
16. Gandhi, M. K., From Yervada Mandir, Ahmedabad: Navajivan Publishing House, 1932, p. 31.
17. *Speeches and Writings of Mahatma Gandhi*, p. 387.
18. *Harijan*, March 2, 1934.
19. *Young India*, December 8, 1920.
20. *Ibid*, July 11, 1927.
21. *Harijan*, July 20, 1936.
22. *Ibid.*, July 20, 1936.
23. Tendulkar, Mahatma, Vol. III, p. 203.
24. Tendulkar, D. G. Mahatma, Vol. III. p. 209.
25. Gandhi, M. K, From Yervada Mandir, Ahmedabad: Navajivan Publishing House, 1932. p. 33.
26. *Babu-Ke-Ashirvad*, November 28, 1944.
27. *Young India*, May 13, 1926.
28. *Speeches and Writings of Mahatma Gandhi*, p. 930.
29. *The Diary of Mahadev Desai*, p. 286.
30. *Conversations of Gandhiji*, p. 60.
31. *Harijan*, March 25, 1933.
32. *Ibid.*, February 16, 1934.
33. *Ibid.*, September 12, 1936.
34. Ram, Jagjivan, *Mahatma Gandhi and Social Change* in S. Radhakrishnan (Ed.), Mahatma Gandhi—100 Years, New Delhi, Gandhi Peace Foundation, 1968, pp. 156–160.

Summary

- Gandhi was the pioneer leader who made the removal of untouchability his life's mission. Gandhi desired to deliver the untouchables, whom he called Harijans, from the slavery of centuries by means of changing the hearts of the high-caste Hindus. Gandhi aroused the people's attention more widely than anyone had done before in history, to the evils of untouchability.
- Gandhi said that the attainment of *swaraj* was a must, but that would not be complete unless a social order based on equality and fraternity was established.
- Through non-violent action, Gandhi wanted to remove the untouchability from its very roots.
- Gandhi's ultimate search was for righteous conduct. According to him, India's real emancipation depended on the abolition of untouchability. Gandhi's influence over the masses was tremendous. The people of India had unflinching faith in him. The most remarkable feature of his leadership was that he was able to lead and direct the movement without holding any position of power of any high office.
- In 1931, Gandhi named the untouchables, Shudras, and Chandalas as 'Harijan' i.e. men of god.

- Gandhi was of the view that untouchability, as it was practiced in Hinduism, was a sin against god and man and was, therefore, like a poison slowly eating into the very vitals of Hinduism.
- Gandhi did not believe the caste system, even as distinguished from varna-ashram, to be an odious and vicious dogma.
- Untouchability, Gandhi was convinced, could not be removed even through the force of law. It can only be removed when the majority of Hindus realized that this is a crime against god and man and felt ashamed of it.
- Gandhi was an honest follower of non-violence. So, he sought to change the hearts of the high-caste Hindus by applying moral pressure.
- Gandhi was strongly committed to a social philosophy which consolidated his faith in persuasion and he opposed what he called 'reform by compulsion'.
- Gandhi's entire life was dedicated to the cause of Harijans. His efforts were unique. He struck the root of untouchability.
- What is remarkable about Gandhi is that instead of falsely glorifying the past he, in fact, infused the past with his very modern ideas of truth, justice, fearlessness, fraternity, absence of hierarchy and dignity of the individual values, which he thought were essential for the revivification of our ancient but also decadent society.

Further Reading

Bandyopadhyaya, J., *Social and Political Thought of Gandhi*, Calcutta: Allied Publishers, 1969.

Biswas, S. C., (Ed.), *Gandhi: Theory and Practice Social Impact and Contemporary Relevance*, Shimla: Indian Institute of Advance Study, 1969.

Ganguli, B. N., *Gandhi's Social Philosophy; Perspective and Relevance*, Delhi: Vikas Publishing House Pvt. Ltd., 1973.

Parekh, Bhikhu, *Colonialism, Tradition and Reform: An Analysis of Gandhi's Political Discourse*, New Delhi: Sage Publications, 1989.

Raghuramaraju, A., (Ed), *Debating Gandhi: A Reader*, New Delhi: Oxford University Press, 2006.

17

Gandhi and Environment

Introduction

The Human Development Report, 1990 clearly stated that, 'The real wealth of a nation is its people. And the purpose of development is to create an enabling environment for people to enjoy long, healthy and creative lives.' This simple but powerful truth is too often forgotten in the pursuit of material and financial wealth. The moot question is in the development syndrome: Where are the people? Where is environmental protection and care for mother earth? Are human beings enjoying long, healthy and creative lives? If not who is responsible for this situation?

The conflict that is inherent to man's quest for happiness through material advancement has taken a variety of forms. There are World Wars, there are religious wars, there are social conflicts, and there are psychological tensions. The entire human society is being torn into pieces. But above all these issues, man has waged a continuous war against nature, endangering the very survival of life on the earth. Man has survived the fury of the two world wars, but he will not survive the fury of the war he has waged against nature. The eco disaster is visible to those who can see. Before it is too late, man must return to sanity. The other name of this sanity is the conduct of life in consonance with the laws of ecology.

In the present situation, man finds himself under severe strain and feels compelled to sit up and reassess his environment, nature, culture and future. Development, the credo of modern age, has become a dubious proposition. The short-term euphoria that it vouchsafed to mankind is turning into a long-term incubus. Humanity today faces an environmental crisis of global dimension, which has threatened the very survival of mankind due to the rape of the mother earth and nature in the name of modernization and development. The whole planet is in danger due to over exploitation of nature. It is a crisis that is threatening the survival of all in exactly the same manner—the rich countries as well as the developing countries. Environmental degradation in both the rich and poor countries is proceeding at an alarming rate—all in the name of more and more development. Development as a process of modernization has proved inimical or antithetical to our environment. Greater development means increased environmental deterioration.

Environment is a global concern and its protection is one of the most challenging tasks facing mankind today. 'Consumption for today and conservation for tomorrow" has become the slogan of humankind all over the world. It is correct to say that 'no technological intervention, however, brilliant, no socio-economic reform, however profound, will be able to save us from the impending catastrophe, if living natural resources are reduced below the sustainable levels and the environmental elements are degraded to the point of dysfunctional".

Therefore, from the Gandhian perspective, the need of the hour is to radically change our life style and learn to live in a harmonious relationship with nature. In reality, the Gandhian perspective is an ecological one and involves not only reassertion of the ancient beliefs but also involves the rejection of the existing paradigm—capitalism, industrialism, consumerism, patriarchal order and reconstructing a new order of values that is more environmental friendly.

Issues and Challenges

The environmental problems of the earth began with its very birth, some 4.6 billion years ago. Environmental degradation has been associated with most human endeavours, leading to changes in the chemistry of nature. All these can be traced to ecologically unsustainable human development. The human being has, thus, become—according to John Mc Hall—the most dangerous organism that the planet has ever hosted.

It is widely recognized that the race to rapid industrialization has left with us polluted rivers, contaminated soil, depleted wildlife and exhausted natural resources. It is a crisis that not only threatens the survival of the poorest one billion inhabitants of this mother earth, but one that threatens all of humanity and which has come to be known as the global ecological crises.

Highly industrialized west consume 80 per cent of world's resources even though they constitute only 20 per cent of world population. This is due to high level of consumerism and sophisticated life style of modern man. Resulting in war for domination.

The question of greenhouse effect, warming of the earth and resultant damage to the ozone layer, scarcity of water, and the pollution of air, water and food through increasing chemical and industrial wastes, has given a jolt to all concerned. But the irony is that the pampered West is unwilling to put a restraint on its pattern and level of consumerism, and seeks a remedy for the environmental degradation in further technological innovations.

If environmental problems are to be solved, then there must be a change in the way individuals think about and interact with their environment. It is for this reason that the cultural and spiritual underpinnings of *dharma*, which is the primary virtue in the active life of all individuals, can be of benefit to all people.

The powers of the world indulge in the great sins which affect us in everyday life in the developing world. The six sins are:

- **Greed:** A little over 16 per cent of the world's population, mainly the affluent seven countries, consumes 81 per cent of the world's resources.
- **Sloth:** No government has substantially altered its path despite the necessary changes called by the Brundtland Report of 1987.
- **Anger:** Annual global military spending total $ 600 billion. NATO accounts for 80 per cent. Every minute, the world spends $1.7 million on arms, and 57 people die from hunger-related illnesses.
- **Covetousness:** In 1989, the poor southern nations paid $ 52 billion more to rich northern countries than they received by way of loan or aid.
- **Pride:** The affluent countries arrogantly believe that their path to development is the only one worthwhile.
- **Lust:** Where tourism is often the largest earner of vital foreign currency for poor developing countries, the underprivileged people living in cities find themselves forced to sell sex for tourists from wealthy countries.

Lifestyles in the United States of America and other countries are based on high levels of consumption. And high consumption levels ultimately lead to high environmental damage and problems of waste disposal.

Per capita consumption of energy, which is a good indicator of the consumption levels of nations, shows that the USA uses 10127 kg of coal, West Germany 5377 kg, Japan 4032 kg, China 810 kg, India 307 kg and Bangladesh 69 kg. In other words, an average USA citizen uses over 30 times more energy than an average Indian, and in extreme cases the difference is likely to be 1: 150. Further in terms of use of resources, the average USA citizen consumes 20 times more steel, 100 times more paper, 15 times more cement than per capita use in India.

India's environmental crisis has been forcefully highlighted by P. Dayanandan in the following statistical data:

- Population reaching one billion by 2000.
- Urban population increasing from 160 to 350 million.
- 250 million suffering from malnutrition.
- 70 per cent of population below 35 years: demands for education and employment.
- Urban-Rural and Rich-Poor gap widening.
- Severe soil erosion [5 million tonnes per year].
- Intensifying droughts and floods [6.4 to 9 million hectares in three decades].
- Land degraded [50 per cent], surface water contaminated [70 per cent].
- Fodder shortage [60 percent]; 500 million livestock; grazing land 3.5 per cent.
- Forest cover decreasing at a rate of 34 per cent loss in one decade.
- At 0.47 hectare per person, forest available only for 150 million.

- More than 1500 plants and animals endangered.
- Conflicts in land use and resources sharing.

Near about 424 nuclear reactors are operating worldwide and more have been planned for the future, which are neither safe nor environment friendly. The principal factor behind these maladies has been the need of the poor, greed of the rich and careless application of technology in each and every field of economic activities.

Almost all the consumer items that are being promoted to sustain the economic growth have significant impact on society, either directly or indirectly. Consumerism is based on more and more consumption of natural resources. The natural resources are limited. The result is increase of violence—at individual level, family level, societal level, and national level. Data shows that violence is increasing every year not only in India but in other countries also. By 2050, it is estimated that two-thirds of the world's people will be short of water. The former secretary General of the United Nations Organizations, Mr. Boutros Boutros Ghali has warned that the war will not be waged over oil, but over water, which is becoming the scarcest natural resource. His predictions are echoed by the World Bank Vice-President Ismail Serageldin, who said: 'Be under no illusion; the impact of general water shortages is going to hit over cities. In the next century, wars will be fought over water.'

A lot of literature exists on the current scenario with regard to the natural resources. Some of them that have summarized the environmental problems facing humankind and way out include *Silent Spring* (Rachel Carson, 1962), *The Limits to Growth* (Meadows et al., 1972), The Report of World Commission on Environment and Development (1987). The Rio de Janeiro conference of UNCED (United Nations Conference on Environment and Development) is a landmark event. The result of the conference was the release of five documents, the principle one being Agenda 21. It is a blueprint for the future.

Gone is the time when environmental protection was synonymous with caring for the big cats; today, on it depends the well-being of the planet as a whole, together with all its inhabitants (including human beings) and non-living things. There is a tremendous connectivity and interdependence among various components—like natural living and non-living resources—with considerable social, economic, historical, cultural, philosophical, ethical and moral dimensions. All these aspects are now under the purview of environment.

The enemy of our environment is within each one of us because we want more and more at the expense of nature, and we consume more than our share of materials. There is undeclared war against nature, culture and future. Today, the human race is at the crossroads; the present eco-degradation and pollution are the result of greed of the rich, need of the poor to eke out an existence, and the careless application of technology.

The importance of the environment is ever increasing and there is no compartment of life which is unaffected by it. Years ago, Gandhi was asked if he would like to have the same standard of living for India's teeming millions as was prevalent in England. He quipped: 'It took Britain half the resources of planet to achieve this prosperity. How many planets will a country like India require?'

The industrial countries have an eye on developing countries. The fixing of targets by industrial countries for population stabilization in the developing countries, must now be backed by their [industrial countries] willingly fixing targets for controlling and bringing down resource use in their own countries. The silver lining is that the ethics of environment and resource use are now being increasingly and openly talked about by thinkers even in the North. Contrarily, in India, saint and philosophers have not only been talking about resource conservation, but also practicing it since the dawn of human history. They lived the life of simplicity. In the present context, the modern visionary Gandhi rightly said long back: 'The earth provides enough to satisfy every man's need but not for every man's greed'.

The 20th century is undoubtedly an era of unprecedented economic growth. The optimum production was the key to peace and prosperity. Nature becomes a commodity and society is only of the human beings. It is our primary duty to sublimate nature with the help of science and technology so that she does not lose her capacity to sustain all forms of life on the earth. The basic needs of all beings should be fulfilled from their surroundings with the least efforts. The present system, which relies more and more upon the use of non-renewable resources like metals and minerals cannot survive because their supply is limited. The ancient cultures survived because they sustained on renewable resources. Ivan Illyich was asked: What was the way out of the crisis of the civilization? He replied, 'Perhaps the Eskimos can show us the way'. Edward Goldsmith, on the basis of his study conducted for 32 years, also arrived at a similar conclusion, when he said, 'Inspiration must come from the world view of vernacular societies, in particular the Chatholic world view of the earliest period when people everywhere lived in harmony with the natural world.'

Modern life has become so complex and complicated that we cannot do without certain things. So the next step should be to find out the alternatives. There is an urgent need to replace the present energy system which is inhuman, hazardous and temporary. The energy priorities should be human, animal, bio, solar, wind, tidal, geothermal and hydrothermal from the rivers. The real development will take the society from *vikriti* (perversion) to *sanskriti* (culture). It is not going back, but going in the right direction.

Sustainable Development

The Brundtland Commission on Environment and Development in its report 'Our Common Future' called for application of sustainability as a criterion for all development initiatives. 'In order for development to be sustainable, it must meet the needs of the present without compromising the ability of future generations to meet their own needs,' said the commission. This definition is highly generalized and, hence, has been subjected to a variety of interpretations. Broadly speaking, developed countries lay emphasis on economic and technological aspects—How to integrate environmental costs into economic decision-making while protecting and enhancing their industrial competitiveness and employment opportunities? In contrast, the perspectives of developing counties are understandably different. In their view, poverty is the greatest polluter of environment and hence they must accelerate economic growth to meet the basic needs of the people. And if the industrialized rich countries are really serious about environment, they should realize that it is they who have created the present environmental crisis, not the poor countries, and hence they should assist the latter with finance and latest environment-friendly technological know-how to promote economic growth.

Each country and each region assigns different weights to different approaches to achieve a sustainable future. Sustainable development cannot be a static concept. It is a dynamic process and will be applied by different countries in tune with their own cultural, political and economic perspectives. Sustainable development has to be a long-term process, and one may say even a continuing process. The economic, political, technological and social structure and superstructure built during the last few centuries the world over, particularly in industrialized countries of the world, cannot be dismantled in a day.

Equity and justice are the sine qua non of sustainable development. It is four dimensional: (i) Equity among nations—rich nations, poor nations, developed nations, developing nations; (ii) Equity with countries—between regions, social classes, genders, sectors of activities; (iii) Equity between generations; and (iv) Equity between economics and ecology and science and spirituality.

Sustainable development has a fixed set of goals. Approaches and means to achieve them can differ.

- Basic needs of all human beings—food, clothing, shelter, education, health, security, and self-esteem must be met adequately. Priority must go to these needs. Level of these needs will be determined by natural and technological resources available and the global socio- economic context.
- Development process should be so articulated that ecological balance and environmental purity is least disturbed, if at all
- All nations and people must join hands to support each other and work with each other to create a world in which the above two goals are optimized.

Sustainable development demands a change in our attitude towards nature. There is an urgent need to move away from the Cartesian world view and post ourselves in the ecological world view. The idea is not to go back to the past, but to create a new future out of the present, the present as it is. The past can help in the shaping of the new future.

Sustainable development is not the business of the government and private companies alone. It is the business of the people in general. It is a process, which has to be initiated at each level of human endeavour and life. It has to be a movement, because it involves paradigmatic change, which is difficult to bring about unless a great many people get involved.

The Western perspectives relate to the incompatibility of the Western capitalist system with the idea of conservation. On the other hand, the Indian perspective relates to the obvious need of prescribing a way of life based on simplicity and self-restraint as the panacea for all our ecological and environmental problems. All cultures have in-built customs, manners and mores which preserve and conserve the environment. How to use various natural resources so that these resources are not destroyed or wasted is given in all cultures. We should have to examine codify them. And this code should be self-imposed.

Each society has certain value systems which are part of their lives. Eastern and Western societies have different social values systems. In most of the cases, we radically differ from each other in so far as social values are concerned. Western society has a materialistic outlook, whereas Indian society has a spiritual outlook.

India has the unique concept of preserving forests. People worship trees. Some trees which have great medicinal values are associated with some god or goddess. Similarly, India has the distinction of developing a unique irrigation system as early as 3000 years ago which conserved and replenished surface and groundwater and improved the living environment of the people. One can find hundreds of examples of water management, particularly watershed planning and water harvesting in Rajasthan and other parts of India.

In India, the Constitution lays down the foundation of sustainable development through Article 48 A and 51 A (9) which state that the 'State shall endeavour to protect and improve the environment and safeguard the forests and wildlife in the country' and the duty of the citizen was 'to protect and improve the natural environment including forests, lakes and rivers and wildlife, and to have compassion for the living creatures'.

Gandhian Perspective

Mahatma's ideas about the dangers of Western civilization have assumed significance in the context of several issues concerning the survival of the humanity and evolution of a just and viable world order. Gandhi clearly saw the moral degradation and cultural decay long back. The *Hind Swaraj* by Gandhi published in 1909—long before the negative consequences of industrial civilization were exposed to the common experience—must have appeared to the generation of his times as a book of reaction and retreat from modernity and civilization. The fact is that long before the people in the new millennium were awakened to the peril and limits of unrestrained economic growth and technological innovations, Gandhi pointed out the pitfalls of industrialism and the damage to nature and man. He strongly criticized the emerging trends of consumer culture in all spheres of life and emphasized austerity and the moral principle in development, which is essential for the present millennium.

The environmental challenges of the new millennium require total newness on all fronts. The holistic analysis, churning of knowledge, ruthless codification of lessons of past and total transparency, viability and replicability are some issues for a clear accelerated plan of action. With the passage of time, the need to look at Mahatma Gandhi's views and beliefs from practical utility with reference to action becomes important. What a gamut of synergy of truth, non-violence, simplicity, characteristics, mission and on the whole a personification of action!

Gandhi said that since a human being has no power to create life, he has, therefore, no right to destroy it either. Man's happiness lies in contentment. He who is discontented, however much be possesses, becomes a slave to his desires. Gandhi's underlying philosophy was need but not greed, and comfort but not luxury. Gandhi's entire life and work is an environmental legacy for all humanity. This was not because he wrote a big treatise on the environment, or led a movement to stall a dam or some industry, or clean a river, or some such mentionable cause. This was because he was a practitioner of sustainable development in the real sense of the word. In brief, his whole life was his message and a lesson on environment and development for Indians and the world at large to follow.

- Humankind would act in a manner that is part of nature rather than apart from nature
- Materials available on the earth (humankind's only home), are not used with an element of greed
- Human beings practice non-violence not only towards fellow humans but also towards other living organisms and inanimate materials, because over use of such materials also amounts to violence
- Bottom-up shared view is preferred over the top down totalitarian overview
- Conservationist and sustainable life-saving approach prevails over the unsustainable consumerist self-destructive approach
- Humans care for and share with the poor and the destitute in society as a moral obligation towards them
- The human race thinks about how much is enough for a simple need-based, austere and comfortable life style
- All development, as far as is possible, leads to local self-reliance and equity with social justice
- Ethics and self-discipline in resource use is an over-riding criterion of development

Dalia Lama put it beautifully when he wrote: 'If we care for nature, it can be rich, bountiful and inexhaustibly sustainable'.

The Gandhian concepts of *sarvodaya*, *satyagraha* and *swadeshi* will be very useful for solving the social economic and political challenges of the new millennium. The concept of *sarvodaya* can be interpreted as the 'awakening of one and all'. In addition to the awakening of everyone, it refers to the awakening of the total human spirit and personality. The *sarvodaya* concept stresses on the duty of individuals to themselves and beyond their immediate families to the entire world. *Sarvodaya* believes that by tapping their inner most beliefs and values, one can awaken people to their *swashakti* (personal awakening or power) and *janashakti* (collective awaking of people's power)' in order that their *dharma* can be realized. The *sarvodaya* ideal, apart from standing for the meaning of the welfare of all, implies the moving of the universal welfare and integrated development of all. As a universal ideal, it aims at not only fulfilling the material needs but also developing the ethico-spiritual aspects of all people.

Similarly, *swadeshi* will be the greatest tool for solving the economic problems of the new millennium. *Swadeshi* means self-reliance in every filled. In other words, *swadeshi* is service and if we understand it, we will simultaneously benefit ourselves, our families, our country and the world. Gandhi delimited the modus operandi of *swadeshi* in terms of limited wants and the capacity of social surroundings and resources to meet the need of the people. In his famous sentence, he laid down his dictum: Our motto in new millennium should be simple living and high thinking so that we can stop the evils of the society. In fact, the *swadeshi* movement may become part of renaissance in the new millennium. Because it conveys the idea of returning to one's own country—to its culture and heritage, its own tradition and screens the mud of the next door neighbor. This is the appropriate times for us to understand the concept of *swadeshi* and implement it in every possible manner. We will be managing this progress by making ourselves self-reliant and self-suffocate in every field and we would be free frown moral degradation, economic exploitation and political subjugation.

Satyagraha will be also an important means by which individuals and groups can have an immediate effect on government policy and programmes related to conservation. Individuals and groups can organize the people and draw the attention of the Government and masses of issues of environment. At a personal level also, a lot of people can work. To operationalize the '*Satyagraha* for better future', it would be desirable to bring like minded people under one umbrella to fight against injustice and wrong governmental policies which are creating social tensions, alienation and polluting the environment.

Summing Up

The present environmental crises are consequence of follies, and of greed, exploitation and domination. Therefore, the present exigency demands that one acquires the basic wisdom of nature, that is to follow its laws and learn to manage according to its principles. Therefore, the present developmental crisis demands a different world view on Gandhian lines that is give up the present life style and reduction in consumerism. The message is simple and very clear. People have no choice but to move towards a secure future and that it has to keep note of the imperatives as well as the potentials of sustainable environment.

If there is anything that can solve the environmental problems, it is the Gandhian path, along with the opportunities, which will emerge from modern science and technology. Our approach to development and economic growth must be harmonized with human value. Our aim should be to have a worth living place and worth living life, which can be achieved through change of our life style, and controlling our unlimited needs and greeds.

We cannot erect the city of peace on the foundation of violence. If mankind is to live in peace and achieve progress in all spheres, it has to eschew violence and develop a way of life anchored in the philosophy of love and cooperation. We should be cautious to those who want to reach heaven by creating hell on earth. It is high time that the individual change the chemistry of thought and action by adopting Gandhian values in our daily life. We have to start from somewhere to overcome the hurdles coming in the way of promoting environmental awareness. In other words, there is need to reiterate Gandhian values and instead of merely garlanding the portraits of Gandhi, people must translate his ideals into real life.

Notes and References

1. World Commission on Environment and Development, Our Common Future, New Delhi, Oxford University Press, 1987
2. Human Development Report, New Delhi, Oxford University Press, 1999.
3. Special Issue on Towards Sustainable Development of Society: Imperatives and Perspectives, The Indian Journal of Public Administration, Vol. 39, No. 3, July-September, 1993.
4. Mishra, Anil Dutta, Gandhian Approach to Contemporary Problems, New Delhi: Mittal Publications, 1996.
5. Berry, Thomas, The Dream of the Earth, San Francisco: Sierra Club, 1988.
6. The Hindu Survey of the Environment, 1999.

Summary

- The conflict that is inherent to the man's quest for happiness through material advancement has taken a variety of forms.
- Development as a process of modernization has proved inimical or antithetical to our environment. Greater development means increased environmental deteriorations.
- From Gandhian perspective, the need of the hour is to radically change our life style and learn to live in a harmonious relationship with nature.
- Gandhian perspectives is an ecological one and involves a not mere reassertion of the ancient beliefs but involves the rejection of the existing paradigms—capitalism, industrialism, consumerism, patriarchal order and reconstructing a new set of values that is more environmental friendly.
- Sanity is the conduct of life in consonance with the laws of ecology.
- If environmental problems are to be solved, then a change in the way that individuals think about and interact with their environment must occur.
- The great powers of the world indulge in the great sins which affect us in everyday life in the developing world. These six sins are: Greed, sloth, anger, covetousness, pride, and lust.
- Gone is the time when environmental protection was synonymous with caring for the big cats; today, it depends the well-being of the planet as a whole, together with all its inhabitants (including human beings) and non-living things.
- The enemy of our environment is within each one of us because we want more and more at the expense of nature, and consume more than our share of materials. There is an undeclared war against nature, culture and future.
- The present eco-degradation and pollution are the result of greed of the rich, the need of the poor to eke out an existence, and careless application of technology.
- The step should be to find out the alternatives. There is an urgent need to replace the present energy system which is inhuman, hazardous and temporary. The real development will take the society from *vikriti* (perversion) to *sanskriti* (culture). It is not going back, but going forward in the right direction.

- Equity and justice are the sine qua non of sustainable development. It is four dimensional: (i) Equity among nations-rich nations, poor nations, developed nations, developing nations; (ii) Equity with countries—between regions, social classes, genders, sectors of activities; (iii) Equity between generations; and (iv) Equity between economics and ecology and science and spirituality.
- Sustainable development has a fixed set of goals. Approaches and means to achieve them can differ. These goals are: (i) Basic needs of all human beings; i.e., food, clothing, shelter, education, health, security, and self- esteem must be met adequately. (ii) Development process should be so articulated that ecological balance and environmental purity is least disturbed, if at all; and (iii) All nations and people must join hands to support each other and work with each other to create a world in which the above two goals are optimized.
- The Western perspectives relates to the incompatibility of the Western capitalist system with the idea of conservation, whereas the Indian perspective relates to the obvious need of prescribing a way of life based on simplicity and self-restraint.
- Gandhi's underlying philosophy was need but not greed, and comfort but not luxury.
- The present environmental crisis is consequence of follies, of greed, exploitation and domination. The present exigency demands that one acquires the basic wisdom of nature that is to follow its laws and learn to manage according to its principles.
- The present developmental crisis demands a different world view on Gandhian line that is give up the present life style and reduction in consumerism. Development and economic growth must be harmonized with human values.

Further Readings

Biswas, S. C., (Ed.), *Gandhi: Theory and Practice Social Impact and Contemporary Relevance*, Shimla: Indian Institute of Advance Study, 1969.

Chakrabarty, Bidyut, *Social and Political Thought of Mahatma Gandhi,* London: Rutledge, 2006.

George, S. K., and Ramchandran, G., *The Economics of Peace: The Cause and the Man,* Peace Publishers, New Delhi, 1992.

Mishra, Anil Dutta, (Ed.), *Gandhian Approach to Contemporary Problems,* New Delhi: Mittal Publications, 1996.Roy, Ramashray, *Contemporary Crisis and Gandhi,* Delhi: Discovery Publishing House, 1986.

18

Relevance of Mahatma Gandhi

Mahatma Gandhi, popularly known as Bapu or Father of the Nation, is the tallest among the leaders of the world of the 20th century ever produced. He is remembered all over the world for his love of peace, non-violence, truth, honesty, pristine purity, compassion and his success in using these instruments to bring together the entire population and helping the country to attain independence from the colonial power and show the new way to the world. Gandhi was a creative man and responded to the challenges of his time and set an example for both present and future generations. Albert Einstein, the great scientist had rightly said that 'Generations to come will scarce believe that such a one as this ever in flesh and blood walked upon this earth'

Gandhi changed the course of history and himself created history. He was a man of principles, great convictions and always practiced what he preached. There was no dichotomy between theory and practice and between public and private life. He left an everlasting impact on the world at large because he always spoke and understood the language of the masses, primarily the socially deprived and downtrodden. Even after sixty-three years of his death, Gandhi continues to attract the attention of scholars, social activists, media, policy makers and dreamers not only in India but throughout the globe.

The present world is passing through a critical phase of human history and is in search of an alternative. Liberalization, privatization and globalization are not only reshaping the economy of the people and nation but fundamentally reshaping the culture, ideology, attitude and life style of the people across the world. Every where, one can see the fundamental change. Small is being replaced by mega. The invisible has become visible. There is a mad race for materialistic development, resulting in alienation of people from society and nature and resorting to violence of different types. Every where, structural violence has increased. Service and need is replaced by greed. Ethics and honesty are no longer pivotal in public life. There is crisis after crises, corruption after corruption and, ultimately, people are the sufferers. Marxism provided an alternative to capitalism. Due to its inherent contradiction, Marxian experiments failed. Liberalism and neo-liberalism are also unable to solve the human miseries. People's hope lies in the Gandhian ideology which has provided an alternative.

The Gandhian principles are capable of mitigating the greatest challenge of the modern age. The most urgent need of the day is the abolition of human suffering. Gandhi's philosophy becomes pertinent in the present world due to the complexity of human behaviour. His philosophy, laying stress on the goodness of human nature, unity of mankind, service of man, application of moral principles considered valid for individuals to group life and inter-state relations, the non-violent process of change, social and economic equality, economic and political decentralization, tries to resolve the various kinds of tensions that disturb domestic and international harmony. It is capable of strengthening the forces of love, creativeness and joy of life and beauty. It takes an integrated view of man and emphasizes his spiritual nature. Gandhi provided an answer and an alternative, which is, above all, a ray of hope, a vision for future and a blue print for individual, state and society. The interpretations of Gandhian thought and perspective needs to be reiterated again and again till the masses learn to adopt and practice it in their thought and deed.

Gandhi provided solutions to the contemporary dilemmas and conflicts arising out from the failure of developmental paradigms and leadership. Even the welfare state is not responding as expected. The tragedy of modern India is that the important aspects of the Gandhian philosophy are not given serious attention. The ruling elite never realized that Gandhi was far ahead of his time. The quest of humanity for social justice and sustainability will remain a dream until and unless humanity realizes what Gandhi meant when he said that economics is untrue, which ignores and disregards moral values. Gandhi, in his various speeches and in his articles written throughout the freedom struggle, spoke highly of democratic decentralization and rural development. In the July 22, 1946 issue of *Harijan*, Gandhi stated that 'Independence must begin at the bottom'. He had also written, 'the *swaraj* of my dreams is the poor man's *swaraj*. The necessaries of life should be enjoyed by you in common with those enjoyed by the princes and the moneyed men. But that does not mean that you should have palaces like theirs. They are not necessary for happiness. You or I would be lost in them. But you ought to get all the ordinary amenities of life that a rich man enjoys. I have not the slightest doubt that *swaraj* is not *Poorna Swaraj* until these amenities are guaranteed to you under it'.

Gandhi found the picture of his free India in its essentials embodied in a song that was sung at one of his evening prayers in Bhangi Colony, New Delhi. What emerged was a picture of the India of his dreams. It was as follows:

We are inhabitants of a country
where there is no sorrow and no suffering,
Where there is no illusion nor anguish,
no delusion nor desire,
Where flows the Ganges of love
and the whole creation is full of joy,
Where all minds flow in one direction,

and where there is no occasion for sense of time,
All there wants satisfied;
Here all barter is just,
Here all are cast in same mould,
Here is no lack nor care,
No selfishness in any shape or form,
No high no low, no master no slave;
All is light, yet no burning heat,
That country is within you-
It is *Swaraj, Swadeshi*,
The home within you-
Victory! Victory! Victory!
He realizes it who longs for it.

India achieved independence on August 15, 1947. From a subject, Indian man became a citizen. But, in Gandhi/s words, we did not get freedom, that is, *swaraj* (self-rule). He wanted not only a new citizen for India but for the rest of the world who would be 'vision-ary'. His vision was to consider the whole world as a single 'family'. His philosophy and goal of development had to be inspired by *sarvodaya* (development of all). His principles and methods were to be based on 'Truth and Non-violence'. He was to wage a relentless battle against injustice. He was to use *Satyagraha* (self-suffering) to change the heart of the opponent.

Such a new man will be able to replace hatred with love, competition with cooperation, and interdependence will be his basic principle of life. He will bring peace, tranquility and harmony in the world. The new man will tell India and the world that we need not adopt war or flee, or be subservient to others in order to resolve conflicts and differences. He will tell us that we can match our soul force against the physical force and wear the other down with goodwill. It is possible to have the 'new man' by internalizing and practicing Gandhi's thoughts, words and deeds. Salvation for a strife-ridden world lies in Gandhi's 'New Man' who will consider the whole world a joint family.

The objective of the governance in India was set by the Pandit Jawaharlal Nehru in his soul-stirring speech in the midnight of August 14–15, 1947. He spoke on the 'ending of poverty and ignorance and disease and inequality of opportunity'. Mahatma Gandhi also prescribed a set of stiff yardsticks for judging the efficacy of public policies in a system of good governance, when he wrote: 'Will it restore to him (the poorest and the weakest man) control over his own life and destiny? In other words, will it lead to *swaraj* for the hungry and spiritually starving millions?' To achieve these objectives, the Directive Principles of State Policy was provided in the Constitution, which are non-justiciable but nonetheless are fundamental to the governance of the country. But the Indian state has without a doubt failed in its responsibilities towards its citizens over the last 60 odd years.

To re-establish and reaffirm the faith, Gandhi wrote *Hind Swaraj*. *Hind Swaraj* is a manifesto for a new world order based on the supremacy of ethics and morality over matter. It represents the voice of the voiceless, that of the common man of India, and even of the common people of the whole world. *Hind Swaraj* raises certain fundamental questions. India's encounter with Britain was not political and economic but civilizational. Even today, the situation is no different from the one when Gandhi wrote *Hind Swaraj. Hind Swaraj* was a Gandhi's response to the immediate, contemporary problems arising out of inner and outer conflicts at the individual, state and society level. *Hind Swaraj* also provides a vision, a strategy and a blueprint for the future and an alternative to solve the contemporary problems. Future hope lies in *Hind Swaraj.* In fact, *Hind Swaraj* is the Gandhian bible; it is the sacred book that the Father of the Nation gave to country. Truly, it is the *Gita* of the nationalist era. Through *Hind Swaraj,* Gandhi wanted to establish the self esteem of individual and moral regeneration of India. In other words, Gandhi through his treatise wanted to transform firstly India as a nation and polity and all Indians. *Hind Swaraj* is a source book for evaluation of India and Indians. It is a manual of action for people. *Hind Swaraj* is a critique of the excessiveness of materialistic Western society. It is a pointer to the down side of modern civilization, i.e., colonialism, neo-colonialism, violence and alienation. It is also a pointer to political democracy because political democracy without social democracy is not a democracy at all. Gandhi's criticism on the railways, lawyer and doctors must be seen as the down side of colonialism and neo-colonialism. *Hind Swaraj* provides an alternative to the manner in which an oppressed class can fight. It provides a way to fight against oppression, injustice, extremism and violence. It also provides an alternative to individual, society and state. One can honestly say that Indians love to talk about *Hind Swaraj* but have not understood it properly nor transformed its idea or philosophy on ground. It is a source book for evaluation of India and Indians in the post independent India.

Among the tributes received in New Delhi within hours of Mahatma Gandhi's assassination on January 30, 1948 was one from Sarojini Naidu who said: 'May the soul of my master, my leader, my father, rest not in peace. Not in peace my father do not rest. Keep us to our pledge. Give us strength to fulfill our promises to our heirs, your descendants, guardians of your dreams, and fulfillers of India's destiny.'

The force of her words reminds us that we should not rest till we are able to internalize in ourselves the twin principles of truth and non-violence in our thought and action. We should be optimistic and hope that we would be able to overcome the present crises facing the world.

According to Gandhi, real democracy should have meaning not for a few but for all, including the poorest and even for the maimed, the blind and the deaf. He did not believe in mere lip sympathy for the ideal which comes so easily to most present-day politicians and leaders. The entire social order should be such that this ideal should be achieved in practice. A genuine democracy calls for a higher degree of seriousness of purpose along with a sense of urgency. Gandhi realized that once the people are awakened, they will become a revolutionary force. Their minimum expectations will have to be satisfied; otherwise they will explode. This explosion could take many unpleasant and ugly forms.

Today, one of the basic questions is whether the rulers and political parties have a high level of seriousness or a sense of urgency. The answer is obviously no. Despite many laws, the entire electoral process and system in India is becoming less and less an honest mirror of public opinion. This is true of all other parts of the world as well. Even criminals are acquiring political respectability. This power is assuming more and more credible forms. The situation in other countries is not bright either. The voters are bribed and often elections are rigged. The candidates are merchandized rather than elected. One of the saddest aspects of election times is that politics overrides all human considerations.

Of course, in order to come out of the present malaise and dilemma, the most viable remedy lies is in adopting the Gandhian path to resolve conflicts. Arnold Toynbee has rightly observed: 'At this supremely dangerous moment in human history, the only way of salvation for mankind is the Indian way—Emperor Ashok's and Mahatma Gandhi's principles of non-violence and Sri Ramakrishna's testimony to the harmony of religions. Here we have an attitude and spirit that can make it possible for the human race to grow together into a single family and in the Atomic Age. this is the only alternative to destroying ourselves.'

Politicians in India—instead of giving moral leadership for which people are yearning and waiting—are only occupied in maintaining a system which is poisoned by collective bad faith and polluted by individual self-interest. People are served by deception and craftiness instead of vision and imagination. The duty of a citizen is not merely to vote but to vote wisely. He must be guided by reason and by reason alone. He must vote for the best man, irrespective of any other consideration and regardless of the party label. The right man in the wrong party is any day preferable to the wrong man in the right party. Time has gone when 'Congress' was a word to conjure with.

Indians, by and large, are 'low arousal' people. They tolerate injustice and unfairness with feudalistic servility and fatalistic resignation. On August 15, 1947 India achieved Independence. But Gandhi was not present in New Delhi. At that time, he was working among the poor people of Bengal. The reason for his absence was simple. He had two dreams in his life. The first dream was liberation of India from the British rule, while the second was liberation of Indians from oppression and injustice, from inequity and inequality, from discord and disharmony. To quote his own words: 'I shall work for an India in which the poorest shall feel that it is their country in whose making they have an effective voice, an India in which there should be no rich class and no poor class of people, and an India in which all communities shall live in perfect harmony. This is the India of my dream.' His first dream was fulfilled but not the second. According to the Mahatma, the true time for celebration would be when the second dream is fulfilled. Gandhi was a leader of his people, unsupported by any authority; a politician whose success rested, not upon craft or guile, but simply upon the moral grandeur of his soul; a fighter who pushed back the mightiest empire on earth without the use of force; a spirit of profound wisdom and captivating humility, armed with only an iron will and inflexible resolve; and a frail man who confronted the brutality of military strength with the dignity of a simple human being. To the Mahatma, truth was god and non-violence was religion. At his memorable trial for sedition in 1922, he said: 'Non-violence is the first article of my faith. It is also, the last article of my creed. In non-violence, bravery consists in dying, not in killing'. His compassion and humanity were as boundless as the universe. 'Gather together', he said, 'under one banner all men from all religions and races of India and infuse into them the spirit of solidarity and oneness to the utter exclusion of all communal and parochial sentiments.' And again: 'My Hinduism is not secularism. It includes all that I know to the best of Islam, Christianity, Buddhism and Zoroastrianism. Truth is my religion and *ahimsa* (the principle of non-violence) is the only way of its realization.' Gandhi held the view that the life of a good citizen was the life of Karma, action in the service of the country. 'My writings should be cremated with my body', he said. 'What I have done will endure, not what I have said or written.'

The hatred and fanaticism which consumed the body of the Mahatma did not touch his great soul. Indian systems and ideologies may be relevant at one time and irrelevant at others. But the teachings of this great and benign lamp of wisdom and humanity are for an endless time. Gandhi gave us the priceless gift of self-respect and the sense of dignity as a nation. The last interview which the Mahatma gave was in the early afternoon of January 30, 1948 to Margaret Bourke an American from the *Life* magazine. She asked him whether he would persist in his theory of non-violence in the event of a nuclear attack on a city. The Mahatma's reply was that 'if the defenseless citizens died in a spirit of non-violence, their sacrifice would not go in vain. They might well pray for the soul of the pilot who thoughtlessly sprayed death on the city.' This was his last message of compassion to mankind. He completely identified himself with the Indian masses. He observed: 'We must first come in living touch with them by working with them and in their midst, we must share their sorrows, understand their difficulties and anticipate their wants. With the pariahs we must be pariahs and see how we feel when we have to clean the toilets of the upper classes and have their wastes to be thrown at us. We must see how we like being in the boxes, miscalled houses, of the labourers of Bombay. We must identify with the villagers who toil under the hot sun beating on their bent back and see how we would like to drink water from the pool in which the villagers bathe, wash their clothes and pots, and in which their cattle drink and roll. Then and not till then shall we truly represent the masses and they will, as surely as I am writing this, respond to every call.'

The Indian masses responded to the Mahatma's call in a spirit of total surrender. He said to them that 'Real *swaraj* will come not by the acquisition of authority by a few but by the acquisition of the capacity by all to resist authority when it is abused'. He repeatedly used to mention that through realization of freedom for India, we would try to carry on and fulfill the mission of the universal brotherhood. He was really involved in achieving the broadest good of humanity at large.

Gandhi showed the way to harmonize the values of *artha* and *moksha*, secularism and spirituality, power and justice. *Purusharthas*, as interpreted by Gandhi, provided a set of values and ideals within which public discourse in India can (and should) be conducted. He presented a balanced view of life. Wealth, power, pleasure, aesthetic beauty, ethical integrity and freedom of the spirit, the *purusharthas*, are goals that all Indians seek. Gandhi explained how and why that seeking should be the basis of modern India's public philosophy.[1]

The concept of *purushartha* has three related meanings. First, it means any human striving towards some achievement. Secondly, it refers to human striving directed towards overcoming fate and *karma.* And thirdly, it refers to any one of the four canonically recognized aims of life, viz., *dharma* (ethics and religion), *artha* (wealth and power), *karma* (pleasure) and *moksha* (liberation from s*amsara*, the cycle of birth, death and rebirth.[2]

Gandhi himself beautifully sum up, he alone is religious, he alone is happy and he alone is wealthy, who is sincere in himself, bears no malice, exploits no one and always acts with a pure mind. Such men alone can serve mankind the best.

The present problems, according to the former Prime Minister P. V. Narasimha Rao, can be traced to a single source: the near complete alienation between the political establishment the bureaucracy, and the money elite on the one hand and civil society on the other. The former seeks self-aggrandizement: the politician through the electoral system and the bureaucrat through manipulating rules, regulations and procedures, and the moneyed elite, thanks to a promiscuous relationship it has built up with the former in an exploitative system.

Citizens find that the state has progressively abandoned its writ to goons and hoodlums. The district collector, the corporator, the M. L. A., the M. P., and the minister no longer command the respect they once did. In the eyes of the common citizen, courts and Parliament serve merely to lend a measure of legitimacy to fraud and crookedness and profligate wheeling dealing.

The leaders of the ruling as well as of other parties, out of their self-interest, fail to understand the basic fact that no party in the country can survive, let alone thrive, if politics is merely a matter of vote banks. In India, the political situation has become so grave and politics has become criminalized to such an extent that crime is slowly but very steadily becoming politicized.

There are three factors responsible which have distorted a rational development of citizenship in India. One is poverty, creating the need for economic security at any price and its corollary, the widening gap between the rich and the poor; the second is the galloping population growth; and the third is the conflict between ethnicity and the doctrine of unity. In reconciling the implications of these pressures upon the public psyche, a self-centered society has emerged. This society seems unable to look farther than narrow self-interest, self-promotion and selfish ambition. This is the rule rather than the exception which leaves a particularly heavy burden on all disinterested citizens who are acutely aware that we shall have no nation worth the name in the near future unless we can do something to restore the confidence of the people in a life-style that shows concern for others.

There is not a single one of us that is not enriched by our composite culture—whether it be in music, food, or dress—to take a few everyday examples. For example, the image of the unseen thread in the garland is an excellent metaphor for what nationality or internationality can be linked to. If the thread is cut at one point, the garland ceases to exist. How is the thread to be safeguarded? I suggest that we need to shift to a language of a different kind in order to answer this question. The nations of the world can only survive if there is a new socio-economic order where the biggest gulf of all, i.e., the one between the rich and poor, is removed to cease the yawning gap between one citizen and another.

The moral authority of most of the politicians has almost disappeared, since they are seen as opportunists in league with criminals and crooked businessmen. It is, therefore, not possible for politicians to impose discipline in a society which sees them as examples of indiscipline. The common man is alarmed at the moral sickness that is enveloping the world and lowering our ethical standards. Money power seems to have an all-pervasive effect.

One hopes that we do not reach a level where indifference by contagion or lassitude slowly engulfs the nation and after a certain point of conditioning violence becomes acceptable, scandal becomes routine, and militant resistance turns into a film script. Education must be shaped as a potent weapon to reverse the process from seeking pleasure, acquisition, and violence to self-control, sharing, and compassion. We Indians must first integrate ourselves to achieve our ultimate motto of *Vasudhaiva Kutumbakam* (the world is one family).

Political parties ought to work for the unity and integrity of India. Unfortunately, all parties with rare exception have used caste, religion and language, to their electoral advantage. Unfortunately, during the last five years or more, a situation has emerged, particularly in India, wherein it is difficult to say whether a particular offence of misdemeanour is opposed or tolerated.

India's success will be measured not by homogenizing a heterogeneous situation, but by the success with which diverse societies can be harmonized and co-exist and become mutually reinforcing and supportive; where traditions and modernity are appropriately blended, and where man-made capital does not become destructive of the natural capital. Both models have their specific constituencies in India.

Summing Up

We must go back to the sprit and ideals of those halcyon days when we practiced the philosophy of nation first and foremost; when we spoke the language of the heart; when we breathed the air of idealism; when we walked hand in hand on the path of selfless service and sacrifice; when all sons and daughters of the motherland took pride in themselves in being 'Indian first, Indians last and Indians always'. The need of the hour is that leaders and people of the country be inspired by the ideals and teachings of Mahatma Gandhi. We need a man of values at the head of the government. We need a philosopher king, whose head is clear and whose heart is in the right place. If this be true, then Gandhi is of relevance. If the policies of tomorrow are to be freed from the corrosiveness of purely personal ambition and raised to the level of serving great causes—such as liberating men from poverty, disease and hunger, both of body and mind—then Gandhi is of relevance. If kindness, magnanimity, gentleness and concern for others are the virtues which should inform public life, then Gandhi is of relevance. With the passage of time, Gandhi will be of greater relevance, and not merely to India, but to the world at large. I have no doubt that so far as my own countrymen are concerned, especially the younger generation to whom Gandhi is a mere name, they will, in the fullness of time and in the measure they address themselves to the real problems of India's historic transformation. The relevance of Gandhi remains undiminished today. In fact, his ideas and approach to political, economic and social issues are more relevant now than even in his life time. The policy makers, politicians, intellectuals and scientists must remember in thought and action the talisman of Mahatma Gandhi:

I will give you a talisman. Whenever you are in doubt, or when the self becomes too much with you, apply the following test.

'Recall the face of the poorest and the weakest man whom you may have seen, and ask yourself, if the step you contemplate is going to be of any use to him? Will he gain anything by it? Will it restore him to a control over his own life and destiny? In other words, will it lead to *swaraj* for the hungry and spiritually starving millions? Then you will find your doubts and yourself melting away.'

I would like to conclude with Gandhi's spoken words, writings, and work done by him that will resonate for centuries to come. At the same time, we must remember the seven social sins which Gandhi wrote in *Young India* of October 22, 1925.

Politics without principles
Wealth without work
Pleasure without consciences
Knowledge without character
Commerce without morality
Science without humanity
Worship without sacrifice.

What breath is to life, Gandhi is to humanity and civilization. As long as there is strife, hostilities, ethnic cleansing, religious unrest, internal conflicts and threats of military occupation, people will turn to Gandhi. His usefulness will not end unless conflict ceases, radical discrimination ends, women are empowered and the poor live with dignity.

References

1. Parel, Anthony J., *Gandhi's Philosophy and the Quest for Harmony,* Cambridge: Cambridge University Press, 2006, p. 5.
2. *Ibid.*

Summary

- Gandhi was a creative man who responded to the challenges of his time.
- Gandhi changed the course of history and himself created history. He was a man of principles, great convictions and always practiced what he preached. There was no dichotomy between theory and practice and between public and private life. He left an everlasting impact on the world at large because he always spoke and understood the language of the masses, the socially deprived sections and the downtrodden.
- The interpretations of Gandhian thought and perspective need to be reiterated again and again till the masses learn to adopt and practice it in their thought and deed.
- India achieved independence on August 15, 1947. From a subject, Indian man became a citizen. But, in Gandhi's words, we did not get freedom, that is, swaraj (self-rule).
- Mahatma Gandhi also prescribed a set of stiff yardsticks for judging the efficacy of public policies in a system of good governance. He said, 'Will it restore to him (the

poorest and the weakest man) control over his own life and destiny? In other words, will it lead to *swaraj* for the hungry and spiritually starving millions?'

- According to Gandhi, real democracy should have meaning not for a few but for all, including the poorest and even for the maimed, the blind and the deaf. He did not believe in mere lip sympathy for the ideal which comes so easily to most present-day politicians and leaders.
- Gandhi had two dreams in his life. The first dream was liberation of India from the British rule, while the second was liberation of Indians from oppression and injustice, from inequity and inequality, from discord and disharmony.
- Gandhi showed the way to harmonize the values of *artha* and *moksha*, secularism and spirituality, power and justice.
- We need a man of values at the head of a government. We need a philosopher king whose head is clear and whose heart is in the right place. If this be true, then Gandhi is of relevance.
- Gandhi's usefulness will not end unless conflict ceases, radical discrimination ends, women are empowered and the poor live with dignity.

Further Readings

Biswas, S. C., (Ed.), *Gandhi: Theory and Practise Social Impact and Contemporary Relevance*, Shimla: Indian Institute of Advance Study, 1969.

Brown, M. Judith, *Gandhi Prisoner of Hope*, New Delhi: Oxford University Press, 1992.

Chakrabarty, Bidyut, *Social and Political Thought of Mahatma Gandhi*, London: Rutledge, 2006.

Choudhuri, Manmohan, *Exploring Gandhi*, New Delhi: The Gandhi Peace Foundation, 1987.

Gangal, S. C., *Gandhian Thought and Techniques in the Modern World*, New Delhi: Criterion Publications, 1988.

Ganguli, B. N., *Gandhi's Social Philosophy; Perspective and Relevance*, Delhi: Vikas Publishing House Pvt. Ltd., 1973.

Mishra Anil Dutta, *Revisiting Hind Swaraj*, New Delhi: Concept, 2010.

Mishra, Anil Dutta, (Ed.), *Gandhian Approach to Contemporary Problems*, New Delhi: Mittal Publications, 1996.

Parel, Anthony J., *Gandhi's Philosophy and the Quest for Harmony*, Cambridge: Cambridge University Press, 2006.

Weber, Thomas, *Gandhi as Disciple and Mentor*, New Delhi: Cambridge University Press, 2004.

Appendix 1: Important Events in Gandhi's Life

1869	Born at Porbandar, now in Gujarat, India, on October 2.
1876	Betrothed to Kasturbai.
1883	Married to Kasturbai
1887	Passed Matriculation Examination; Entered the Sanwaldas College at Bhavnagar.
1888	Proceeded to England on September 4, to study Law.
1889	First public speech in England to a gathering of vegetarians.
1891	Became Barrister on June 10; Sailed back to India: Reached Bombay on July 7, where he received news of his mother's death.
1892	Started legal practice at Rajkot and Bombay.
1893	First time left for South Africa in April to appear in a civil suit.
1894	Civil suit decided by compromise.
1895	Enrolled as an Advocate of Natal Supreme Court; organized the Natal Indian Congress.
1896	Returned from South Africa to India, where he remained for six months and met Indian leaders, Tilak, Gokhale and others; went to South Africa again on November 28.
1897	Anti-Gandhi demonstrations in Durban, which marked the beginning of a great change in his life.
1899	Helped the British in the Boer War.
1901	Returned to India; Organized public service in plague-affected areas of Rajkot, Participated in Calcutta Congress.
1902	Went to Burma; Started travelling across India in a third class railway compartment; Opened an office in Bombay in July; Again proceeded after 3 months to South Africa.
1903	Established the Transvaal British India Association; Started editing *Indian Opinions*.

1904 Studied the *Bhagvad Gita* and Ruskin's *Unto This Last* which led to a revolutionary change in his life; Established the Phoenix Ashram.

1906 During the Zulu Revolt, Rendered service to the injured in the revolt; Took a vow to observe *Brahmacharya*; The word *satyagraha* was coined for the first time; Proceeded to England as a member of the Indian deputation.

1907 Started *satyagraha* against 'Black Act.'

1908 Interim agreement with British; attacked by a Pathan; Restarting of *satyagraha*, resulting in his arrest.

1909 Wrote his first latter to Tolstoy; Proceeded to England as a member of the second Indian deputation. While returning from England, he wrote *Hind Swaraj* or *Indian Home Rule*.

1910 Established Tolstoy Farm in Johannesburg.

1912 Gokhale arrived in South Africa; *Niti Dharma* was published: wrote another book of general information on nature cure for health.

1913 Restarting of *satyagraha*: Arrested and released; observed fast for seven days and thereafter took one meal a day for four and a half months.

1914 Began a fast for 14 days; Success of satyagraha, proceeded to England on July; First World War broke out on August 4; Meeting with Sarojini Naidu; Service in the First World War.

1915 Awarded Kaiser-e-Hind medal on return to India; widely travelled in India; Meeting with Kaka Kalelkar and Acharya Kripalani; Death of Gokhale on February 19; on May 25 Sabarmati Ashram was established.

1916 Gave a historical speech on the occasion of the establishment of Kashi Vishwavidyalaya; First meeting with Jawaharlal Nehru in the Lucknow Congress.

1917 First meeting with Dr. Rajendra Prasad; Started Champaran Satyagraha on April 10; Abolition of Indentured Labour Act on May 31; First meeting with Mahadev Desai.

1918 Mill Worker's strike in Ahmedabad, followed by three days' fast; Khera Satyagraha; Revival of the spinning wheel.

1919 Enforcement of the Rowlatt Act; observed April 6, as prayer-cum-fast day; Jallianwala Bagh massacre on April 13; Started editing of *Young India* and *Navajivan*; Khilafat Movement; Amritsar Congress

1920 Death of Lokmanya Tilak on August 1; Tilak Swaraj Fund was established on October 2; Congress constitution prepared by Gandhi was approved; Started Non-cooperation Movement; Establishment of Gujarat Vidyapeeth.

1921 Establishment of other national educational institutions; Boycott of the visit of Prince of Wales, followed by riots; Five-day fast; Ahmedabad Congress.

1922 Revolt of Chauri Chaura on February 5; Satyagraha suspended, five days' fast; Arrested on March 10; Six years of imprisonment.

1924 Operated for appendicitis; Released from jail on February 5; Twenty-one days fast from September 24; Presided over the Belgaum Congress.

1925 Death of Deshbandu Chittaranjan Das on June 16; One-week fast; Kanpur Congress; Establishment of Charkha Sangh.

1927 Extensively toured throughout India for the revival of khadi; Death of Hakim Ajmal Khan on September 19.

1928 Simon Commission; Bardoli Satyagraha; Death of Maganlal Gandhi in Patna on April 22; Death of Lala Lajpat Rai on November 17; Nehru Report, Compromise resolution in the Calcutta Congress.

1929 Resolution for complete independence passed in the Lahore Congress.

1930 Pledge for complete Independence on January 26; Dandi March on March 12 to break the Salt Law; Arrested on May 5.

1931 Death of Mohammed Ali in England on January 4; Gandhi released from jail on January 25; Death of Pandit Motilal Nehru on February 6; Gandhi-Irwin Pact on March 4; Bhagat Singh hanged on March 23; Karachi Congress; Martyrdom of Ganesh Shankar Vidyarthi on March 25; Participated in the Second Round Table Conference as the sole representative of India, but returned disappointed in December.

1932 Congress declared an unlawful organization; Restarted *satyagraha*; Arrested on January 4, Publication of *Young India* and *Navajivan* stopped; From September 20 started a fast unto death against communal award; Yeravada Pact on September 24; fast ended on September 26.

1933 Twenty-one days fast from 8th May; Started *Harijan* weekly; Released from jail and arrested again; one year's imprisonment; Fast unto death from August 16, which ended after one week; Released from jail on August 23; Death of Annie Besant on September 30; Death of Vitthalbhai Patel on September 22; Left Sabarmati Ashram to live at Wardha; Undertook tour from November 7for *Harijan* upliftment.

1934 Bihar earthquake; *Satyagraha* suspended on May 7; Seven days' fast; Gram Udyog Sangh established on October 26; Bombay Congress.

1935 Golden Jubilee of the Indian National Congress.

1936 Sewagram Ashram established.

1937 Accepted Congress membership in July; Started 'Nai Talim' programme.

1939 Death of Maulana Shaukat Ali on January 4; Fast unto death in Rajkot, which ended after 4 days on the intervention of the Viceroy; Tripura Congress; Subhash Chandra Bose resigned from the presidentship of the Indian National Congress; Second World War broke out on September 3; Congress Government in all provinces resigned on November 8.

1940 Individual Satyagraha started from October 11, Vinoba offered arrest as the first *satyagrahi*; Publication of *Harijan* weekly suspended.

1941	Death of Rabindranath Tagore on August 7; Gave up leadership of the Indian National Congress; Established 'Go-Seva-Sangh' on September 30.
1942	Again accepted the leadership of the Indian National Congress; Death of Shri Jamnalal Bajaj on February 11; Cripps Mission; established Hindustani Prachar Sabha; 'Quit India' resolution on August 8; Collective arrest of Indian leaders all over India on August 9; Death of Mahadev Desai on August 15.
1943	Twenty-one days' fast in Agha Khan Palace.
1944	Death of Kasturba Gandhi on February 22; Released from Jail on May 6; Gandhi-Jinnah talks.
1945	Indian leaders released from jail; First Shimla Conference. 1946 Cabinet Mission; 'Direct Action' Programme of the Muslim League from August 16; Communal riots; Padyatra in Noakhali; Death of Madan Mohan Malaviya on November 12.
1947	India declared independent on August 15; Seventy three hours' fast for peace in Calcutta.
1948	Fast unto death undertaken to establish peace in Delhi, which continued for five days; Martyrdom on January 30, with last words; 'Hey Ram', 'Hey Ram'.

Appendix 2: Gandhi's *Satyagraha* Movements

I

1. South African *Satyagraha* Movement: July 1, 1907 to June 30, 1914.

Cause: The racial segregation policy of the South African colonies and the various measures resulting therefrom.

Directed Against: (1) Officials of the Transvaal Asiatic Department, and subsequently also those of the Imperial Government; and (2) The White Population (Europeans)

Technique Employed: (1) Wait and watch; (2) Negotiations; (3) Protest Meetings; (4) Formation of political associations; (5) *Satyagraha* pledge; (6) Prayer for self-purification, (7) Ultimatum; (8) ceremonial March; (9) Pamphlets and newspapers; (10) *Hartals* (strikes); (11) Strikes; (12) Civil Disobedience (13) Courting Imprisonment; (14) Boycott; (15) Picketing; (16) *Satyagrahi Sahayog*; and (7) Symbolic acts of *satyagraha.*

Results: (1) The Indian Relief Act of July 1, 1914, finally and successfully closed the struggle. General Louis Botha, the Prime Minister of the Union of South Africa admitted that it was solely due to the *satyagraha* efforts of the Indian community that the Government had to revise or repeal the discriminatory laws and prevent their further enactment; (2) General Smuts (The Union Minister of Interior), Patrick Duncan (author of the Asiatic Registration Act), Percy Fitzpatrick (the worst opponent of the Indian cause), the Government officials; the legislators, the Magistrates, jail authorities, police, and a very large number of white Europeans realized that the India's cause was just, and they not only co-operated with them in several ways, but also conceded their demands substantially; (3) His method not only roused public opinion in favour of the Indian cause, but also brought considerable political awakening among the masses and knit them together; and (4) The movement strengthened Gandhi's belief in the efficacy of *satyagraha* as a sure way of solving social and political conflicts.

2. I Penitential Fast: November 10, 1913 to November 16, 1913

Cause: Moral lapse of two of his Ashram inmate Phoenix.

Directed Against: The erring Ashram inmates.

Techniques Employed: (1) Prayer for self-purification; and (2) fasting for seven days.

Result: The Ashram inmates realized 'What a terrible thing it was to be sinful.'

3. II Penitential Fast: April 1914

Cause: Moral lapse of an inmate at the Phoenix Ashram.

Directed Against: The erring Ashram inmate.

Technique Employed: (1) Prayer for self-purification; and (2) Fasting for fourteen days.

Result: The Ashram inmates realized 'what a terrible thing it was to be sinful.'

4. Viramgam Question: January 16, 1915 to November 4, 1917

Cause: Harassment of passengers proceeding from Kathiawad and other villages bordering Gujarat, by levying customs duties on them.

Directed Against: Officials of the Government of India.

Technique Employed: (1) Assessment of facts by Public Inquiry; (2) Negotiations; and (3) Protest Meetings.

Results: In view of the imminent possibility of *satyagraha*, Lord Chelmsford announced the abolition of Viramgam customs on November 11, 1917.

5. Indenture Immigration Question: March 20, 1916 to March 12, 1917.

Cause: India's demand for the abolition of the Indenture immigration question.

Directed Against: Officials of the Government of India. Technique Employed: (1) Negotiations; (2) Protest meetings; and (3) ultimatum.

Results: In view of the imminent possibility of Satyagraha, the Governor-General-in-Council's decision prohibiting labour immigration from India under Defense of India Act was gazetted on March 12, 1917.

6. Champaran *Satyagraha*: April 16, 1917, to October 6, 1917.

Cause: Harassment of and unfair impositions on the Champaran ryots by the British indigo planters.

Directed Against: (1) British indigo planters; (2) Officials of the Bihar Government.

Technique Employed: (1) Assessment of facts by public inquiry; (2) Negotiations; (3) Protest meetings; (4) Prayer for self-purification; (5) Ultimatum; (6) Personal disobedience of the District Magistrates' orders (restraints); (7) Technical trespass on the wrongly forfeited fields, squatting there upon and looting the onion crops there from; and (8) *Satyagrahi Sahayog*.

Results: (1) Champaran Agrarian Inquiry Committee with Gandhi as one of its members was appointed by the Government. The recommendations of this Committee were subsequently carried out through the enabling Act of 26th April 1918; and (2)The Movement brought social and political awakening amongst the peasantry and knit them together.

7. Ahmedabad *Satyagraha*: February 26, 1918 to March 18, 1918.

Cause: Ahmedabad mill workers' demand for increase in their wages to make up for the special wartime plague bonus, which was arbitrarily withdrawn by the mill owners.

Directed Against: The mill owners of Ahmedabad.

Technique Employed: (1) Negotiations; (2) Protest meetings; (3) Arbitration; (4) *Satyagraha* pledge; (5) Prayer for self-purification; (6) Ultimatum; (7) Pamphlets; (8) Strike; (9) Fasting for three days; and (10) *Satyagrahi Sahayog*.

Results: (1) On Arbitrator's Award, workers' demand for 35 per cent increase in the wages was accepted by the mill owners; (2) The *satyagraha* brought social and political awakening among the workers and knit them together; and (3) The indefinite fast undertaken by Gandhi against the mill workers in order to encourage them in their strike indirectly exercised moral pressure on the mill owners and Gandhi had with them very close and cordial relations.

8. Kheda *Satyagraha*: March 22, 1918 to June 6, 1918.

Cause: Kheda peasants' demand for suspension of land revenue recovery on account of failure of crops and the Government's refusal thereto.

Directed Against: Officials of the Government of Bombay.

Technique Employed: (1) Assessment of facts by public inquiry; (2) Negotiations; (3) Protest Meetings; (4) Formation of Political associations; (5) Satyagraha pledge; (6) Prayer for self-purification; (7) Ultimatum; (8) Pamphlets; (9) No-tax Campaign; (10) Courting imprisonment; and (11) *Satyagrahi Sahayog*.

Results: (1) The recovery of land revenue was suspended from those peasants who were unable to pay it; and (2) There was widespread awakening among the peasantry in Gujarat. In fact, they shed their lethargy and learnt the lesson of self-reliance and self-confidence. They realized that they had certain rights which they could enforce by mass action.

9. Rowlatt Act *Satyagraha*: March 1, 1919 to April 18, 1919.

Causes: (1) Indian's demand for the withdrawal of the Anarchical Crimes Act of 1919 and prevention of the passage of the II Bill of the similar character; and (2) Intensification of political awareness for independence.

Directed Against: Officials of the Government of India.

Technique Employed: (1) Negotiations; (2) Protest-meetings; (3) Formation of political associations; (4) Satyagraha Training Centres; (5) Satyagraha pledge; (6) Prayer for self-purification; (7) Ultimatum; (8) National days and weeks; (9) Pamphlets; (10) *Hartals*; (11) Civil Disobedience; (12) Protest Resignations; and (13) *Satyagrahi Sahayog*.

Results: (1) The Anarchical Crimes Act was never implemented and the second bill was never brought before the Central Legislature; (2) Through Satyagraha Sabhas, Gandhi raised a corps of volunteers and commenced the work of reeducating the public with regard to the meaning and practice of *satyagraha*; (3) The campaign brought unprecedented political awakening among the masses; and (4) Gandhi had to suspend the Civil Disobedience Movement in order to effectively assist the Government in restoring law and order despite the fact that *satyagraha* had neither been the cause nor the occasion for the outbreak of violence.

10. I Anti-violence Fast: April 14, 1919 to April 16, 1919.

Cause: Derailment of a train at Nadiad by some anarchists.

Directed Against: The anarchists and the Ahmedabad mill labourers on whose behalf Gandhi had earlier offered *satyagraha.*

Technique Employed: (1) Prayer for self-purification; and (2) Fasting for three days.

Result: The disturbances at Ahmedabad came to an end on April 14, and the Government withdrew the military proclamation.

11. I Non-violent Non-co-operation Movement: August 1, 1920 to February 12, 1922.

Causes: (1) Government of India's failure to protect the innocent people of Punjab and punish offenders guilty of unsoldierly and barbarous behaviour towards them; (2) Imperial and Indian Governments' failure to allow the authority of the Turkish Empire to remain as it was at the commencement of the First World War; and (3) The attainment of *swaraj* for India.

Directed Against: Officials of the Government of India.

Technique Employed: (1) Assessment of facts through public inquiry; (2) Negotiations; (3) Protest meetings; (4) Formation of political associations; (5) Satyagraha training camps; (6) Satyagraha pledge; (7) Prayer for self-purification; (8) Ultimatum; (9) National Days and weeks; (10) Pamphlets and Newspapers; (11) *Hartals*; 12) Civil Disobedience; (13) Courting imprisonment; (14) Boycott; (15) Picketing; (16) *Dharnas*; (17) Protest meetings; (18) Constructive Programme; (19) *Satyagrahi Sahayog*; and (20) Symbolic acts of *satyagraha.*

Results: (1) The movement failed in its immediate objectives and had to be suspended due to the violence at Chauri Chaura; 2) The whole of India, particularly the hitherto politically indifferent and inert peasantry, became acquainted, as never before, with the deep-seated disease of alien domination; (3) The people learnt lessons in the practical art of fearlessness and self-restraint; and (4) The spirit of religious unity was created between the Hindus and Muslims, which was Gandhi's biggest sin in the eyes of the British bureaucracy.

12. II Anti-violence Fast: November 19, 1921 to November 22, 1921.

Causes: Anarchists' activities in protest of the visit of the Prince of Wales to India.

Directed Against: The Anarchists.

Technique Employed: (1) Prayer for self-purification; (2) Fasting for three days; and (3) Newspaper propaganda.

Results: Peace was restored and, consequently, on November 22, Gandhi broke his fast in the midst of Hindus, Muslims and Parsis.

13. III Anti-violence Fast: February 12, 1922 to February 17, 1922.

Cause: Outbreak of violence at Chauri Chaura.

Directed Against: The Anarchist Technique Employed: (1) Prayer for self-purification; (2) Fasting for five days; and (3) Newspaper propaganda.

Results: Riots rapidly subsided.

14. Vykom *Satyagraha*: March 1924 to June 17, 1925.

Causes: (1) Prohibition upon the use by untouchables of roadways passing the Vykom Shiva temple; and (2) To rid Hinduism of the blot of untouchability.

Directed Against: (1) The orthodox Hindus of Travancore; and (2) The Maharaja, the Dewan, and the members of the Legislative Council of Travancore.

Technique Employed: (1) Negotiations; (2) Protest meetings; (3) Newspaper propaganda; and (4) Courting of imprisonment.

Results: (1) Roads were declared open for all on June 17, 1925; and (2) Subsequently, on November 12, 1937, the Maharaja of Travancore declared all the temples open for all, and the so-called untouchables were willingly welcomed by both the priests and the Savarna Hindus.

15. I Hindu-Muslim Unity Fast: September 18, 1924 to October 8, 1924.

Cause: Hindu-Muslim riots in Delhi, Gulbarga, Kohat and Lucknow.

Directed Against: The communal fanatics.

Technique Employed: (1) Negotiations; (2) Protest meetings; (3) Prayer for self-purification; (4) Newspaper-propaganda; and (5) Fasting for twenty-one days.

Results: (1) The riots rapidly subsided; and (2) The unity conference of Delhi passed a resolution appointing a National Panchayat Board of 15 members for setting communal disturbances.

16. III Penitential Fast: November 24, 1925 to November 30, 1925.

Cause: Moral lapse of some of his Ashram inmates at Sabarmati.

Directed Against: The erring Ashramites.

Technique Employed: (1) Prayer for self-purification; and (2) Fasting for seven days.

Result: Gandhi Succeeded in bringing the youngsters to the sense of their error.

17. Neill Statue *Satyagraha*: September 1, 1927 to October 13, 1927.

Cause: People's demand for the removal of the statue of Neill, a British General responsible for the brutalities during the 1857 rebellion.

Directed Against: Officials of the Madras Government.

Technique Employed: (1) Negotiations; (2) Protest meetings; (3) Newspaper propaganda; and (4) Courting imprisonment.

Results: (1) The Satyagraha had to be discontinued after some time due to lack of public enthusiasm; and (2) Eventually, in 1937, the Congress Ministry got the statue removed.

18. Bardoli *Satyagraha*: February 12, 1928 to August 4, 1928.

Cause: Bardoli peasants' demand for the revision and suspension of land revenue assessment, arbitrarily enhanced by the Government by 22 Per cent.

Directed Against: Officials of the Revenue Department, the Police of the Bardoli District and the Government of Bombay.

Technique Employed: (1) Protest Meetings; (2) Negotiations; (3) Satyagraha Training camps; (4) Satyagraha pledge; (5) Ultimatum; (6) Pamphlets and newspapers; (7) No-tax campaign; (8) Courting, imprisonment; (9) Boycott; (10) *Dharnas*; (11) Protests and Resignations; (12) Non-possession; (13) Constructive programme; (14) *Satyagrahi sahayog*; and (15) Symbolic acts of *satyagraha*.

Results: (1) Broomfield Enquiry Committee appointed and on its recommendations the enhanced rate was reduced to 6.25 per cent; (2) Closer co-operation was established between the Hindus and Muslims; and (3) There was widespread awakening among the peasantry.

19. Salt *Satyagraha*: March 12, 1930 to March 4, 1931.

Causes: (1) Demand for the repeal of Salt Acts providing for Government monopoly of salt, resulting in hardships especially to the poor; and (2) Demand for Poorna Swaraj for India.

Directed Against: The officials of the Government of India.

Technique Employed: (1) Protest meetings; (2) Formation of political associations; (3) Satyagraha training centres; (4) *Satyagraha* pledge; (5) Prayer for self purification; (6) Negotiations; (7) Ultimatum; (8) Ceremonial march (9) Pamphlets and newspapers; (10) *Hartals*; (11) National Days and weeks; (12) Non-violent non-co-operation; (13) Civil Disobedience; (14) No-tax campaign; (15) Courting imprisonment; (16) Boycott; (17) Picketing; (18) *Dharna*; (19) Peaceful Raids on Salt pans and works; (20) Protest resignations; (21) Non-possession; (22) Constructive programme; (23) *Satyagrahi sahayog*; and (24) Symbolic acts of *satyagraha*.

Results: (1) The *satyagraha* was discontinued in order to enable the government to implement the Gandhi-Irwin Pact; (2) The Pact provided that in further discussions on Indian constitutional reforms, the Congress representatives would be associated; (3) The campaign marked a distinct moral victory which created self-confidence among the people and confidence in the weapon of Satyagraha; (4) Young Muslims and Hindus showed increased toleration towards each other. They came to realize that the prevailing Hindu-Muslim antagonism was due to the extremists (on both sides) who were 'advanced in age and few in number'; and (5) Though the immediate and the long-range objectives of the *satyagraha* were not realized, the Government did permit certain classes of people to collect or make salt for domestic consumption or for sale within their villages.

20. Karnataka *Satyagraha*: March 1931 to May 1931.

Cause: Demand of the peasants of Sirsi, Siddapur and Hirekerur Talukas of Karnataka for the suspension of land revenue recovery on account of failure of crops and the government's refusal thereto.

Directed Against: Officials of the local government.

Technique Employed: (1) Protest meetings; (2) Negotiations; (3) No-tax campaigns; (4) Courting imprisonment; and (5) Peaceful picketing.

Result: Relief was granted to those who were unable to pay the assessed land revenue.

21. II Non-violent Non-cooperation Movement: January 4, 1932 to April 7, 1934.

Cause: Attainment of Poorna Swaraj for India.

Directed Against: Officials of the Imperial and Indian Governments.

Technique Employed: (1) Negotiations; (2) Protest meetings; (3) Political associations; (4) Prayers for self-purification; (5) Ultimatum; (6) Holding of banned meetings and processions; (7) Ceremonial march; (8) National days and weeks; (9) Non-violent Non-cooperation; (10) Courting imprisonment; (11) Boycott; (12) Picketing; (13) *Satyagrahi sahayog*; and (14) The symbolic acts of *satyagraha*.

Results: (1) Due to unprecedented all-round repression by the Government, the movement failed to achieve its objective of Poorna Swaraj and had finally to be abandoned; and (2) Phenomenal mass awakening throughout the country.

22. I Anti-Untouchability Fast: September 20, 1932 to September 26, 1932.

Cause: To lodge protests against the Macdonald Award aimed at creating separate electorates for the depressed classes.

Directed Against: Officials of the Imperial and Indian Governments.

Technique Employed: (1) Negotiations; (2) Prayer for self-purification; (3) Ultimatum; and (4) Fasting for six days.

Results: (1) On September 24, 1932, a complete agreement was reached between Gandhi and the British officials, and on September 26, the British Prime Minister announced his acceptance of the Yeravada pact, substituting the Macdonald Award; and (2) The fast 'roused mass consciousness, directing public opinion to the field of social reform'.

23. II Anti-untouchability Fast: December 3, 1932.

Cause: To express sympathy with Appasaheb Patwardhan who had asked for the scavenger's work in the Ratnagiri Jail, but was refused by the authorities.

Directed Against: Officials of the Government of India.

Technique Employed: (1) Negotiations; (2) Prayers for self-purification; (3) Ultimatum; and (4) Fasting for one day.

Result: Exercised moral influence on the adversaries.

24. III Anti-Untouchability Fast: May 8, 1933 to May 29, 1933.

Cause: To hasten the removal of untouchability.
Directed Against: The Savarna Hindus.

Technique Employed: (1) Negotiations with the Government of India; (2) Prayer for self-purification; and (3) Fasting for 21 days.

Results: (1) The fast exerted a sort of purifying influence on the adversaries and on those in whose behalf it was undertaken; and (2) In view of his fast, he was unconditionally released on May 8, 1933.

25. IV Anti-Untouchability Fast: August 16, 1933 to August 23, 1933.

Cause: Bombay Government's is refusal to permit Gandhi to continue Harijan work from inside the jail.

Directed Against: Officials of the Government of India.

Technique Employed: (1) Negotiations; (2) Prayer for self-purification; (3) Ultimatum; (4) Newspaper propaganda; and (5) Fasting for seven days.

Result: In view of the seriousness of his condition, Gandhi was unconditionally released on August 23, 1933.

26. IV Anti-Violence Fast: August 7, 1934 to August 14, 1934

Cause: An act of violence on the part of a young Congressman, who had struck Swami Lal Nath (a Sanatani Hindu) on his head.

Directed Against: The young Congressman.

Technique Employed: (1) Prayers for self-purification; (2) Newspaper propaganda; (3) Fasting for seven days.

Result: Enabled him to realize more fully that untouchability could be removed only by those who had a pure character.

27. Rajkot *Satyagraha*: March 3, 1939 to May 17, 1939.

Cause: (1.) Breach by Rajkot Ruler of an agreement entered into between him and his people, and his subsequent ordinances aimed at suppressing the Satyagraha activities; and (2) People's demand for representative Government in princely states.

Directed Against: The native British rulers of Rajkot.

Technique Employed: (1) Assessment of facts by public enquiry; (2) Negotiations; (3) Protest meetings; (4) Prayer of self-purification; (5) Ultimatum; (6) Newspaper propaganda; (7) Fasting for four days; and (8) *Satyagrahi sahayog.*

Result: Failed in achieving its immediate objective and Gandhi had to renounce the Gwyer Award for he realized his unconscious fault of offending the Rajkot Thakore and Durbar Shri Virawala by seeking the Viceroy's intervention.

28. Individual *Satyagraha*: October 17, 1940 to December 4, 1941.

Causes: (1) Indians' demand for the freedom to preach Non co-operation, with the Government in the Second World War efforts; and (2) To attain Poorna Swaraj in India.

Directed Against: Officials of the British Government in India.

Technique Employed: (1) Negotiations; (2) Protest meetings; (3) Political associations; (4) I pledge; 5) Prayer for self-purification; (6) Ultimatum; (7) Newspaper propaganda; (8) Courting imprisonment; (9) Non-violent Non-co-operation; and (10) *Satyagrahi sahayog*.

Results: (1) The *satyagrahis* successfully preached non-co-operation and cheerfully courted imprisonment; (2) Towards the end of 1941, public enthusiasm had waned and, consequently, the movement was discontinued.

29. Quit India Movement: August 9, 1942 to June 21, 1945.

Causes: Indians' demand for the immediate ending of the British Rule in India and the attainment of the Poorna Swaraj.

Directed Against: The officials of the British Government in India.

Technique Employed: (1) Negotiations; (2) Protest meetings; (3) Political association; (4) *Satyagraha* pledge; (5) Prayer for self-purification; (6) Holding of banned meetings, processions and demonstration; (7) *Hartals*; (8) Fasting for 21 days; (9) Non-violent Non-co-operation; and (10) *Satyagrahi sahayog*.

Result: The Government crushed the movement with all the weight at their command.

30. II Hindu-Muslim Unity Fast: September 1, 1947 to September 4, 1947.

Cause: Hindu-Muslim riots in Calcutta and Punjab.

Directed Against: The communal fanatics, particularly the militant Hindus.

Techniques Employed: (1) Negotiations; (2) Protest meetings; (3) Tours, including the *pad yatra*; (4) Prayer for self-purification; (5) Newspaper propaganda; and (6) Fasting for three days.

Result: The fast stirred the people and the riots rapidly subsided.

31. III Hindu-Muslim Unity Fast: January 13, 1948 to January 18, 1948.

Cause: Hindu-Muslim riots in Delhi.

Directed Against: The communal fanatics, particularly the militant Hindus.

Technique Employed: (1) Negotiations; (2) Protest meetings; (3) Prayers for self-purification; (4) Newspaper propaganda; and (5) Fasting for five days.

Results: (1) Representatives of Hindus and Muslims signed a joint declaration assuring Gandhi the restoration of peace; and (2) Riots rapidly subsided.

II

COLLECTIVE MOVEMENTS

A: On National Questions

1. South-African Satyagraha Movement: July 1, 1907 to June 30, 1914.
2. Rowlatt Act Satyagraha: March 1, 1919 to April 18, 1919.
3. I Non-violent Non-co-operation Movement: August 1, 1920 to February 12, 1922.
4. Salt Satyagraha: March 12, 1930 to March 4, 1931.
5. II Non-violent Non-co-operation Movement: January 4, 1932 to April 7, 1934.
6. Quit India Movement: August 9, 1942 to June 21, 1945.

B: On Local Questions

1. Champaran Satyagraha: April 16, 1917 to October 6, 1917.
2. Ahmedabad Satyagraha: February 26, 1918 to March 18, 1918.
3. Kheda Satyagraha: March 22, 1918 to June 6, 1918.
4. Rajkot Satyagraha: March 3, 1939 to May 17, 1939.

Individual Movements

A: On National Questions

1. I Hindu-Muslim Unity Fast: September 18, 1924 to October 8, 1924.
2. I Anti-Untouchability Fast: September 20, 1932 to September 26, 1932.
3. II Anti-Untouchability Fast: December 3, 1932.
4. III Anti-Untouchability Fast: May 8, 1933 to May 29, 1933.
5. IV Anti-Untouchability Fast: August 16, 1933 to August 23, 1933.
6. Individual Satyagraha: October 17, 1940 to December 4, 1941.
7. II Hindu-Muslim Unity Fast: September 1, 1947 to September 4, 1947.
8. III Hindu-Muslim Unity Fast: January 13, 1948 to January 18, 1948.

B: On Other Questions

1. I Penitential Fast: November 10, 1913 to November 16, 1913.
2. II Penitential Fast: April 1914.
3. I Anti-Violence Fast: April 14, 1919 to April 16, 1919.
4. II Anti-Violence Fast: November 19, 1921 to November 22, 1921.
5. III Anti-Violence Fast: February 12, 1922 to February 17, 1922.
6. III Penitential Fast: November 24, 1925 to November 30, 1925.
7. Anti-Violence Fast: August 7, 1934 to August 19, 1934.

Movements Short of *Satyagraha* Methods

1. Viramgam Question: January 16, 1915 to November 4, 1917.
2. Indenture Immigration Question: March 20, 1916 to March 12, 1917.

Movements Started by Others and Supported by Gandhi

1. Vykom Satyagraha: March 1924 to June 17, 1925.
2. Neill Statue Satyagraha: September 1, 1927 to October 13, 1927.
3. Bardoli Satyagraha: February 12, 1928 to April 4, 1928.
4. Karnataka Satyagraha: March 1931 to May 1931.

Appendix 3: Gandhi's Periods of Imprisonments

Total Period of Imprisonment

Total Imprisonment Awarded: Twelve years, two months, six days.
Total Simple Imprisonment Awarded: Eleven years, three months, six days.
Total Rigorous Imprisonment Awarded: Eleven months.
Total Actual Imprisonment: Six years, four months, twenty four days.
Total Actual Simple Imprisonment: Six years, one month, sixteen days.
Total Actual Rigorous Imprisonment: Three months, and eight days.
Total Actual Rigorous Imprisonment in South Africa: Seven months and eight days.
Total Actual Imprisonment in India: Five years; nine months and sixteen days.

Details of the Imprisonment

1. Johannesburg Imprisonment

Method of Courting Imprisonment: By disobeying the orders to leave the colony within the prescribed time limit.

Imprisonment Awarded: Two months' simple imprisonment.

Actual Duration of Imprisonment: Twenty days simple imprisonment (January 10 to January 30, 1908).

Ground of Release: In view of the Gandhi-Smuts Agreement regarding the voluntary registration and its validation.

2. Volksrust Imprisonment

Method of Courting Imprisonment: By entering Transvaal without registration certificates and by refusing to give his finger and thumb impressions.

Imprisonment Awarded: Seven days' simple and two months' rigorous imprisonment.

Actual Duration of Imprisonment: Seven days' simple and two months' rigorous imprisonment. (October 7 to October 14, 1908) and (October 14 to December 12, 1908) Ground of release: Completion of the awarded imprisonment.

3. Volksrust-Pretoria Imprisonment

Method of Courting Imprisonment: By entering Transvaal without registration certificates and by refusing to give his finger and thumb impressions.

Imprisonment Awarded: Three months' simple imprisonment.

Actual Duration of Imprisonment: Three months' simple imprisonment (February 25 to May 24, 1909).

Ground of Release: Completion of the awarded imprisonment.

4. Palmford-Volksrust Imprisonment

Method of Courting Imprisonment: By inducing strike of Ballengeich Indian miners and Ladysmith Railway men and by taking them to stage a march from New Castle to the Transvaal without requisite registration certificates to protest against f-3 tax.

Imprisonment Awarded: Nine months' rigorous imprisonment.

Actual Duration of Imprisonment: One month and eight days' rigorous and three days' simple imprisonment (November 6, 9 and 10, 1913 and November 11 to December 18, 1913).

Ground of Release: Recommendations of the Solomon Commission.

5. I Yeravada Imprisonment

Method of Courting Imprisonment: By writing four articles in *Young India*, amounting in the Government's opinion to sedition.

Imprisonment Awarded: Six years' simple imprisonment.

Actual Duration of Imprisonment: One year, ten months and twenty-seven days' simple imprisonment (March 10 to March 17, 1922 and March 18, 1922 to February 5, 1924).

Ground of Release: In view of the seriousness of his health.

6. II Yeravada Imprisonment

Method of Courting Imprisonment: By violating the salt laws at Dandi and by asking others to do the same for achieving Poorna Swaraj or complete independence for India.

Imprisonment Awarded: During Government's pleasure

Actual Duration of Imprisonment: Eight months' and twenty two days' simple imprisonment (May 4, 1930 to January 25, 1931).

Ground of Release: In the 'hope of restoration of peaceful conditions.'

7. III Yeravada Imprisonment

Method of Courting Imprisonment: By dispatching to the Viceroy an ultimatum to review the Civil Disobedience Movement of the attainment of Poorna Swaraj for India.

Imprisonment Awarded: During Government's pleasure.

Actual Duration of Imprisonment: One year, four months and five days (January 4, 1932, to May 8, 1933).

Ground of Release: 'In view of the nature and object of the fast' which Gandhi imposed on himself on this day.

8. IV Yeravada Imprisonment

Method of Courting Imprisonment: By continuing and intensifying the Civil Disobedience Movement for the attainment of Poorna Swaraj for India.

Imprisonment Awarded: During Government's pleasure. Actual duration of imprisonment: Three days (August 1 to August 4, 1933).

Ground of Release: After being served with a restraint order requiring him to reside within the limits of Poona City.

9. V Yeravada Imprisonment

Method of Courting Imprisonment: By disobeying the restraint orders requiring him to reside within the limits of the Poona city.

Imprisonment Awarded: One year's simple imprisonment.

Actual Duration of Imprisonment: Twenty days' simple imprisonment (August 4 to August 23, 1933).

Ground of Release: When he was considered to have entered the danger zone, he was released unconditionally (on medical grounds).

10. Aga Khan Palace Imprisonment

Method of Courting Imprisonment: Although this time Gandhi did not want court imprisonment, the Government, by precipitating the inauguration of Quit India Movement, arrested and detained him under the Defense India Rules.

Imprisonment Awarded: During the Government's pleasure.

Actual Duration of Imprisonment: One year, eight months and twenty-nine days. (August 9, 1942 to May 6, 1944).

Ground of release: His anaemic condition had worsened and blood-pressure fallen.

Appendix 4: Gandhi's Fasts

Gandhi fasted on 17 different occasions in his life time.

Total Actual Period of Fasting: 138 days (4 months, 18 days).

1. I Penitential Fast (March 10 to March 16, 1913)

Issue of Fast: Against moral lapse of two of his Phoenix Ashram inmates.
Announced Duration of Fast: Seven days.
Actual Duration of Fast: Seven days (March 10 to March 16, 1913)
Ground of Terminating Fast: Expiry of the period for which the fast was undertaken.

2. II Penitential Fast

Issue of Fast: Against second moral lapse of an inmate of his Phoenix-Ashram.
Announced Duration of Fast: Fourteen days.
Actual Duration of Fast: Fourteen days (April 1914).
Ground of Terminating Fast: Expiry of the period for which the fast was undertaken.

3. Ahmedabad Fast (March 15 to March 18, 1918)

Issue of Fast: In order to encourage the Ahmedabad mill workers in their strike.
Announced Duration of Fast: Indefinite.
Actual Duration of Fast: Three days.
Ground of Terminating Fast: Settlement between the mill workers and the owners was arrived at, and Mr. A. B. Dhuma was appointed the arbitrator.

4. I Anti-violence Fast (April 14 to April 16, 1919)

Issue of Fast: Against the attempts of some anarchists to derail a train at Nadiad.
Announced Duration of Fast: Three days.

Actual Duration of the Fast: Three days.

Ground of Terminating Fast: Expiry of the period for which the fast was undertaken.

5. II Anti-violence Fast (November 19 to November 22, 1921)

Issue of Fast: In order to check the anarchists' activities on the occasion of the arrival of the Prince of Wales.

Announced Duration of Fast: Indefinite.

Actual Duration of Fast: Three days.

Ground of Terminating Fast: Peace was restored.

6. III Anti-violence Fast (February 12 to February 17, 1922)

Issue of Fast: Against violent activities of Chauri Chaura.

Announced Duration of Fast: Five days.

Actual Duration of Fast: Five days.

Ground of Terminating Fast: Expiry of the period for which the fast was undertaken.

7. I Hindu-Muslim Unity Fast (September 18 to October 8, 1924)

Issue of Fast: Against Hindu-Muslim riots in Delhi, Gulbarga, Kohat and Lucknow.

Announced Duration of Fast: Twenty-one days.

Actual Duration of Fast: Twenty-one days.

Ground of Terminating Fast: Expiry of the period for which the fast was undertaken.

8. III Penitential Fast (November 24 to November 30, 1925)

Issue of Fast: Against moral lapse of some of his Sabarmati Ashram inmates.

Announced Duration of Fast: Seven days.

Actual Duration of Fast: Seven days.

Ground of Terminating Fast: Expiry of the period for which the fast was undertaken.

9. I Anti-Untouchability Fast

Issue of Fast: Against MacDonald Award creating separate electorates for the depressed classes.

Announced Duration of Fast: Unto death.

Actual Duration of Fast: Six days (September 20 to September 26, 1932).

Ground of Terminating Fast: British Prime Minister accepted the Yeravada Pact in place of the MacDonald Award.

10. II Anti-Untouchability Fast (December 3, 1932)

Issue of Fast: Sympathetic fast with Appasaheb Patwardhan who asked for scavenger's work in jail but was refused by the jail authorities.

Announced Duration of Fast: One day.

Actual Duration of Fast: One day.

Ground of Terminating Fast: Expiry of the period for which the fast was undertaken.

11. III Anti-Untouchability Fast (May 8 to May 29, 1933)

Issue of Fast: A purificatory fast for Harijan work and welfare.

Announced Duration of Fast: Twenty-one days.

Actual Duration of Fast: Twenty-one days.

Ground of Terminating Fast: Expiry of the period for which the fast was undertaken.

12. IV Anti-Untouchability Fast (August 16 to August 23, 1933)

Issue of Fast: Against Government's refusal to allow him to continue Harijan work from inside the Yeravada prison.

Announced Duration of Fast: Unto death.

Actual Duration of Fast: Seven days.

Ground of Terminating Fast: On his unconditional release from jail on medical grounds.

13. IV Anti-violence Fast (August 7 to August 14, 1934)

Issue of Fast: Against a young Congressman who had struck a sanatani on the head.

Announced Duration of Fast: Seven days.

Actual Duration of Fast: Seven days.

Ground of Terminating Fast: Expiry of the period for which the fast was undertaken.

14. Rajkot Fast (March 3 to March 7, 1939)

Issue of Fast: Against the Rajkot Thakore's refusal to honour his agreement with the people, to release *satyagrahi* prisoners, and to withdraw the repressive ordinances.

Announced Duration of Fast: Unto death.

Actual Duration of Fast: Four days.

Ground of Terminating Fast: The Viceroy conceded to intervene and appointed Chief Justice Maurie Gwyer to resolve the deadlock between the Rajkot ruler and Sardar Patel (and also Gandhi.)

15. Aga-Khan Palace Fast (February 10 to March 3, 1943)

Issue of Fast: As a protest to the Viceroy's refusal to convince him of his errors or to release him from the prison so that he does not remain a helpless witness to what was going on in the country.

Announced Duration of Fast: Twenty-one days.

Actual Duration of Fast: Twenty-one days.

Ground of Terminating Fast: Expiry of the period for which the fast was undertaken.

16. II Hindu-Muslim Unity Fast (September 1 to September 4, 1947)

Issue of Fast: To prevent Hindu-Muslim riots in Calcutta and Punjab and particularly to protect the Muslim minority against the Hindu majority.

Announced Duration of Fast: Unto death.

Actual Duration of Fast: Three days.

Ground of Terminating Fast: Peace was restored and a pledge was signed by the representatives of the Hindus and Muslims, a car-load of hand grenades and arms were surrendered to him as a token of repentance on the part of those who had taken part in the reprisals and counter-reprisals.

17. III Hindus-Muslim Unity Fast (January 13 to January .18, 1948)

Issue of Fast: To prevent Hindu-Muslim riots in Delhi, and particularly to protect Muslims from being forcibly turned out of Delhi by their Hindu brethren.

Announced Duration of Fast: Unto death.

Actual Duration of Fast: Five days.

Ground of Terminating Fast: Peace was restored and pledge was signed by the representatives of various communities to prevent their future outbreak.

Appendix 5: Eleven Vows

1. *Ahimsa*—Non-violence
2. *Satya*—Truth
3. *Asteya*—Non-stealing
4. *Brahmacharya*—Celibacy
5. *Aparigraha*—Non-possession
6. *Sharirashrama*—Bread labour
7. *Aswada*—Control over palate
8. *Sarvatrabhayavarjana*—Fearlessness
9. *Sarva Dharma Samatva*—Equality of all religions
10. *Swadeshi*—use locally made goods
11. *Sparshbhavana*—Remove untouchability

Glossary

Ahimsa	Non-violence
Anasakti	Non-attachment
Aparigraha	Non-possession
Ashram	Stages of life-Brahamacharya, Grihasatha, Banaprashtha and Sanaysha
Atman	Soul
Bania	Person of commercial caste
Bhakti	Devotion
Bhangi	Sweeper
Brahmacharya	Celibacy
Brahman	The ultimate reality
Brahmin	The highest caste in Hindu society
Charkha	Spinning wheel
Daridranarayan	God embodied as the poor
Darshan	The sight of a holy person
Dewan	Prime Minister
Dharma	Duty; one of the four purusharthas-Dharma, Artha, Kama and Moksha
Dharna	A form of sit-down strike
Dhoti	Loin cloth worn by men
Duragraha	Stubborn persistence
Gram	Village
Gram-Pradhan	Head man of the Village
Guru	Holy man, teacher
Hartal	Strike
Karma	The ethical law of causation

Khadi	Hand-spun cloth
Khilafat	Movement in support of Khalifah
Kisan	Farmer
Mandir	Temple
Moksha	Salvation, release from the cycle of rebirth; one of the four purusharthas-Dharma, Artha, Kama and Moksha
Purdha	The custom of veiling women
Poorna Swaraj	Complete Independence
Praja	People
Ramrajya	The rule of Ram, the rule of God
Sanatani	Follower of Vedic dharma(religion)
Sanyasi	One who has renounce from ordinary life for religious meditation
Satyagraha	Truth force; Insistence on Truth
Swadeshi	Insistence on local products
Swaraj	Self rule, Home Rule, Self- government
Varna	Caste
Varnashrama	Four fold division in Hindu society
Vaishnava	Follower of Lord Vishnu
Yajna	sacrificial offering to Fire God
Yogi	One who practices yoga

Bibliography

Axelrod, Alan, Gandhi, Ceo New York: Sterling, 2010.

Agarwal, Shriman Narayan, *Gandhian Constitution For Free India*, Allahabad: Kitabistan, 1946.

Alexander, Horace, *Gandhi Through Western Eyes*, Bombay: Asia Publishing House, 1969.

Andrews, C. F., *Mahatma Gandhi's Ideas,* London: George Allen & Unwin Ltd., 1949.

Andrews, C. F., *Mahatma Gandhi at Work Ideas*, London: George Allen & Unwin Ltd., 1931.

Anjaria, J. J., *An Essay on Gandhian Economics*, Bombay: Vora and Co., 1944.

Appadorai, A., *Documents on Political Thought in Modern India*, Vol. 1, New Delhi: Oxford University Press, 1981.

Ashe, Geoffrey, Gandhi*: A Study in Revolution*, Bombay: Asia Publishing House, 1968.

Bandyopadhyaya, J., *Social and Political Thought of Gandhi*, Calcutta, Allied Publishers, 1969.

Bhattacharyya, Buddhadeva, *Evolution of Political Thought of Gandhi,* Calcutta: Calcutta Book House, 1969.

Birla, G. D., *In the Shadow of the Mahatma*, Bombay: Orient Longmans Ltd., 1953.

Biswas, S. C., (Ed.), *Gandhi: Theory and Practice Social Impact and Contemporary Relevance,* Shimla; Indian Institute of Advance Study, 1969.

Bondurant, Joan *Conquest of Violence The Gandhian Philosophy of Conflict,* Bombay: Oxford University Press, 1959.

Bose, Anima, *Dimensions of Peace and Non-violence: The Gandhian Perspective,* New Delhi: Gian Publishing House, 1987.

Bose, N. K., *Studies in Gandhism*, Ahmedabad: Navajivan Publishing House, 1962.

Bose, N. K., *Gandhiji The Man And His Mission,* Bombay: Bharatiya Vidya Bhawan, 1966.

Bose, N. K., *Selections from Gandhi*, Ahmedbad: Navajivan Publishing House, 1972.

Brown, Judith M., *Gandhi and Civil-Disobedience,* London: Cambridge University Press, 1977.

Brown, Judith M., *Gandhi's Rise to Power, Indian Politics, 1915-22,* London: Cambridge University Press, 1972.

Brown, M. Judith, *Gandhi Prisoner of Hope*, New Delhi: Oxford University Press, 1992.

Chakrabarty, Bidyut, *Social and Political Thought of Mahatma Gandhi,* London: Rutledge, 2006.

Chatterjee, Partha, *Nationalist Thought and the Colonial World,* New Delhi: Oxford University Press, 1986.

Chatterjee, Margaret, *Gandhi's Religious Thought*, London: Macmillan, 1992.

Chopra, Pran, *The Sage in Revolt: A Remembrance*, New Delhi: Gandhi Peace Foundation, 1972.

Choudhuri, Manmohan, *Exploring Gandhi*, New Delhi: The Gandhi Peace Foundation, 1987.

Datta, D. M., *The Philosophy of Mahatma Gandhi*, Madison: University of Wisconsin Press, 1953.

Dhawan, Gopi Nath, *The Political Philosophy of Mahatma Gandhi*, Ahmedabad: Navajivan Publishing House, 1962.

Diwakar, R. R., *Saga of Satyagraha*, New Delhi, Gandhi Peace Foundation, 1969

Doke, J. J., *M. K. Gandhi: An Indian Patriot*, Madras: Natesan, 1909.

Durgadas, *India from Curzon to Nehru and After*, London: Collins, 1969.

Erikson, Erik H., *Gandhi's Truth: On the Origins of Militant Non-violence*, London: Faber and Faber Limited, 1970.

Fischer, Louis, *The Essential Gandhi*, London ;George Allen and Union Limited, 1962.

Gandhi, M. K., *An Autobiography or the Story of My Experiments With Truth*, Ahmedabad: Navajivan Publishing House, 1988.

Gandhi, M. K., *Hind Swaraj or Indian Home Rule*, Ahmedabad: Navajivan Publishing House, 1975.

Gandhi, M. K., *Satyagraha in South Africa*, Ahmedabad: Navajivan, Publishing House, 1975.

Gandhi, Rajmohan, *Mohandas: A true Story of a Man, his People and an Empire*, New Delhi: Penguin, 2006

Gandhi, Rajmohan, *The Good Boatman: A Portrait of Gandhi*, New Delhi: Penguin Books, 1995.

Gandhi, Tushar A., *Let's Kill Gandhi!: A Chronicle of his Last Days, The Conspiracy, Murder, Investigation and Trial*, New Delhi: Rupa, 2007.

Gangal, S. C., *Gandhian Thought and Techniques in the Modern World,* New Delhi: Criterion, Publications, 1988.

Gangrade, K. D. and Misra, R. P., *Conflict Resolution Through Non-violence Role of the Universities,* New Delhi: Concept Publishing Company, 1990.

Ganguli, B. N., *Gandhi's Social Philosophy; Perspective and Relevance*, Delhi: Vikas Publishing House Pvt. Ltd., 1973.

George, S. K., and Ramchandran G., *The Economics of Peace : The Cause and the Man,* New Delhi: Peace Publishers, 1992.

Ghosh, Sudhir, *Gandhi's Emissary*, London, Cresset Press, 1967.

Gregg, Richard B., *The Power of Non-Violence*, Ahmedabad: Navajivan Publishing House, 1960.

Green, Martin, *Gandhi: Voice of a New Age Revolution*, New York: Continuum, 1993.

Hardiman, David, *Gandhi In His Time and Ours*, New Delhi: Permanent Black, 2003.

Hunter, Doris A., and Mallick Krishna, *Non-violence A reader in the Ethics of Action*, New Delhi: Gandhi Peace Foundation, 1990.

Huttenback, Robert A., *Gandhi In South Africa: British Imperialism and The Indian Question, 1860-1914*, London: Cornell University Press, 1971.

Huxley, A., *Ends and Means*, London: Kegan Paul, 1937.

Guha, Ramachandra, *India After Gandhi:The History of the World's Largest Democracy,* New Delhi: Picador, 2008.

Iyer, Raghavan, *The Moral and Political Thought of Mahatma Gandhi,* Chicago: Oxford University Press, 1973.

Jack, A. Homer, (Ed.), *The Gandhi Reader,* Madras: Samata Books, 1984.

Kalelkar, Kaka, *Stray Glimpses of Bapu*, Ahmedabad: Navajivan Publishing House, 1957.

Karunakaran, K. P., *Gandhi-Interpretations,* New Delhi: Gitanjali Publishing House, 1985.

Keer, Dhananjay, *Mahatma Gandhi: Political Saint and Unarmed Prophet*, Bombay: Popular Prakashan, 1973.

Khan, Afaque, *Gandhian Approach to Communalism A Critical Study,* Delhi: Ajanta Publications, 1986.

Kripalani, J. B., *Gandhi: His Life and Thoughts*, New Delhi, Publications Division, Ministry of Information and Broadcasting, Government of India, 1968.

Lohia, Rammanohar, *Marx, Gandhi and Socialism*, Hyderabad: Rammanohar Lohia Samata Vidylaya Nyasa, 1978.

Mehta, P. J., *Gandhi and South African Question*, Madaras, 1911.

Mishra, Anil Dutta, *Understanding Mahatma Gandhi: Speeches and Writings that Reveal his Mind Methods and Mission*, New Delhi: Concept, 2012.

Mishra, Anil Dutta, Pravin kumar and Sohan Raj Tater, et. al. *Revisiting Gandhi*, New Delhi: Abhijeet Publications, 2011.

Mishra, Anil Dutta, *Mahatma on Ethics,* New Delhi: Concept, 2010.

Mishra Anil Dutta, *Revisiting Hind Swaraj*, New Delhi: Concept, 2010.

Mishra, A. D., (ed.), *Perspectives on Human Rights,* New Delhi: Radha Publications, 2002.

Mishra, Anil Dutta, (Ed.), *Gandhian Approach to Contemporary Problems*, New Delhi: Mittal Publications, 1996.

Mishra, Anil Dutta, and Dadage, M. S., *Panchayati Raj: Gandhian Perspective,* New Delhi: Mittal Publications, 2000.

Mishra, Anil Dutta, *Challenges of 21st Century and Gandhian Alternative,* New Delhi: Mittal Publications, 2003.

Mishra, Anil Dutta, *Fundamentals of Gandhism,* New Delhi: Mittal Publications, 1995.

Mishra, Anil Dutta, *Rediscovering Gandhi,* New Delhi: Mittal Publications, 2002.

Mishra, Anil Dutta, *Gandhian Approach to Contemporary Problems,* New Delhi: Mittal Publications, 1996.

Mishra, Anil Dutta, *Gandhism After Gandhi*, New Delhi: Mittal Publications, 1999.

Mishra, R. P., *Gandhian Model of Development and World Peace,* New Delhi: Concept Publishing Company, 1988.

Mishra, Sweta, *Democratic Decentralisation in India*, New Delhi: Mittal Publications, 1994.

Misra, K. P., and Gangal, S. C., *Gandhi and the Contemporary World : Studies in Peace and War*, New Delhi: Chanakya Publications, 1981.

Mukerjee, Hiren, *Gandhi: A Study*, New Delhi: People's Publishing House, 1960.

Namboodiripad, E. M. S., *The Mahatma and the Ism*, New Delhi: People Publishing House, 1959.

Nanda, B. R., *Gandhi Pan-Islamism Imperialism and Nationalism,* Bombay: Oxford University Press, 1989.

Nanda, B. R., *Mahatma Gandhi: A Biography*, London: George Allen and Unwin Ltd., 1959.

Narayan, Shriman, *Selected Works of Mahatma Gandhi*, Ahmedabad: Navajivan Publishing House, 1956.

Nehru, Jawahar Lal, *Mahatma Gandhi*, Calcutta: Signet Press, 1949.

Ostergaard Geoffrey, *Non-violent Revolution in India,* New Delhi: Gandhi Peace Foundation, 1985.

Parekh, Bhikhu, *Colonialism, Tradition and Reform : An Analysis of Gandhi's Political Discourse*, New Delhi: Sage Publications, 1989.

Parel, Anthony J., *Gandhi's Philosophy and the Quest for Harmony*, Cambridge, Cambridge University Press, 2006.

Parel, Anthony J., *Hind Swaraj and other Writings*, Cambridge: , Cambridge University Press, 1997.

Parel, Anthony J., *Gandhi, Freedom, and Self-Rule*, New Delhi: Vistaar Publications, 2000.

Polak, H. S. C.; H. N. Brailsford and Lord Pethick, Lawrence, *Mahatma Gandhi,* London: Oldham Press Limited, 1949.

Prabhu, R. K., and Rao, U. R., *The Mind of Mahatma*, Ahmedabad: Navajivan Publishing House, 1967.

Prasad, Nageshwar, *Hind Swaraj A Fresh Look,* New Delhi: Gandhi Peace Foundation, 1985.

Pyare Lal, *Mahatma Gandhi: The Early Phase,* Volume 1, Ahmedabad: Navajivan Publishing House, 1965.

Pyare Lal, *Mahatma Gandhi: The Last Phase*, in 2 volumes, Ahmedabad: Navajivan Publishing House, 1956, 1958.

Pyarelal and Nayar Sushila, *In Gandhiji's Mirror*, New Delhi: Oxford University Press, 1991.
Pyarelal, *Mahatma Gandhi, The Last Phase*, Ahmedabad: Navajivan Publishing House, 1958.
Radhakrishnan, S., (ed.), *Mahatma Gandhi: Essays and Reflections on His Life and Thought*, Allahabad: Kitabistan, 1944.
Radhakrishnan, S., (Ed.), *Mahatma Gandhi 100 Years*, New Delhi: Gandhi Peace Foundation, 1968.
Rajendra Prashad, *At the Feet of Mahatma Gandhi*, Bombay: Asia Publishing House, 1961.
Rao, U. R., *The Way to Communal Harmony*, Ahmedabad: Navajivan Publishing House, 1963.
Rao, U. S., Mohan (Ed.), *The Message of Mahatma Gandhi*, Publication Division, Ministry of Information and Broadcasting, Govt. of India, New Delhi, 1968.
Raghuramaraju, A., (Ed), *Debating Gandhi: A Reader*, New Delhi: Oxford University Press, 2006.
Rolland, Romain, *Mahatma Gandhi*, London: Allen and Unwin, 1924.
Roy, Ramashray, *Contemporary Crisis and Gandhi*, New Delhi: Discovery Publishing House, 1986.
Roy, Ramashray, *Gandhi: Soundings in Political Philosophy*, New Delhi: Chanakya Publications, 1984.
Rudolph, Lloyd, I., and Rudoulh, Susanne Hoeber, *Postmodern Gandhi and Other Essays: Gandhi in the World and at Home*, New Delhi: Oxford University Press, 2006.
Sethi, J. D., *Gandhi Today*, New Delhi: Vikas Publishing House Pvt. Ltd., 1978.
Sharp, Gene, *Gandhi Wields the Weapon of Moral Power Three Case Histories*, Ahmedabad: Navajivan Publishing House, 1960.
Sharp, Gene, *The Politics of Non- Violent Action: Power and Struggle*, Part 1, Boston: Porter Sarget Publishers, 1973.
Sheean Vincent, *Mahatma Gandhi A Great Life in Brief*, New Delhi: Publication Division, 1990.
Shukla, Chandrashanker, *Reminiscences of Gandhiji*, Bombay: Vora and Company, 1951.
Sitaramayya, Pattabhi, *Gandhi and Gandhism*, Allahabad: Kitabistan, 1942, in 2 volumes.
Tendulkar, D. G, *Mahatma*, New Delhi, Publications Division, Ministry of Information and Broadcasting, Government of India, 1952.
The Collected Works of Mahatma Gandhi, New Delhi, Publications Division, Ministry of Information and Broadcasting, Government of India, 1965, (Vols. 1-100).
Verma, V. P., *The Political philosophy of Mahatma Gandhi and Sarvodaya*, Agra: Lakshmi Narain Aggarwal, 1981.
Vinobha, Bhave, *Swaraj Sastra*, Varanasi: Sarva Seva Sangh Prakashan, 1963.
Watson, Francis, and Tennyson Hallam, *Talking of Gandhi*, Bombay: Sangam Books, 1957.
Weber, Thomas, *Conflict Resolution and Gandhian Ethics*, New Delhi: The Gandhi Peace Foundation, 1991.
Weber, Thomas, *On the Salt March*, New Delhi: Harper Colliings, 1997.
Weber, Thomas, *Gandhi As Disciple And Mentor*, New Delhi: Cambridge University Press, 2004.

Index

L

M

N

O

P

U

V

W

Y